# Data Science on the
# Google Cloud Platform

*Implementing End-to-End Real-Time*
*Data Pipelines: From Ingest to Machine Learning*

*Valliappa Lakshmanan*

Beijing · Boston · Farnham · Sebastopol · Tokyo

**Data Science on the Google Cloud Platform, Second Edition**

by Valliappa Lakshmanan

Copyright © 2022 Google LLC. All rights reserved.

Published by O'Reilly Media, Inc., 1005 Gravenstein Highway North, Sebastopol, CA 95472.

O'Reilly books may be purchased for educational, business, or sales promotional use. Online editions are also available for most titles (*http://oreilly.com*). For more information, contact our corporate/institutional sales department: 800-998-9938 or *corporate@oreilly.com*.

| | |
|---|---|
| **Acquisition Editor:** Jessica Haberman | **Indexer:** WordCo Indexing Services, Inc. |
| **Development Editor:** Michele Cronin | **Interior Designer:** David Futato |
| **Production Editor:** Katherine Tozer | **Cover Designer:** Karen Montgomery |
| **Copyeditor:** Tom Sullivan | **Illustrator:** Kate Dullea |
| **Proofreader:** Piper Editorial Consulting, LLC | |

| | |
|---|---|
| January 2018: | First Edition |
| April 2022: | Second Edition |

**Revision History for the Second Edition**

2022-03-29:   First Release

See *http://oreilly.com/catalog/errata.csp?isbn=9781098118952* for release details.

978-1-098-11895-2

LSI

# Table of Contents

# Preface

In my current role at Google, I get to work alongside data scientists and data engineers in a variety of industries as they move their data processing and analysis methods to the public cloud. Some try to do the same things they do on premises, the same way they do them, just on rented computing resources. The visionary users, though, rethink their systems, transform how they work with data, and thereby are able to innovate faster.

As early as 2011, an article in *Harvard Business Review* (*https://oreil.ly/vaQlk*) recognized that some of cloud computing's greatest successes come from allowing groups and communities to work together in ways that were not previously possible. This is now much more widely recognized. An MIT survey in 2017 (*https://oreil.ly/tlk6B*) found that more respondents (45%) cited increased agility rather than cost savings (34%) as the reason to move to the public cloud. However, it is still not widely achieved. McKinsey estimated in 2021 (*https://oreil.ly/sDRJR*) that companies are leaving behind nearly $1 trillion of value by not looking at the public cloud as a source of transformative value. Therefore, being able to work on a data science project in the cloud is a skill well worth investing in.

In this book, we walk through an example of a cloud-native, transformative, collaborative way of doing data science. You will learn how to implement an end-to-end data pipeline—we will begin with ingesting the data in a serverless way and work our way through data exploration, dashboards, relational databases, and streaming data all the way to training and making an operational machine learning model. I cover all these aspects of data-based services because data engineers will be involved in designing the services, developing the statistical and machine learning models, and implementing them in large-scale production and in real time.

## Who This Book Is For

If you use computers to work with data, this book is for you. You might go by the title of data analyst, database administrator, data engineer, data scientist, or systems programmer today. Although your role might be narrower today (perhaps you do only data analysis, or only model building, or only DevOps), you want to stretch your wings a bit—you want to learn how to create data science models as well as how to implement them at scale in production systems.

Google Cloud Platform is designed to make you forget about infrastructure. The marquee data services—Google BigQuery, Cloud Dataflow, Cloud Pub/Sub, and Vertex AI—are all serverless and autoscaling. When you submit a query to BigQuery, it is run on thousands of nodes, and you get your result back; you don't spin up a cluster or install any software. Similarly, in Cloud Dataflow, when you submit a data pipeline, and in Vertex AI, when you submit a machine learning job, you can process data at scale and train models at scale without worrying about cluster management or failure recovery. Cloud Pub/Sub is a global messaging service that autoscales to the through-put and number of subscribers and publishers without any work on your part. Even when you're running open source software like Apache Spark that's designed to oper-ate on a cluster, Google Cloud Platform makes it easy with job-specific clusters and serverless Spark. Because of this job-specific infrastructure, there's no need to fear overprovisioning hardware or running out of capacity to run a job when you need it. Plus, data is encrypted, both at rest and in transit, and kept secure. As a data scientist, not having to manage infrastructure is incredibly liberating.

These autoscaled, fully managed services make it easier to implement data science models at scale—which is why data scientists no longer need to hand off their models to data engineers. Instead, they can write a data science workload, submit it to the cloud, and have that workload executed automatically in an autoscaled manner. At the same time, data science packages are becoming simpler and simpler. So, it has become extremely easy for an engineer to slurp in data and use a canned model to get an initial (and often very good) model up and running. With well-designed packages and easy-to-consume APIs, you don't need to know the esoteric details of data science algorithms—only what each algorithm does and how to link algorithms together to solve realistic problems. This convergence between data science and data engineering is why you can stretch your wings beyond your current role.

Rather than simply read this book cover-to-cover, I strongly encourage you to follow along with me by trying out the code. The full source code for the end-to-end pipe-line I build in this book is on GitHub (*https://github.com/GoogleCloudPlatform/data-science-on-gcp*). Create a Google Cloud Platform project (*https://cloud.google.com*), and after reading each chapter, try to repeat what I did by referring to the code and to the *README.md* file in each folder of the GitHub repository.

 Follow the instructions in the *README.md* files in GitHub to try out the code. The code snippets in the book are often incomplete—for example, I may omit some arguments to cloud commands for clarity or conciseness.

Note that this is not a reference book—the best reference to Google Cloud is its documentation, and there is very little value to be had by simply reproducing that in a book. Instead, this book shows you how to use a variety of tools together to solve a problem. My goal here is to teach you how to think about a problem in order to solve it using Google Cloud, not to comprehensively cover any particular product.

If you find yourself fascinated by a topic in this book and want to dive deeper, you can find a few selected resources at the end of every chapter that provide a deeper dive into topics covered in the chapter. Don't feel obligated to watch every video or read every article.

## Conventions Used in This Book

The following typographical conventions are used in this book:

*Italic*
> Indicates new terms, URLs, email addresses, filenames, and file extensions.

`Constant width`
> Used for program listings, as well as within paragraphs to refer to program elements such as variable or function names, databases, data types, environment variables, statements, and keywords.

**`Constant width bold`**
> Shows commands or other text that should be typed literally by the user.

*Constant width italic*
> Shows text that should be replaced with user-supplied values or by values determined by context.

 This element signifies a tip or suggestion.

 This element signifies a general note.

 This element indicates a warning or caution.

# Using Code Examples

Supplemental material (code examples, exercises, etc.) is available for download at *https://github.com/GoogleCloudPlatform/data-science-on-gcp*.

If you have a technical question or a problem using the code examples, please email *bookquestions@oreilly.com*.

This book is here to help you get your job done. In general, if example code is offered with this book, you may use it in your programs and documentation. You do not need to contact us for permission unless you're reproducing a significant portion of the code. For example, writing a program that uses several chunks of code from this book does not require permission. Selling or distributing examples from O'Reilly books does require permission. Answering a question by citing this book and quoting example code does not require permission. Incorporating a significant amount of example code from this book into your product's documentation does require permission.

We appreciate, but do not require, attribution. An attribution usually includes the title, author, publisher, and ISBN. For example: "*Data Science on the Google Cloud Platform* by Valliappa Lakshmanan (O'Reilly). Copyright 2022 Google LLC, 978-1-098-11895-2."

If you feel your use of code examples falls outside fair use or the permission given above, feel free to contact us at *permissions@oreilly.com*.

# O'Reilly Online Learning

 For more than 40 years, *O'Reilly Media* has provided technology and business training, knowledge, and insight to help companies succeed.

Our unique network of experts and innovators share their knowledge and expertise through books, articles, and our online learning platform. O'Reilly's online learning platform gives you on-demand access to live training courses, in-depth learning paths, interactive coding environments, and a vast collection of text and video from O'Reilly and 200+ other publishers. For more information, visit *https://oreilly.com*.

# How to Contact Us

Please address comments and questions concerning this book to the publisher:

O'Reilly Media, Inc.
1005 Gravenstein Highway North

---

Sebastopol, CA 95472
800-998-9938 (in the United States or Canada)
707-829-0515 (international or local)
707-829-0104 (fax)

We have a web page for this book, where we list errata, examples, and any additional information. You can access this page at *https://oreil.ly/data-science-on-gcp*.

Email *bookquestions@oreilly.com* to comment or ask technical questions about this book.

For news and information about our books and courses, visit *https://oreilly.com*.

Find us on Facebook: *https://facebook.com/oreilly*.

Follow us on Twitter: *https://twitter.com/oreillymedia*.

Watch us on YouTube: *https://www.youtube.com/oreillymedia*.

# Acknowledgments

When I took the job at Google in 2014, I had used the public cloud simply as a way to rent infrastructure—so I was spinning up virtual machines, installing the software I needed on those machines, and then running my data processing jobs using my usual workflow. Fortunately, I realized that Google's big data stack was different, and so I set out to learn how to take full advantage of all the data and machine learning tools on Google Cloud Platform.

The way I learn best is to write code, and so that's what I did. When a Python meetup group asked me to talk about Google Cloud Platform, I did a show-and-tell of the code that I had written. It turned out that a walk-through of the code to build an end-to-end system while contrasting different approaches to a data science problem was quite educational for the attendees. I wrote up the essence of my talk as a book proposal and sent it to O'Reilly Media.

A book, of course, needs to have a lot more depth than a 60-minute code walk-through. Imagine that you come to work one day to find an email from a new employee at your company, someone who's been at the company less than six months. Somehow, he's decided he's going to write a book on the pretty sophisticated platform that you've had a hand in building and is asking for your help. He is not part of your team, helping him is not part of your job, and he is not even located in the same office as you. What is your response? Would you volunteer?

What makes Google such a great place to work is the people who work here. It is a testament to the company's culture that so many people—engineers, technical leads, product managers, solutions architects, data scientists, legal counsel, directors—across so many different teams happily gave of their expertise to someone they had never met (in fact, I still haven't met many of these people in person). This book, thus, is immeasurably better because of (in alphabetical order of last names) William Brockman, Mike Dahlin, Tony DiLoreto, Bob Evans, Roland Hess, Brett Hesterberg, Dennis Huo, Chad Jennings, Puneith Kaul, Dinesh Kulkarni, Manish Kurse, Reuven Lax, Jonathan Liu, James Malone, Dave Oleson, Mosha Pasumansky, Kevin Peterson, Olivia Puerta, Reza Rokni, Karn Seth, Sergei Sokolenko, and Amy Unruh. In particular, thanks to Mike Dahlin, Manish Kurse, and Olivia Puerta for reviewing every single chapter. When the first edition of the book was in early access, I received valuable error reports from Anthonios Partheniou and David Schwantner. Needless to say, I am responsible for any errors that remain.

A few times during the writing of the book, I found myself completely stuck. Sometimes, the problems were technical. Thanks to (in alphabetical order) Ahmet Altay, Eli Bixby, Ben Chambers, Slava Chernyak, Marián Dvorský, Robbie Haertel, Felipe Hoffa, Amir Hormati, Qiming (Bradley) Jiang, Kenneth Knowles, Nikhil Kothari, and Chris Meyers for showing me the way forward. At other times, the problems were related to figuring out company policy or getting access to the right team, document, or statistic. This book would have been a lot poorer had these colleagues not unblocked me at critical points (again alphabetically): Louise Byrne, Apurva Desai, Rochana Golani, Fausto Ibarra, Jason Martin, Neal Mueller, Philippe Poutonnet, Brad Svee, Jordan Tigani, William Vampenebe, and Miles Ward. Thank you all for your help and encouragement.

Five years on, I continue to be humbled by the incredible talent and collaboration of my colleagues. Sagar Baliyara, Filipe Gracio, Polong Lin, and Krishnan Saidapet (in alphabetical order of last names) brought a close eye to the second edition and made many great suggestions.

Thanks also to the O'Reilly team—Marie Beaugureau, Kristen Brown, Ben Lorica, Tim McGovern, Rachel Roumeliotis, and Heather Scherer for believing in me and making the process of moving from draft to the first edition of the book painless. Producing the second edition was greatly streamlined by Katherine Tozer, Michele Cronin, and Tom Sullivan.

The second edition has also greatly benefited from fresh outside perspectives. Colin Dietrich verified much of the code in the book and made numerous pull requests to the GitHub repository. Joy Payton suggested many improvements to make the book more accessible to beginners in data science. Michael Hopkins and Margaret Maynard-Reid scrutinized the book for areas that needed updating. Thanks also to readers of the first edition who left reviews of the book on Amazon, filed issues on GitHub, and reached out to me via email and on Twitter. Your feedback has greatly improved this edition of the book.

Finally, and most important, thanks to Abirami, Sidharth, and Sarada for your understanding and patience even as I became engrossed in writing and coding. You make it all worthwhile.

I am donating 100% of the royalties from this book to United Way of King County (*https://www.uwkc.org*), where I live. I strongly encourage you to get involved with a local charity to give, volunteer, and take action to help solve your community's toughest challenges.

# CHAPTER 1

# Making Better Decisions Based on Data

The primary purpose of data analysis is to make better decisions. There is rarely any need for us to spend time analyzing data if we aren't under pressure to make a decision based on the results of that analysis. When you are purchasing a car, you might ask the seller what year the car was manufactured and the odometer reading. Knowing the age of the car allows you to estimate the potential value of the car. Dividing the odometer reading by the age of the car allows you to discern how hard the car has been driven, and whether it is likely to last the five years you plan to keep it. Had you not cared about purchasing the car, there would have been no need for you to do this data analysis.

In fact, we can go further—the purpose of collecting data is, in many cases, only so that you can later perform data analysis and make decisions based on that analysis (see Figure 1-1). When you asked the seller the age of the car and its mileage, you were collecting data to carry out your data analysis. But it goes beyond your data collection. The car has an odometer in the first place because many people, not just potential buyers, will need to make decisions based on the mileage of the car. The odometer reading needs to support many decisions—should the manufacturer pay for a failed transmission? Is it time for an oil change? The analysis for each of these decisions is different, but they all rely on the fact that the mileage data has been collected.

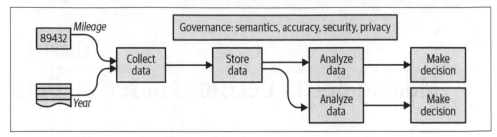

*Figure 1-1. The purpose of collecting data is to make decisions with it.*

If you are in the business of making a lot of decisions using car mileage, it makes sense to store the data that you have collected so that future decisions are easier to make. Collecting data takes time and effort, whereas storing it is relatively inexpensive. Of course, you have to plan on storing the data in a way that you will know what it *means* when you need it later. This is called capturing the *semantics* of the data and is an important aspect of *data governance*, to ensure that data is useful for decision making.

Collecting data in a form that enables decisions to be made places requirements on the collecting infrastructure and the security of such infrastructure. How does the insurance company that receives an accident claim and needs to pay its customer the car's value know that the odometer reading is accurate? How are odometers calibrated? What kinds of safeguards are in place to ensure that the odometer has not been tampered with? What happens if the tampering is inadvertent, such as installing tires whose size is different from what was used to calibrate the odometer? The *auditability* of data is important whenever there are multiple parties involved, and ownership and use of the data are separate. When data is unverifiable, markets fail, optimal decisions cannot be made, and the parties involved need to resort to signaling and screening.[1]

---

1 The classic paper on this is George Akerlof's 1970 paper titled "The Market for Lemons" (*https:// www.jstor.org/stable/1879431*). Akerlof, Michael Spence (who explained signaling), and Joseph Stiglitz (who explained screening) jointly received the 2001 Nobel Prize in Economics for describing this problem. In a transaction that involves asymmetric information, the party with good information signals, whereas the party with poor information screens. For example, the seller of a car (who has good information) might signal that they have a great car by publishing the repair record of the car. The buyer (who has poor information) might screen cars by rejecting any cars from cities that recently experienced a flood.

Not all data is as expensive to collect and secure as the odometer reading of a car.[2] The cost of sensors has dropped dramatically in recent decades, and many of our daily processes produce so much data that we find ourselves in possession of data that we had no intention of explicitly collecting. Because the hardware to collect, ingest, and store the data has become cheaper, we often default to retaining the data indefinitely, keeping it around for no discernible reason. As the size of data within an organization increases, it becomes more and more essential to organize and catalog it carefully. So, if we're to perform analysis on all of this data that we somehow managed to collect and store, we better have a purpose for it. Labor remains expensive.

Another reason to be purposeful about the data we collect and store is that a lot of it is about people. Knowing the mileage of the car that someone drives gives us a lot of information about them, and this is information that they may not want to share other than for the specific purpose of estimating the market price of their car. Privacy and confidentiality need to be considered even before any data is collected, so that appropriate decisions can be made about what data to collect, how to control access to it, and how long to retain it. This is even more important when the data is provided at significant cost, risk, and/or loss of bodily autonomy, as is the case for much biomedical patient data. Having a data privacy expert examine your schema and data protection practices is an investment that will pay for itself manyfold in terms of regulatory compliance and public relations.

Data analysis is usually triggered because a decision needs to be made. To move into a market or not? To pay a commission or not? How high to bid up the price? How many bags to purchase? Whether to buy now or wait a week? The decisions keep multiplying, and because data is so ubiquitous now, we no longer need to make those decisions based on *heuristics* or simple rules of thumb. We can now make those decisions in a data-driven manner.

Of course, we don't need to create the systems and tools to make every data-driven decision ourselves. The use case of estimating the value of a car that has been driven a certain distance is common enough that there are several companies that provide this as a service—they will verify that an odometer is accurate, confirm that the car hasn't been in an accident, and compare the asking price against the typical selling price of

---

2 The odometer itself might not be all that expensive, but collecting that information and ensuring that it is correct has considerable costs. The last time I sold a car, I had to sign a statement that I had not tampered with the odometer, and that statement had to be notarized by a bank employee with a financial guarantee. This was required by the company that was loaning the purchase amount on the car to the buyer. Every auto mechanic is supposed to report odometer tampering, and there is a state government agency that enforces this rule. All of these costs are significant. Even if you disregard all these external costs, and assume that the hardware and infrastructure exists such that each car has an odometer, there is still a significant cost associated with streaming that data from cars into a central location so that you have real-time odometer readings from all the cars in your fleet. The cost of securing that data to respect the privacy of the drivers can also be quite significant.

cars in your market. The real value, therefore, comes not in making a data-driven decision once, but in being able to do it systematically and provide it as a service.[3] This also allows companies to specialize in different business areas and continuously improve the accuracy and value of the decisions that can be made.

# Many Similar Decisions

Because of the low costs associated with sensors and storage, there are many industries and use cases that have the potential to support data-driven decision making. If you are working in such an industry, or you want to start a company that will address such a use case, the possibilities for supporting data-driven decision making have just become wider. In some cases, you will need to collect the data. In others, you will have access to data that was already collected, and, in many cases, you will need to supplement the data you have with other datasets that you will need to hunt down. In all these cases, being able to carry out data analysis to support decision making systematically on behalf of users is one of the most important skills to possess.

In this book, I will take a decision that needs to be made and apply different statistical and machine learning methods to gain insight into making that decision. However, we don't want to make that decision just once, even though we might occasionally pose it that way. Instead, we will look at how to make the decision in a systematic manner so that we use the same algorithm to make the decision many, many, many times. Our ultimate goal will be to provide this decision-making capability as a service to our customers—they will tell us the things they reasonably can be expected to know, and we will either know or infer the rest (because we have been systematically collecting data). Based on this data, we will suggest the optimal decision.

Whether or not a decision is a one-off is the primary difference between data analytics and data science. Data analytics is about manually analyzing data to make a single decision or answer a single question. Data science is about developing a technique (called a model or algorithm) so that similar decisions can be made in a systematic way. Often, data science is about automating and optimizing the decision-making process that was first determined through data analysis.[4]

When we are collecting the data, we will need to look at how to make the data secure. This will include how to ensure not only that the data has not been tampered with but also that users' private information is not compromised—for example, if we are systematically collecting odometer mileage and know the precise mileage of the car at

---

3 Providing it as a service is often the only way to meet the mission of your organization—whether it is to monetize it, support thousands of users, or provide it at low cost to decision makers.

4 Contrary to what you may hear, it is not about whether you use SQL or Python! You can do data science in SQL—we will see BigQuery ML later on in the book, and you can use Python for one-off data analysis.

any point in time, this knowledge becomes extremely sensitive information. Given enough other information about the customer (such as the home address and traffic patterns in the city in which the customer lives), the mileage is enough to be able to infer that person's location at all times.[5] So, the privacy implications of hosting something as seemingly innocuous as the mileage of a car can become enormous. Security implies that we need to control access to the data, and we need to maintain immutable audit logs on who has viewed or changed the data.

It is not enough to simply collect the data or use it as-is. We must understand the data. Just as we needed to know the kinds of problems associated with odometer tampering to understand the factors that go into estimating a vehicle's value based on mileage, our analysis methods will need to consider how the data was collected in real time and the kinds of errors that could be associated with that data. Intimate knowledge of the data and its quirks is invaluable when it comes to doing data science— often the difference between a data-science startup idea that works and one that doesn't is whether the appropriate nuances have all been thoroughly evaluated and taken into account.

When it comes to providing the decision-support capability as a service, it is not enough to simply have a way to do it in some offline system somewhere. Enabling it as a service implies a whole host of other concerns. The first set of concerns is about the quality of the decision itself—how accurate is it typically? What are the typical sources of errors? In what situations should this system not be used? The next set of concerns, however, is about the quality of service. How reliable is it? How many queries per second can it support? What is the latency between some piece of data being available and it being incorporated into the model that is used to provide systematic decision making? In short, we will use this single use case as a way to explore many different facets of practical data science.

# The Role of Data Scientists

"Wait a second," I imagine you saying, "I never signed up for queries-per-second of a web service. We have people who do that kind of stuff. My job is to write SQL queries and create reports. I don't recognize this thing you are talking about. It's not what I do at all." Or perhaps the first part of the discussion was what puzzled you. "Decision

---

5 In 2014, New York City officials released a public dataset (*https://oreil.ly/Xvflt*) of New York City taxi trips in response to a Freedom of Information request. However, because it was improperly anonymized, a brute force attack was able to find out the trips associated with any specific driver (*https://oreil.ly/8v8Sy*). It got worse. Privacy researchers were able to cross-reference paparazzi photos (*https://oreil.ly/F3SGD*) (which revealed the exact location of celebrities at specific times) and figure out which celebrities don't tip. It got even worse. By looking at people who picked up a taxi cab at the same location every morning, and correlating it with the location from where they got dropped back, they were able to identify New Yorkers who frequented strip clubs.

making? That's for the business people. Me? What I do is to design data processing systems. I can provision infrastructure, tell you what our systems are doing right now, and keep it all secure. Data science sure sounds fancy, but I do engineering. When you said Data Science on the Google Cloud Platform, I was thinking that you were going to talk about how to keep the systems humming and how to offload bursts of activity to the cloud." A third set of people are wondering, "How is any of this data science? Where's the discussion of different types of models and of how to make statistical inferences and evaluate them? Where's the math? Why are you talking to data analysts and engineers? Talk to me, I've got a PhD." These are fair points—I seem to be mixing up the jobs done by different sets of people in your organization.

In other words, you might agree with the following:

- Data analysis is there to support decision making.
- Decision making in a data-driven manner can be superior to heuristics.
- The accuracy of the decision models depends on your choice of the right statistical or machine learning approach.
- Nuances in the data can completely invalidate your modeling, so understanding the data and its quirks is crucial.
- There are large market opportunities in supporting decision making systematically and providing it as a service.
- Such services require ongoing data collection and model updates.
- Ongoing data collection implies robust security and auditing.
- Customers of the service require reliability, accuracy, and latency assurances.

What you might not agree with is whether these aspects are all things that you, personally and professionally, need to be concerned about. Instead, you might think of yourself as a data analyst, a data engineer, or a data scientist and not care about how the other roles do whatever it is that they do.

There are three answers to this objection:

- In any situation where you have small numbers of people doing ambitious things—a scrappy company, an innovative startup, an underfunded nonprofit, or an overextended research lab—you will find yourself playing all these roles, so learn the full lifecycle.
- The public cloud makes it relatively easy to learn all the roles, so why not be a full stack data scientist?

- Even if you work in a large company where these tasks are carried out by different roles, it is helpful to understand the end-to-end process and concerns at each stage. This will help you collaborate with other teams better.

Let's take these answers one by one.

## Scrappy Environment

At Google, we look at the role of a data engineer quite expansively. Just as we refer to all our technical staff as engineers, we look at data engineers as an inclusive term for anyone who can "shape business outcomes by performing data analysis." To perform data analysis, you begin by preparing the data so that you can analyze it at scale. It is not enough to simply count and sum and graph the results using SQL queries and charting software—you must understand the nuances of the data and the statistical framework within which you are interpreting the results. This ability to prepare the data and carry out statistically valid data analysis to solve specific business problems is of paramount importance—the queries, the reports, and the graphs are not the end goal. A verifiably accurate decision is.

Of course, it is not enough to do one-off data analysis. That data analysis needs to scale. In other words, an accurate decision-making process must be repeatable and be capable of being carried out by many users, not just you. The way to scale up one-off data analysis is to make it automated. After a data engineer has devised the algorithm, they should be able to make it systematic and repeatable. Just as it is a lot easier when the folks in charge of systems reliability can make code changes themselves,[6] it is considerably easier when people who understand statistics and machine learning can code those models themselves. A data engineer, Google believes, should be able to go from building statistical and machine learning models to automating them. They can do this only if they are capable of designing, building, and troubleshooting data processing systems that are secure, responsible, reliable, fault-tolerant, scalable, and efficient.

This desire to have engineers who know data science and data scientists who can code is not Google's alone—it's common at technologically sophisticated organizations and at small companies. When a scrappy company advertises for data engineers or for data scientists, what they are looking for is a person who can do all the three tasks—data preparation, data analysis, and automation—that are needed to make repeatable, scalable decisions on the basis of data.

---

6 Google invented the role of Site Reliability Engineers (SREs (*https://oreil.ly/X6XH6*))—these are folks in charge of keeping systems running. Unlike traditional IT, though, they know the software they are operating and are quite capable of making changes to it.

How realistic is it for companies to expect a Renaissance person, a virtuoso in different fields? Can they reasonably expect to hire data engineers who can do data science? How likely is it that they will find someone who can design a database schema, write SQL queries, train machine learning models, code up a data processing pipeline, and figure out how to scale it all up? Surprisingly, this is a very reasonable expectation because the amount of knowledge you need in order to do these jobs has become a lot less than what you needed a few years ago.

## Full Stack Cloud Data Scientists

Because of the ongoing movement to the cloud, data scientists can do the job that used to be done by several people with different sets of skills. With the advent of autoscaling, serverless, managed infrastructure that is easy to program, there are more and more people who can build scalable systems. Therefore, it is now reasonable to expect to be able to hire data scientists who are capable of creating holistic data-driven solutions to your thorniest problems. You don't need to be a polymath to be a full stack data scientist—you simply need to learn how to do data science on the cloud.

Saying that the cloud is what makes full stack data scientists possible seems like a very tall claim. This hinges on what I mean by "cloud"—I don't mean simply migrating workloads that run on premises to infrastructure that is owned by a public cloud vendor. I'm talking, instead, about truly autoscaling, managed services that automate a lot of the infrastructure provisioning, monitoring, and management—services such as Google BigQuery, Vertex AI, Cloud Dataflow, and Cloud Run on Google Cloud Platform. When you consider that the scaling and fault-tolerance of many data analysis and processing workloads can be effectively automated, provided the right set of tools is being used, it is clear that the amount of IT support that a data scientist needs dramatically reduces with a migration to the cloud.

At the same time, data science tools are becoming simpler and simpler to use. The wide availability of frameworks like Spark, Pandas, and Keras has made data science and data science tools extremely accessible to the average developer—no longer do you need to be a specialist in data science to create a statistical model or train a random forest. This has opened up the field of data science to people in more traditional IT roles.

Similarly, data analysts and database administrators today can have completely different backgrounds and skill sets because data analysis has usually involved serious SQL wizardry, and database administration has typically involved deep knowledge of database indices and tuning. With the introduction of tools like BigQuery, in which tables are denormalized and the administration overhead is minimal, the role of a database administrator is considerably diminished. The growing availability of turnkey visualization tools like Tableau and Looker that connect to all the data stores within an enterprise makes it possible for a wider range of people to directly interact with enterprise warehouses and pull together compelling reports and insights.

The reason that all these data-related roles are merging together, then, is because the infrastructure problem is becoming less intense and the data analysis and modeling domain is becoming more democratized.

If you think of yourself today as a data scientist, or a data analyst, or a database administrator, or a systems programmer, this is either totally exhilarating or totally unrealistic. It is exhilarating if you can't wait to do all the other tasks that you've considered beyond your ken if the barriers to entry have fallen as low as I claim they have. If you are excited and raring to learn the things you will need to know in this new world of data, welcome![7] This book is for you.

If my vision of a blend of roles strikes you as an unlikely dystopian future, hear me out. The vision of autoscaling services that require very little in the form of infrastructure management might be completely alien to your experience if you are in an enterprise environment that is notoriously slow moving—there is no way, you might think, that data roles are going to change as dramatically as all that by the time you retire.

Well, maybe. I don't know where you work or how open to change your organization is. What I believe, though, is that more and more organizations and more and more industries are going to be like digital natives. There will be increasingly more openings for full stack data scientists, and data engineers will be as sought after as data scientists are today. This is because data engineers will be people who can do data science and know enough about infrastructure so as to be able to run their data science workloads on the public cloud. It will be worthwhile for you to learn data science terminology and data science frameworks, and make yourself more valuable for the next decade.

## Collaboration

Even if you work in a company with strict separation of responsibilities, it can be helpful to know how the other teams do their work. This is because there are many

---

7 The words "need to know" are important here. It can sometimes be intimidating to see the breadth and depth of data science and despair of ever understanding everything. Here's the truth: there is no one who knows the entire field in-and-out. Everyone is, at some level, glossing over some areas. Which areas? Areas that are not important to the problems that they are currently working on. This then gives you a strategy to approach data science—rather than try to learn topics ("I will learn RNNs this month") or learn how to solve problems ("I will learn how to use AI to complete phrases"). Start with simple approaches, and stop once things become difficult and unintelligible. In most fields of AI, the simple approaches will get you quite far. Also, a deep understanding of the underlying mathematics is usually not required to implement a complex approach using frameworks like Keras.

artifacts that they create that you will use, or that you will create and they will use. Knowing their requirements and constraints will help you be more effective at communicating across organizational boundaries.

The various job roles related to data and machine learning are shown in Figure 1-2. All these roles collaborate in creating a production machine learning model. Between data ingestion and the end-user interface, there are multiple handoffs. Every such handoff presents an opportunity for misunderstanding the requirements of the next stage or for an inability to take over what's been created at the previous stage.

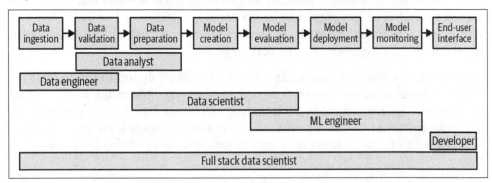

*Figure 1-2. There are many job roles that need to collaborate to take a data science solution from idea to production. Every handoff carries a risk of failure.*

Understanding the adjacent roles, the tools they work with, and the infrastructure that they use can help you reduce the chances of the baton getting dropped.

That said, it is very difficult to get a clean separation of responsibilities—the best organizations that I know, the ones that have hundreds to thousands of machine learning models in production, employ full stack data scientists that work on a problem from inception to production. They may have specialist data analysts, data engineers, data scientists, or ML engineers, but mostly in a maintenance capacity—the innovation tends to be done by the full stack folks. Even the full stack data scientists have areas in which they are stronger and areas where they collaborate with specialists.

# Best Practices

This entire book consists of an extended case study. Solving a real-world, practical problem will help cut through all the hype that surrounds big data, machine learning, cloud computing, and so on. Pulling a case study apart and putting it together in multiple ways illuminates the capabilities and shortcomings of the various big data and machine learning tools that are available to you. A case study can help you identify the kinds of data-driven decisions that you can make in your business and illuminate the considerations behind the data you need to collect and curate, as well as the kinds of statistical and machine learning models you can use. I will attempt, through-out this book, to apply current best practices.

## Simple to Complex Solutions

One of the ways that this book mirrors practice is that I use a real-world dataset to solve a realistic scenario and address problems as they come up. So, I will begin with a decision that needs to be made and apply different statistical and machine learning methods to gain insight into making that decision in a data-driven manner. This will give you the ability to explore other problems and the confidence to solve them from first principles. As with most things, I will begin with simple solutions and work my way to more complex ones. Starting with a complex solution will only obscure details about the problem that are better understood when solving it in simpler ways. Of course, the simpler solutions will have drawbacks, and these will help to motivate the need for additional complexity.

One thing that I do not do, however, is to go back and retrofit earlier solutions based on knowledge that I gain in the process of carrying out more sophisticated approaches. In your practical work, however, I strongly recommend that you main-tain the software associated with early attempts at a problem, and that you go back and continuously enhance those early attempts with what you learn along the way. Parallel experimentation is the name of the game. Due to the linear nature of a book, I don't do it, but I heartily recommend that you continue to actively maintain several models. Given the choice of two models with similar accuracy measures, you can then choose the simpler one—it makes no sense to use more complex models if a simpler approach can work with some modifications.[8] Another reason to have multi-ple models is that a drop-in replacement is useful to have if you discover that the cur-rent production model drops in accuracy or is discovered to have unwanted behaviors.

## Cloud Computing

Before I joined Google, I was a research scientist working on machine learning algo-rithms for weather diagnosis and prediction. The machine learning models involved multiple weather sensors, but were highly dependent on weather radar data. A few years ago, when we undertook a project to reanalyze historical weather radar data (*https://oreil.ly/8HPoR*) using the latest algorithms, it took us four years to do. How-ever, more recently, my team was able to build rainfall estimates off the same dataset,

---

8 This goes by the name Principle of Parsimony or Occam's Razor and holds that the simplest explanation, with the fewest assumptions, is best. This is because simpler models are likely to fail less often because they depend on fewer assumptions. In engineering terms, another advantage of simpler models is that they tend to be less costly to implement.

but were able to traverse the dataset in about two weeks. You can imagine the pace of innovation that results when you take something that used to take four years and make it doable in two weeks.

Four years to two weeks. The reason was that much of the work as recently as five years ago involved moving data around. We'd retrieve data from tape drives, stage it to disk, process it, and move it off to make way for the next set of data. Figuring out what jobs had failed was time consuming, and retrying failed jobs involved multiple steps including a human in the loop. We were running it on a cluster of machines that had a fixed size. The combination of all these things meant that it took incredibly long periods of time to process the historical archive. After we began doing everything on the public cloud, we found that we could store all of the radar data on cloud storage and, as long as we were accessing it from virtual machines (VMs) in the same region, data transfer speeds were fast enough. We still had to stage the data to disks, carry out the computation, and bring down the VMs, but this was a lot more manageable. Simply lowering the amount of data movement between tape and disk and running the processes on many more machines enabled us to carry out processing much faster; to the credit of *elasticity* (the ability to seamlessly increase the number of resources we can assign to a job in the public cloud.

Was it more expensive to run the jobs on 10 times more machines than we did when we did the processing on premises? No, because the economics are usually in favor of renting on demand rather than buying the processing power outright, especially if you will not be using the machines 24-7. Whether you run 10 machines for 10 hours or 100 machines for 1 hour, the cost remains the same. Why not, then, get your answers in an hour rather than 10 hours?

In this book, we will do all our data science on Google Cloud in order to take advantage of the near-infinite scale that the public cloud offers.

## Serverless

When we did our weather data preparation using cloud-based VMs, we were still not taking full advantage of what the cloud has to offer. We should have completely foregone the process of spinning up VMs, installing software on them, and looking for failed jobs—what we should have done was to use an autoscaling data processing framework such as BigQuery or Cloud Dataflow. Had we done that, we would have been able to run our jobs on thousands of machines and might have brought our processing time from two weeks to a few hours. Not having to manage any infrastructure is itself a huge benefit when it comes to trawling through terabytes of data. Having the data processing, analysis, and machine learning autoscale to thousands of machines is a bonus.

The key benefit of performing data engineering in the cloud is the amount of time that it saves you.[9] You shouldn't need to wait days or months—instead, because many jobs are embarrassingly parallel, you can get your results in minutes to hours by having them run on thousands of machines. You might not be able to afford permanently owning so many machines, but it is definitely possible to rent them for minutes at a time. These time savings make autoscaled services on a public cloud the logical choice to carry out data processing.

Running data jobs on thousands of machines for minutes at a time requires fully managed services. Storing the data locally on the virtual machines or persistent disks as with the Apache Hadoop cluster doesn't scale unless you know precisely what jobs are going to be run, when, and where. You will not be able to downsize the cluster of machines if you don't have automatic retries for failed jobs and more importantly, shuffle the data around in remaining data nodes (assuming there is enough free space). The total computation time will be the time taken by the most overloaded worker unless you have dynamic task shifting among the nodes in the cluster. All of these point to the need for autoscaling services that dynamically resize the cluster, split jobs down into tasks, move tasks between compute nodes, and can rely on highly efficient networks to move data to the nodes that are doing the processing.

On Google Cloud Platform, the key autoscaling, fully managed, "serverless" services are BigQuery (for data analytics), Cloud Spanner (for databases), Cloud Dataflow (for data processing pipelines), Cloud Pub/Sub (for message-driven systems), Cloud Bigtable (for high-throughput ingest), Cloud Run or Cloud Functions (for applications, tasks), and Vertex AI (for machine learning).[10] Using autoscaled services like these makes it possible for a data engineer to begin tackling more complex business problems because they have been freed from the world of managing their own machines and software installations whether in the form of bare hardware, virtual machines, or containers. Given the choice between a product that requires you to first configure a container, server, or cluster, and another product that frees you from those considerations, choose the serverless one. You will have more time to solve the problems that actually matter to your business.

# A Probabilistic Decision

Imagine that you are about to take a flight and, just before the flight takes off from the runway (and you are asked to switch off your phone), you have the opportunity to

---

9 For your organization, any time you save translates to budget savings. You get more accomplished with a smaller budget.

10 For a word that gets bandied about quite a lot, there is not much agreement on what exactly *serverless* means. In this book, I'll call a service serverless if users of the service have to supply only code and not have to manage the lifecycle of the machines that the code runs on.

send one last text message. It is past the published departure time and you are a bit anxious. Figure 1-3 presents a graphic view of the scenario.

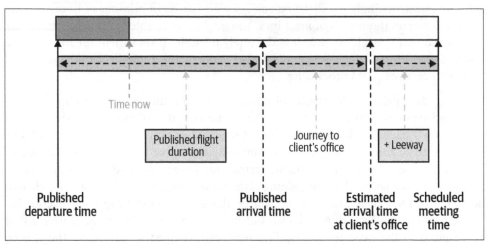

*Figure 1-3. A graphic illustration of the case study: if the flight departs late, should the road warrior cancel the meeting?*

The reason for your anxiety is that you have scheduled an important meeting with a client at its offices. As befits a rational data scientist,[11] you scheduled things rather precisely. You have taken the airline at its word with respect to when the flight would arrive, accounted for the time to hail a taxi, and used an online mapping tool to estimate the time to the client's office. Then, you added some leeway (say 30 minutes) and told the client what time you'd meet them. And now, it turns out that the flight is departing late. So, should you send a text informing your client that you will not be able to make the meeting because your flight will be late or should you not?

This decision could be made in many ways, including by gut instinct and using heuristics. Being very rational people, we (you and I) will make this decision informed by data. Also, we see that this is a decision made by many of the road warriors in our company day in and day out. It would be a good thing if we could do it in a systematic way and have a corporate server send out an alert to travelers about anticipated delays if we see events on their calendar that they are likely to miss. Let's build a data framework to solve this problem.

---

11 Perhaps I'm simply rationalizing my own behavior—if I'm getting to the departure gate with more than 15 minutes to spare at least once in about five flights, I decide that I must be getting to the airport too early and adjust accordingly. Fifteen minutes and 20% tend to capture my risk aversion. If you are wondering why my risk aversion threshold is not simply 15 minutes but includes an associated probabilistic threshold, read on.

## Probabilistic Approach

If we decide to make the decision in a data-driven way, there are several approaches we can take. Should we cancel the meeting if there is greater than a 30% chance that you will miss it? Or should we assign a cost to postponing the meeting (the client might go with our competition before we get a chance to demonstrate our great product) versus not making it to a scheduled meeting (the client might never take our calls again) and minimize our expected loss in revenue? The probabilistic approach translates to risk, and many practical decisions hinge on risk. In addition, the probabilistic approach is more general because if we know the probability and the monetary loss associated with missing the meeting, it is possible to compute the expected value of any decision that we make. For example, suppose the chance of missing the meeting is 20% and we decide to not cancel the meeting (because 20% is less than our decision threshold of 30%). But there is only a 25% chance that the client will sign the big deal (worth a cool million bucks) for which you are meeting them. Because there is an 80% chance that we will make the meeting, the expected upside value of not canceling the meeting is $0.8 \times 0.25 \times 1$ million, or \$200,000. The downside value of not canceling is that we do miss the meeting. Assuming that the client is 90% likely to blow us off in the future if we miss a meeting with them, the expected downside is $0.2 \times 0.9 \times 0.25 \times 1$ million, or \$45,000. This yields an expected value of \$155,000 in favor of not canceling the meeting. We can adjust these numbers to come up with an appropriate probabilistic decision threshold.

Another advantage of a probabilistic approach is that we can directly take into account human psychology. You might feel frazzled if you arrive at a meeting only two minutes before it starts and, as a result, might not be able to perform at your best. It could be that arriving only two minutes early to a very important meeting doesn't feel like being on time. This obviously varies from person to person, but let's say that this time interval that you need to settle down is 15 minutes. You want to cancel a meeting for which you cannot arrive 15 minutes early. You could also treat this time interval as your personal risk aversion threshold, a final bit of headroom if you will. Thus, you want to arrive at the client's site 15 minutes before the meeting and you want to cancel the meeting if there is a less than 70% chance of doing that. This, then, is our decision criterion:

> Cancel the client meeting if the probability of arriving 15 minutes early is 70% or less.

I've explained the 15 minutes, but I haven't explained the 70%. Surely, you can use the aforementioned model diagram (Figure 1-3, in which we modeled our journey from the airport to the client's office), plug in the actual departure delay, and figure out what time you will arrive at the client's offices. If that is less than 15 minutes before the meeting starts, you should cancel! Where does the 70% come from?

## Probability Density Function

It is important to realize that the model diagram (Figure 1-3) of times is not exact. The probabilistic decision framework gives you a way to treat this in a principled way. For example, although the airline company says that the flight duration is 127 minutes and publishes an arrival time, not all flights are exactly 127 minutes long. If the plane happens to take off with the wind, catch a tail wind, and land against the wind, the flight might take only 90 minutes. Flights for which the winds are all precisely wrong might take 127 minutes (i.e., the airline might be publishing worst-case scenarios for the route). Google Maps predicts journey times based on historical data, and the actual journeys by taxi will be centered around those times. Your estimate of how long it takes to walk from the airport gate to the taxi stand might be predicated on landing at a specific gate, and actual times may vary. So, even though the model depicts a certain time between airline departure and your arrival at the client site, this is not an exact number. The actual time between departure and arrival might have a distribution that looks like that shown in Figure 1-4.

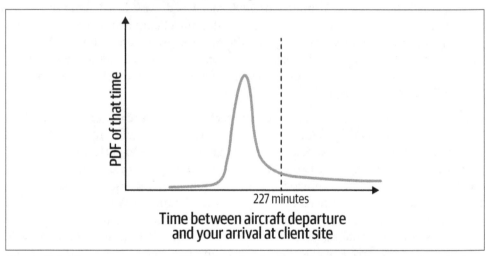

*Figure 1-4. There are many possible values for the time differences between aircraft departure and your arrival at a client site, and the distribution of that value is called the probability density function.*

The curve in Figure 1-4 is referred to as the probability density function (abbreviated as the PDF). In fact, the PDF can be (and often is) greater than one. In order to get a probability, you will need to integrate the probability density function.[12] A simple way to do this integration is provided by the cumulative distribution function (CDF).

---

12 To integrate a function is to compute the area under the curve of that function up to a specific x-value, as shown in Figure 1-5.

# Cumulative Distribution Function

The cumulative probability distribution function of a value x is the probability that the observed value X is less than the threshold x. For example, you can get the cumulative distribution function (CDF) for 227 minutes by finding the fraction of flights for which the time difference is less than 227 minutes, as shown in Figure 1-5.

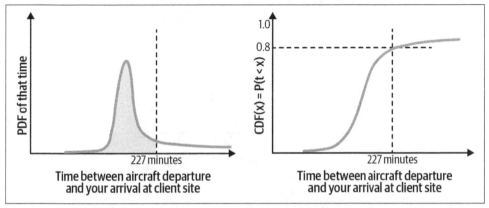

*Figure 1-5. The CDF is the area under the curve of the PDF. It is easier to understand and keep track of than the PDF. In particular, it is bounded between 0 and 1, whereas the PDF could be greater than 1.*

Let's interpret the graph in Figure 1-5. What does a CDF (227 minutes) = 0.8 mean? It means that 80% of flights will arrive such that we will make it to the client's site in less than 227 minutes—this includes both the situation in which we can make it in 100 minutes and the situation in which it takes us 226 minutes. The CDF, unlike the PDF, is bounded between 0 and 1. The y-axis value is a probability, just not the probability of an exact value. It is, instead, the probability of observing all values less than that value.

Because the time to get from the arrival airport to the client's office is unaffected by the flight's departure delay,[13] we can ignore it in our modeling. We can similarly ignore the time to walk through the airport, hail the taxi, and get ready for the meeting. So, we need only to find the probability of the arrival delay being more than 15 minutes. If that probability is 0.3 or more, we will need to cancel the meeting. In terms of the CDF, that means that the probability of arrival delays of less than 15 minutes has to be at least 0.7, as presented in Figure 1-6.

Thus, our decision criteria translate to the following:

---

13  This is a simplifying assumption—if the flight was supposed to arrive at 2 p.m., and instead arrives at 4 p.m., the traveler is more likely to hit rush hour traffic.

---

Cancel the client meeting if the CDF of an arrival delay of 15 minutes is less than 70%.

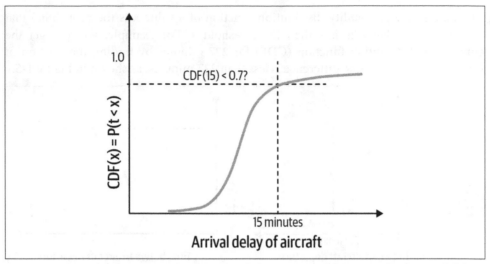

*Figure 1-6. Our decision criterion is to cancel the meeting if the CDF of an arrival delay of 15 minutes is less than 70%. Loosely speaking, we want to be 70% sure of the aircraft arriving no more than 15 minutes late.*

The rest of this book is going to be about building data pipelines that enable us to compute the CDF of arrival delays using statistical and machine learning models. From the computed CDF of arrival delays, we can look up the CDF of a 15-minute arrival delay and check whether it is less than 70%.

## Choices Made

What data do we need to predict the probability of a specific flight delay? What tools shall we use? Should we use Hadoop? BigQuery? Should we do it on my laptop or should we do it in the public cloud? The question about data is easily answered—we will use historical flight arrival data (*https://oreil.ly/Dk3jc*) published by the US Bureau of Transportation Statistics, analyze it, and use it to inform our decision. Often, a data scientist would choose the best tool based on their experience and just use that one tool to help make the decision, but here, I will take you on a tour of several ways that we could carry out the analysis. This will also allow us to model best practice in the sense of picking the simplest tool and analysis that suffices.

## Choosing Cloud

On a cursory examination of the data, we discover that there were more than 30.6 million flights in 2015–2019.[14] My laptop, nice as it is, is not going to cut it. We will do the data analysis on the public cloud. Which cloud? We will use the Google Cloud Platform (GCP). Although some of the tools we use in this book (notably Hadoop, Spark, Beam, TensorFlow, etc.) are available on other cloud platforms, the managed services I use (BigQuery, Cloud Dataproc, Cloud Dataflow, Vertex AI, etc.) are specific to GCP. Using GCP will allow me to avoid fiddling around with virtual machines and machine configuration and focus solely on the data analysis. Also, I do work at Google, so this is the platform I know best.

## Not a Reference Book

This book is not an exhaustive look at data science—there are other books (often based on university courses) that do that. It is also not a reference book on Google Cloud—the documentation is much more timely and comprehensive. Instead, this book allows you to look over my shoulder as I solve one particular data science problem using a variety of methods and tools. I promise to be quite chatty and tell you what I am thinking and why I am doing what I am doing. Instead of presenting you with fully formed solutions and code, I will show you intermediate steps as I build up to a solution.

This learning material is presented to you in three forms:

- This book that you are reading.
- The code referenced throughout the book on GitHub (*https://github.com/Google CloudPlatform/data-science-on-gcp*). Note in particular, the *README.md* file in each folder of the GitHub repository.
- Labs with instructions that allow you to try the code of this book in a sandbox environment, available at *https://qwiklabs.com*.

Rather than simply read this book cover to cover, I strongly encourage you to follow along with me by also taking advantage of the code. After reading each chapter, or major section in each chapter, try to repeat what I did, referring to the code if something's not clear.

---

14  Yes, this is the second edition of the book, published in 2022. The first edition of the book used only 2015 data. Here, I'll use 2015–2019. I stopped with 2019 because 2020 was the year of the COVID-19 pandemic, and flights were rather spotty.

## Getting Started with the Code

To begin working with the code, follow these steps:

- Sign up (*https://console.cloud.google.com*) for the free trial if you haven't already done so. Otherwise, use your existing GCP account.

- Create a new project and give it any name you want. I suggest calling it ds-on-gcp. GCP will assign a unique project ID to your project (see Figure 1-7). You will need to provide this unique ID whenever you do anything that is billable. Once you are finished working through this book, simply delete the project to stop getting billed.

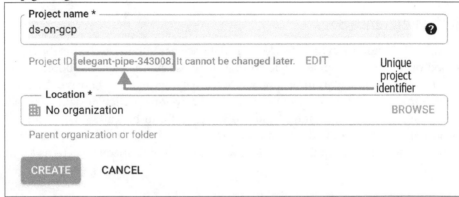

*Figure 1-7. When you create a new project, GCP will assign it a unique project identifier. Use this unique identifier whenever a script or program asks for a project ID. You will also be able to get the unique identifier from the dashboard (see Figure 1-8).*

- Open Cloud Shell, your terminal access to GCP. To open Cloud Shell, on the menu bar, click the Activate Cloud Shell icon, as shown in Figure 1-8. Even though the web console is very nice, I typically prefer to script things rather than go through a GUI. To me, web GUIs are great for occasional and/or first-time use, but for repeatable tasks, nothing beats the terminal.

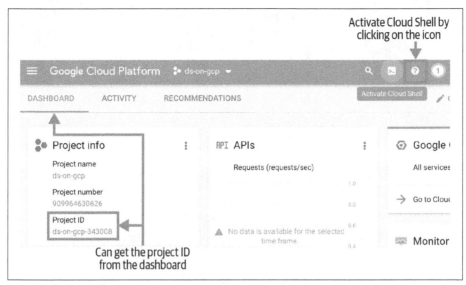

*Figure 1-8. Activate Cloud Shell by clicking on the highlighted icon in the top right corner of the GCP web console. Note that the unique project identifier can be obtained at any time from the dashboard.*

Cloud Shell is a micro-VM that is alive for the duration of the browser window and gives you terminal access to the micro-VM. Close the browser window, and the micro-VM goes away. The Cloud Shell VM is free and comes loaded with many of the tools that developers on Google Cloud Platform will need. For example, it has Python, Git, the Google Cloud SDK, and Orion (a web-based code editor) installed on it. Although the Cloud Shell VM is ephemeral, it is attached to a persistent disk that is tied to your user account. Files that you store in your home directory are saved across different Cloud Shell sessions.

- In the Cloud Shell window, git clone my repository by typing the following:

```
git clone \
    https://github.com/GoogleCloudPlatform/data-science-on-gcp
    cd data-science-on-gcp
```

Because the Git repository was checked out to the home directory of the Cloud Shell micro-VM, it will be persistent across browser sessions.

- Note that there is a directory corresponding to each chapter of this book (other than Chapters 1 and 12). In each directory, you will find a *README.md* file with directions on how to replicate the steps in that chapter.

Do not copy-paste code snippets from the book. Read the chapters and *then* try out the code by following the steps in each chapter's *README.md* using the *code in the repository*. I recommend that you not copy-paste from electronic versions of this book.

- The book is written for readability, not for completeness. Some flags to cloud tools may be omitted so that we can focus on the key aspect being discussed. The GitHub code will have the full command.
- The GitHub repo will be kept up to date with new versions of cloud tools, Python, etc.
- When following along in the book, it's easy to miss a step.
- Copy-paste of special characters from PDF is problematic.

---

### Developing Locally

If you prefer to do development on your local machine (rather than in Cloud Shell), you will need to install three pieces of software (all three are already present on Cloud Shell, so this is only if you wish to develop on your own laptop):

1. Python version 3.6 or higher
2. The Google Cloud SDK (*https://oreil.ly/eRUX6*)
3. The version control software Git

---

That's it. You are now ready to follow along with me. As you do, remember that you need to change my project ID to the ID of your project (you can find this on the dashboard of the Google Cloud web console, as shown in Figure 1-8) and my bucket-name to your bucket on Cloud Storage (you will create this in Chapter 2; we'll introduce buckets at that time).

## Agile Architecture for Data Science on Google Cloud

I will introduce Google Cloud products and technologies as we go along. In this section, I will provide a high-level overview of why I choose what I choose. Do not worry if you don't recognize the names of these technologies (e.g., data warehouse) or products (e.g., BigQuery) since we will cover them in detail as we go along.

# What Is Agile Architecture?

One of the principles of Agile software (*https://oreil.ly/95PKa*) is that simplicity, by which we mean maximizing the amount of work not done, is essential. Another is that requirements change frequently, and so flexibility is important. An Agile architecture, therefore, is one that gives you:

- Speed of development. You should be able to go from idea to deployment as quickly as possible.

- Flexibility to quickly implement new features. Sometimes speed comes at the expense of flexibility—the architecture might shoehorn you into a very limited set of use cases. You don't want that.

- Low-maintenance. Don't spend your time managing infrastructure.

- Autoscaling and resiliency so that you are not spending your time monitoring infrastructure.

What does such an architecture look like on Google Cloud when it comes to Data Analytics and AI? It will use low-code and no-code services (pre-built connectors, automatic replication, ELT [extract-load-transform], AutoML) so that you get speed of development. For flexibility, the architecture will allow you to drop down to developer-friendly, powerful code (Apache Beam, SQL, TensorFlow) whenever needed. These will run on serverless infrastructure (Pub/Sub, Dataflow, BigQuery, Vertex AI) so that you get low-maintenance, autoscaling, and resiliency.

## No-Code, Low-Code

When it comes to architecture, choose no-code over low-code and low-code over writing custom code. Rather than writing ETL (extract-transform-load) pipelines to transform the data you need before you land it into BigQuery, use pre-built connectors to directly land the raw data into BigQuery (see Figure 1-9). Then, transform the data into the form you need using SQL views directly in the data warehouse. You will be a lot more agile if you choose an ELT approach over an ETL approach.

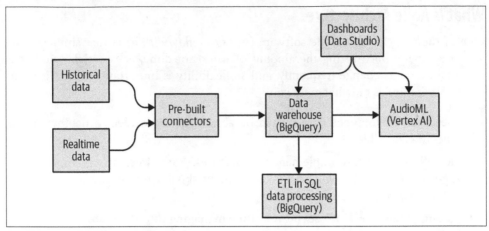

*Figure 1-9. Agile architecture for most use cases.*

Another place is when you choose your ML modeling framework. Don't start with custom TensorFlow models. Start with AutoML. That's no-code. You can invoke AutoML directly from BigQuery, avoiding the need to build complex data and ML pipelines. If necessary, move on to pre-built models from TensorFlow Hub and pre-built containers on Vertex AI. That's low-code. Build your own custom ML models only as a last resort.

## Use Managed Services

You will want to be able to drop down to code if the low-code approach is too restrictive. Fortunately, the no-code architecture described previously is a subset of the full architecture, shown in Figure 1-10, that gives you all the flexibility you need.

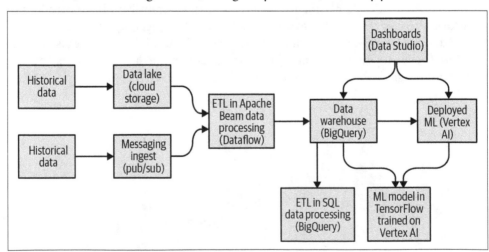

*Figure 1-10. Agile architecture for analytics and AI.*

When the use case warrants it, you will have the full flexibility of Apache Beam, SQL, and TensorFlow. This is critical—for use cases where the ELT + AutoML approach is too restrictive, you have the ability to drop to a ETL/Dataflow + Keras/Vertex approach.

Best of all, the architecture is unified, so you are not maintaining two stacks. Because the first architecture is a subset of the second, you can accomplish both easy and hard use cases in a unified way.

It is this architecture that we build in this book.

## Summary

A key goal of data analysis is to be able to provide data-driven guidance toward making accurate decisions systematically. Ideally, this guidance can be provided as a service, and providing as a service gives rise to questions of service quality—both in terms of the accuracy of the guidance and the reliability, latency, and security of the implementation.

A data engineer needs to be able to go from designing data-based services and building statistical and machine learning models to implementing them as reliable, high-quality services. This has become easier with the advent of cloud services that provide an autoscaling, serverless, managed infrastructure. Also, the wide availability of data science tools has made it so that you don't need to be a specialist in data science to create a statistical or machine learning model. As a result, the ability to work with data has spread throughout an enterprise—no longer is it a restricted skill.

Our case study involves a traveler who needs to decide whether to cancel a meeting depending on whether the flight they are on will arrive late. The decision criterion is that the meeting should be canceled if the probability of an arriving within 15 minutes of the scheduled time is less than 70%. To estimate the probability of this arrival delay, we will use historical data from the US Bureau of Transportation Statistics.

To follow along with me throughout the book, create a project on Google Cloud Platform and a clone of the GitHub repository of the source code listings in this book. Alternatively, try the code of this book in a sandbox environment using Qwiklabs. The folder for each of the chapters in GitHub contains a *README.md* file that lists the steps to be able to replicate what I do in the chapters. So, if you get stuck, refer to those README files.

Incidentally, the footnotes in this book are footnotes because they break the flow of the chapter. Some readers of the first edition noted that they realized only toward the middle of the book that many of the footnotes contained useful information. So, this might be a good time to read the footnotes if you have been skipping them.

## Suggested Resources

What is data science on Google Cloud? What does the toolkit consist of? The data science website in Google Cloud (*https://oreil.ly/UbRIB*) contains a set of whitepapers and reference guides that address these topics. Bookmark this page and use it as a starting point for everything data science on GCP.

There are five key autoscaling, fully managed, serverless products for data analytics and AI on Google Cloud. We'll cover them later in the book, but these videos and articles are a great starting point if you want to dive deeper immediately:

- BigQuery is the serverless data warehouse that forms the heart of most data architectures built in Google Cloud. I recommend watching "Google BigQuery Introduction by Jordan Tigani" (*https://oreil.ly/NYP5H*), one of the founding engineers of BigQuery, even though it is a few years old now.

- Dataflow is the execution service for batch and streaming pipelines written using Apache Beam. Start with "What Is Dataflow?" (*https://oreil.ly/eyeW1*) by Google Cloud Tech, a 5-minute video that introduces what Dataflow is and how it works. This is part of the Google Cloud Drawing Board (*https://oreil.ly/6a1t1*) series of videos—they are quick and informative ways to learn about various topics on Google Cloud.

- Pub/Sub is the global messaging service that can be used for use cases ranging from user interaction and real-time event distribution to refreshing distributed caches. Start from the overview documentation page (*https://oreil.ly/5X1ys*). All Google Cloud products have an overview page that can serve as a launching point to learning not only what a product does but also what it can be used for and how to choose between it and other alternatives.

- Cloud Run provides an autoscaling, serverless platform for containerized applications. You can use it for all kinds of automation and lightweight data transformation. The best way to learn Cloud Run is to try it out, and Qwiklabs provides a great set of hands-on labs (*https://oreil.ly/r6rFM*) in a sandbox environment. While you are there, check out the Catalog for other quests and labs on the topic of choice.

- Vertex AI is the end-to-end ML development, deployment, and automation platform on Google Cloud. A good place to learn about it is to watch the video that accompanied its announcement at Google I/O, "Build End-to-End Solutions with Vertex AI" (*https://oreil.ly/MRZy9*), by the Google Cloud Tech YouTube channel.

There are two key fully managed transaction processing databases on Google Cloud:

- Bigtable is a distributed NoSQL database. You could, of course, learn about it from Google Cloud Tech's overview video, "What Is Cloud Bigtable?" (*https://oreil.ly/V6z5j*), or the Bigtable documentation (*https://oreil.ly/cJZjq*), but I recommend you read the famous research paper that introduced the idea to the world: Fay Chang et al., "Bigtable: A Distributed Storage System for Structured Data" (*https://research.google/pubs/pub27898*), *7th USENIX Symposium on Operating Systems Design and Implementation (OSDI)*, USENIX (2006): 205–218.

- Spanner is a distributed SQL database that provides global strong consistency and five nines (99.999%) availability—something that greatly simplifies your architecture if you are in a domain like banking or gaming where you have concurrent users all over the world. "Why You Should Use Google's Cloud Spanner for Your Next Game" (*https://oreil.ly/TiImw*), a 2019 blog post by Miles Ward, CTO of Google's partner SADA, is a great starting point for Spanner and Spanner best practices.

For more on probability as applied in information theory and artificial intelligence, read either Chapter 3 of *Deep Learning* (*https://oreil.ly/c90dI*), "Probability and Information Theory," by Ian Goodfellow et al. (MIT Press) or a summary of that chapter (*https://oreil.ly/hd899*) by William Green on *Medium*. The foundation of information theory was laid by Claude Shannon in a classic 1948 paper (*https://oreil.ly/Lw7Hg*). He is also famous for perhaps the most influential masters thesis in history (*https://oreil.ly/b6jdc*)—showing how to use Boolean algebra to test circuit designs without even building the circuits in the first place.

# CHAPTER 2

# Ingesting Data into the Cloud

In Chapter 1, we explored the idea of deciding whether to cancel a meeting in a data-driven way. We decided on a probabilistic decision criterion: to cancel the meeting with a client if the probability of the flight arriving within 15 minutes of the scheduled arrival time was less than 70%. To model the arrival delay given a variety of attributes about the flight, we need historical data that covers a large number of flights. Historical data that includes this information from 1987 onward is available from the US Bureau of Transportation Statistics (*https://oreil.ly/g03E2*) (BTS). One of the reasons that the government captures this data is to monitor the fraction of flights by a carrier that are on-time (defined as flights that arrive less than 15 minutes late), so as to be able to hold airlines accountable.[1] Because the key use case is to compute on-time performance, the dataset that captures flight delays is called Airline On-Time Performance Data (*https://oreil.ly/91or5*). That's the dataset we will use in this book.

 All of the code snippets in this chapter are available in the folder *02_ingest* of the book's GitHub repository (*https://github.com/GoogleCloudPlatform/data-science-on-gcp*). See the last section of Chapter 1 for instructions on how to clone the repository, and see the *README.md* file in the *02_ingest* directory for instructions on how to do the steps described in this chapter.

---

1 See, for example, this US Senate committee report (*https://oreil.ly/IfJNo*) on the proposed Airline Customer Service Improvement Act. The bill referenced in the report was not enacted into law, but it illustrates Congress's monitoring function based on the statistics collected by the Department of Transportation.

# Airline On-Time Performance Data

For nearly 40 years, all major US air carriers have been required to file statistics about each of their domestic flights with the BTS. The data they are required to file includes the scheduled departure and arrival times as well as the actual departure and arrival times. From the scheduled and actual arrival times, the arrival delay associated with each flight can be calculated. Therefore, this dataset can give us the true value or "label" for building a model to predict arrival delay.

The actual departure and arrival times are defined rather precisely, based on when the parking brake of the aircraft is released and when it is later reactivated at the destination. The rules even go as far as to define what happens if the pilot forgets to engage the parking brake—in that case, the time that the passenger door is closed or opened is used instead. Because of the precise nature of the rules, and the fact that they are enforced, we can treat arrival and departure times from all carriers uniformly. Had this not been the case, we would have to dig deeper into the quirks of how each carrier defines "departure" and "arrival," and do the appropriate translations.[2] Good data science begins with such standardized, repeatable, trustable data collection rules; you should use the BTS's very well-defined data collection rules as a model when creating standards for your own data collection, whether it is log files, web impressions, or sensor data that you are collecting. The airlines report this particular data monthly, and it is collated by the BTS across all carriers and published as a free dataset on the web.

In addition to the scheduled and actual departure and arrival times, the data includes information such as the origin and destination airports, flight numbers, and nonstop distance between the two airports. It is unclear from the documentation whether this distance is the distance taken by the flight in question or whether it is simply a precomputed distance—if the flight needs to go around a thunderstorm, is the distance in the dataset the actual distance traveled by the flight or the great-circle distance between the airports?[3] This is something that we will need to examine—it should be easy to ascertain whether the distance between a pair of airports remains the same or changes. In addition, a flight is broken into three parts (Figure 2-1)—taxi-out duration, air time, and taxi-in duration—and all three time intervals are reported.

---

2 For example, weather radar data from before 2000 had timestamps assigned by a radar engineer. Essentially, the engineers would look at their wristwatches and enter a time into the radar products generator. Naturally, this was subject to all kinds of human errors—dates could be many hours off. The underlying problem was fixed by the introduction of network clocks to ensure consistent times between all the radars on the US weather radar network. When using historical weather data, though, time correction is an important preprocessing step.

3 The shortest path between two points on the globe is an arc that passes through the two points and whose focus point is the center of the globe.

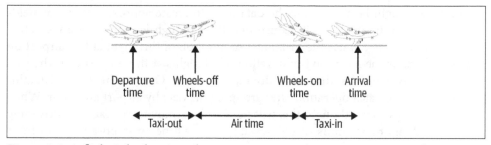

*Figure 2-1. A flight is broken into three parts: taxi-out duration, air time, and taxi-in duration.*

## Knowability

Before we get started with ingesting data, we need to decide what it is that we have to ingest into our model. There are two potential traps—causality and training–serving skew (I'll define them shortly). We should take care to avoid these problems during the ingest phase, in order to save us a lot of heartburn later.

## Causality

The causality principle boils down to this key question: what data will we be able to provide to the model at the time that we need to make predictions? If we won't know some piece of information about the flight during prediction, we cannot use that information as an input during training.

Some of the fields in the dataset could form the inputs to our model to help us predict the arrival delay as a function of these variables. Some, but not all. Why? It should be clear that we cannot use taxi-in duration or actual flight distance because at the time the aircraft is taking off, which is when we want to make our decision on whether to cancel the meeting, we will not know either of these things. The in-air flight time between two airports is not known a priori given that pilots have the ability to speed up or slow down. Thus, even though we have these fields in our historical dataset, we should not use them in our prediction model. This is called a causality constraint.

The causality constraint is one instance of a more general principle. Before using any field as input to a model, we should consider whether the data will be known at the time we want to make the decision. It is not always a matter of logic as with the taxi-in duration. Sometimes, practical considerations such as security (is the decision maker allowed to know this data?), the latency between the time the data is collected and the time it is available to the model, and the cost of obtaining the information also play a part in making some data unusable. At the same time, it is possible that approximations might be available for fields that we cannot use because of causality—even though, for example, we cannot use the actual flight distance, we should be able to use the great-circle distance between the airports in our model.

Similarly, we might be able to use the data itself to create approximations for fields that are obviated by the causality constraint. Even though we cannot use the actual taxi-in duration, we can use the mean taxi-in duration of this flight at this airport on previous days, or the mean taxi-in duration of all flights at this airport over the past hour, to approximate what the taxi-in duration might be. Over the historical data, this could be a simple batch operation after grouping the data by airport and hour. When predicting in real time, though, this will need to be a moving average on streaming data. Indeed, approximations of unknowable data will be an important part of our models.

## Training–Serving Skew

A training–serving skew is the condition in which you use a variable that's computed differently in your training dataset than in the production model. For example, suppose that you train a model with the distance between cities in miles, but when you predict, the distance that you receive as input is actually in kilometers. That is obviously a bad thing and will result in a bad result from the model because the model will be providing predictions based on the distances being 1.6 times their actual value. Although it is obvious in clear-cut cases such as unit mismatches, the same principle (that the training dataset has to reflect what is done to inputs at prediction time) applies to more subtle scenarios as well.

For example, suppose we determine whether the flight is on a weekday or a weekend and use it as an input to the model. We need to ensure that this calculation is carried out precisely the same way during both training and prediction. For example, if we use the wheels-off time during training but the departure time during prediction, we will suffer from training–serving skew. If the time library we use during training treats the timestamp as being local time, but the library we use during prediction treats the timestamp as being in Coordinated Universal Time (UTC), we will run into training–serving skew.

As our models become increasingly sophisticated—and more and more of a black box—it will become extremely difficult to troubleshoot errors that are caused by a training–serving skew. This is especially true if the code bases for computing inputs for training and during prediction are different and begin to diverge over time. We will always attempt to design our systems in such a way that the possibilities of a training–serving skew are minimized. In particular, we will gravitate toward solutions in which we can use the same code in training (building a model) as in prediction.

The dataset includes codes for the airports (such as ATL for Atlanta) from which and to which the flight is scheduled to depart and land. Planes might land at an airport other than the one they are scheduled to land at if there are in-flight emergencies or if weather conditions cause a deviation. In addition, the flight might be canceled. It is important for us to ascertain how these circumstances are reflected in the dataset—

although they are relatively rare occurrences, our analysis could be adversely affected if we don't deal with them in a reasonable way. The way we deal with these out-of-the-ordinary situations also must be consistent between training and prediction.

The dataset also includes airline codes (such as AA for American Airlines), but it should be noted that airline codes can change over time (for example, United Airlines and Continental Airlines merged and the combined entity began reporting as United Airlines in 2012). If we use airline codes in our prediction, we will need to cope with these changes in a consistent way, too.

## Downloading Data

As of August 2021, there were nearly 200 million records in the on-time performance dataset, with records starting in 1987. The last available data was June 2021, indicating that there is more than a month's delay in updating the dataset—this is going to be important when we automate the process of getting new data.

This is not the most helpful way to provide data for download. For one thing, the data can be downloaded only one month at a time. For another, going through a web form is pretty error-prone. Imagine that you want to download all of the data for 2015. In that scenario, you'd painstakingly select the fields you want for January 2015, submit the form, and then have to repeat the process for February 2015. If you forgot to select a field in February, that field would be missing, and you wouldn't know until you began analyzing the data!

Obviously, we can script the download to make it less tiresome and ensure consistency.[4] However, it is better to download all the raw data, not just a few selected fields. Why? Won't the files be larger if we ask for all the fields? Won't larger files take longer to download?

In this book, our model will use input fields drawn mostly from this dataset, but where feasible and necessary, we will include other datasets such as airport locations and weather. We can download the on-time performance data from the BTS website as comma-separated value (CSV) files. The web interface requires you to filter by geography and period, as illustrated in Figure 2-2. The data itself is offered in two ways: one with all the data in a zipped file and the other containing just the fields that we select in the form.

---

[4] Indeed, scripting the field selection and download is what I did in the first edition of the book. If interested, see the select-and-download code (*https://oreil.ly/GmcNu*) in GitHub in the branch `edition1_tf2`—the key thing is that the web request sends the selected fields inside the POST request and handles the resulting client-side redirect to obtain the ZIP file that is created on demand.

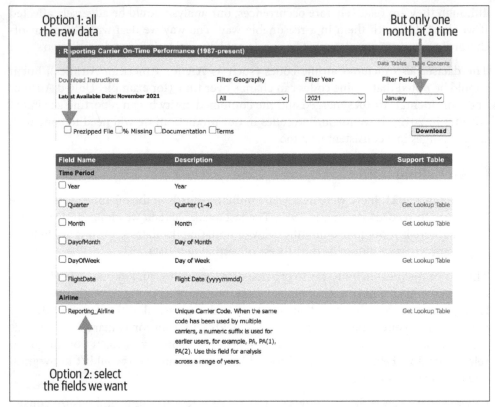

*Figure 2-2. The BTS web interface to download the flights on-time arrival dataset.*

## Hub-and-Spoke Architecture

Yes, the files will be larger if we download all the fields using the static link. But there is a significant drawback to doing preselection. In order to support the interactive capability of selecting fields, the BTS does server-side processing—it extracts the fields we want, creates a custom ZIP file, and makes the ZIP file available for download. This would make our code reliant on the BTS servers having the necessary uptime and reliability.[5] Avoiding the server-side processing should help reduce this dependency.[6]

---

5 Over the last 5 years, I have observed that the BTS server that does this ZIP file creation is frequently down. I know, I know. Ideally, they'd use a public cloud to host their website and/or data, but *you* try telling the US government what to do.

6 Another thing I am doing to limit the dependence on the BTS website is to host the ZIP files on Google Cloud and have my code hit the Google Cloud server. The code by default will not hit the BTS server anymore. The original BTS URL is still present in the code, just commented out, so change it back if you want to try it out.

An even more salient reason is that best practice in data engineering now is to build ELT (extract-load-transform) pipelines, rather than ETL (extract-transform-load) pipelines. What this means is that we will extract the data from BTS and immediately load the data into a data warehouse rather than rely on the BTS server to do transformation for us before loading it into Google Cloud. This point is important. The recommended modern data architecture is to minimize the preprocessing of data—instead, land all available data as-is into the enterprise data warehouse (EDW) and then carry out whatever transformations are necessary for different use cases (see Figure 2-3). This is called a hub-and-spoke architecture, with the EDW functioning as the hub.

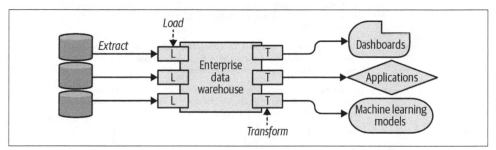

*Figure 2-3. The recommended data architecture, whenever you can make it work, is the hub-and-spoke architecture.*

## Dataset Fields

Even though I'm going to download all the fields, it's worthwhile reading through the column descriptions provided by BTS (*https://oreil.ly/EE9MH*) to learn more about the dataset and get a preliminary idea about what fields are relevant to our problem and whether there are any caveats. For example, Table 2-1 shows three ways in which the airline is recorded. Which of these should we use?

*Table 2-1. The airline operating the flight is recorded in three separate columns*

| Column name | Description (copied from BTS website) |
|---|---|
| Reporting_Airline | Unique Carrier Code. When the same code has been used by multiple carriers, a numeric suffix is used for earlier users; for example, PA, PA(1), PA(2). Use this field for analysis across a range of years. |
| DOT_ID_Reporting_Airline | An identification number assigned by the US Department of Transportation (DOT) to identify a unique airline (carrier). A unique airline (carrier) is defined as one holding and reporting under the same DOT certificate regardless of its Code, Name, or holding company/corporation. |
| IATA_CODE_Reporting_Airline | Assigned by the International Air Transport Association (IATA) and commonly used to identify a carrier. Because the same code might have been assigned to different carriers over time, the code is not always unique. For analysis, use the Unique Carrier Code. |

It's clear that we could use either the `Reporting_Airline` or the `DOT_ID_Report ing_Airline` since they are both unique. Ideally, we'd use whichever one of these corresponds to the common nomenclature (for example, UA or United Airlines). Fortunately, the BTS provides an Analysis link for the columns (see Figure 2-4), so we don't have to wait until we explore the data to make this decision. It turns out that the `Reporting_Airline` is what we want—the IATA code consists of the number 19977 for United Airlines whereas the `Reporting_Airline` is UA as we would like.

**Airline**

| Reporting_Airline | Unique Carrier Code. When the same code has been used by multiple carriers, a numeric suffix is used for earlier users, for example, PA, PA(1), PA(2). Use this field for analysis across a range of years. | Analysis |
| DOT_ID_Reporting_Airline | An identification number assigned by US DOT to identify a unique airline (carrier). A unique airline (carrier) is defined as one holding and reporting under the same DOT certificate regardless of its Code, Name, or holding company/corporation. | Analysis |
| IATA_CODE_Reporting_Airline | Code assigned by IATA and commonly used to identify a carrier. As the same code may have been assigned to different carriers over time, the code is not always unique. For analysis, use the Unique Carrier Code. | |
| Tail_Number | Tail Number | |
| Flight_Number_Reporting_Airline | Flight Number | |

*Figure 2-4. The BTS provides an Analysis link for some of the columns. These provide a handy way to learn what values a field can take.*

The first thing to do in any real-world problem where we are fortunate enough to be provided documentation is to read it![7] After reading through the descriptions of the 100-plus fields in the dataset, there are a few fields that appear relevant to the problem of training, predicting, or evaluating flight arrival delay. Table 2-2 presents the fields I shortlisted.

*Table 2-2. Selected fields from the airline on-time performance dataset downloaded from the BTS (there is a separate table for each month)*

| Column name | Description (copied from BTS website) |
| --- | --- |
| `FlightDate` | Flight date (yyyymmdd) |
| `Reporting_Airline` | Unique Carrier Code. When the same code has been used by multiple carriers, a numeric suffix is used for earlier users; for example, PA, PA(1), PA(2). Use this field for analysis across a range of years. |
| `Origin` | Origin airport |

---

7 Normally, you will also have to verify the description since data dictionaries are quite often outdated. The BTS documentation doesn't have this problem—it is correct and corresponds to the version of the data that BTS publishes.

| Column name | Description (copied from BTS website) |
|---|---|
| Dest | Destination airport |
| CRSDepTime | Computerized reservation system (CRS) departure time (local time: hhmm) |
| DepTime | Actual departure time (local time: hhmm) |
| DepDelay | Difference in minutes between scheduled and actual departure time. Early departures show negative numbers. |
| TaxiOut | Taxi-out duration, in minutes |
| WheelsOff | Wheels-off time (local time: hhmm) |
| WheelsOn | Wheels-on time (local time: hhmm) |
| TaxiIn | Taxi-in duration (minutes) |
| CRSArrTime | CRS arrival time (local time: hhmm) |
| ArrTime | Actual arrival time (local time: hhmm) |
| ArrDelay | Difference in minutes between scheduled and actual arrival time. Early arrivals show negative numbers. |
| Cancelled | Cancelled flight indicator (1 = Yes) |
| CancellationCode | Specifies the reason for cancellation |
| Diverted | Diverted flight indicator (1 = Yes) |
| Distance | Distance between airports (miles) |

# Separation of Compute and Storage

There are essentially three options when it comes to processing large datasets (see Table 2-3), and all three are possible on GCP. Which one you use depends on the problem—in this book, we'll use the third option because it is the most flexible. However, this option requires a bit of preplanning on our part—we will have to store our data in Google Cloud Storage and in Google BigQuery. To see why we choose this, let's consider the other two options also.

*Table 2-3. How to choose between scaling up, scaling out with data sharding, or scaling out with data in situ*

| Option | Performance and cost | Required platform capabilities | How to implement on Google Cloud Platform | Example use case |
|---|---|---|---|---|
| Scaling up | Expensive on both compute and storage; fast, but limited to capability of most powerful machine | Very powerful machines; ability to rent machines by the minute; attachable persistent SSDs | Compute Engine with persistent SSDs Vertex AI Notebooks | Job that requires rereading of data (e.g., training an ML model) |

| Option | Performance and cost | Required platform capabilities | How to implement on Google Cloud Platform | Example use case |
|--------|---------------------|-------------------------------|--------------------------------------------|------------------|
| Scaling out with sharding | High storage costs; inexpensive compute; add machines to achieve desired speed, but limited to ability to preshard the data on a cluster of desired size | Data local to the compute nodes; attachable persistent SSDs | Cloud Dataproc (with Spark) and Hadoop Distributed File System (HDFS) | Light compute on a splittable dataset (e.g., creating a search index from thousands of documents). Many data analytics use cases used to be in this segment. |
| Scaling out with data in situ | Inexpensive storage, compute; add machines to achieve desired speed | Extremely fast networking, cluster-wide filesystem | Cloud Dataproc + Spark on Cloud Storage, BigQuery, Cloud Dataflow, Vertex AI Training, etc. | Any use case where we can configure datasets so that I/O keeps up with computation. Data analytics use cases are increasingly falling into this segment. |

Even if you are used to downloading data to your laptop for data analysis and development, you should realize that this is a suboptimal solution. Wouldn't it be great to directly ingest the BTS files into our data analysis programs without having to go through a step of downloading them? Having a single source of truth has many advantages, ranging from security (providing and denying access) to error correction (no need to worry about stale copies of the data lying around). Of course, the reason we don't do this is that we'd have to read the BTS data over the internet, and the public internet typically has speeds of 3 to 10 MBps.[8] If you are carrying out analysis on your laptop, accessing data via the internet every time you need it will become a serious bottleneck.

Downloading the data has the benefit that subsequent reads happen on the local drive and this is both inexpensive and fast (see Figure 2-5). For small datasets and short, quick computation, it's perfectly acceptable to download data to your laptop and do the work there. This doesn't scale, though. What if our data analysis is very complex or the data is so large that a single laptop is no longer enough? We have two options: scale up or scale out.

---

8 Public internet as opposed to traffic traveling on private fiber. For example, communication between machines in Google Cloud travels on Google's own cables.

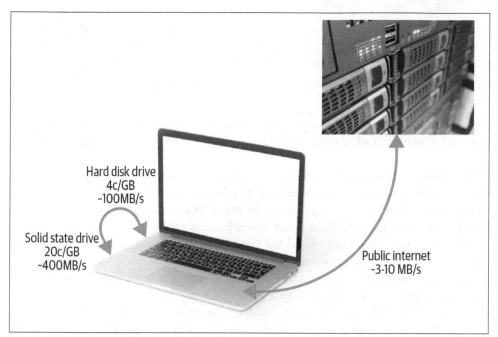

*Figure 2-5. Comparison of data access speeds if data is accessed over the public internet versus from a disk drive.*

## Scaling Up

One option to deal with larger datasets or more difficult computation jobs is to use a larger, more powerful machine with many CPUs/GPUs, lots of RAM, and many terabytes of drive space. This is called *scaling up*, and it is a perfectly valid solution. However, such a computer is likely to be quite expensive. Because we are unlikely to be using it 24 hours a day, we might choose to rent an appropriately large computer from a public cloud provider. In addition, the public cloud offers persistent drives that can be shared between multiple instances and whose data is geo-replicated to guard against data loss (*https://oreil.ly/wlKNY*). In short, then, if you want to do your analysis on one large machine but keep your data permanently in the cloud, a good solution would be to marry a powerful, high-memory Compute Engine instance with a persistent drive, download the data from the external data center (BTS's computer in our case) onto the persistent drive, and start up compute instances on demand, as depicted in Figure 2-6 (cloud prices in Figure 2-6 are estimated monthly charges; actual costs may be higher or lower than the estimate).

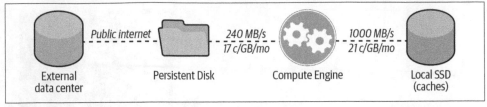

*Figure 2-6. One solution to cost-effective and fast data analysis is to store data on a persistent disk that is attached to an ephemeral, high-memory Compute Engine instance.*

When you are done with the analysis, you can delete the Compute Engine instance.[9] Provision the smallest persistent drive that adequately holds your data—temporary storage (or caches) during analysis can be made to an attached SSD that is deleted along with the instance, and persistent drives can always be resized if your initial size proves too small. This gives you all the benefits of doing local analysis but with the ability to use a much more powerful machine at a lower cost. I will note here that this recommendation assumes several things: the ability to rent powerful machines by the minute, to attach resizeable persistent drives to compute instances, and to achieve good-enough performance by using solid-state persistent drives. These are true of Google Cloud and other public cloud providers, but are unlikely to be true on premises.

Scaling up is a common approach whenever you have a job that needs to read the data multiple times. This is quite common when training machine learning models, and so scaling up is a common approach in machine learning, especially machine learning on images and video. Indeed, Google Cloud offers special Compute Engine instances, called Deep Learning VM (*https://oreil.ly/WXaZW*), that have accelerators like GPUs and come preinstalled with the libraries that are needed for machine learning. Jupyter Notebook instances are also frequently scaled up as necessary to fit the job. You'd create a Deep Learning VM, and attach to it a network-based persistent disk containing the training data or use local SSD for improved performance.

---

9 You could also just stop (and not delete) the Google Compute Engine instance. Stopping the instance stops the bill associated with the compute machine, but you will continue to pay for storage. In particular, you will continue to pay for the SSD associated with the Compute Engine instance. The key advantage of a stopped instance is that you get to resume exactly where you left off, but this might not be important if you always start from a clean (known) state each time.

# Scaling Out with Sharded Data

The solution of using a high-memory Compute Engine instance along with persistent drives and caches might be reasonable for jobs that can be done on a single machine, but it doesn't work for jobs that are bigger than that. Configuring a job into smaller parts so that processing can be carried out on multiple machines is called *scaling out*. One way to scale out a data processing job is to shard the data and store the pieces on the drives attached to multiple compute instances or persistent drives that will be attached to multiple instances.[10] Then, each compute instance can carry out analysis on a small chunk of data at high speeds—these operations are called the *map* operations. The results of the analysis on the small chunks can be combined, after some suitable collation, on a different set of compute nodes—these combination operations are called the *reduce* operations. Together, this model is known as *MapReduce*. This approach also requires an initial download of the data from the external data center to the cloud. In addition, we also need to split the data onto preassigned drives or nodes.

Whenever we need to carry out analysis, we will need to spin up the entire cluster of nodes, reattach the persistent drives, and carry out the computation. Fortunately, we don't need to build the infrastructure to do the sharding or cluster creation ourselves. We could store the data on the Hadoop Distributed File System (HDFS), which will do the sharding for us, spin up a Cloud Dataproc cluster (which has Hadoop, Presto, Spark, etc., preinstalled on a cluster of Compute Engine VMs), and run our analysis job on that cluster. Figure 2-7 presents an overview of this approach.

---

10 To shard a large database is to partition it into smaller, more easily managed parts. Whereas normalization of a database table places the columns of a database into different tables, sharding splits the rows of the database and uses different database server instances to handle each part. For more information, go to the Wikipedia entry for the Shard database architecture (*https://oreil.ly/OSw9s*).

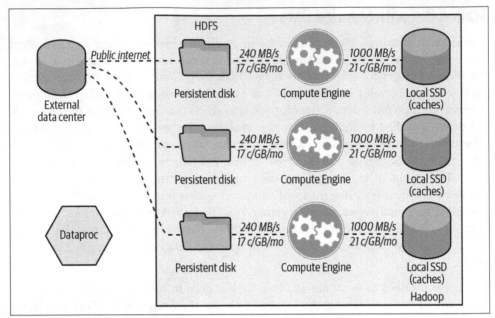

*Figure 2-7. For larger datasets, one potential solution is to store data on the HDFS and use an ephemeral Dataproc cluster to carry out the analysis.*

A MapReduce framework like the Hadoop ecosystem requires data to be presharded. Because the presharded data must be stored on drives that are attached to compute instances, the scheme can be highly wasteful unless all the data happens to get used all the time by those compute instances. In essence, whenever you need to run a job, the framework ships the code to whichever nodes happen to be storing the data. What the framework should be doing, however, is try to find a machine that has free capacity. Shipping the analysis code to run on storage nodes regardless of their computational load leads to poor efficiency because it is likely that there are long periods during which a node might have nothing to do, and other periods when it is subject to resource contention.

In summary, we have two options to work with large datasets: keep the data as-is and scale up by using a large-enough computer, or scale out by sharding the data and shipping code to the nodes that store the data. Both of these options have some drawbacks. Scaling up is subject to the limitations of whatever the most powerful machine available to you can do. Scaling out is subject to the inefficiencies of resource allocation. Is there a way to keep data-in-place and scale out?

## Scaling Out with Data-in-Place

Recall that much of the economics of our case for downloading the data onto nodes on which we can do the compute relied on the slowness of an internet connection as compared to drive speeds—it is because the public internet operates at only 3 to 10 MBps, whereas drives offer two orders of magnitude faster access, that we moved the data to a large Compute Engine instance (scaling up) or sharded it onto persistent drives attached to Compute Engine instances (scaling out).

What if, though, you are operating in an environment in which networking speeds are higher, and files are available to all compute instances at those high speeds? For example, what if you had a job that uses 100,000 servers and those servers could communicate with one another at 1 GBps? This is seriously fast—it is twice the speed of SSDs, 10 times the speed of a local hard drive, and 100 times faster than the public internet. What if, in addition, you have a cluster-level filesystem (not node-by-node) whose metadata is sharded across the data center and replicated on write for durability? Because the total bisection bandwidth of Google's Andromeda and Jupiter networks (*https://oreil.ly/sRQqU*) in Google's data centers is 125,000 GBps,[11] and because Google's next-generation Colossus filesystem operates at the cluster level, this is the scenario that operates if your data is available in Google Cloud Storage and your jobs are running on Compute Engine instances in the same data center as the file. At that point, it becomes worthwhile to treat the entire data center as a single computer. The speed of the network and the design of the storage make both compute and data fungible resources that can be allocated to whichever part of the data center is most free. Scheduling a set of jobs over a single large data center provides much higher utilization than scheduling the same set of jobs over many smaller clusters. This resource allocation can be automatic—there is no need to preshard the data, and if we use an appropriate computation framework (such as BigQuery, Cloud Dataflow, or Vertex AI), we don't even need to instantiate a Compute Engine instance ourselves. Figure 2-8 presents this framework, in which compute and storage are separate.

Therefore, choose between scaling up, scaling out with data sharding, or scaling out with data-in-place depending on the problem that you are solving (see Table 2-3).

---

11 The blog on Google's networking infrastructure (*https://oreil.ly/y60F5*) is worth a read. One petabit is 1 million gigabits, so the 1 Pbps quoted in the article works out to 125,000 GBps. Networking has only gotten better since 2015, of course.

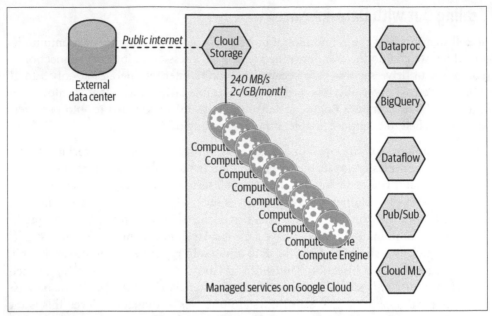

*Figure 2-8. On the Google Cloud Platform, the speed of the networking within a data center allows us to store the data persistently and cheaply on Cloud Storage and access it as needed from a variety of ephemeral managed services. This is called separation of compute and storage.*

## Google Cloud Data Centers Are Different

Google data centers, unlike most other data centers, are optimized for total bisection bandwidth. They are optimized to maximize the network bandwidth between nodes on the backend ("East-West communications" in networking parlance). Most other data centers are optimized to minimize the network time with an outside client sending, for example, a web request ("North-South communications").

Why would anybody design a data center for East-West communications? Aren't most applications web applications? You would design a data center for East-West networking only if the amount of network calls you do on the backend in response to a user request is several times the traffic of the request itself. That is true of Google Search (very simple user interface, very complex business logic). Fortunately, this design also comes in extremely useful for data science because it is not necessary to *preshard* the data.

What's presharding? The Google File System (or GFS, on which the HDFS is based) was built for batch operations and involves storing data in shards close to processing nodes. Colossus (GFS's successor that is in use in Google data centers) was designed for real-time updates. Although GFS/HDFS suffices for batch processing operations that happen over a few days, Colossus is required to update Google's search index in real time—this is why Google Search can now reflect current events. There are several other innovations that were necessary to get to this data processing architecture in which data does not need to be presharded. For example, when performing large fan-out operations, you must be tolerant of latency and design around it. This involves slicing up requests to reduce head-of-line blocking,[12] creating hundreds of partitions per machine to make it easy to move partitions elsewhere, making replicas of heavily used data chunks, using backup requests, and canceling other requests as soon as one is completed, among other strategies. To build a cluster-wide filesystem with high throughput speeds to any compute instance within the data center, it is necessary to minimize the number of network hops within the data center by changing the network definitions through software. Within the Google Cloud Platform, any two machines in the same zone are only one network hop away.

The innovation in networking, compute, and storage at Google and elsewhere is by no means over. Even though the Jupiter network provides bisection bandwidths of 125,000 GBps (the last time Google published this number publicly was in the mid-2010s and it's probably higher now), engineers estimate that 600,000 GBps is what's required to match the performance of local disks. Moreover, jobs are not being sliced finely enough—because I/O devices have response times on the order of microseconds, decisions should be scheduled even more finely than the current milliseconds. Next-generation flash storage is still largely untapped within the data center. Colossus addresses the issue of building a cluster-level filesystem, but there are applications that need global consistency, not just consistency within a single-region cluster. The challenge of building a globally distributed database is being addressed by Cloud Spanner. The ongoing innovations in computational infrastructure promise exciting times ahead.

All of this is in the way of noting (again!) that your mileage will vary if you do your data processing on other infrastructure—there is a reason why the title of this book includes the words "on the Google Cloud Platform." The hardware optimizations if you implement your data pipelines on premises or in a different cloud provider will typically target different things.[13] The APIs might look the same, and in many cases, you can run the same software as I do, but the performance characteristics will be different. Google TensorFlow, Apache Beam, and others are open source and portable to on-premises infrastructure and across different cloud providers, but the execution frameworks that make Vertex AI and Cloud Dataflow so powerful may not translate well to infrastructure that is not built the same way as Google Cloud Platform.

---

12 *Head-of-line blocking* is a condition in which network packets need to be delivered in order; thus, a slow packet holds up delivery of later packets.

13 Microsoft Azure seems to involve a centralized host layer (*https://oreil.ly/X5E5w*), for example, while AWS S3 seems to prioritize network latency (*https://oreil.ly/qDXKp*). You'd design your software for such infrastructure differently.

Another way to see this is that multicloud software works faster on Google Cloud than on other cloud platforms. BigQuery Omni, although available on Amazon Web Services (AWS) and Azure, does not get the performance of BigQuery on GCP. This performance difference is not limited to multicloud software developed by Google. Databricks notes (*https://oreil.ly/VNIZu*) that startup and certain Spark workloads are faster on GCP than on other clouds. Actian Avalanche notes (*https://oreil.ly/8WOeh*) that their implementation on GCP is 20% faster than on other cloud platforms.

# Ingesting Data

To carry out our data analysis on the on-time performance dataset, we will need to download the monthly data from the BTS website and then upload it to Google Cloud Storage. Doing this manually will be tedious and error-prone, so let's script this operation.

## Reverse Engineering a Web Form

How would you script filling out the BTS web form shown in Figure 2-2? First, verify that the website's terms of use do not bar you from automated downloads! Then, use the Chrome browser's developer tools to find what web calls the form makes. Once you know that, you can repeat those web calls in a script.

The BTS web form is a simple HTML form with no dynamic behavior. This type of form collects all the user selections into a single GET or POST request. If we can create that same request from a script, we will be able to obtain the data without going through the web form.

We can find out the exact HTTP command sent by the browser after we make our selections on the BTS website. You can do this while on the BTS download website (*https://oreil.ly/quDJ7*) in the Chrome web browser—in the upper-right menu bar of the browser, navigate to the Developer Tools menu, as shown in Figure 2-9.

Now, on the BTS website, select the Prezipped File option, select 2015 and January in the drop-down boxes, and click Download.[14] The Developer tools menu shows us that the browser is now making a GET request for *https://transtats.bts.gov/PREZIP/ On_Time_Reporting_Carrier_On_Time_Performance_1987_present_2015_1.zip*.

---

14 The BTS website is frequently down. Do not be alarmed if you get an error here. You will not need the website to work in order to go through the remaining chapters. If the BTS server is down, you can copy the necessary files from my bucket. Consult the *README.md* file in the GitHub repository for details.

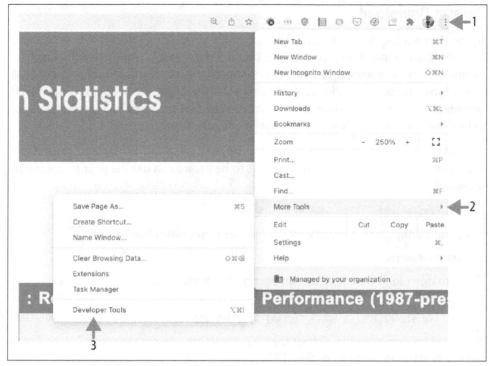

*Figure 2-9. Navigating to the Developer Tools menu in Chrome.*

It is pretty obvious what the pattern here is. If we issue an HTTP GET for a file with the pattern:

```
${BASEURL}_${YEAR}_${MONTH}.zip
```

we should get the data corresponding to a single month. Let's try it from the command line of Cloud Shell:

```
BTS=https://transtats.bts.gov/PREZIP
BASEURL="${BTS}/On_Time_Reporting_Carrier_On_Time_Performance_1987_present"
YEAR=2015
MONTH=3
curl -k -o temp.zip ${BASEURL}_${YEAR}_${MONTH}.zip
```

We see the data for March 2015 starting to get downloaded. Once the file is downloaded, we can unzip it:

```
unzip temp.zip
```

We then notice that the ZIP file contains a comma-separated values (CSV) file. Peeking at the first few lines of the file using:

```
head -5 *.csv
```

confirms that the file contains flight data from the month of January 2015.

## Dataset Download

In the data exploration phase, I'll do most of my processing interactively with Linux command-line tools. I will assume that this is what you are using as well. Adapt the commands as necessary if you are working locally in some other environment (e.g., where I ask you to do a `sudo apt-get install`, you might use the appropriate install command for your Linux-like environment). When we have settled on the processing to be done, we'll look at how to make this more automated.

Instead of calling the downloaded file *temp.zip*, let's call it *201501.zip* and place it into a temporary directory. To pad the month 1 to be 01, we can use the `printf` command in bash:[15]

```
MONTH2=$(printf "%02d" $MONTH)
```

To create a temporary directory, we can use the Linux command `mktemp`:

```
TMPDIR=$(mktemp -d)
```

Then, to download the file to the temporary directory, we can do:

```
ZIPFILE=${TMPDIR}/${YEAR}_${MONTH2}.zip
curl -o $ZIPFILE ${BASEURL}_${YEAR}_${MONTH}.zip
```

Now, we can unzip the file, extract the CSV file to the current directory (*./*), and blow out the remaining contents of the ZIP file:

```
unzip -d $TMPDIR $ZIPFILE
mv $TMPDIR/*.csv ./${YEAR}${MONTH2}.csv
rm -rf $TMPDIR
```

I put the preceding commands into a file called *download.sh*, and then in the script `ingest.sh`, I call it from within a for loop:

```
for MONTH in `seq 1 12`; do
    bash download.sh $YEAR $MONTH
done
```

On running this, we get a set of CSV files, one for each month in 2015 (see Figure 2-11).

The complete download script is on GitHub (*https://oreil.ly/Kjrm1*)—if you want to follow along with me, perform these steps:

- Go to *https://console.cloud.google.com*.
- Select the GCP project that you will be working on. This is accomplished by using the drop-down box next to "Example Project" in Figure 2-10.

---

[15] See the script *02_ingest/download.sh* in the course repository.

---

- On the top strip, activate Cloud Shell using the button shown in Figure 2-10.

*Figure 2-10. The Cloud Shell button on the Google Cloud Platform web console.*

- In Cloud Shell, type the following:

```
git clone \
    https://github.com/GoogleCloudPlatform/data-science-on-gcp
```

This downloads the GitHub code to your Cloud Shell home directory.

- Navigate into the flights folder:

```
cd data-science-on-gcp
```

- Make a new directory to hold the data, and then change into that directory:

```
mkdir data

cd data
```

- Run the code to download the files:

```
for MONTH in `seq 1 12`; do
        bash download.sh 2015 $MONTH
done
```

- When the script completes, run `ls -lrt` to view the downloaded ZIP files, shown in Figure 2-11.

```
vlakshmanan@cloudshell:~/data-science-on-gcp/data (data-science-on-gcp-180606)$ ls -lrt
total 2561352
-rw-r--r-- 1 vlakshmanan vlakshmanan 211633508 Sep 19  2018 201501.csv
-rw-r--r-- 1 vlakshmanan vlakshmanan 192791832 Sep 19  2018 201502.csv
-rw-r--r-- 1 vlakshmanan vlakshmanan 227017003 Sep 19  2018 201503.csv
-rw-r--r-- 1 vlakshmanan vlakshmanan 218600101 Sep 19  2018 201504.csv
-rw-r--r-- 1 vlakshmanan vlakshmanan 224003621 Sep 19  2018 201505.csv
-rw-r--r-- 1 vlakshmanan vlakshmanan 227418851 Sep 19  2018 201506.csv
-rw-r--r-- 1 vlakshmanan vlakshmanan 235038069 Sep 19  2018 201507.csv
-rw-r--r-- 1 vlakshmanan vlakshmanan 230183745 Sep 19  2018 201508.csv
-rw-r--r-- 1 vlakshmanan vlakshmanan 209229804 Sep 19  2018 201509.csv
-rw-r--r-- 1 vlakshmanan vlakshmanan 219158206 Sep 19  2018 201510.csv
-rw-r--r-- 1 vlakshmanan vlakshmanan 211122691 Sep 19  2018 201511.csv
-rw-r--r-- 1 vlakshmanan vlakshmanan 216562989 Sep 19  2018 201512.csv
```

*Figure 2-11. The `ls -lrt` command shows details of the downloaded files.*

This looks quite reasonable—all the files have different sizes and the sizes are robust enough that one would assume they are not just error messages.

## Exploration and Cleanup

At this point, I have 12 CSV files. Let's look at the first two lines of one of them to ensure the data matches what we think it ought to be:

```
head -2 201503.csv
```

The result is shown in Figure 2-12.

```
vlakshmanan@cloudshell:~/data-science-on-gcp/data (data-science-on-gcp-180606)$ head -2 201503.csv
"Year","Quarter","Month","DayofMonth","DayOfWeek","FlightDate","Reporting_Airline","DOT_ID_Reporting_Airline","IATA_CODE_
Reporting_Airline","Tail_Number","Flight_Number_Reporting_Airline","OriginAirportID","OriginAirportSeqID","OriginCityMark
etID","Origin","OriginCityName","OriginState","OriginStateFips","OriginStateName","OriginWac","DestAirportID","DestAirpor
tSeqID","DestCityMarketID","Dest","DestCityName","DestState","DestStateFips","DestStateName","DestWac","CRSDepTime","DepT
ime","DepDelay","DepDelayMinutes","DepDel15","DepartureDelayGroups","DepTimeBlk","TaxiOut","WheelsOff","WheelsOn","TaxiIn
","CRSArrTime","ArrTime","ArrDelay","ArrDelayMinutes","ArrDel15","ArrivalDelayGroups","ArrTimeBlk","Cancelled","Cancellat
ionCode","Diverted","CRSElapsedTime","ActualElapsedTime","AirTime","Flights","Distance","DistanceGroup","CarrierDelay","W
eatherDelay","NASDelay","SecurityDelay","LateAircraftDelay","FirstDepTime","TotalAddGTime","LongestAddGTime","DivAirportL
andings","DivReachedDest","DivActualElapsedTime","DivArrDelay","DivDistance","Div1Airport","Div1AirportID","Div1AirportSe
qID","Div1WheelsOn","Div1TotalGTime","Div1LongestGTime","Div1WheelsOff","Div1TailNum","Div2Airport","Div2AirportID","Div2
AirportSeqID","Div2WheelsOn","Div2TotalGTime","Div2LongestGTime","Div2WheelsOff","Div2TailNum","Div3Airport","Div3Airport
ID","Div3AirportSeqID","Div3WheelsOn","Div3TotalGTime","Div3LongestGTime","Div3WheelsOff","Div3TailNum","Div4Airport","Di
v4AirportID","Div4AirportSeqID","Div4WheelsOn","Div4TotalGTime","Div4LongestGTime","Div4WheelsOff","Div4TailNum","Div5Air
port","Div5AirportID","Div5AirportSeqID","Div5WheelsOn","Div5TotalGTime","Div5LongestGTime","Div5WheelsOff","Div5TailNum"
,
2015,1,3,3,2,2015-03-03,"WN",19393,"WN","N258WN","1254",11066,1106603,31066,"CMH","Columbus, OH","OH","39","Ohio",44,1463
5,1463502,31714,"RSW","Fort Myers, FL","FL","12","Florida",33,"0610","0605",-5.00,0.00,0.00,-1,"0600-0659",12.00,"0617","
0823",5.00,"0900","0828",-32.00,0.00,0.00,-2,"0900-0959",0.00,"",0.00,170.00,143.00,126.00,1.00,930.00,4,,,,,,"",,,0,,,,,
"",,,"",,,,"","","",,,"",,,,"","","",,,"",,,,"","","",,,"",,,,"","","",,,"",,,,"","",
```

*Figure 2-12. The first two lines of the CSV file containing March 2015 data.*

There is a header in each CSV file, and the second line looks like data. Some of the fields are enclosed by quotes (perhaps in case the strings themselves have commas), and there are some fields that are missing (there is nothing between successive commas toward the end of the line). There seems to be a pesky extra comma at the end as well.

How many fields are there? Because the second line doesn't have any commas between the quotes, we can check using:

```
head -2 201503.csv  | tail -1 | sed 's/,/ /g' | wc -w
```

The number of words is 81, so there are 81 columns (remember there's a comma at the end of the line). Here's how the command works. It first gets the first two lines of the data file (with `head -2`), and the last line of that (with `tail -1`) so that we are looking at the second line of *201503.csv*. Then, we replace all the commas by spaces and count the number of words with `wc -w`.

How much data is there? A quick shell command (`wc` for word count, with an `-l` [lowercase letter L] to display only the line count) informs us that there are between ~43,000 and ~52,000 flights per month:

```
$ wc -l *.csv
  469969 201501.csv
  429192 201502.csv
  504313 201503.csv
  485152 201504.csv
  496994 201505.csv
```

```
 503898 201506.csv
 520719 201507.csv
 510537 201508.csv
 464947 201509.csv
 486166 201510.csv
 467973 201511.csv
 479231 201512.csv
5819091 total
```

This adds up to nearly six million flights in 2015! The slowness of this command should tell us that any kind of analysis that involves reading all the data is going to be quite cumbersome. You can repeat this for other years (2016–2019), but let's wait until we have the whole process complete for one year before we add more years.

You might have realized by now that knowing a little Unix Shell scripting can come in very handy at this initial stage of data analysis.[16]

## Uploading Data to Google Cloud Storage

For durability of this raw dataset, let's upload it to Google Cloud Storage. To do that, you first need to create a *bucket*, essentially a namespace for binary large objects (blobs) stored in Cloud Storage that you typically want to treat similarly from a permissions perspective. You can create a bucket from the Google Cloud Platform Console (*https://oreil.ly/09lCP*). For reasons that we will talk about shortly, make the bucket a single-region bucket.

---

### Setting Up a Cost Budget

It is likely that when you create a bucket, you will be prompted to enable billing or connect to a billing account. This is because storage is chargeable. I suggest that you create a brand new Google Cloud project for this book and delete the project once you are done to stop all billing. If you want total peace of mind, you can set up a cost budget (*https://oreil.ly/k6a8s*) and ask Google Cloud to cap resource usage (*https://oreil.ly/i5dUG*) once you exceed that budget.

---

Bucket names must be globally unique (i.e., unique not just within your project or organization, but across Google Cloud Platform). This means that bucket names are globally knowable even if the contents of the bucket are not accessible. This can be problematic. For example, if you created a bucket named acme_gizmo, a competitor might later try to create a bucket also named acme_gizmo, but fail because the name already exists. This failure can alert your competitor to the possibility that Acme Corp. is developing a new Gizmo. It might seem like it would take Sherlock Holmes–

---

16 Software Carpentry provides a good intro to Unix and shell scripting (*https://oreil.ly/M3cet*).

like powers of deduction to arrive at this conclusion, but it's simply best that you avoid revealing sensitive information in bucket names. A common pattern to create unique bucket names is to use suffixes on the project ID. Project IDs are globally unique,[17] and thus a bucket name such as *projectid*-dsongcp will also tend to be unique. In my case, my project ID is cloud-training-demos and my bucket name is cloud-training-demos-ml.

You can create a unique bucket on the command line using:

```
PROJECT=$(gcloud config get-value project)
BUCKET=${PROJECT}-dsongcp
REGION=us-central1 #See https://cloud.google.com/storage/docs/locations
gsutil mb -l $REGION gs://$BUCKET
```

where the first line retrieves the project ID and the second line uses it to form a bucket name that is hopefully unique.

Cloud Storage will also serve as the staging ground to many of the GCP tools and enable collaborative sharing of the data with our colleagues. In my case, to upload the files to Cloud Storage, I type the following in Cloud Shell:

```
gsutil -m cp *.csv gs://cloud-training-demos-ml/flights/raw/
```

This uploads the files to Cloud Storage, specifically to my bucket cloud-training-demos-ml in a multithreaded manner (-m) and makes me the owner. If you are working locally, another way to upload the files would be to use the Cloud Platform Console (*https://oreil.ly/dzVgF*).

It is better to keep these as separate files instead of concatenating them into a single large file because Cloud Storage is a blob store (*https://oreil.ly/WzTBl*), not a regular filesystem. In particular, it is not possible to append to a file on Cloud Storage; you can only replace it. Therefore, although concatenating all 12 files into a single file containing the entire year of data will work for this batch dataset, it won't work as well if we want to later add to the dataset one month at a time, as new data becomes available. Second, because Cloud Storage is blob storage,[18] storing the files separately will permit us to more easily process parts of the entire archive (for example, only the

---

17 You can get your unique project ID from the Cloud Platform Console dashboard; it could be different from the common name that you assigned to your project. By default, Google Cloud Platform tries to give you a project ID that is the same as your project name, but if that name is already taken, you will get an autogenerated, unique project ID. Because of this default, you should be similarly careful about giving projects sensitive names.

18 In an object store, we don't have random access to data in the middle (technically, this is called a seek), as we would in a filesystem. Rather, we have to download an entire object in order to work with it. Tools such as GCS FUSE (*https://oreil.ly/yKyA8*) allow you to treat the object store, in certain ways, like a filesystem, but the abstraction is not perfect. There is no seek capability.

summer months) without having to build slicing into our data processing pipeline. Third, it is generally a good idea to keep ingested data in as raw a form as possible.

It is preferable that this bucket to which we upload the data is a single-region bucket. There are four reasons: first, we will create Compute Engine instances in the same region as the bucket and access it only from this one region. A multiregion bucket would be overkill because we don't need global availability. Second, a single-region bucket is less expensive than a multiregion one. Third, single-region buckets are optimized for low latency and high throughput for data consumers, whereas dual-region and multiregion buckets are optimized for high availability, serving content outside of the Google network (think data analytics versus web traffic). All three of the preceding factors point to using single region buckets for data analytics and machine learning. The fourth reason is helpful here, although it won't come into play for "real-world" uses: at the time of writing, certain US single regions (us-east1, us-west1, and us-central1) offer 5 GB of storage free (*https://oreil.ly/tsncz*).

Note that both single-region and multiregion buckets in Google Cloud Platform offer strong consistency, so this does not seem like a consideration to choose one over the other. However, the speed differences inherent in being able to offer strong consistency on global buckets points to using single-region buckets if you can. What exactly is strong versus eventual consistency, and why does it matter? Suppose that a worker in a distributed application updates a piece of data, and another worker views that piece of data immediately afterward. Does the second worker always see the updated value? Then, what you have is *strong consistency*. If, on the other hand, there could be a potential lag between an update and availability (i.e., if different viewers can see potentially different values of the data at the same instant in time), what you have is *eventual consistency*. Eventually, all viewers of the data will see the updated value, but that lag will be different for different viewers. Strong consistency is an implicit assumption that is made in a number of programming paradigms. However, to achieve strong consistency, we have to make compromises on scalability and performance (this is called *Brewer's theorem*). For example, we might need to lock readers out of the data while it is being updated so that simultaneous readers always see a consistent and correct value.

Brewer's theorem, also called the CAP theorem, states that no computer system can simultaneously guarantee consistency, availability, and partition resilience. *Consistency* is the guarantee that every reader sees the latest written information. *Availability* is the guarantee that a response is sent to every request (regardless of whether it is the most current information or not). *Partition resilience* is the guarantee that the system continues to operate even if the network connecting readers, writers, and storage drops an arbitrary number of messages. Because network failures are a fact of life in distributed systems, the CAP theorem essentially says that you need to choose between consistency and availability. Neither multiregion buckets nor Cloud Spanner change this: they essentially make choices during partitioning—Cloud Spanner is always consistent and achieves five nines (99.999%, but not perfect) availability despite operating over a wide area. For more details, see this 2017 research paper by Eric Brewer (*https://oreil.ly/qGX93*).

If you need the performance of a regional bucket, but need to be tolerant to failure (for example, you want to be able to carry out your workload even if a region goes down), there are two options: eventual consistency and dual-region buckets. As an example of eventual consistency consider how DNS servers cache values and have their values replicated across many DNS servers all over the internet. If a DNS value is updated, it takes some time for this modified value to become replicated at every DNS server. Eventually, this does happen, though. Having a centralized DNS server that is locked whenever any DNS value is modified would have led to an extremely brittle system. Because the DNS system is based on eventual consistency, it is highly available and extremely scalable, enabling name lookups for/to millions of internet-capable devices. The other option is to have a dual-region bucket in a multiregion location, so that the metadata remains the same. If, for whatever reason, one region is not available for analytics, computation can be migrated to the other region in a multiregion location (US, EU, Asia). Dual-region buckets are more expensive than either single-region buckets or multiregion buckets, but offer both high performance and reliability.

This being public data, I will ensure that my colleagues can use this data without having to wait on me:

```
gsutil acl ch -R -g google.com:R \
    gs://cloud-training-demos-ml/flights/raw/
```

That changes the access control list (`acl`) recursively (`-R`), applying to the group *google.com* read permission (`:R`) on everything starting from the Cloud Storage URL supplied. You'd of course replace *google.com* with your company's domain in order to share data with your own colleagues. Had there been sensitive information in the dataset, I would have to be more careful. We'll discuss fine-grained security, by providing views with different columns to different roles in my organization, when we talk about putting the data in BigQuery.

# Loading Data into Google BigQuery

On Google Cloud, the best place for structured and semi-structured data is BigQuery, a serverless data warehouse and SQL engine.

## Advantages of a Serverless Columnar Database

Most relational database systems, whether commercial or open source, are row oriented in that the data is stored row by row. This makes it easy to append new rows of data to the database and allows for features such as row-level locking when updating the value of a row. For example, if you have an inventory table, you'd lock the row corresponding to the item being purchased so that you can ensure the item is shipped to the person who paid for it.

The drawback is that queries that involve table scans (i.e., any aggregation that requires reading every row in the entire table) can be expensive. For example, if we want to find the number of times an item was purchased by someone living in Belgium, that will involve a table scan. Indexing counteracts this expense by creating a lookup table to map rows to column values, so that SELECT queries that involve indexed columns do not have to load unnecessary rows from storage into memory— we might index the country column, for example, if purchases by country is a common query. If you can rely on indexes for fast lookup of your data, a traditional relational database management system (RDBMS) works well. For example, if your queries tend to come from software applications, you will know the queries that will come in (and the columns they are likely to access). So, you can create the appropriate indexes beforehand. This is not an option for use cases like business intelligence for which human users are writing ad hoc queries; therefore, a different architecture is needed.

BigQuery, unlike an RDBMS, is a columnar database—data is stored column by column and each column's data is stored in a highly efficient compressed format (*https:// oreil.ly/UgK1w*) that enables fast querying. Because of the way data is stored, many common queries can be carried out such that the query processing time is linear on the size of the relevant data (*https://oreil.ly/YALB2*). For applications such as data warehousing and business intelligence for which the predominant operations are read-only SELECT queries requiring full table scans, columnar databases are a better fit. BigQuery, for example, can scan terabytes of data in a matter of seconds. The trade-off is that INSERT, UPDATE, and DELETE statements, although possible in Big-Query, are significantly more expensive to process (*https://oreil.ly/QVVoQ*) than SELECT statements. BigQuery is tuned toward analytics use cases.

BigQuery is serverless, so you don't actually spin up a BigQuery server in your project. You simply submit a SQL query, and it's executed on the cloud. SQL queries that you submit to BigQuery are executed on a large number of compute nodes (called *slots*) in parallel. These slots do not need to be statically allocated beforehand —instead, they are "always on" available on demand, and scale to the size of your job. Because data is kept in-place and not sharded (i.e., not broken into small chunks that are attached to individual compute instances), the total power of the data center can be brought to bear on the problem. Because these resources are elastic and used only for the duration of the query, BigQuery is more powerful and less expensive than a statically preallocated cluster because preallocated clusters will typically be provisioned for the average use case—BigQuery can bring more resources to bear on the above-average computational jobs and utilize fewer resources for below-average ones.

In addition, because you don't need to reserve any compute resources for your data when you are not querying your data, it is extremely cost effective to just keep your data in BigQuery (you'll pay for storage, but storage is inexpensive). Whenever you do need to query the data, the data is immediately available—you can query it without the need to start project-specific compute resources. This on-demand, autoscaling of compute resources is incredibly liberating.

---

## BigQuery Pricing

If an on-demand cost structure (you pay per query) concerns you because costs can fluctuate month over month, you can specify a billing cap for users. For even more cost predictability, it is possible to pay a fixed monthly price for BigQuery—flat-rate pricing means you get a predictable cost regardless of the number of queries run or data processed by those queries. The fixed monthly price essentially buys you access to a specific number of slots.

In short, BigQuery has two pricing models for analysis (*https://oreil.ly/NXnDT*): an on-demand pricing model in which your cost depends on the quantity of data processed, and a flat-rate model in which you pay a fixed amount per month for an unlimited number of queries that will run on a specific set of compute resources. You can augment either with flex slots (*https://oreil.ly/h8Ytl*) you pay for by the minute. In all these cases, storage is a separate cost and depends on data size.

---

In summary, BigQuery is a columnar database, making it particularly effective for read-only queries that process all of the data. Because it is serverless, can autoscale to thousands of compute nodes, and doesn't require clusters to be preallocated, it is also very powerful and quite inexpensive.

## Staging on Cloud Storage

Although it is possible to ingest files from on-premises hardware directly into Big-Query using the bq command-line tool (*https://oreil.ly/gwVzC*) that comes with the Google Cloud Software Development Kit (SDK), aka gcloud, you should use that capability only for small datasets. To ingest data from outside Google Cloud Platform to BigQuery, it is preferable to first load it into Cloud Storage and use Cloud Storage as the staging ground for BigQuery, as demonstrated in Figure 2-13.

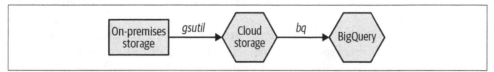

*Figure 2-13. Use Cloud Storage as a staging ground to ingest data into BigQuery.*

For larger files, it is better to ingest the files into Cloud Storage using gsutil first because gsutil takes advantage of multithreaded, resumable uploads and is better suited to the public internet. In our case, this is what we did in the previous section when we used gsutil to copy the extracted flights CSV files to Cloud Storage. Now that we have the CSV files in Cloud Storage, we can load them into BigQuery.

---

### Cloud Storage or BigQuery?

When should you save your data in Cloud Storage, and when should you store it in BigQuery? First, if the data is not tabular-like (that is: images, videos, and other arbitrary file types), then Google Cloud Storage (GCS) is the right choice. For tabular-like data, the answer boils down to what you want to do with the data and the kinds of analyses you want to perform. If you'll mostly be running custom code that expects to read plain files, or your analysis involves reading the entire dataset, use Cloud Storage. On the other hand, if your desired access pattern is to run interactive SQL queries on the data, store your data in BigQuery. To summarize, if in the pre-cloud world you would use flat files, use Cloud Storage. If you'd put the data in a relational database, put it in BigQuery.

---

## Access Control

The first step to ingest data into BigQuery is to create a BigQuery dataset—a dataset is a container for tables. You can have multiple datasets within a project. Go to the web console (*https://oreil.ly/JOPN5*) and choose the Create Dataset option. Then, create a dataset called dsongcp.

You can also do this from the command line:

```
bq mk dsongcp
```

---

Datasets in BigQuery are mostly just an organizational convenience—tables are where data resides, and it is the columns of the table that dictate the queries we write. Besides providing a way to organize tables, though, datasets also serve as a convenient *access control point*. You can conveniently provide view or edit access at the dataset level to control access to all the tables in the dataset. Cloud Identity and Access Management (Cloud IAM) on Google Cloud Platform provides a mechanism to control *who* can carry out *what* actions on *which* resource (Figure 2-14).

The "who" can be specified in terms of an individual user (identified by their Google account such as a *gmail.com* address, or company email address if the company is a Google Workspace customer), a Google Group (i.e., all current members of the group), or a Google Workspace or Google Identity domain (*https://oreil.ly/uKVDD*) (anyone with a Google account in that domain). Google Groups and Google Identity/Workspace domains provide a convenient mechanism for aggregating a number of users and providing similar access to all of them.

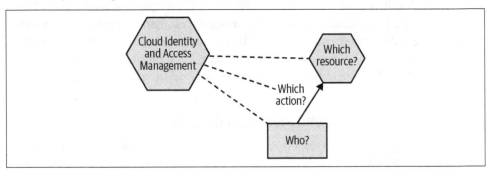

*Figure 2-14. Cloud IAM provides a mechanism to control access to resources.*

In addition, different logical parts of an application can be assigned separate identities (linked to email addresses) called *service accounts*. Service accounts are a very powerful concept because they allow different parts of a codebase to have permissions that are independent of the access level of the person running that application. For example, you might want an application to be able to query a table but not delete it even if the developer who created the application and the person running the application have that authority.

## Careful with Service Accounts

You should use service accounts with care for scenarios in which audit records are mandatory. Providing access at the Google Groups level provides more of an audit trail; because Google Groups don't have login credentials (only individual users do), the user who made a request or action is always recorded, even if their access is provided at the level of a Google Group or Google Workspace domain. However, service accounts are themselves login credentials, and so the audit trail turns cold if you provide access to service accounts—you will no longer know which user initiated the application request unless that application in turn logs this information.[19] Keep this in mind when granting access to service accounts.

Try to avoid providing service account access to resources that require auditability. If you do provide service account access, you should ensure that the application to which you have provided access itself provides the necessary audit trail by keeping track of the user on behalf of whom it is executing the request. The same considerations apply to service accounts that are part of Google Groups or Google Workspace domains. Because audit trails go cold with service accounts, you should restrict Google Groups and Google Workspace domains to only human users and service accounts that belong to applications that provide any necessary legal auditability guarantees.

Creating single-user projects is another way to ensure that service accounts map cleanly to users, but this can lead to significant administrative overhead associated with shared resources and departing personnel. Essentially, you would create a project that is billed to the same company billing account, but each individual user would have their own project in which they work. You can use the gcloud command to script the creation of such single-user projects in which the user in question is an editor (not an owner).

In addition to specific users, groups, domains, and service accounts, there are two wildcard options available. Access can be provided to allAuthenticatedUsers, in which case anyone authenticated with either a Google account or a service account is provided access. Because allAuthenticatedUsers includes service accounts, it should not be used for resources for which a clear audit trail is required. The other wildcard option is to provide access to allUsers, in which case anyone on the internet has access—a common use case for this is to provide highly available static web resources by storing them on Cloud Storage. Be careful about doing this indiscriminately—egress of data from Google Cloud Platform is not free, so you will pay for the bandwidth consumed by the download of your cloud-hosted datasets.

The "what" actions depend on the resource access that is being controlled. The resources themselves fall into a policy hierarchy.

Policies can be specified at an organization level (i.e., to all projects in the organization), at the project level (i.e., to all resources in the project), or at the resource level (i.e., to a Compute Engine instance or a BigQuery dataset). As Figure 2-15 shows,

---

19 A service account is tied to a project, but project membership evolves over time. So, even the subset of users who could have invoked the action might not be known unless you have strict governance over who is allowed to be an owner/editor/viewer of a project.

policies specified at higher levels are inherited at lower levels, and the policy in effect is the union of all the permissions granted—there is no way to restrict some access to a dataset to a user who has that access inherited from the project level. Moving a project from one organization to another automatically updates that project's Cloud IAM policy and ends up affecting all the resources owned by that project.

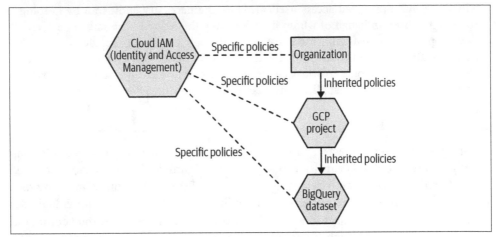

*Figure 2-15. Policies specified at higher levels are inherited at lower levels.*

What type of actions can be carried out depends on the resource in question. Before Cloud IAM was introduced on the Google Cloud Platform, there were only three roles: owner, editor, and viewer/reader for all resources. Cloud IAM brought with it finer-grained roles, but the original three roles were grandfathered in as primitive roles. Table 2-4 lists some of the roles that are possible for BigQuery datasets. Cloud IAM roles for BigQuery (and by extension for all GCP products) are continuously updated to cater to new use cases. Please refer to BigQuery access control (*https:// oreil.ly/0EtiW*) for the current roles and permissions.

*Table 2-4. Some of the available roles in BigQuery*

| Role | Capabilities | Inherits from |
|---|---|---|
| Project Viewer | Execute a query<br>List datasets | |
| Project Editor | Create a new dataset | Project Viewer |
| Project Owner | List/delete datasets<br>View jobs run by other project users | Project Editor |
| bigquery.user | Execute a query<br>List datasets | |
| bigquery.dataViewer | Read, query, copy, export tables in the dataset | |
| bigquery.dataEditor | Append, load data into tables in the dataset | Project Editor<br>bigquery.dataViewer |

| Role | Capabilities | Inherits from |
|---|---|---|
| bigquery.dataOwner | Update, delete on tables in the dataset | Project Owner bigquery.dataEditor |
| bigquery.admin | All | |

## Ingesting CSV Files

We can load the data directly into BigQuery's native storage using the command-line utility bq that comes with the gcloud SDK:

```
BUCKET=${PROJECT}-dsongcp
bq load --autodetect --source_format=CSV \
    dsongcp.flights_auto \
    gs://${BUCKET}/flights/raw/201501.csv
```

Here, we are asking BigQuery to autodetect the schema from the CSV file and load the January data into a table named flights_auto (if you are following along with me, make sure to change the bucket to reflect the bucket that your files are in).[20] Since we are asking BigQuery to autodetect the schema using --autodetect, it will read the header line of the CSV and use them as column names. However, the CSV header doesn't specify the column types (string, integer, float, etc.), and so BigQuery will sample a few hundred lines and attempt to guess at the type. This guess will not be perfect, and we might have to fix it.

If you now go to the BigQuery web console (*https://oreil.ly/jPapd*) and examine the dataset dsongcp, you will see that there is a table named flights_auto in it. You can examine the autodetected schema and preview the contents of the table.

We can try querying the data to find the average departure and arrival delays at the busiest airports:

```
SELECT
    ORIGIN,
    AVG(DEP_DELAY) AS dep_delay,
    AVG(ARR_DELAY) AS arr_delay,
    COUNT(ARR_DELAY) AS num_flights
  FROM
    dsongcp.flights_auto
  GROUP BY
    ORIGIN
ORDER BY num_flights DESC
LIMIT 10
```

The result (see Table 2-5) starts with Atlanta (ATL), Dallas (DFW), and Chicago (ORD), which is what we would expect.

---

20 If this is your first time working in BigQuery for the project, you might have to authorize the proper API. That's expected behavior.

*Table 2-5. Average arrival and departure delays in January 2015 at the busiest 10 airports*

| Row | ORIGIN | dep_delay | arr_delay | num_flights |
|-----|--------|-----------|-----------|-------------|
| 1 | ATL | 7.265885087329549 | 1.0802479706819135 | 29,197 |
| 2 | DFW | 11.761812240572308 | 9.37162730937924 | 22,571 |
| 3 | ORD | 19.96205128205128 | 17.016131923283645 | 22,316 |
| 4 | LAX | 7.476340878516738 | 5.542057719380547 | 17,048 |
| 5 | DEN | 15.506798076352176 | 11.842324888226543 | 16,775 |
| 6 | IAH | 9.07378596782721 | 5.353498597528596 | 13,191 |
| 7 | PHX | 8.066722908198505 | 6.197786998616902 | 13,014 |
| 8 | SFO | 10.328127477406069 | 9.038424821002382 | 12,570 |
| 9 | LAS | 8.566096692995435 | 5.0543525523958595 | 11,499 |
| 10 | MCO | 9.887440638577354 | 5.820512820512793 | 9,867 |

Autodetection is hit-and-miss, though. This is because the way it works is that Big-Query samples about a hundred rows of data in order to determine what the data type needs to be. If the arrival delay was an integer for all one hundred rows that it saw, but there turns out to be a string (NA) somewhere else in the file, the loading will fail. Autodetection may also fail if many of the fields are empty.

## Partitioning

Because of this, autodetection is okay during initial exploration, but we should quickly pivot to actually specifying the schema. At that time, it may be worthwhile to also consider whether this table should be partitioned by date—if most of our queries will be not on the full table, but only a few days, then partitioning will lead to cost savings. If that were the case, we would create the table first, specifying that it should be partitioned by date (don't do this—we have already created the table and we don't need daywise partitioning):

```
bq mk --time_partitioning_type=DAY dsongcp.flights_auto
```

When loading the data, we'd need to load each partition separately (partitions are named `flights_auto$20150101`, for example). We can also partition by a column in the data (FlightsDate, for example).

Currently, we don't know much about the fields, so we can ask BigQuery to treat all the columns except the FlightDate as a string:

```
SCHEMA=Year:STRING,...,FlightDate:DATE,Reporting_Airline:STRING,...
```

Putting all these together, the loading becomes (see *bqload.sh* in the book's repo):

```
for MONTH in `seq -w 1 12`; do
  CSVFILE=gs://${BUCKET}/flights/raw/${YEAR}${MONTH}.csv
  bq --project_id $PROJECT \
     load --time_partitioning_field=FlightDate \
```

```
    --time_partitioning_type=MONTH \
    --source_format=CSV --ignore_unknown_values \
    --skip_leading_rows=1 --schema=$SCHEMA \
  ${PROJECT}:dsongcp.flights_raw\$${YEAR}${MONTH} $CSVFILE
done
```

At this point, we have the CSV files in Cloud Storage and the raw data in BigQuery. We have successfully ingested the 2015 flights data into GCP! If you want, you can repeat this for years 2016–2019 by changing the for loop in *ingest.sh* to:[21]

```
for YEAR in `seq 2016 2019`; do
```

Cloud Shell comes with a text editor. You can use it to edit files. Alternatively, use a Unix editor tool such as nano or vim. However, don't do it just yet—let's develop the code in this book with just 2015 data so that we can move faster. In Chapter 12, we'll expand the analysis and ML models to 2015–2019 data. In Chapter 3, we will start to look at the 2015 data and do useful things with it.

But before we move on, let's digress a little and consider automation.

# Scheduling Monthly Downloads

Now that we have some historical flight data in our Cloud Storage bucket, it is natural to wonder how to keep the bucket current. After all, airlines didn't stop flying in 2021, and the BTS continues to refresh its website on a monthly basis. It would be good if we could schedule monthly downloads to keep ourselves synchronized with the BTS.

There are two scenarios to consider here. The BTS could let us know when it has new data, and we could then proceed to ingest the data. The other option is that we periodically monitor the BTS website and ingest new data as it becomes available. The BTS doesn't offer a mechanism by which we can be notified about data updates, so we will need to resort to *polling*. We can, of course, be smart about how we do the polling. For example, if the BTS tends to update its website around the 5th of every month, we could poll at that time.

Where should this ingest program be executed? Realizing that this is a program that will be invoked only once a month (more often if retries are needed if an ingest fails), we realize that this is not a long-running job, but is instead something that should be scheduled to run periodically. The traditional way to do this is to schedule a *cron* job in Unix/Linux.[22] To schedule a cron job, you add a line to a *crontab* file and then

---

21 Let's ignore 2020 and 2021 because those were the years of the COVID-19 pandemic and historical data would not be very helpful in predicting arrival delays in 2020 or 2021.

22 A shortened form of a misspelling of chronos, Greek for time, cron is the name of the Unix daemon process that executes scheduled jobs at specific times.

register it with a Unix daemon that takes care of the scheduling.[23] For example, adding this line:

```
1 2 10 * * /etc/bin/ingest_flights.py
```

to crontab will cause the Python program */etc/bin/ingest_flights.py* (that would carry out the same steps to ingest the flights data that we did on the command line in the previous section) to be run by the system at 02:01 on the 10th of every month.

Although cron jobs are a straightforward solution, there are several problems that all come down to resilience and repeatability:

- The cron job is scheduled on a particular server. If that server happens to be rebooted around 2 a.m. on April 10, the ingest might never take place that month.

- The environment that cron executes in is very restricted. Our task will need to download data from BTS, uncompress it, clean it up, and upload it to the cloud. These impose a variety of requirements in terms of memory, space, and permissions, and it can be difficult to configure cron appropriately. In practice, system administrators configure cron jobs on particular machines and find it difficult to port them to other machines that do not have the same system paths.

- If the ingest job fails (if, for example, the network is down), there is no way to retry it. Retries and other such failure-recovery efforts will have to be explicitly coded in our Python program.

- Remote monitoring and one-time, ad hoc executions are not part of the cron interface. If you need to monitor, troubleshoot, and restart the ingest from a mobile device, good luck.

This litany of drawbacks is not unique to cron. They are implicit in any solution that is tied to specific servers. So, how would you do it on the cloud? What you should not do is to create a Compute Engine VM and schedule a cron job on it—that will be subject to some of the same problems!

For resilience and reliability, we need a serverless way to schedule ingest jobs. Obviously, the ingest job will need to be run on some machine somewhere. However, we shouldn't need to manage that machine at all. This is a job that needs perhaps two minutes of compute resources a month. We should be looking for a way to write the ingest code and let the cloud infrastructure take care of provisioning resources, making retries, and providing for remote monitoring and ad hoc execution.

On Google Cloud Platform, Cloud Scheduler provides a way to schedule periodic jobs in a serverless manner. These jobs can involve hitting an HTTP endpoint (which

---

23 Shortened form of cron table.

is what we will do), but can also send a message via Cloud Pub/Sub or trigger a Google Kubernetes Engine or Cloud Dataflow job. Figure 2-16 presents our architecture for the monthly ingest job.

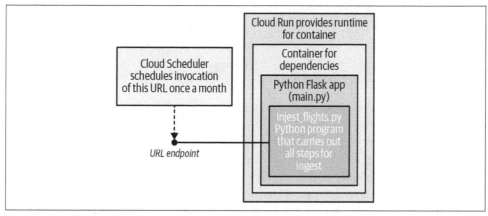

*Figure 2-16. The architecture of the monthly ingest job.*

First, we will write a standalone *ingest_flights.py* application that is capable of downloading the data for a specific year/month and uploading the data to Cloud Storage. We will invoke the ingest code from a Python Flask application making sure to explicitly capture our dependencies in a `Dockerfile` which describes a Docker container. Cloud Run will run our container.[24]

The way scheduling works in Cloud Scheduler is that we must specify a URL that will be invoked or a Cloud Pub/Sub topic that must be monitored. Whereas in the previous Linux cron example we specified a script on the server that was running the cron daemon, the Cloud Scheduler endpoint will be a URL that will be visited according to the schedule that we specify (this can be any URL; it doesn't need to be a service that we write). Because our ingest code is a standalone Python program, we will wrap that ingest code into a Python Flask application (`main.py`) so that we can invoke it by using a URL (Flask is a web application framework).

## Ingesting in Python

While exploring the data, we carried out the ingest on the command line in Bash. We saved our commands as we went along in the form of Bash scripts. We created our

---

24 Docker containers (*https://www.docker.com*) are lightweight wrappers around a piece of software (here, the Flask endpoint `main.py`) that contain everything needed to run that software—code (e.g., *ingest_flights.py*), runtime (Python dependencies, etc.), configuration files, and system libraries (here, a specific Linux distribution). Unlike a virtual machine, different containers running on the same machine can share layers of operating system dependencies.

ingest program by simply making a Bash script (*02_ingest/ingest.sh*) that invokes those intermediate steps:

```bash
#!/bin/bash
for MONTH in `seq 1 12`; do
    bash download.sh $YEAR $MONTH
done

# upload the raw CSV files to our GCS bucket
bash upload.sh

# load the CSV files into BigQuery as string columns
bash bqload.sh
```

This is the sort of decision that leads to spaghetti-like code that is difficult to unravel and to maintain. There are many assumptions made by this set of Bash scripts in terms of what to download, where the temporary storage resides, and where to upload it. Changing any of these will involve changing multiple scripts. Using Bash to quickly get a handle on the data is a good idea, as is the idea of saving these scripts so as to continue the exploration. But when it comes to making the ingest more systematic and routine, you do not want to use a shell scripting language; a more formal programming language is better.

In this book, we will use Python wherever we can because of its ability to span a wide range of computing tasks, from systems programming to statistics and machine learning. Python is currently the best choice if you need to pick a single language in which to do most of your work. Java is typesafe and performant. Its object-orientation and packaging architectures are suitable for large, multideveloper programs, but it makes the code too verbose. Moreover, the lack of a read–eval–print loop (REPL) interpreter makes Java unwieldy for quick experimentation. C++ is numerically very efficient, but standard libraries for nonnumerical computing are often nonexistent. Scala combines the benefits of Python (easy scriptability, conciseness) with the benefits of Java (type safety, speed), but the tooling for Scala (such as for statistics and visualization) is not as pervasive as it is for Python. Today, therefore, the best choice of programming language is Python. For certain use cases for which speed is important and Python is not performant enough, it might be necessary to use Java.

The ingest program in Python goes through the same four steps as before when we did it manually on the command line:

- Download data from the BTS website to a local file.
- Unzip the downloaded ZIP file and extract the CSV file it contains.
- Upload the CSV file to Google Cloud Storage.
- Load the CSV data into a BigQuery partitioned table.

Whereas our download Bash script got all 12 months of a hardcoded year (2015), our download subroutine in Python will take as input the year and month:

```python
def download(YEAR, MONTH, destdir):
    url = os.path.join("https://transtats.bts.gov/PREZIP",
                       "_{}_{}.zip".format(YEAR, int(MONTH)))

    filename = os.path.join(destdir, "{}{}.zip".format(YEAR, MONTH))
    with open(filename, "wb") as fp:
        response = urlopen(url)
        fp.write(response.read())
    return filename
```

Another thing to note is that our Bash script simply downloaded the ZIP file from BTS to the current working directory of the user. However, since our Python script is meant to be executed on demand by the scheduler service, we cannot make assumptions about the directory in which the script will be run. In particular, we don't know whether that directory will be writable and have enough space. Hence, we ask the caller of the function to provide an appropriate destination directory in which to store the downloaded ZIP file.

Here's how to unzip the file and extract the CSV contents:

```python
def zip_to_csv(filename, destdir):
    zip_ref = zipfile.ZipFile(filename, 'r')
    cwd = os.getcwd()
    os.chdir(destdir)
    zip_ref.extractall()
    os.chdir(cwd)
    csvfile = os.path.join(destdir, zip_ref.namelist()[0])
    zip_ref.close()
```

Unzipping explodes the size of the file. We can optimize things slightly. Rather than upload the text file, we can gzip it because BigQuery knows how to load gzipped CSV files:

```python
    gzipped = csvfile + ".gz"
    with open(csvfile, 'rb') as ifp:
        with gzip.open(gzipped, 'wb') as ofp:
            shutil.copyfileobj(ifp, ofp)
    return gzipped
```

Here's the code to upload the CSV file for a given month to Cloud Storage:

```python
def upload(csvfile, bucketname, blobname):
    client = storage.Client()
    bucket = client.get_bucket(bucketname)
    blob = Blob(blobname, bucket)
    blob.upload_from_filename(csvfile)
    gcslocation = 'gs://{}/{}'.format(bucketname, blobname)
    print ('Uploaded {} ...'.format(gcslocation))
    return gcslocation
```

The code asks for the `bucketname` (the single-region bucket that was created during our exploration) and a `blobname` (e.g., *flights/201501.csv*) and carries out the upload using the Cloud Storage Python library. Although it can be tempting to simply use the `subprocess` module in Python to invoke `gsutil` operations, it is better not to do so. If you go the `subprocess` route, you will then need to ensure that the Cloud SDK (which `gsutil` comes with) is installed on whichever machine this is going to run on. This won't be a problem in Cloud Run, but might pose problems if you switch the way you provide URL access later (to, say, Google App Engine or Cloud Functions). It is preferable to use pure Python modules when possible and add those modules to *requirements.txt*, as follows:[25]

```
Flask
google-cloud-storage
google-cloud-bigquery
gunicorn==20.1.0
```

The Flask library will help us handle HTTP requests (covered shortly), and Google Cloud Storage is needed so as to invoke the `get_bucket()` and `upload_from_file name()` operations. While using the latest version of libraries is okay, it poses the problem that an upgrade to those dependencies might break our code. For production code, it is better to pin the library versions to the ones with which the code has been tested:

```
Flask==2.0.1
google-cloud-storage==1.42.0
google-cloud-bigquery==2.25.1
gunicorn==20.1.0
```

If you do pin libraries, though, you will have to have a process in place to periodically test and upgrade to the latest stable version of your dependencies. Otherwise, your code might go stale or, worse, be insecure because it's using library versions with known vulnerabilities.

We can now write an `ingest()` method that calls the four major steps, plus the verification, in order:

```
def ingest(year, month, bucket):
    '''
    ingest flights data from BTS website to Google Cloud Storage
    return cloud-storage-blob-name on success.
    raises DataUnavailable if this data is not on BTS website
    '''
    tempdir = tempfile.mkdtemp(prefix='ingest_flights')
    try:
```

---

25  Hopefully, you know what the required packages are because you installed them using a package manager such as conda or pip. To find the packages in your development environment, you can use pip freeze.

```
        zipfile = download(year, month, tempdir)
        bts_csv = zip_to_csv(zipfile, tempdir)
        gcsloc = f'flights/raw/{year}{month}.csv.gz'
        gcsloc = upload(bts_csv, bucket, gcsloc)
        return bqload(gcsloc, year, month)
    finally:
        print ('Cleaning up by removing {}'.format(tempdir))
        shutil.rmtree(tempdir)
```

The destination directory that we use to stage the downloaded data before uploading to Cloud Storage is obtained using the `tempfile` package in Python. This ensures that if, for whatever reason, there are two instances of this program running at the same time, they will not cause contention issues.

We can try out the code by writing a `main()` that is executed if this program is run on the command line:[26]

```
if __name__ == '__main__':
    import argparse
    parser = argparse.ArgumentParser(
     description='ingest flights data from BTS website to GCS')
    parser.add_argument('--bucket', help='GCS bucket to upload data to',
                        required=True)
    parser.add_argument('--year', help='Example: 2015.', required=True)
    parser.add_argument('--month', help='01 for Jan.', required=True)
    try:
        args = parser.parse_args()
        gcsfile = ingest(args.year, args.month, args.bucket)
        print (f'Success ... ingested to {gcsfile}')
    except DataUnavailable as e:
        print ('Try again later: {}'.format(e.message))
```

Specifying a valid month ends with a new (or replaced) file on Cloud Storage:

```
$ ./ingest_flights.py  --bucket cloud-training-demos-ml \
                --year 2015 --month 01
...
Success ... ingested to gs://cloud-training-demos-ml/flights/201501.csv
```

Trying to download a month that is not yet available results in an error message:

```
$ ./ingest_flights.py --bucket cloud-training-demos-ml \
                --year 2029 --month 01
...
HTTP Error 403: Forbidden
```

On Cloud Scheduler, this will result in the call failing and being retried subject to a maximum number of retries. Retries will also happen if the BTS web server cannot be reached.

---

26 The full program is available as *ingest_flights.py* in the book's GitHub repository—try it out.

At this point, we have the equivalent of our exploratory Bash scripts, but with some additional resilience, repeatability, and fault tolerance built in. Our Python program expects us to provide a year, month, and bucket. However, if we are doing monthly ingests, we already know which year and month we need to ingest. No, not the current month—recall that there is a time lag between the flight events and the data being reported by the carriers to the BTS. Instead, it is simply the month after whatever files we already have on Cloud Storage![27] So, we can automate this, too:

```python
def next_month(bucketname):
    '''
      Finds which months are on GCS, and returns next year,month to download
    '''
    client = storage.Client()
    bucket = client.get_bucket(bucketname)
    blobs = list(bucket.list_blobs(prefix='flights/raw/'))
    files = [blob.name for blob in blobs if 'csv' in blob.name] # csv files only
    lastfile = os.path.basename(files[-1]) # e.g. 201503.csv
    year = lastfile[:4]
    month = lastfile[4:6]
    dt = datetime.datetime(int(year), int(month), 15) # 15th of month
    dt = dt + datetime.timedelta(30) # will always go to next month
    return '{}'.format(dt.year), '{:02d}'.format(dt.month)
```

To get the next month given that there is a file, say *201503.csv*, on Cloud Storage, we add 30 days to the Ides of March—this gets around the fact that there can be anywhere from 28 days to 31 days in a month, and that timedelta requires a precise number of days to add to a date.

By changing the year and month to be optional parameters, we can try out the ingest program's ability to find the next month and ingest it to Cloud Storage. We simply add:

```python
if args.year is None or args.month is None:
    year, month = next_month(args.bucket)
else:
    year = args.year
    month = args.month
gcsfile = ingest(year, month, args.bucket)
```

Having ingested the data, it is a good idea to verify that the end-to-end pipeline worked as intended. We could count the number of rows in the CSV file and assert that this is appropriately large (at least 10,000, for example) and equal to the number of rows corresponding to the month in BigQuery.

---

27 Our decision earlier to name the files as <*YYYYMM.csv*> (with zero padding month) was a good data engineering choice. By doing that, we can reliably count the number of months in our archive and check if the data for a specific month has already been downloaded.

Now that we have an ingest program that is capable of updating our Cloud Storage bucket one month at a time, we can move on to building the scaffolding to have it be executed in a serverless way.

## Cloud Run

Cloud Run (*https://oreil.ly/mUpzR*) is a serverless framework that provides an autoscaling, resilient runtime for containerized code. The container (see Figure 2-16) will consist of code that listens for requests or events. Cloud Run abstracts away all the infrastructure management that would otherwise be needed.

Now that we have a Python function that will do the ingest, we will wrap it inside a web application. To write the web application, we will use Flask (*https://oreil.ly/WS0xk*), which is a lightweight Python web application framework, and as a web server, we will use Gunicorn (*https://gunicorn.org*). Flask provides the ability to invoke Python code in response to an HTTP request, while Gunicorn will listen to HTTP requests and send them to the Flask app. Our container will consist of the Gunicorn server, Flask application, and its dependencies. This is expressed in the form of a Dockerfile:

```
FROM python:3.8-slim

# Copy local code to the container image.
ENV APP_HOME /app
WORKDIR $APP_HOME
COPY . ./

# Install production dependencies.
RUN pip install --no-cache-dir -r requirements.txt

# Run the web service on container startup.
# Timeout is set to 0 to disable the timeouts of
# the workers to allow Cloud Run to handle instance scaling.
CMD exec gunicorn --bind :$PORT --workers 1 \
                  --threads 8 --timeout 0 main:app
```

In our `main.py`, we have a function that gets invoked in response to the URL trigger:

```
import logging
from flask import escape
from ingest_flights import *

app = Flask(__name__)


@app.route("/", methods=['POST'])
def ingest_flights(request):
   try:
      json = request.get_json()
```

```
    year = escape(json['year']) if 'year' in json else None
    month = escape(json['month']) if 'month' in json else None
    bucket = escape(json['bucket']) # required

    if year is None or month is None or len(year) == 0 or len(month) == 0:
        year, month = next_month(bucket)
    tableref, numrows = ingest(year, month, bucket)
    ok = 'Success ... ingested {} rows to {}'.format(numrows, tableref)
    return ok
except Exception as e:
    logging.exception('Try again later')
```

Essentially, `main.py` has a single function that receives a Flask request object, from which we can extract the JSON (JavaScript Object Notation) payload of the HTTP POST by which the Cloud Run will be triggered. We get the next month by looking to see what months are already in the bucket and then ingest the necessary data using the existing code in the module `ingest_flights`. We can deploy the our codebase as a container to Cloud Run using:

```
NAME=ingest-flights-monthly
REGION=us-central1

gcloud run deploy $NAME --region $REGION --source=$(pwd) \
    --platform=managed --timeout 12m
```

But there are a couple of serious security and governance problems if we do this.

## Securing Cloud Run

What are the security problems?

- Anyone can invoke the URL and cause our dataset to get updated. We have to disallow unauthenticated users.

- Allowing this code to run with our user account's permissions will pollute any audit logs since we are not actually running the ingest interactively. We need to create a separate account so that the Cloud Run service can run with that identity.

- Allowing this code to run with our user account's permissions is also quite dangerous because our user account will typically have very broad permissions. We'd like to restrict the tasks that this automated service can do: we want it to be able to write only to specific Cloud Storage buckets and BigQuery tables.

The way to address the first point is to disallow unauthenticated users. The way to accomplish the second requirement is to specify that the Cloud Run service will have to run as a service account. A service account is an account whose identity is meant to be taken on by automated services. Like any identity, it can be configured to have specific and limited permissions. Therefore, before we can deploy the Cloud Run service, we will need to create a service account. Service accounts have email addresses of the form ${*service-account-name*}@${*project-id*}.iam.gserviceaccount.com. In our case, the service name is svc-monthly-ingest@cloud-training-demos. iam. gser viceaccount.com.

You can create a service account by going to the IAM area in the web console, but as usual, I prefer to script things:[28]

```
SVC_ACCT=svc-monthly-ingest
PROJECT_ID=$(gcloud config get-value project)
BUCKET=${PROJECT_ID}-cf-staging
REGION=us-central1
SVC_PRINCIPAL=serviceAccount:${SVC_ACCT}@${PROJECT_ID}.iam.gserviceaccount.com


gcloud iam service-accounts create $SVC_ACCT \
        --display-name "flights monthly ingest"
```

Then, we make the service account the admin of the staging GCS bucket so that it can read, write, list, delete, etc., on this bucket (and only this bucket):

```
gsutil mb -l $REGION gs://$BUCKET
gsutil uniformbucketlevelaccess set on gs://$BUCKET
gsutil iam ch ${SVC_PRINCIPAL}:roles/storage.admin gs://$BUCKET
```

We will also allow the service account to create and delete partitions on tables in just the BigQuery dataset dsongcp (and no other datasets):

```
bq --project_id=${PROJECT_ID} query --nouse_legacy_sql \
  "GRANT \`roles/bigquery.dataOwner\` ON SCHEMA dsongcp TO '$SVC_PRINCIPAL' "

gcloud projects add-iam-policy-binding ${PROJECT_ID} \
  --member ${SVC_PRINCIPAL} \
  --role roles/bigquery.jobUser
```

Are these permissions sufficient to carry out all the steps of our data processing pipeline? One way to check is to try to ingest a month of data when running as this service account. To do so, we will have to *impersonate* the service account:[29]

- Visit the Service Accounts section (*https://oreil.ly/V7U1L*) of the GCP Console.

- Select the newly created service account svc-monthly-ingest and click Manage Keys.

- Add key (Create a new JSON key) and download it to a file named *tempkey.json*. Transfer this key file to your Cloud Shell instance.

---

28 See *02_ingest/monthlyupdate/01_setup_svc_acct.sh*.

29 See the instructions in *README.md* in *02_ingest*.

- Run:

```
gcloud auth activate-service-account \
    --key-file tempkey.json
```

- Try ingesting one month:

```
./ingest_flights.py --bucket $BUCKET \
    --year 2015 --month 03 --debug
```

Once you have ensured that the service account has all the necessary permissions, go back to running commands as yourself using `gcloud auth login`.

## Deploying and Invoking Cloud Run

Now that we have the code for the Flask application and a service account with the right permissions, we can deploy the code to Cloud Run to run as this service account:[30]

```
NAME=ingest-flights-monthly
SVC_ACCT=svc-monthly-ingest
PROJECT_ID=$(gcloud config get-value project)
REGION=us-central1
SVC_EMAIL=${SVC_ACCT}@${PROJECT_ID}.iam.gserviceaccount.com

gcloud run deploy $NAME --region $REGION --source=$(pwd) \
    --platform=managed --service-account ${SVC_EMAIL} \
    --no-allow-unauthenticated --timeout 12m
```

Recall that we started the discussion on securing the Cloud Run instance by saying that we would disallow unauthenticated users and have the Cloud Run service run as a service account. Note how we are turning on both these options when we deploy to Cloud Run.

Once the application has been deployed to Cloud Run, we can try accessing the URL of the service with our authentication details in the header of the web request and a JSON message as its POST:[31]

```
# Feb 2015
echo {\"year\":\"2015\"\,\"month\":\"02\"\,\"bucket\":\"${BUCKET}\"\}\
    > /tmp/message

curl -k -X POST $URL \
    -H "Authorization: Bearer $(gcloud auth print-identity-token)" \
    -H "Content-Type:application/json" --data-binary @/tmp/message
```

---

30  See *02_ingest/monthlyupdate/02_deploy_cr.sh*.

31  See *02_ingest/monthlyupdate/03_call_cr.sh*.

But what is the URL? Cloud Run generates the URL when we deploy the container, and we can obtain it using:

```
gcloud run services describe ingest-flights-monthly \
    --format 'value(status.url)')
```

Changing the message to provide only the bucket (no year or month) will make the service get the next month:

```
echo {\"bucket\":\"${BUCKET}\"\} > /tmp/message
curl -k -X POST $URL \
    -H "Authorization: Bearer $(gcloud auth print-identity-token)" \
    -H "Content-Type:application/json" --data-binary @/tmp/message
```

## Scheduling Cloud Run

Our intent is to automatically invoke CloudRun once a month. We can do that using Cloud Scheduler, which is also serverless and doesn't require us to manage any infrastructure. We simply specify the schedule and the URL to hit. This URL is what came from the output of the Cloud Run deployment command in the previous section:

```
echo {\"bucket\":\"${BUCKET}\"\} > /tmp/message
cat /tmp/message

gcloud scheduler jobs create http monthlyupdate \
        --description "Ingest flights using Cloud Run" \
        --schedule="8 of month 10:00" \
        --time-zone "America/New_York" \
        --uri=$SVC_URL --http-method POST \
        --oidc-service-account-email $SVC_EMAIL \
        --oidc-token-audience=$SVC_URL \
        --max-backoff=7d \
        --max-retry-attempts=5 \
        --max-retry-duration=2d \
        --min-backoff=12h \
        --headers="Content-Type=application/json" \
        --message-body-from-file=/tmp/message
```

The preceding parameters would make the first retry happen after 12 hours. Subsequent retries are increasingly farther apart, up to a maximum of 2 days between attempts. We fail the task permanently if it fails five times within a defined time period and the task is more than 7 days old (both limits must be passed for the task to fail).

To try out the Cloud Scheduler, we could wait for the 8th of the month to roll around. Or we could go to the GCP web console and click on Run Now. Unfortunately, when I tried it, it wouldn't work because Cloud Scheduler wanted to run as the service account while I was logged in as myself. So, I gave myself the ability to impersonate the service account by going to the Service Accounts part of the web console. Once I did that, I was able to get Run Now to work.

The monthly update mechanism works if you have the previous month's data on Cloud Storage. If you start out with only 2015 data, updating it monthly means that you will inevitably be many months behind. So, you will need to run it ad hoc until your data is up-to-date and then let the cron service take care of things after that. Alternatively, you can take advantage of the fact that the ingest task is cheap and non-intrusive when there is no new data. So, you can change the schedule to be every day instead of every month. A better solution is to change the ingest task so that if it is successful in ingesting a new month of data, it immediately tries to ingest the next month. This way, your program will crawl month-by-month to the latest available month and then keep itself always up-to-date.

At this point, it is worth reflecting a bit on what we have accomplished. We are able to ingest data and keep it up-to-date by doing just these steps:

- Write some Python code.
- Deploy that Python code to the Google Cloud Platform.

We did not need to manage any infrastructure in order to do this. We didn't install any OS, manage accounts on those machines, keep them up-to-date with security patches, maintain failover systems, and so on—a serverless solution that consists simply of deploying code to the cloud is incredibly liberating. Not only is our ingest convenient, it is also very inexpensive—everything scales down to zero when it is not being used. All this falls comfortably within the free tier or might cost less than 5¢ a month.

# Summary

The US BTS collects, and makes publicly available, a dataset of flight information. It includes nearly a hundred fields, including scheduled and actual departure and arrival times, origin and destination airports, and flight numbers of every domestic flight scheduled by every major carrier. We will use this dataset to estimate the likelihood of an arrival delay of more than 15 minutes of the specific flight whose outcome needs to be known in order for us to decide whether to cancel the meeting.

There are three possible data processing architectures on the cloud for large datasets: scaling up, scaling out with sharded data, and scaling out with data in situ. Scaling up is very efficient, but is limited by the size of the largest machine you can get a hold of. Scaling out is very popular but requires that you preshard your data by splitting it among compute nodes, which leads to maintaining expensive clusters unless you can hit sustained high utilization. Keeping data in situ is possible only if your data center supports petabits per second of bisectional bandwidth so that any file can be moved to any compute node in the data center on demand. Because Google Cloud Platform has this capability, we will upload our data to Google Cloud Storage (a blob storage that is not presharded) and to BigQuery, which will allow us to carry out interactive exploration on large datasets.

To automate the ingest of the files, we reverse engineered the BTS's web form and obtained the format of the POST request that we need to make. With that request in hand, we were able to write a Bash script to pull down 12 months of data, uncompress the ZIP file, and load the data into BigQuery. It is quite straightforward to change this script to loop through multiple years.

We discussed the difference between strong consistency and eventual consistency and how to make the appropriate trade-off imposed by Brewer's CAP theorem. In this case, we wanted strong consistency and did not need global availability. Hence, we chose to use a single-region bucket. We then uploaded the downloaded, unzipped, and cleaned CSV files to Google Cloud Storage.

To schedule monthly downloads of the BTS dataset, we made our download and cleanup Python program and made it callable from Cloud Run so that it was completely serverless. We used Cloud Scheduler to periodically request the Cloud Run application to download BTS data, unzip it, and upload it to both Cloud Storage and BigQuery.

# Code Break

This is the point at which you should put this book off to the side and attempt to repeat all the things I've talked about. All the code snippets in this book have corresponding code in the GitHub repository.

I strongly encourage you to play around with the code in *02_ingest* with the goal of understanding why it is organized that way and being able to write similar code yourself. At minimum, though, you should do the following:

- Open Cloud Shell and git clone the book's code repository as explained in Chapter 1.
- Go to the *02_ingest* folder of the repository.
- Go to the Storage section of the GCP web console and create a new regional bucket—choose the region (such as us-central1) that is closest to where you live.
- Run ./ingest.sh providing the name of the bucket that you just created. This will populate your bucket and BigQuery dataset with data from 2015. Although you can change the year loop in this file to download all the data corresponding to 2015–2019, I recommend that you hold off on downloading all the data until Chapter 12 because processing 5 years of data will make every subsequent thing in this book take five times longer.

- Because software changes, an up-to-date list of the preceding steps is available in the course repository in *02_ingest/README.md*. This is true for all the following chapters.

## Suggested Resources

A key aspect of cloud-native architectures is reliance on fully managed, autoscaling services. That is Principle 3 from Tom Grey's short, but informative 2019 blog post, "5 Principles for Cloud-Native Architecture" (*https://oreil.ly/WtRO6*). How do you think the other principles apply to data analytics and AI?

When every department in your organization uses a hub-and-spoke architecture, and provides data access to other departments, the architecture you will have across the entire organization is a *data mesh*. This 2020 article from Medium.com, "Building a Data Platform to Enable Analytics and AI-Driven Innovation" (*https://oreil.ly/v8ihb*), describes the journey to get there.

Cloud Storage is a blob store. This 2020 article from Netapp, "Storage Options in Google Cloud: Block, Network File, and Object Storage" (*https://oreil.ly/8EJrL*) by Bruno Almeida, is a great introduction to the various storage options available on Google Cloud.

This handy flowchart (*https://oreil.ly/1ULUq*) summarizes the key considerations when deciding where to store your data. While you are there, take a look at some of the other flowcharts.

Google BigQuery (*https://cloud.google.com/bigquery*) is the heart of data analytics and AI architectures on Google Cloud. The O'Reilly Media book *BigQuery: The Definitive Guide* by Valliappa Lakshmanan and Jordan Tigani is a great place to learn about BigQuery.

Cloud Run (*https://oreil.ly/TaKkD*) is a serverless execution environment for containerized applications. Cloud Scheduler (*https://oreil.ly/CQs50*) provides a serverless way to invoke services on a schedule. Having Cloud Scheduler trigger Cloud Run is a common pattern that is documented (*https://oreil.ly/waw1P*). There is a list of guides for Cloud Run (*https://oreil.ly/OsU1I*) and a list of guides for Cloud Storage (*https://oreil.ly/a05aj*). Do you see the pattern? Try to find the list of guides for BigQuery.

A lot of data wrangling and early exploration involves Unix tools. A good introduction to the Unix shell and tools is this online tutorial (*https://oreil.ly/cwyaB*). How to use command-line tools to do data science is the focus of *Data Science at the Command Line* by Jeroen Janssens (O'Reilly).

"Scaling up" and "scaling out" seem very easy when we say the words or draw neat pictures. However, they are extremely hard problems to solve. As described in this 2018 *CIO* article by Stephen Watts (*https://oreil.ly/9Unyh*), scaling up requires being able to design application-specific integrated circuits (ASICs) when running into limits on how many transistors we can pack into a chip. The fundamental algorithm that underlies scaling out is the Paxos consensus protocol, which is fiendishly complicated to get right (see Deniz Altınbüken's website (*https://oreil.ly/3ft5y*), Paxos Made Moderately Complex). This is another reason to choose a public cloud.

# CHAPTER 3

# Creating Compelling Dashboards

In Chapter 2, we ingested on-time performance data from the US Bureau of Transportation Statistics (BTS) so as to be able to model the arrival delay given various attributes of an airline flight—the purpose of the analysis is to cancel a meeting if the probability of the flight arriving within 15 minutes of the scheduled arrival time is less than 70%.

Before we delve into building statistical and machine learning models, it is important to explore the dataset and gain an intuitive understanding of the data—this is called *exploratory data analysis*, and it's covered in more detail in Chapter 5. You should always carry out exploratory data analysis for any dataset that will be used as the basis for decision making. In this chapter, though, I talk about a different aspect of depicting data—of depicting data to end users and decision makers so that they can understand the recommendation that you are making. The audience of these visual representations, called *dashboards*, that we talk about in this chapter is not other data scientists, but is instead the end users. Keep the audience in mind as we go through this chapter, especially if you come from a data science background—the purpose of a dashboard is to explain an existing model, not to develop it. A dashboard is an end-user report that is interactive, tailored to end users, and continually refreshed with new data. See Table 3-1.

*Table 3-1. A dashboard is different from exploratory data analysis*

|  | For decision makers | For data scientists |
| --- | --- | --- |
| Usage pattern | Dashboards | Exploratory data analysis |
| Kinds of depictions | Current status, gauges, trendlines | Model fits with error bars, kernel density estimates |
| What does it explain? | Model recommendations and confidence | Input data, feature importance, model performance, etc. |

|  | For decision makers | For data scientists |
|---|---|---|
| Data represented | Subset of dataset, tailored to user's context | Aggregate of historical data |
| Typical tools | Data Studio, Tableau, Qlik, Looker, plotly, D3, shiny apps, etc. | Jupyter, Python, R Studio, S-plus, matplotlib, seaborn, Matlab, etc. |
| Mode of interaction | GUI-driven | Code-driven |
| Update | Real time | Not real time |
| Covered in | Chapter 3 , Chapter 4 | Chapter 5 |
| Example |

From AAA fuel gage report, May 2013 | From AAA safety and educational foundation (*https://oreil.ly/YMeHv*) |

Very often, this step of creating end-user visual depictions goes by the anodyne name of "visualization," as in visualizing data. However, I have purposefully chosen not to call it by that name because there is more to this than throwing together a few bar graphs and charts. Dashboards are highly visual, interactive reports that have been designed to depict data and explain models. When used in this way, dashboards provide business intelligence (BI).

All of the code snippets in this chapter are available in the folder *03_sqlstudio* of the book's GitHub repository (*https://github.com/GoogleCloudPlatform/data-science-on-gcp*). See the *README.md* file in that directory for instructions on how to do the steps described in this chapter.

# Explain Your Model with Dashboards

The purpose of this step in the modeling process is not simply to depict the data but to improve your users' understanding of how the model behaves. Whenever you are designing the display of a dataset, evaluate the design in terms of three aspects:

- Does it accurately and honestly depict the data? This is important when the raw data itself can be a basis for decision making.

- How well does it help envision not just the raw data, but the information content embodied in the data? Will the typical user know whether they need to take action after looking at the graphic? This is crucial for the cases when you are relying on human pattern recognition and interaction to help reveal insights about the environment in which the data was collected.

- Is it constructed in such a way that it explains the model being used to provide recommendations?

You want to build displays that are always accurate and honest. At the same time, the displays need to be interactive so as to provide viewers with the ability to play with the data and gain insights. Insights that users have gained should be part of the display of that information going forward in such a way that those insights can be used to explain the data.

The last point, that of explanatory power, is very important. The idea is to disseminate data understanding throughout your company. A statistical or machine learning model that you build for your users will be considered a black box, and while you might get feedback on when it works well and when it doesn't, you will rarely get pointed suggestions on how to actually improve that model in the field. In many cases, your users will use your model at a much more fine-grained level than you ever will because they will use your model to make a single decision, whereas in both training and evaluation, you would have been looking at model performance as a whole. Explainability is also critical to catch situations where the model is amplifying unfair bias.[1]

Although this holistic overview is useful for statistical rigor, you need people taking a close look at individual cases, too. Because users are making decisions one at a time, they are analyzing the data one scenario at a time. If you provide your users not just with your recommendation, but also with an explanation of why you are

---

[1] When Amazon built a hiring tool to help select resumes using machine learning, they were able to use explainability to recognize what the model was keying off—apparently, the machine learning model penalized resumes (*https://oreil.ly/wCxIV*) that included terms more commonly found in women's resumes. Amazon was able to catch this error and not use the ML model to actually evaluate candidates. Had explainability not been part of the workflow, many women would have been unfairly not considered for jobs at Amazon.

recommending it, they will begin to develop insights into your model. However, your users will only be able to develop such insights into the problem and your recommendations if you give them ways to observe the data that went into your model. Give enough users ways to view and interact with your data, and you will have unleashed a never-ending wave of innovation as users suggest improvements and factors the model should be considering.

Your users have other activities that require their attention. Why would they spend their time looking at your data? One of the ways to entice them to do that is by making the depiction of the information compelling. In my experience,[2] the most compelling displays are displays of real-time information in context. You can show people the average airline delay at JFK on January 12, 2012, and no one will care. But show a traveler in Chicago the average airline delay at ORD *right now* and you will have their interest—the difference is that the data is in context (O'Hare Airport, or ORD, for a traveler in Chicago) and that it is real-time information.

In this chapter, therefore, we will look at building dashboards that combine accurate depictions with explanatory power and interactivity in a compelling package. This seems to be a strange time to be talking about building dashboards—shouldn't the building of a dashboard wait until after we have built the best possible predictive model?

## Why Build a Dashboard First?

Building a dashboard when building a machine learning model is akin to building a form or survey tool to help you build the machine learning model. To build powerful machine learning models, you need to understand the dataset and devise features that help with prediction. By building a dashboard, you get to rope in the eventual users of the predictive model to take a close look at your data. Their fine-grained look at the data (remember that everyone is looking at the data corresponding to their context) will complement your overarching look at it. As they look at the data and keep sending suggestions and insights about the data to your team, you will be able to incorporate them into the machine learning model that you actually build.

---

2 When I worked on developing machine learning algorithms for weather prediction, nearly every one of the suggestions and feature requests that I received emerged when the person in question was looking at the real-time radar feed. There would be a storm, my colleague would watch it go up on radar, observe that the tracking of the storm was patchy, and let me know what aspect of the storm made it difficult to track. Or, someone would wake up, look at the radar image, and discover that birds leaving to forage from their roost had been wrongly tagged as a mesocyclone. It was all about real-time data. No matter how many times I asked, I never ever got anyone to look at how the algorithms performed on historical data. It was also often about Oklahoma (where our office was) because that's what my colleagues would concentrate on. Forecasters from around the country would derisively refer to algorithms that had been hypertuned to Oklahoma supercells.

In addition, when presented with a dataset, you should be careful that the data is the way you imagine it to be. There is no substitute for exposing and exploring the data to ensure that. Doing such exploratory data analysis with an immediately attainable milestone—building a dashboard from your dataset—is a fine way to do something real with the data and develop awareness of the subtleties of your data. Just as you often understand a concept best when you explain it to someone, building an explanatory display for your data is one of the best ways to develop your understanding of a dataset. The fact that you have to visualize the data in order to do basic pre-processing such as outlier detection makes it clear that building visual representations is work you will be doing anyway. If you are going to be doing it, you might as well do it well, with an eye toward its eventual use in production.

Eventual use in production is the third reason why you should develop the dashboard first instead of leaving it as an afterthought. Building explanatory power should be constantly on your mind as you develop the machine learning model. Giving users just the machine learning model will often go down poorly—they have no insight into why the system is recommending whatever it does. Adding explanations to the recommendations is more likely to succeed. For example, if you accompany your model prediction with five of the most salient features presented in an explanatory way, it will help make the model output more believable and trustworthy.

Even for cases in which the system performs poorly, you will receive feedback along the lines of "the prediction was wrong, but it is because Feature #3 was fishy. I think maybe you should also look at Factor Y." In other words, shipping your machine learning model along with an explanation of its behavior gets you more satisfied users, and users whose criticism will be a lot more constructive. It can be tempting to ship the machine learning model as soon as it is ready, but if there is a dashboard already available (because you were building it in parallel), it is easier to counsel that product designers consider the machine learning model and its explanatory dashboard as the complete product.

Finally, creating a dashboard is fun. It will help you build a user base quickly and show end users what's in it for them.

Explanations can be a double-edged sword because humans are not fully rational beings. Explanations can be the result of *apophenia*— the tendency of humans to see meaningful patterns even when there are none. This can lead to *motivated reasoning*—the tendency of humans to create justifications for decisions that are more desirable at an emotional level. The combination of apophenia and motivated reasoning can lead to just-so stories that attempt to justify whatever the state of the world is on the basis of spurious explanations. As data scientists, we should realize that we too are human. We need to be careful to set aside these biases, consider counterfactuals, and be willing to revise our initial judgments. Easier said than done, of course.

Where should these dashboards be implemented? Find out the environment that gets the largest audience of experts and eventual users and build your dashboard to target that environment.

Your users might already have a visualization interface with which they are familiar. Especially when it comes to real-time data, your users might spend their entire workday facing a visualization program that is targeted toward power users—this is true of weather forecasts, air traffic controllers, and options traders. If that is the case, look for ways to embed your visualizations into that interface. In other cases, your users might prefer that your visualizations be available from the convenience of their web browser. If this is the case, look for a visualization tool that lets you share the report as an interactive, commentable document (not just a static web page). In many cases, you might have to build multiple dashboards for different sets of users (don't shoehorn everything into the same dashboard).

## Accuracy, Honesty, and Good Design

Because the explanatory power of a good dashboard is why we are building visualizations, it is important to ensure that our explanations are not misleading. In this regard, it is best not to do anything too surprising. Although modern-day visualization programs are chock-full of types of graphs and palettes, it is best to pair any graphic with the idiom for which it is appropriate. For example, some types of graphics are better suited to relational data than others, and some graphics are better suited to categorical data than to numerical data.

Broadly, there are four fundamental types of graphics: relational (illustrating the relationship between pairs of variables), time series (illustrating the change of a variable over time), geographical maps (illustrating the variation of a variable by location), and narratives (to support an argument). Narrative graphics are the ones in magazine spreads, which win major design awards. The other three are more worker-like.

You have likely seen enough graphical representations to realize intuitively that the graph is somehow wrong when you violate an accuracy, honesty, or aesthetic principle,[3] but this section of the book lists a few of the canonical ones. For example, it is advisable to choose line graphs or scatter plots for relational graphics and to ensure that autoscaling of the axes doesn't portray a misleading story about your data. A good design principle is that your time series graphs should be more horizontal than vertical, and that it is the data lines and not "chart junk" (grid lines, labels, etc.) that ought to dominate your graphics. Maximizing the ratio of data to space and ink is a principle that will stand you in good stead when it comes to geographical data—ensure that the domain is clipped to the region of interest, and go easy on place names and other text labels.

Just as you probably learned to write well by reading good writers, one of the best ways to develop a feel for accurate and compelling graphics is to increase your exposure to good exemplars. *The Economist* newspaper has a Graphic Detail blog (*https://oreil.ly/AnPgC*)[4] that is worth following—they publish a chart, map, or infographic every weekday, and these run the gamut of the fundamental graphics types. Figure 3-1 shows a graphic from the blog published on Nov. 25, 2016 (*https://oreil.ly/YipcK*).

The graphic depicts the increase in the number of coauthors on scientific papers over the past two decades. The graphic itself illustrates several principles of good design. It is a time series, and as you'd expect of this type of graphic, the time is on the horizontal axis and the time-varying quantity (number of authors per article or the number of articles per author) is on the vertical axis. The vertical axis values start out at zero, so that the height of the graphs is an accurate indicator of magnitude. Note how minimal the chart junk is—the axes labels and gridlines are very subtle and the title doesn't draw attention to itself. The data lines, on the other hand, are what pop out. Note also the effective use of repetition—instead of all the different disciplines (Economics, Engineering, etc.) being on the same graph, each discipline is displayed on its own panel. This serves to reduce clutter and makes the graphs easy to interpret. Each panel has two graphs, one for authors per article and the other for articles per author. The colors remain consistent across the panels for easy comparison, and the placement of the panels also encourages such comparisons. We see, for example, that the increase in number of authors per article is not accompanied by an increase in articles per author in any of the disciplines, except for Physics & Astronomy. Perhaps the physicists and astronomers are gaming the system?

---

3 If you are not familiar with design principles, I recommend *The Visual Display of Quantitative Information* by Edward Tufte (Graphics Press).

4 *The Economist* is published weekly as an 80-page booklet stapled in the center, and each page is about the size of a letter paper. However, for historical reasons, the company refers to itself as a newspaper rather than a magazine.

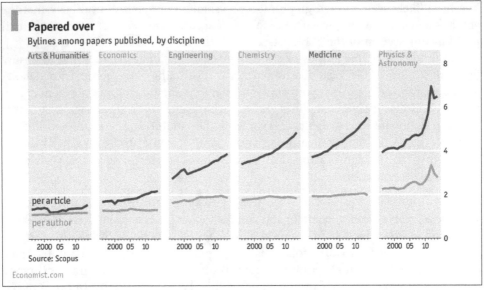

Figure 3-1. *This graphic from* The Economist *shows an increase in the number of authors of papers in various academic disciplines over time.*

The graphic does, however, subtly mislead viewers who are in a hurry. Take a moment and try to critique the graphic—figure out how a viewer might have been misled. It has to do with the arrangement of the panels. It appears that the creator of the graphic has arranged the panels to provide a pleasing upward trend between the panels, but this upward trend is misleading because there is no relationship between the number of authors per article in Economics in 2016 and the same quantity in Engineering in 1996. This misdirection is concerning because the graph is supposed to support the narrative of an increasing number of authors, but the increase is not from one author to six authors over two decades—the actual increase is much less dramatic (for example, from four to six in Medicine). However, a viewer who only glances at the data might wrongly believe that the increase in the number of authors is depicted by the whole graph and is therefore much more than it really is.

# Loading Data into Cloud SQL

To create dashboards to allow interactive analysis of the data, we will need to store the data in a manner that permits fast random access and aggregations. Because our flight data is tabular, SQL is a natural choice, and if we are going to be using SQL, we should consider whether a relational database meets our needs. Relational databases are a mature technology and remain the tool of choice for many business problems. Relational database technology is well known and comes with a rich ecosystem of interoperable tools. The problem of standardized access to relational databases from high-level programming languages is pretty much solved.

PostgreSQL (*https://www.postgresql.org*) is a very popular open source relational database that is used in production at many enterprises. In addition to its high performance, PostgreSQL is easy to program against—it supports ANSI SQL, geographic information system (GIS) functionality, client libraries in a variety of programming languages, and standard connector technologies such as Open Database Connectivity (ODBC) and Java Database Connectivity (JDBC).

## Create a Google Cloud SQL Instance

Google Cloud SQL (*https://cloud.google.com/sql*) offers a managed database service that supports PostgreSQL, MySQL, and SQL Server. Cloud SQL manages backups, patches, updates, and even replication while providing for global availability, automatic failover, and high uptime. For best performance, choose a machine whose RAM is large enough to hold your largest table in memory—as of this writing, available machine types range from a single CPU with less than 4 GB of memory all the way to a 96 CPU machine with 624 GB of memory. Balance this desire for speed with the monthly cost of a machine, of course.

Let's configure a Cloud SQL instance, create a database table in it, and load the table with the data we ingested into Cloud Storage. You can do all these things on the command line using `gcloud`, but let's begin by using the SQL section of Cloud Platform Console (*https://oreil.ly/Q4OaT*) and select Create Instance. Choose PostgreSQL and then fill out the form as follows (see Figure 3-2):

- Call the instance "flights."
- Generate a strong password by clicking on the GENERATE button.
- Choose the default PostgreSQL version.
- Choose the region where your bucket of CSV data exists.
- Choose a single zone instance since we are just trying it out. We won't take this to production.
- Choose a Standard machine type with 2 vCPU.
- Click Create Instance, accepting all the other defaults.

*Figure 3-2. Creating a PostgreSQL instance using the web console.*

## Interacting with Google Cloud Platform

Instead of filling out the dialog box by hand, we could have used the command-line tool `gcloud` from Cloud Shell (or any other machine that has `gcloud` installed); here's how to do that:

```
gcloud sql instances create flights \
    --database-version=POSTGRES_13 --cpu=2 --memory=8GiB \
    --region=us-central1 --root-password=somestrongpassword
```

In the rest of the book, I will show you just the `gcloud` commands, but you don't need to memorize them. You can use `--help` at any time on `gcloud` to get a list of options. For example:

```
gcloud sql instances create --help
```

will give you all the options available to create Cloud SQL instances (the database-version, its zone, etc.), whereas:

```
gcloud sql instances --help
```

will give you all the ways in which you can work with Cloud SQL instances (create, delete, restart, export, etc.).

In general, everything you can do on the command line is doable using the Cloud Platform Console, and vice versa. In fact, both the Cloud Platform Console and the gcloud command invoke representational state transfer (REST) API actions. You can invoke the same REST APIs from your programs (the APIs are documented on the Google Cloud Platform website). Here is the REST API call to create an instance from Bash:[5]

```
ACCESS_TOKEN="$(gcloud auth application-default print-access-token)"
curl --header "Authorization: Bearer ${ACCESS_TOKEN}" \
     --header 'Content-Type: application/json' \
     --data '{"name":"flights", "settings":
            {"database-version":"POSTGRES_13", ...}' \
     https://www.googleapis.com/sql/v1beta4/projects/[PROJECT-ID]/instances \
     -X POST
```

Alternatively, you can use the Cloud Client Library (available for a variety of programming languages (*https://oreil.ly/ZUpit*)) to issue the REST API calls. We saw this in Chapter 2 when we used the google.cloud.storage Python package to interact with Cloud Storage.

In summary, there are three ways to interact with Google Cloud Platform:

1. The web console:

   ```
   The gcloud command from the command line in Cloud Shell
   or a machine that has the gcloud SDK installed
   ```

2. Directly invoke the REST API

3. Google Cloud Client Library (available as of this writing for Go, Java, Node.js, Python, Ruby, PHP, and C#)

   In this book, I use primarily Option 2 (from the shell) and Option 4 (from Python programs).

---

[5] I looked up the URL and the format of the message from the REST API reference documentation (*https://oreil.ly/jD7RC*). All the other methods of interacting with a service (web console, gcloud command line, Cloud Client Library) end up invoking the REST API.

## Create Table of Data

In order to import data into a Postgres table, we first have to create an empty database and a table with the correct schema.

In the Cloud (web) console, navigate to the databases section of Cloud SQL, select instance "flights," and create a new database called `bts`. This will be where we load our data.

Next, we have to create a file with the following syntax, to create a column for every field in the CSV file:

```
drop table if exists flights;

CREATE TABLE flights (
  "Year" TEXT,
  "Quarter" TEXT,
  "Month" TEXT,
  "DayofMonth" TEXT,
  "DayOfWeek" TEXT,
  "FlightDate" DATE,
  "Reporting_Airline" TEXT,
  "DOT_ID_Reporting_Airline" TEXT,
  "IATA_CODE_Reporting_Airline" TEXT,
...
```

For your convenience, the file I created is already in the Git repository, so just go to Cloud Shell, change into the *03_sqlstudio* directory, and do the following steps:

- Stage the file into Google Cloud Storage (changing the bucket to one that you own):

  ```
  gsutil cp create_table.sql \
      gs://cloud-training-demos-ml/flights/ch3/create_table.sql
  ```

- In the web console, navigate to the flights instance of Cloud SQL and select IMPORT. In the form, specify the location of *create_table.sql* and specify that you want to create a table in the database `bts` (see Figure 3-3).

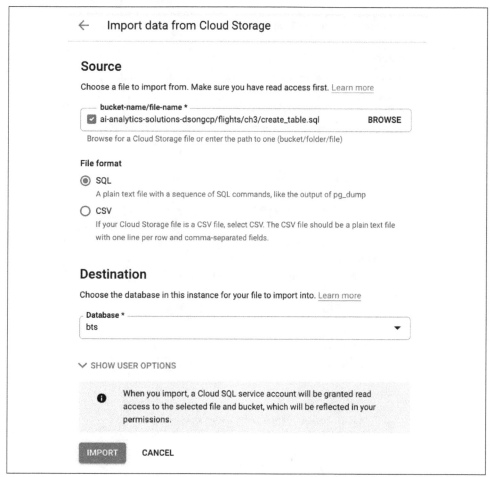

*Figure 3-3. Creating an empty table.*

A few seconds later, the empty table will be created.

We can now load the CSV files into this table. Start by loading the January data by browsing to *201501.csv* in your bucket and specifying CSV as the format, `bts` as the database, and `flights` as the table (see Figure 3-4).

## Import data from Cloud Storage

### Source

Choose a file to import from. Make sure you have read access first. Learn more

bucket-name/file-name *

☑ ai-analytics-solutions-dsongcp/flights/raw/201501.csv          BROWSE

Browse for a Cloud Storage file or enter the path to one (bucket/folder/file)

**File format**

○ SQL
  A plain text file with a sequence of SQL commands, like the output of pg_dump

◉ CSV
  If your Cloud Storage file is a CSV file, select CSV. The CSV file should be a plain text file
  with one line per row and comma-separated fields.

### Destination

Choose the database and table in your instance for this file to import into. Learn more

Database *

bts                                                            ▼

Table *

flights

Enter the name of an existing table in the database to house your CSV file

⌄ SHOW USER OPTIONS

> ❶  When you import, a Cloud SQL service account will be granted read
>     access to the selected file and bucket, which will be reflected in your
>     permissions.

**IMPORT**   CANCEL

*Figure 3-4. Populating the table with data from January.*

 Note that the user interface doesn't provide a way to skip the first line, so the header will also get loaded as a row in the table. Fortunately, our schema calls all the fields as text, so this doesn't pose a problem—after loading the data, we can delete the row corresponding to the header. If we have a more realistic schema, we will have to remove the header line before loading the file.

## Interacting with the Database

We can connect to the Cloud SQL instance from Cloud Shell using:[6]

```
gcloud sql connect flights --user=postgres
```

In the prompt that comes up, we connect to the bts database:

```
\c bts;
```

Then, we can run a query to obtain the five busiest airports:

```
SELECT "Origin", COUNT(*) AS num_flights
FROM flights GROUP BY "Origin"
ORDER BY num_flights DESC
LIMIT 5;
```

While this is performant because the dataset is relatively small (only January!), as I added more months, the database started to slow down.

Relational databases are particularly well suited to smallish datasets on which we wish to do ad hoc queries that involve searching and that return small subsets of data. For larger datasets, we can tune the performance of a relational database by indexing the columns of interest. Further, because relational databases typically support transactions and guarantee strong consistency, they are an excellent choice for data that will be updated often.

However, a relational database is a poor choice if your data is primarily read-only, if your dataset sizes go into the terabyte range, if you have a need to scan the full table (such as to compute the maximum value of a column), or if your data streams in at high rates. This describes our flight delay use case. So, let's switch from a relational database to an analytics data warehouse—BigQuery. The analytics data warehouse will allow us to use SQL and is much more capable of dealing with large datasets and ad hoc queries (i.e., doesn't need the columns to be indexed).

---

6 If your organization has set up a security policy to allow access only from authorized networks, you might have to use a SQL proxy (*https://oreil.ly/cdXyL*) to connect to the instance. At the time of writing, this is available only in the beta version, so use the following command: **gcloud beta sql connect flights -- user=postgres**.

If you are following along with me, delete the Cloud SQL instance. We won't need it any further in this book.[7]

# Querying Using BigQuery

In Chapter 2, we loaded the CSV data into BigQuery into a table named `flights_raw` in the dataset `dsongcp`. Let's explore that dataset a bit—this is not a full exploratory data analysis, which I will do in Chapter 5.

My goal here is to do "just enough" analysis on the data and then quickly pivot to building my first model. Once I have the model, I will be able to build a dashboard to explain that model. The idea is to get a first iteration out in front of users as quickly as possible. Going from ingested data to minimum viable outputs (model, dashboard, etc.) quickly is what agile development in data science looks like.

Teams that wait until they build a fully capable model before incorporating it into decision tools often build the wrong model (i.e., they solve the wrong problem because of misunderstanding how the decision will be used) or choose unviable technology (that is hard to get into production). Avoid these traps by testing your work with real users as quickly as possible!

## Schema Exploration

Navigate to the BigQuery section (*https://oreil.ly/vyCns*) of the Google Cloud (web) console and select the `flights_raw` table. On the right side of the window, select Schema (see Figure 3-5). Which fields do you think are relevant to predicting flight arrival delays?

---

7 Considering that we were using BigQuery and we are going to use BigQuery, what was the point of this detour into Cloud SQL? In many cases, your data will originally be in a relational database management system (RDBMS). If that dataset is small, you can power the dashboard off the RDBMS. Even though BigQuery is the better choice for the flights delay dataset, it won't always be the best choice for all the projects you will work on in Google Cloud. Part of my philosophy in this book is to "show," not "tell." So, the reason for this section was to show this trade-off between RDBMS and a data warehouse. This will be true later on in the book as well. I'll do a Spark ML model in Chapter 7, but it won't scale once we add categorical columns—in that sense, that entire chapter is a digression! I'll stream into Bigtable in Chapter 11 and show that the resulting performance improvement is overkill. In summary, the point of the Cloud SQL detour was to explore the possibilities, show what the problems are, and help you develop the intuition for the trade-offs involved.

---

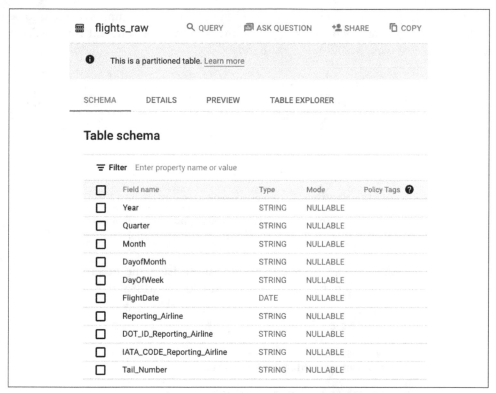

*Figure 3-5. The schema of the* `flights_raw` *table that we loaded into BigQuery in Chapter 2.*

Just looking at the schema is not enough. For example, do we really need the Year, Month, DayofMonth, and so on? Isn't FlightDate enough? It's best to not have duplicative data—the more columns we have, the more work we have to do to keep analysis consistent.

Similarly, which of the various Airline columns do we need? For the Airline columns, we did read the description on the BTS website in Chapter 2, and will probably follow their recommendation that `Reporting_Airline` be the one that we use. Still, it's worth verifying why that is.

To make decisions like this, we can use two features—the Preview tab and the Table Explorer tab (see Figure 3-6).

## Using Preview

The best way to quickly look at a BigQuery table is to use the Preview functionality. The Preview is free, whereas doing a `SELECT * FROM ... LIMIT 10` will incur a querying cost.

Looking at the preview (see Figure 3-6), the Year, Month, etc., columns do seem to be redundant. (If you are following along with me, you may see different rows because the Preview just picks whatever is most handy.)

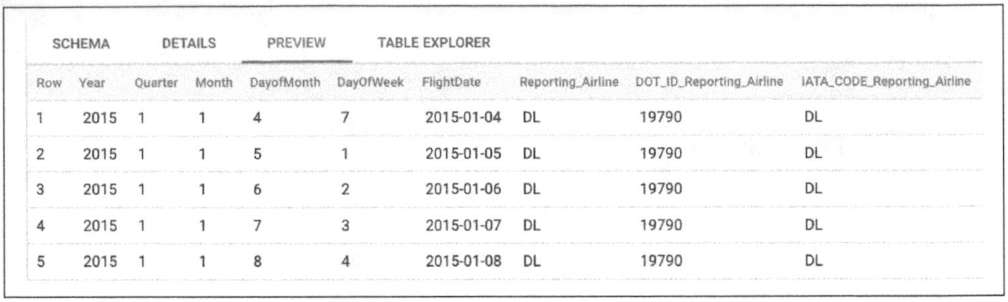

| Row | Year | Quarter | Month | DayofMonth | DayOfWeek | FlightDate | Reporting_Airline | DOT_ID_Reporting_Airline | IATA_CODE_Reporting_Airline |
|-----|------|---------|-------|------------|-----------|------------|-------------------|--------------------------|------------------------------|
| 1 | 2015 | 1 | 1 | 4 | 7 | 2015-01-04 | DL | 19790 | DL |
| 2 | 2015 | 1 | 1 | 5 | 1 | 2015-01-05 | DL | 19790 | DL |
| 3 | 2015 | 1 | 1 | 6 | 2 | 2015-01-06 | DL | 19790 | DL |
| 4 | 2015 | 1 | 1 | 7 | 3 | 2015-01-07 | DL | 19790 | DL |
| 5 | 2015 | 1 | 1 | 8 | 4 | 2015-01-08 | DL | 19790 | DL |

*Figure 3-6. Preview of the `flights_raw` table that we loaded into BigQuery in Chapter 2.*

Let's check whether we can resurrect the FlightDate from the other columns and extract the date pieces from the FlightDate. We can do that with SQL:

```
SELECT
    FORMAT("%s-%02d-%02d",
        Year,
        CAST(Month AS INT64),
        CAST(DayofMonth AS INT64)) AS resurrect,
    FlightDate,
    CAST(EXTRACT(YEAR FROM FlightDate) AS INT64) AS ex_year,
    CAST(EXTRACT(MONTH FROM FlightDate) AS INT64) AS ex_month,
    CAST(EXTRACT(DAY FROM FlightDate) AS INT64) AS ex_day,
FROM dsongcp.flights_raw
LIMIT 5
```

The result appears to bear this out:

| Row | resurrect | FlightDate | ex_year | ex_month | ex_day |
|-----|-----------|------------|---------|----------|--------|
| 1 | 2015-02-19 | 2015-02-19 | 2015 | 2 | 19 |
| 2 | 2015-02-20 | 2015-02-20 | 2015 | 2 | 20 |
| 3 | 2015-02-22 | 2015-02-22 | 2015 | 2 | 22 |
| 4 | 2015-02-23 | 2015-02-23 | 2015 | 2 | 23 |
| 5 | 2015-02-25 | 2015-02-25 | 2015 | 2 | 25 |

But we have to be sure. Let's print out rows where the extracted data from FlightDate is *not* identical:

```
WITH data AS (
SELECT
    FORMAT("%s-%02d-%02d",
        Year,
```

```
        CAST(Month AS INT64),
        CAST(DayofMonth AS INT64)) AS resurrect,
    FlightDate,
    CAST(EXTRACT(YEAR FROM FlightDate) AS INT64) AS ex_year,
    CAST(EXTRACT(MONTH FROM FlightDate) AS INT64) AS ex_month,
    CAST(EXTRACT(DAY FROM FlightDate) AS INT64) AS ex_day,
FROM dsongcp.flights_raw
)
SELECT * FROM data
WHERE resurrect != CAST(FlightDate AS STRING)
```

This query returns an empty result set, so we are sure that we can safely keep only the FlightDate column.

## Using Table Explorer

How about the Airline code? Switch to the Table Explorer tab and select the three airline columns as shown in Figure 3-7.

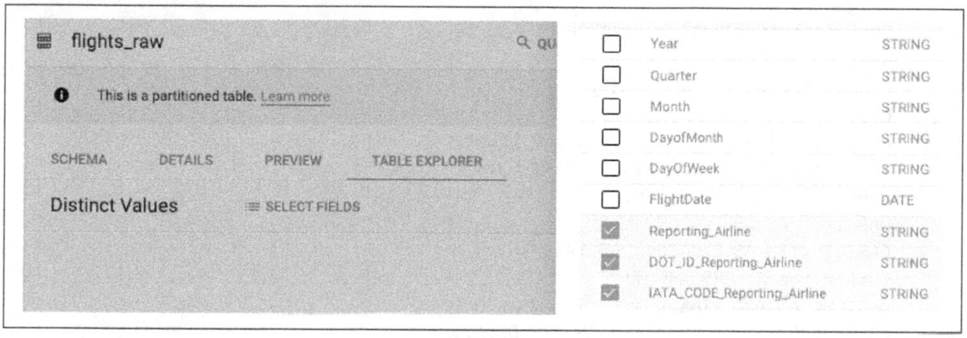

*Figure 3-7. Selecting fields for Table Explorer.*

BigQuery analyzes the full dataset and shows the unique values in the table, as shown in Figure 3-8.

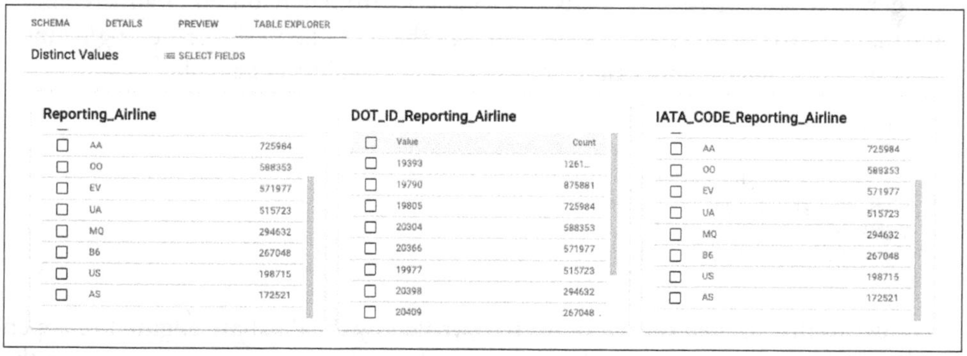

*Figure 3-8. Distinct values for the three Airline fields.*

It is clear from the Table Explorer that we want to use either the `Reporting_Airline` or the `IATA_CODE_Reporting_Airline`. As before, checking to see if there are rows where these are different indicates that `Reporting_Airline` is sufficient.

## Creating BigQuery View

Based on such analysis on the remaining fields, I came up with the following sets of operations I want to do to the raw data to make it more usable. For example, the Departure Delay should be a floating point number and not a string. The Cancellation Code should be a boolean and not 1.00:

```
CREATE OR REPLACE VIEW dsongcp.flights AS

SELECT
  FlightDate AS FL_DATE,
  Reporting_Airline AS UNIQUE_CARRIER,
  OriginAirportSeqID AS ORIGIN_AIRPORT_SEQ_ID,
  Origin AS ORIGIN,
  DestAirportSeqID AS DEST_AIRPORT_SEQ_ID,
  Dest AS DEST,
  CRSDepTime AS CRS_DEP_TIME,
  DepTime AS DEP_TIME,
  CAST(DepDelay AS FLOAT64) AS DEP_DELAY,
  CAST(TaxiOut AS FLOAT64) AS TAXI_OUT,
  WheelsOff AS WHEELS_OFF,
  WheelsOn AS WHEELS_ON,
  CAST(TaxiIn AS FLOAT64) AS TAXI_IN,
  CRSArrTime AS CRS_ARR_TIME,
  ArrTime AS ARR_TIME,
  CAST(ArrDelay AS FLOAT64) AS ARR_DELAY,
  IF(Cancelled = '1.00', True, False) AS CANCELLED,
  IF(Diverted = '1.00', True, False) AS DIVERTED,
  DISTANCE
FROM dsongcp.flights_raw;
```

In order to avoid repeating these casts in all queries from here on out, I am creating a view that consists of the `SELECT` statement (see the first line in the preceding listing). A view is a virtual table—we can query the view just as if it were a table:

```
SELECT
  ORIGIN,
  COUNT(*) AS num_flights
FROM dsongcp.flights
GROUP BY ORIGIN
ORDER BY num_flights DESC
LIMIT 5
```

Any queries that happen on the view are rewritten by the database engine to happen on the original table—conceptually, a view works as if the SQL corresponding to the view was to be inserted into every query that uses the view.

What if the view includes a WHERE clause so that the number of rows is much less? In such cases, it would be far more efficient to export the results into a table and query that table instead:

```
CREATE OR REPLACE TABLE dsongcp.flights AS

SELECT
```

But what if you export the results into a table and then the original table has a new month of data added to it? We'd have to rerun the table creation statement to make the extracted table up-to-date. In the case of a view, we wouldn't have to do anything special—all new queries would automatically be querying the entire raw table and thus include the new month of data.

Can we have our cake and eat it too? Can we get the "live" nature of a view, but the query efficiency of a table? Yes. It's called a *materialized view*:

```
CREATE MATERIALIZED VIEW dsongcp.flights AS

SELECT
```

The view is materialized into a table and kept up-to-date by BigQuery. While views are free, materialized views carry an extra cost because of the extra storage and compute overhead they involve.

In this book, I'll use a regular view during development, since it's easy to come back and add new columns, etc. Later on, once we go to production, it's quite simple to change it over to a materialized view—none of the client code will need to change.

# Building Our First Model

Intuitively, we feel that if the flight departure is delayed by 15 minutes, it will also tend to arrive 15 minutes late. So, our model could be that we cancel the meeting if the departure delay of the flight is 15 minutes or more. Of course, there is nothing here about the probability (recall that we wanted to cancel if the probability of an arrival delay of 15 minutes was greater than 30%). Still, it will be a quick start and give us something that we can ship now and iterate upon.

## Contingency Table

Suppose that we need to know how often we will be making the right decision if our decision rule is the following:

If DEP_DELAY ≥ 15, cancel the meeting; otherwise, go ahead.

There are four possibilities in the *contingency table* or the *confusion matrix*, which you can see in Table 3-2.

*Table 3-2. Confusion matrix for the decision to cancel the meeting*

|  | Arrival delay < 15 minutes | Arrival delay ≥ 15 minutes |
|---|---|---|
| We did not cancel meeting (departure delay < 15 min) | Correct (true positive) | False positive |
| We canceled meeting (departure delay ≥ 15 min) | False negative | Correct (true negative) |

If we cancel the meeting and it turns out that the flight arrived on time (let's call that a "positive"), it is clear that we made a wrong decision. It is arbitrary whether we refer to it as a false positive (treating the on-time arrival as a positive event) or as a false negative (treating the late arrival as a negative event). Because the dataset is called "on-time arrivals," let's term on-time arrival the positive event. How do we find out how often the decision rule of thresholding the departure delay at 15 minutes will tend to be correct? We can evaluate the first box in the confusion matrix using BigQuery:

```
SELECT
    COUNT(*) AS true_positives
FROM dsongcp.flights
WHERE dep_delay < 15 AND arr_delay < 15
```

There are 4,430,885 such flights.

To compute all four values in a single statement, move the WHERE clause into the SELECT itself:

```
SELECT
    COUNTIF(dep_delay < 15 AND arr_delay < 15) AS true_positives,
    COUNTIF(dep_delay < 15 AND arr_delay >= 15) AS false_positives,
    COUNTIF(dep_delay >= 15 AND arr_delay < 15) AS false_negatives,
    COUNTIF(dep_delay >= 15 AND arr_delay >= 15) AS true_negatives,
    COUNT(*) AS total
FROM dsongcp.flights
WHERE arr_delay IS NOT NULL AND dep_delay IS NOT NULL
```

Each of the COUNTIF statements counts the number of rows that match the given criterion, and COUNT(*) counts all rows. This way, we get to scan the table just once, and still manage to collect the four numbers that form the confusion matrix:

| Row | true_positives | false_positives | false_negatives | true_negatives | total |
|---|---|---|---|---|---|
| 1 | 4430885 | 232701 | 219684 | 830738 | 5714008 |

Recall that these numbers assume that we are making a decision by thresholding the departure delay at 15 minutes. But is that the best threshold?

# Threshold Optimization

Ideally, we want to try out different values of the threshold and pick the one that provides the best results. To do so, we can declare a variable called THRESH and use it in the query. This way, there is just one number to change when we want to try out a different threshold:

```
DECLARE THRESH INT64;
SET THRESH = 15;

SELECT
    COUNTIF(dep_delay < THRESH AND arr_delay < 15) AS true_positives,
    COUNTIF(dep_delay < THRESH AND arr_delay >= 15) AS false_positives,
    COUNTIF(dep_delay >= THRESH AND arr_delay < 15) AS false_negatives,
    COUNTIF(dep_delay >= THRESH AND arr_delay >= 15) AS true_negatives,
    COUNT(*) AS total
FROM dsongcp.flights
WHERE arr_delay IS NOT NULL AND dep_delay IS NOT NULL
```

Still, I'd rather not run the query several times, once for each threshold. It's not about the drudgery of it—I could avoid the manual work by using a for loop in a script. What I'm objecting to is scanning the table four times. The better way to do this in SQL is to declare an array of possible thresholds and then group by them:

```
SELECT
    THRESH,
    COUNTIF(dep_delay < THRESH AND arr_delay < 15) AS true_positives,
    COUNTIF(dep_delay < THRESH AND arr_delay >= 15) AS false_positives,
    COUNTIF(dep_delay >= THRESH AND arr_delay < 15) AS false_negatives,
    COUNTIF(dep_delay >= THRESH AND arr_delay >= 15) AS true_negatives,
    COUNT(*) AS total
FROM dsongcp.flights, UNNEST([5, 10, 11, 12, 13, 15, 20]) AS THRESH
WHERE arr_delay IS NOT NULL AND dep_delay IS NOT NULL
GROUP BY THRESH
```

This way, we get to run a single query, which scans the table just once and still manages to create contingency tables for all the thresholds we want to try. The result consists of the four contingency table values for each of the seven values of the threshold:

| Row | THRESH | true_positives | false_positives | false_negatives | true_negatives | total |
|---|---|---|---|---|---|---|
| 1 | 5 | 3931979 | 144669 | 718590 | 918770 | 5714008 |
| 2 | 10 | 4242286 | 184944 | 408283 | 878495 | 5714008 |
| 3 | 11 | 4288279 | 193912 | 362290 | 869527 | 5714008 |
| 4 | 12 | 4329146 | 203068 | 321423 | 860371 | 5714008 |
| 5 | 13 | 4366641 | 212498 | 283928 | 850941 | 5714008 |
| 6 | 15 | 4430885 | 232701 | 219684 | 830738 | 5714008 |
| 7 | 20 | 4542475 | 291791 | 108094 | 771648 | 5714008 |

Learn SQL. You'll thank me later.

This is all well and good, but recall that our goal (see Chapter 1) is to cancel the client meeting if the probability of arriving 15 minutes late is 30% or more. How close do we get with each of these thresholds?

To know this, we need to compute the fraction of times a decision is wrong. We can do this by calling the preceding result the contingency table, and then computing the necessary ratios:

```
WITH contingency_table AS (
 SELECT
   THRESH,
   COUNTIF(dep_delay < THRESH AND arr_delay < 15) AS true_positives,
   COUNTIF(dep_delay < THRESH AND arr_delay >= 15) AS false_positives,
   COUNTIF(dep_delay >= THRESH AND arr_delay < 15) AS false_negatives,
   COUNTIF(dep_delay >= THRESH AND arr_delay >= 15) AS true_negatives,
   COUNT(*) AS total
 FROM dsongcp.flights, UNNEST([5, 10, 11, 12, 13, 15, 20]) AS THRESH
 WHERE arr_delay IS NOT NULL AND dep_delay IS NOT NULL
 GROUP BY THRESH
)

SELECT
   ROUND((true_positives + true_negatives)/total, 2) AS accuracy,
   ROUND(false_positives/(true_positives+false_positives), 2) AS fpr,
   ROUND(false_negatives/(false_negatives+true_negatives), 2) AS fnr,
   *
FROM contingency_table ORDER BY accuracy ASC
```

The result now includes the accuracy, false positive rate, and false negative rate:

| Row | accu racy | fpr | fnr | THRESH | true_posi tives | false_pos itives | false_neg atives | true_nega tives | total |
|---|---|---|---|---|---|---|---|---|---|
| 1 | 0.85 | 0.04 | 0.44 | 5 | 3931979 | 144669 | 718590 | 918770 | 5714008 |
| 2 | 0.9 | 0.04 | 0.32 | 10 | 4242286 | 184944 | 408283 | 878495 | 5714008 |
| 3 | 0.9 | 0.04 | 0.29 | 11 | 4288279 | 193912 | 362290 | 869527 | 5714008 |
| 4 | 0.91 | 0.04 | 0.27 | 12 | 4329146 | 203068 | 321423 | 860371 | 5714008 |
| 5 | 0.91 | 0.05 | 0.25 | 13 | 4366641 | 212498 | 283928 | 850941 | 5714008 |
| 6 | 0.92 | 0.05 | 0.21 | 15 | 4430885 | 232701 | 219684 | 830738 | 5714008 |
| 7 | 0.93 | 0.06 | 0.12 | 20 | 4542475 | 291791 | 108094 | 771648 | 5714008 |

We want to cancel the meeting whenever we think the flight will be late. Our decision will not be perfect. There are times that the decision will be wrong. What is our tolerance for error? It's 30%. This means that:

- Flights should arrive on time (when we cancel the meeting) less than 30% of the time. So, we want the false positive rate to be 0.3 or less.
- Flights should arrive late (when we go ahead with the meeting) less than 30% of the time. So, we want the false negative rate 0.3 or less.

Looking at the preceding contingency table, which of these criteria looks like it could be a problem? That's right—the false negative rate. The false positive rate, at 0.04 or so, is comfortably within our error tolerance.

If we are going to make the decision based on the departure delay, our choice of departure delay threshold will have to be such that the false negative rate is 0.3.

It is clear from the preceding table that if we want our decision to have a false negative rate of 30%, the departure delay threshold needs to be 10 or 11 minutes (in the dataset, departure delay is an integer, so an intermediate threshold like 10.6 minutes does not make sense). We could choose 11 minutes on the grounds that, at 11 minutes, the FNR is less than 0.3. Or we could choose 10 minutes on the grounds that it's a nice, round number and our model is not so sophisticated that we can make decisions at a 1 minute precision.[8]

If we choose a threshold of 10 minutes, we will make the correct decision 96% of the time when we don't cancel the meeting and 68% of the time when we cancel the meeting. Overall, we are correct 90% of the time.

Note that 10 minutes is not the threshold that maximizes the overall accuracy. Had we chosen a threshold of 20 minutes, we'd cancel far fewer meetings (108,000 versus 408,000) and be correct more often overall (93%). However, that would be very conservative. Since it is not our goal to be correct 88% of the times we cancel the meeting—we only want to be correct 70% of the time—10 minutes is the right threshold.

However, we could also consider that if we can increase the threshold to 20 minutes, we would be correct far more often with very little impact on the false negative rate. Until we looked at the data, we didn't know what was achievable, and it is possible that the original target was set in a fog of uncertainty. It might be worthwhile asking

---

8 If this argument surprises you, imagine that we are talking about a threshold of 0.1 versus a threshold of 0.11. It's the same principle—don't use thresholds that have a misleading number of significant digits. This is important because I'm going to show the threshold to end users in a dashboard. If I were not showing the threshold, then I could use arbitrary precision. But when showing numbers to end users, keep the number of significant digits in mind.

our stakeholders whether they are really wedded to the 30% false negative rate and whether we have leeway to change the trade-offs available to users of our application —a dashboard that shows the impact of a threshold is an excellent way to gauge this. If the stakeholders don't know, it might be worth doing an A/B test with a focus group, and that's what we are about to do next.

---

### Is This Machine Learning?

What we did here—trying different thresholds—is at the heart of machine learning. Our model is a simple rule that has a single parameter (the departure delay threshold), and we can tune it to maximize some objective measure (here, the desired precision). We can (and will) use more complex models, and we can definitely make our search through the parameter space a lot more systematic, but this process of devising a model and tuning it is the gist of machine learning. We haven't evaluated the model (we can't take the 70% we got on the 12 months of 2015 data and claim that to be our model performance—we need an independent dataset to do that), and that is a key step in machine learning. However, we can plausibly claim that we have built a simple machine learning model to provide guidance on whether to cancel a meeting based on historical flight data.

---

## Building a Dashboard

Even this simple model is enough for us to begin getting feedback from end users. Recall that my gut instinct at the beginning of the previous section was that I needed to use a 15-minute threshold on the departure delay. Analysis of the contingency table, however, indicated that the right threshold to use was 10 minutes. I'm satisfied with this model as a first step, but will our end users be? Let's go about building a dashboard that explains the model recommendations to end users. Doing so will also help clarify what I mean by explaining a model to end users.

There are a large number of business intelligence and visualization tools available, and many of them connect with data sources like BigQuery and Cloud SQL on Google Cloud Platform. In this chapter, we build dashboards using Data Studio, which is free and comes as part of Google Cloud Platform, but you should be able to do similar things with Tableau, QlikView, Looker, and so on.

---

### Looker or Data Studio?

Google Cloud has two business intelligence tools—Looker and Data Studio. Data Studio is free and much more suitable for self-service use. Looker is much more capable and more suitable for enterprise use.

---

What do I mean by enterprise use? Here are a few examples of things that Looker can do that Data Studio can't:

*Consistency*
> It is possible for one team to define a semantic layer consisting of standard nomenclature for columns and ways of computing key performance metrics. The rest of the organization then builds dashboards starting from the semantic layer rather than from the raw data.

*Multicloud*
> Looker can access data in BigQuery, Amazon Redshift, Azure SQL Data Warehouse, and Snowflake *simultaneously* in the same report.

*Embedded analytics*
> Have you been to a website where you can see charts and graphs of your activity? This is provided by a lot of B2B applications, such as marketplaces allowing sellers to visualize their own data. Looker allows you to embed analytics in another website.

*Alerts and updates*
> Data Studio requires the user to visit the Data Studio web page and refresh the graphics. With Looker, you can push reports on a schedule or whenever an event happens.

> That said, in our case, all we want is a self-serve dashboard, and Data Studio fits the bill perfectly.

For those of you with a data science background, I'd like to set expectations here—a dashboard is a way for end users to quickly come to terms with the current state of a system and is not a full-blown, completely customizable, statistical visualization package. Think about the difference between what's rendered in the dashboard of a car versus what would be rendered in an engineering visualization of the aerodynamics of the car in a wind tunnel—that's the difference between what we will do in Data Studio versus what we will use Vertex AI Notebooks for in later chapters. Here, the emphasis is on providing information effectively to end users—thus, the key aspects are interactivity and collaboration. With Data Studio, you can share reports similarly to Google Workspace documents; that is, you can give different colleagues viewing or editing rights, and colleagues with whom you have shared a visualization can refresh the charts to view the most current data.

## Getting Started with Data Studio

To work with Data Studio, navigate to the Data Studio home page (*https://oreil.ly/ EJq0N*). There are two key concepts in Data Studio: reports and data sources. A report is a set of charts and commentary that you create and share with others. The charts in the report are built from data that is retrieved from a data source. The first step, therefore, is to set up a data source. Because our data is in BigQuery, the data source we need to set up is for Data Studio to connect to BigQuery.

On the Data Studio home page, click on the Create button, click the Data Source menu item, and choose the BigQuery button, as illustrated in Figure 3-9.[9]

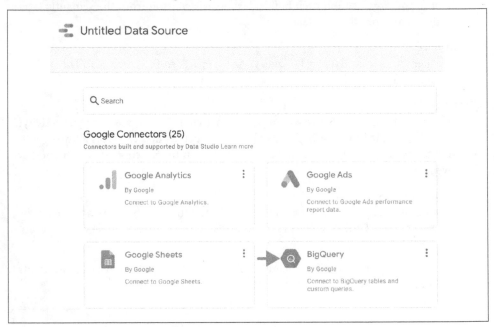

*Figure 3-9. Choose BigQuery from the Data Source menu item in Data Studio.*

Select your project, the `dsongcp` dataset, and `flights` as the table. Then, click on the Connect button. Recall that `flights` is the view that we have set up with the stream-lined set of fields.

A list of fields in the table displays, with Data Studio inferring something about the fields based on a sampling of the data in that table. We'll come back and correct some of these, but for now, just click Create Report, accepting all the prompts.

---

9 Graphical user interfaces are often the fastest-changing parts of any software. So, if the user interface has changed from these screenshots by the time this book gets into your hands, please hunt around a bit. There will be some way to add a new data source.

# Creating Charts

On the top ribbon, select the scatter chart icon from the "Add a chart" pulldown (see Figure 3-10) and draw a rectangle somewhere in the main window; Data Studio will draw a chart. The data that is rendered is pulled from some rather arbitrary columns.

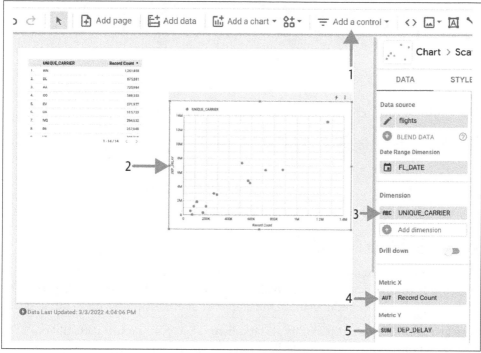

*Figure 3-10. Initial chart rendered by Data Studio.*

Ignoring the Date Range Dimension for now, there are three columns being used: the Dimension is the quantity being plotted; Metric X is along the x-axis; and Metric Y is along the y-axis. Change (if necessary) Dimension to UNIQUE_CARRIER, Metric X to DEP_DELAY, Metric Y to ARR_DELAY, and change the aggregation metric for both Metric X and Metric Y to Average. Ostensibly, this should give us the average departure delay and arrival delay of different carriers. Click the Style tab and add in a linear trendline and show the data labels. Figure 3-11 depicts the resulting chart.

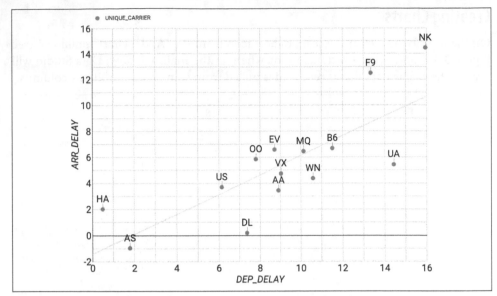

*Figure 3-11. Chart after changing Metric, Dimension, and Style.*

## Adding End-User Controls

So far, our chart is static—there is nothing for end users to interact with. They get to see a pretty picture, but do not get to change anything about our graph. To permit the end user to change something about the graph, we should add *controls* to our graph.

Let's give our end users the ability to set a date range. On the top icon ribbon, click the "Date range control" button, as illustrated in Figure 3-12.

On your chart, place the rectangle where you'd like the control to appear. Change the time window to be Fixed and set the Start Date to Jan. 1, 2015, and end date to Dec. 31, 2019.[10] This is how the report will initially appear to users.

In the upper-right corner, change the toggle to switch to the View mode. This is the mode in which users interact with your report. Change the data range to Jan 1, 2015 to May 31, 2015 (see Figure 3-13) and you should see the chart immediately update.

---

10 Or whatever the last month that you downloaded is. Just so that you don't have to wait a long time for the data to be available in your Google Cloud project, the *ingest.sh* script in Chapter 2, by default, downloads only 2015 data. Change the YEAR loop in that script to download 2015 to 2019.

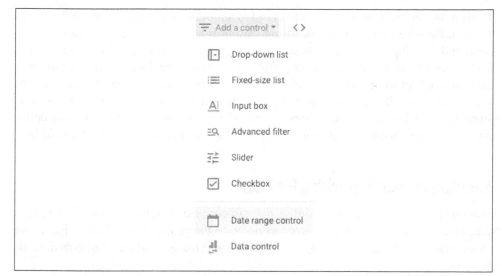

Figure 3-12. The Date range control on the top icon ribbon.

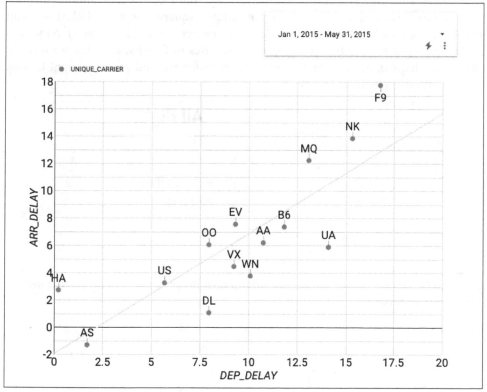

Figure 3-13. The chart in View mode.

Pause a bit here and ask yourself what kind of a model the chart in Figure 3-13 would explain. Because there is a line, it strongly hints at a linear model. If we were to recommend meeting cancellations based on this chart, we'd be suggesting, based on the linear trend of arrival delay with departure delay, that departure delays of more than 20 minutes lead to arrival delays of more than 15 minutes. That, of course, was not our model—we did not do linear regression, and certainly not airline by airline. Instead, we picked a departure threshold based on a contingency table over the entire dataset. So, we should not use the preceding graph in our dashboard—it would be a misleading description of our actual model.

## Showing Proportions with a Pie Chart

How would you explain our contingency table–based thresholds to end users in a dashboard? Recall that the choice comes down to the proportion of flights that arrive more than 15 minutes after their scheduled time. That is what our dashboard needs to show.

One of the best ways to show a proportion is to use a pie chart.[11] Switch back to the Edit mode, and from the pull-down menu, select the Donut Chart button (this is a type of pie chart), and then, on your report, draw a square where you'd like the donut chart to appear (it is probably best to delete the earlier scatter plot from it). As we did earlier, we need to edit the dimensions and metrics to fit what it is that we want to display. Perhaps things will be clearer if you see what the end product ought to look like. Figure 3-14 gives you a glimpse.

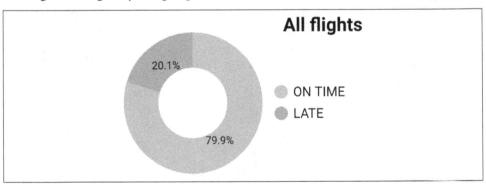

*Figure 3-14. Desired end result is a chart that shows the proportion of flights that are late versus on time.*

---

11 An alternative way to show proportions, especially of a time-varying whole, is a stacked column chart. (*https://oreil.ly/T51MW*)

In this chart, we are displaying the proportion of flights that arrived late versus those that arrived on time. The labeled field ON TIME versus LATE is the Dimension. The number of flights is the metric that will be apportioned between the labels. So, how do you get these values from the BigQuery view?

It is clear that there is no column in the database that indicates the total number of flights. However, Data Studio has a special value Record Count that we can use as the metric, after making sure to change the aggregate from the default Sum to Count.

The "islate" value, though, will have to be computed as a formula. Conceptually, we need to add a new calculated field (*https://oreil.ly/fWZvf*) to the data that looks like this:

```
CASE WHEN
(ARR_DELAY < 15)
THEN
"ON TIME"
ELSE
"LATE"
END
```

Click on the current Dimension column and click on "Create Field." Give the field the name is_late, enter the preceding formula, and change the type to Text (see Figure 3-15).

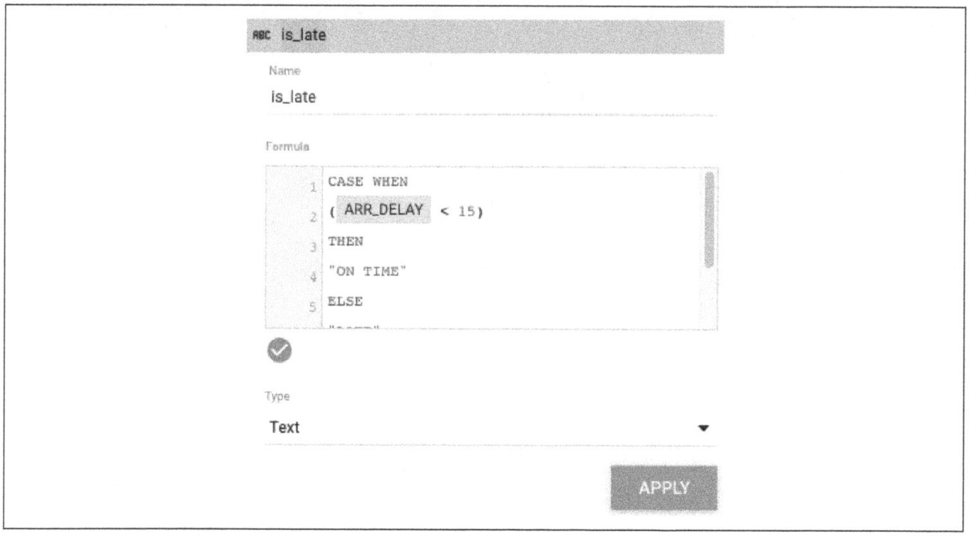

*Figure 3-15. How to set up the is_late definition.*

The pie chart is now complete and reflects the proportion of flights that are late versus those that are on time. You can switch over to the Style tab if you'd like to change the appearance of the pie chart to be similar to mine.

Because the proportion of flights that end up being delayed is the quantity on which we are trying to make decisions, the pie chart translates quite directly to our use case. However, it doesn't tell the user what the typical delay would be. To do that, let's create a bar (column) chart that looks like the one shown in Figure 3-16.

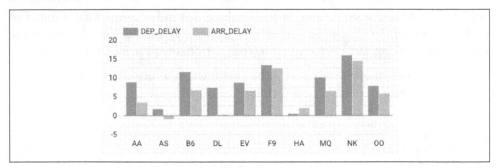

*Figure 3-16. Typical delay for each carrier.*

Here, the labeled quantity (or Dimension) is the Carrier. There are two metrics being displayed: the DEP_DELAY and ARR_DELAY, both of which are aggregated to their averages over the dataset. Figure 3-17 shows the specifications.

Note the Sort column at the end—it is important to have a reliable sort order in dashboards so that users become accustomed to finding the information they want in a known place. Also, the default is to use different axes for the two variables.

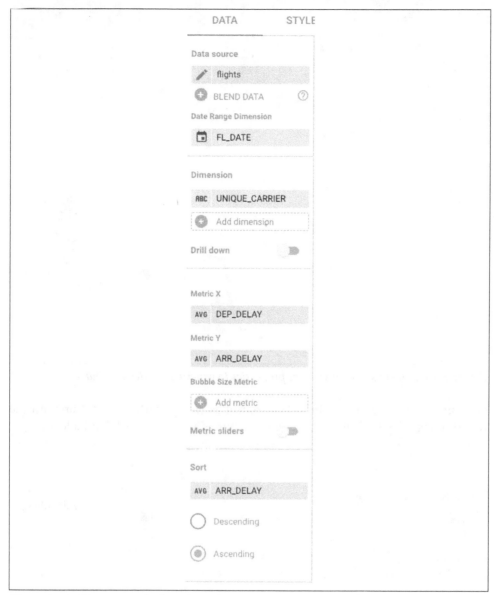

*Figure 3-17. How to set the bar chart properties to generate the desired chart.*

Switch over to the Style tab and change this to use a single axis. Finally, Data Studio defaults to 10 bars. In the Style tab, change this to reflect that we expect to have up to 20 unique carriers (Figure 3-18).

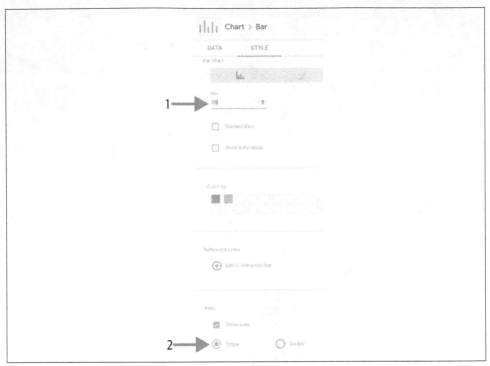

*Figure 3-18. How to set the bar chart properties to generate the desired chart.*

Of course, we can now add in a date control as we did earlier to end up with the report in Figure 3-19 ("All flights" in the diagram is just a text label that I added).

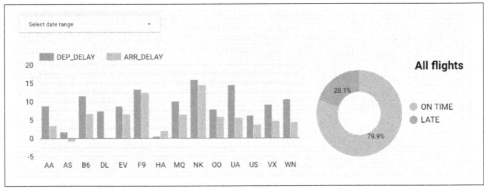

*Figure 3-19. Resulting dashboard consisting of a pie chart and bar chart.*

It appears that, on average, about 80% of flights are on time and that the typical arrival delay varies between airlines but lies in a range of 0 to 15 minutes.

# Explaining a Contingency Table

Even though the dashboard we just created shows users the decision-making criterion (proportion of flights that will be late) and some characteristics of that decision (the typical arrival delay), it doesn't actually show our model. Recall that our model involved a threshold on the departure delay. We need to show that. Figure 3-20 shows what we want the dashboard to look like.

*Figure 3-20. Dashboard consisting of three pairs of pie charts and bar charts along with a date control.*

In other words, we want to show the same two charts, but for the decision thresholds that we considered—departure delays of 10, 15, and 20 minutes or more.

To get there, we need to change our data source. No longer can we populate the chart from the entire table. Instead, we should populate it from a query that pulls only those flights whose departure delay is greater than the relevant threshold. In Big-Query, we can create the views we need and use those views as data sources.[12] Here's how:

```
CREATE OR REPLACE VIEW dsongcp.delayed_10 AS
SELECT * FROM dsongcp.flights WHERE dep_delay >= 10;

CREATE OR REPLACE VIEW dsongcp.delayed_15 AS
SELECT * FROM dsongcp.flights WHERE dep_delay >= 15;

CREATE OR REPLACE VIEW dsongcp.delayed_20 AS
SELECT * FROM dsongcp.flights WHERE dep_delay >= 20;
```

Alternatively, we can add a filter on the departure delay and allow the end user to try out different thresholds. However, because we want to explain the decision model, it is better to ensure that the 10-minute threshold is explicitly present in the dashboard.

Looking at the resulting pie chart for a 10-minute threshold (Figure 3-20), we see that it comes quite close to our target of 30% on-time arrivals. The bar chart for the 10-minute delay explains why the threshold is important. Hint: it is not about the exact numeric value of 10 minutes. It is about what the 10-minute delay is indicative of. Can you decipher what is going on? Still stuck? Look at the y-axis of the three bar charts.

Although the typical departure delay of a flight is only about 5 minutes (see the chart corresponding to all flights that we created earlier), flights that are delayed by more than 10 minutes fall into a separate statistical regime. The typical departure delay of an aircraft that departs more than 10 minutes late is around 50 minutes! A likely explanation is that a flight that is delayed by 10 minutes or more typically has a serious issue that will not be resolved quickly. If you are sitting in an airplane and it is more than 10 minutes late in departing, you might as well cancel your meeting—you are going to be sitting at the gate for a while.[13]

At this point, we have created a very simple model and created dashboards to explain the model to our end users. Our end users have a visual, intuitive way to see how often our model is correct and how often it is wrong. The model might be quite simple, but the explanation of why the model works is a satisfying one.

---

12 Data Studio does support a BigQuery query as a data source, but it is preferable to read from a view because views are more reusable.

13 Road warriors know this well. Ten minutes in, and they whip out their phones to try to get on a different flight.

There is one teeny, tiny thing missing, though. Context. The dashboard that we have built so far is all about historical data, whereas real dashboards need to be timely. Our dashboard shows aggregates of flights all over the country, but our users will probably care only about the airport from which they are departing and the airport to which they are going. We have a wonderfully informative dashboard, but without such time and location context, few users would care. In Chapter 4, we look at how to build real-time, location-aware dashboards—unfortunately, however, there is a problem with our dataset that prevents us from doing so immediately. So, we'll spend the first part of Chapter 4 doing some data wrangling.

Before we move on to Chapter 4, let's expand our discussion of business intelligence beyond dashboards.

# Modern Business Intelligence

Modern business intelligence (BI) is more than dashboards. BI is data science for business users. As such, the trends in BI are toward digitization (there is data on more and more things), democratization (more and more people can get insights from data), and integration (access to sophisticated insights from familiar tools).

Let's look at these trends.

## Digitization

The release notes of Data Studio (*https://oreil.ly/nFLeM*) are a great way to stay up-to-date with product updates and new visualization options. All Google Cloud products have release notes that are published online—take a look at the release notes for Big-Query (*https://oreil.ly/mKo2i*), for example.

Once upon a time, release notes were nothing more than pages of text. But now, they are digitized and queryable. As befits a Data Cloud, the release notes for BigQuery (and all other Google Cloud products) are available as a public dataset in BigQuery (*https://oreil.ly/ItWZp*). Let's query it:

```
SELECT
  product_name,
  DATE_TRUNC(published_at, MONTH) AS month,
  COUNT(*) AS releases
FROM `bigquery-public-data.google_cloud_release_notes.release_notes`
GROUP BY product_name, month
```

The result looks like this:

| Row | product_name | month | releases |
|-----|--------------|------------|----------|
| 1 | BigQuery | 2012-05-01 | 8 |
| 2 | BigQuery | 2012-07-01 | 5 |

| Row | product_name | month | releases |
|-----|--------------|-------|----------|
| 3 | BigQuery | 2012-08-01 | 5 |
| 4 | Dataflow | 2017-10-01 | 6 |
| 5 | Dataflow | 2019-02-01 | 3 |

## Natural Language Queries

We can explore the data with Data Studio, of course, but let's try using natural language queries. At the time of writing, this was still in alpha and one could only query one's own tables (not a public dataset). So let's export the preceding query to a table in our own project:

```
CREATE OR REPLACE TABLE dsongcp.monthly_releases AS

SELECT
  product_name,
  DATE_TRUNC(published_at, MONTH) AS month,
  COUNT(*) AS releases
FROM `bigquery-public-data.google_cloud_release_notes.release_notes`
GROUP BY product_name, month
```

Now, select the option to "Ask Question." The UI immediately proposes a few questions (see Figure 3-21).

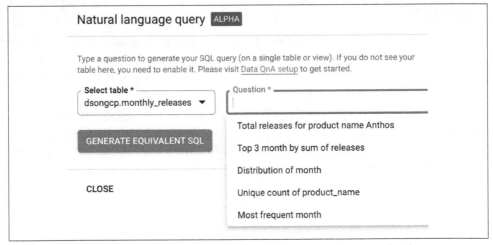

*Figure 3-21. Some of the questions automatically generated based on the dataset.*

Let's pick a different question, though: "top three products by total releases." The UI generates the following SQL query automatically (see Figure 3-22):

```
SELECT
  product_name AS product_name,
  (SUM(releases)) AS SUM_releases
FROM
```

```
  `ai-analytics-solutions.dsongcp.monthly_releases`
GROUP BY product_name
ORDER BY SUM_releases DESC
LIMIT 3;
```

Isn't that something? Notice that even though I said "top three products," the engine was smart enough to pick up the product_name column. The result, in case you are curious, is:

| Row | product_name | SUM_releases |
|---|---|---|
| 1 | Google Kubernetes Engine | 749 |
| 2 | Dataproc | 625 |
| 3 | App Engine standard environment Java | 472 |

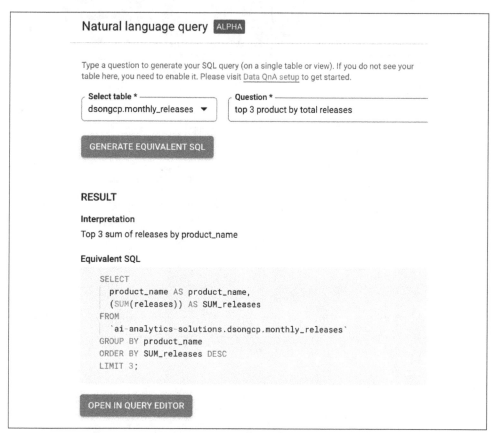

*Figure 3-22. Natural language querying in BigQuery.*

# Connected Sheets

Try this. Open up a new Google Sheet (you can do so by visiting *https://sheets.new*) and select Data > Data Connectors > Connect to BigQuery using the menu.[14]

Connect to the monthly_releases table in your project. What we now have is a *Connected Sheet*—all operations we carry out in the sheet are actually executed in BigQuery! This allows us to interact with tables and query results that may have millions of rows!

Select "Discover Data Insights" and follow the prompts to create a chart of Google Cloud releases over time (see Figure 3-23). The machines are getting smarter, and the pace of change is increasing!

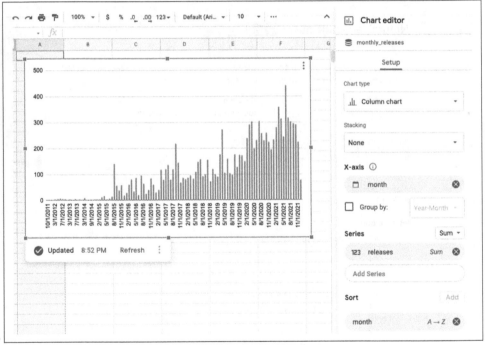

*Figure 3-23. Google Cloud releases over time.*

---

14 Make sure you are using the same Google account as the one you are using for your Google Cloud project. At the time of writing, this capability is only available to Enterprise Google Workspace accounts. If you are trying this section in a personal Google Account, you likely won't have the Data Connectors option in the Data menu.

# Summary

In this chapter, we discussed the importance of bringing the insights of our end users into our data modeling efforts as early as possible. Bringing their insights is possible only if you make it a point to explain your models in context from the get-go.

We tried using Cloud SQL, a transactional, relational database whose management is simplified by virtue of it running on the cloud and being managed by Google Cloud Platform. However, it stopped scaling once we got to millions of flights. Transactional databases are not built for queries that involve scanning the entire table. For such queries, we want to use an analytics data warehouse. Hence, we switched to using BigQuery.

Within BigQuery, we previewed the table, selected a subset of columns, and created a view to make downstream analysis simpler.

The first model that we built was to suggest that our road warriors cancel their immediately scheduled meeting if the departure delay of the flight was more than 10 minutes. At this threshold, flights arrive late (when we go ahead with the meeting) less than 30% of the time. This would enable them to make 70% of their meetings with 15 minutes to spare.

We then built a dashboard in Data Studio to explain the contingency table model. Because our choice of threshold was driven by the proportion of flights that arrived late given a particular threshold, we illustrated the proportion using a pie chart for two different thresholds. We also depicted the average arrival delay given some departure delay—this gives users an intuitive understanding of why we recommend a 10-minute threshold.

Finally, we looked at trends in business intelligence.

# Suggested Resources

An influential three-part series on business intelligence (BI) by Forrester Analyst Boris Evelson (*https://oreil.ly/qEH9y*) recommends a "layer-cake" model for modernizing BI. Unfortunately, at the time of writing, it's behind a $1,495 paywall.[15] So, perhaps read a summary of that article in *Forbes* (*https://oreil.ly/YfkXm*) by Shant Hovsepian. Accordion to Hovsepian, Evelson suggests that organizations modernize their use of BI by:

- Bringing BI to the data, rather that doing BI on extracts of the data (don't do "data cubes" (*https://oreil.ly/LuE4P*))

---

15 No, not a typo. It's not $14.95. It's $1495.

- Infusing AI such as natural language into BI (*https://oreil.ly/EiKHP*)
- Moving BI to the public cloud to take advantage of elasticity and separation of compute and storage

Data Studio is great as a self-service dashboard, but enterprises are often short of SQL experts. Looker provides a self-service business intelligence workflow by interposing a level of indirection, called LookML. This 2021 article by Clay Porter, "Using Big-Query & Data Studio? You Should Check Out Looker" (*https://oreil.ly/bi3Vs*), provides an excellent explanation. There is an online course (*https://oreil.ly/2hqDh*) if you want to learn how to create dashboards in Looker.

Once you create a dashboard, you might want to embed the graphics within a website. This is called embedded analytics—it can be done through iframes or using Looker's application programming interface. See the 2020 Google blog post "A Step-by-Step Guide to Building and Delivering Embedded Analytics" (*https://oreil.ly/alZ2L*) by Sharon Zhang for more information.

# Streaming Data: Publication and Ingest with Pub/Sub and Dataflow

In Chapter 3, we developed a dashboard to explain a contingency table–based model of suggesting whether to cancel a meeting. However, the dashboard that we built lacked immediacy because it was not tied to users' context. Because users need to be able to view a dashboard and see the information that is relevant to them at that point, we need to build a real-time dashboard with location cues.

How would we add context to our dashboard? We'd have to show maps of delays in real time. To do that, we'll need locations of the airports, and we'll need real-time data. Airport locations can be obtained from the US Bureau of Transportation Statistics (BTS; the same US government agency from which we obtained our historical flight data). Real-time flight data, however, is a commercial product. If we were to build a business out of predicting flight arrivals, we'd purchase that data feed. For the purposes of this book, however, let's just simulate it.

Simulating the creation of a real-time feed from historical data has the advantage of allowing us to see both sides of a streaming pipeline (production as well as consumption). In the following section, we look at how we could stream data into the database if we were to receive it in real time.

 All of the code snippets in this chapter are available in the folder *04_streaming* of the book's GitHub repository (*https://github.com/ GoogleCloudPlatform/data-science-on-gcp*). See the *README.md* file in that directory for instructions on how to do the steps described in this chapter.

# Designing the Event Feed

Let's assume that we wish to create an event feed, not with all 100 fields in the raw BTS dataset, but with only the few fields that we selected in Chapter 3 as being relevant to the flight delay prediction problem (see Figure 4-1).

| Field name | Type | Mode | Policy Tags ❓ |
|---|---|---|---|
| ☐ | flights | 🔍 QUERY | 🗐 ASK QUESTION | ➕ SHARE | 🗐 COPY |

SCHEMA  DETAILS  TABLE EXPLORER

| ☐ Field name | Type | Mode | Policy Tags ❓ |
|---|---|---|---|
| ☐ FL_DATE | DATE | NULLABLE | |
| ☐ UNIQUE_CARRIER | STRING | NULLABLE | |
| ☐ ORIGIN_AIRPORT_SEQ_ID | STRING | NULLABLE | |
| ☐ ORIGIN | STRING | NULLABLE | |
| ☐ DEST_AIRPORT_SEQ_ID | STRING | NULLABLE | |
| ☐ DEST | STRING | NULLABLE | |
| ☐ CRS_DEP_TIME | STRING | NULLABLE | |
| ☐ DEP_TIME | STRING | NULLABLE | |
| ☐ DEP_DELAY | FLOAT | NULLABLE | |
| ☐ TAXI_OUT | FLOAT | NULLABLE | |
| ☐ WHEELS_OFF | STRING | NULLABLE | |
| ☐ WHEELS_ON | STRING | NULLABLE | |
| ☐ TAXI_IN | FLOAT | NULLABLE | |
| ☐ CRS_ARR_TIME | STRING | NULLABLE | |
| ☐ ARR_TIME | STRING | NULLABLE | |
| ☐ ARR_DELAY | FLOAT | NULLABLE | |
| ☐ CANCELLED | BOOLEAN | NULLABLE | |
| ☐ DIVERTED | BOOLEAN | NULLABLE | |
| ☐ DISTANCE | STRING | NULLABLE | |

*Figure 4-1. In Chapter 3, we created a view in BigQuery with the fields relevant to the flight delay prediction problem. In this chapter, we will simulate a real-time stream of this information.*

To simulate a real-time stream of the flight information shown in Figure 4-1, we can begin by using the historical data in the `flights` view in BigQuery but will need to transform it further. What kinds of transformations are needed?

# Transformations Needed

Note that FL_DATE is a Date while DEP_TIME is a STRING. This is because FL_DATE is of the form 2015-07-03 for July 3, 2015, whereas DEP_DATE is of the form 1406 for 2:06 p.m. local time. This is unfortunate. I'm not worried about the separation of date and time into two columns—we can remedy that. What's unfortunate is that there is no time zone offset associated with the departure time. Thus, in this dataset, a departure time of 1406 in different rows can be different times depending on the time zone of the origin airport.

The time zone offsets (there are two, one for the origin airport and another for the destination) are not present in the data. Because the offset depends on the airport location, we need to find a dataset that contains the time zone offset of each airport and then mash this data with that dataset.[1] To simplify downstream analysis, we will then put all the times in the data in a common time zone—Coordinated Universal Time (UTC) is the traditional choice of common time zone for datasets. We cannot, however, get rid of the local time—we will need the local time in order to carry out analysis, such as the typical delay associated with morning flights versus evening flights. So, although we will convert the local times to UTC, we will also store the time zone offset (e.g., −3,600 minutes) to retrieve the local time if necessary.

Therefore, we are going to carry out two transformations to the original dataset. First, we will convert all the time fields in the raw dataset to UTC. Second, in addition to the fields present in the raw data, we will add three fields to the dataset for the origin airport and the same three fields for the destination airport: the latitude, longitude, and time zone offset. These fields will be named:

```
DEP_AIRPORT_LAT, DEP_AIRPORT_LON, DEP_AIRPORT_TZOFFSET
ARR_AIRPORT_LAT, ARR_AIRPORT_LON, ARR_AIRPORT_TZOFFSET
```

The third transformation that we will need to carry out is that, for every row in the historical dataset, we will need to publish multiple events. This is because it would be too late if we wait until the aircraft has arrived to send out a single event containing all the row data. If we do this at the time the aircraft departs, our models will be violating causality constraints. Instead, we will need to send out events corresponding to each state the flight is in. Let's choose to send out five events for each flight: when the flight is first scheduled, when the flight departs the gate, when the flight lifts off, when the flight lands, and when the flight arrives. These five events cannot have all the same data associated with them because the knowability of the columns changes during the flight. For example, when sending out an event at the departure time, we will

---

1 This is a common situation. It is only as you start to explore a dataset that you discover you need ancillary datasets. Had I known beforehand, I would have ingested both datasets. But you are following my workflow, and as of this point, I knew that I needed a dataset of time zone offsets but hadn't yet searched for it!

not know the arrival time. For simplicity, we can notify the same structure, but we will need to ensure that unknowable data is marked by a `null` and not with the actual data value.

## Architecture

Table 4-1 lists when those events can be sent out and the fields that will be included in each event.

*Table 4-1. Fields that will be included in each of the five events that will be published. Compare the order of the fields with those in the schema in Figure 4-1.*

| Event | Sent at (UTC) | Fields included in event message |
|-------|---------------|----------------------------------|
| Scheduled | `CRS_DEP_TIME` minus 7 days | `FL_DATE, UNIQUE_CARRIER, ORIGIN_AIRPORT_SEQ_ID, ORIGIN, DEST_AIRPORT_SEQ_ID, DEST, CRS_DEP_TIME [nulls], CRS_ARR_TIME [nulls], DISTANCE` |
| Departed | `DEP_TIME` | All fields available in scheduled message, plus:<br>• `DEP_TIME, DEP_DELAY CANCELLED`<br>• `CANCELLATION_CODE`<br>• `DEP_AIRPORT_LAT, DEP_AIRPORT_LON, DEP_AIRPORT_TZOFFSET` |
| Wheelsoff | `WHEELS_OFF` | All fields available in departed message, plus: `TAXI_OUT` and `WHEELS_OFF` |
| Wheelson | `WHEELS_ON` | All fields available in wheelsoff message, plus:<br>• `WHEELS_ON`<br>• `DIVERTED`<br>• `ARR_AIRPORT_LAT, ARR_AIRPORT_LON, ARR_AIRPORT_TZOFFSET` |
| Arrived | `ARR_TIME` | All fields available in wheelson message, plus: `ARR_TIME` and `ARR_DELAY` |

We will carry out the transformations needed and then store the transformed data in a database so that it is ready for the event simulation code to use. Figure 4-2 shows the steps we are about to carry out in our extract-transform-load (ETL) pipeline and the subsequent steps to simulate an event stream from these events, and then create a real-time dashboard from the simulated event stream.

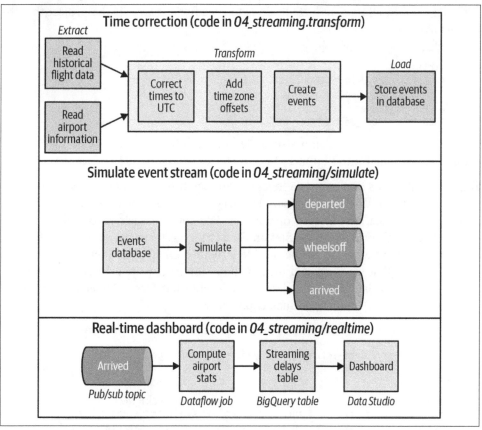

*Figure 4-2. Steps in our ETL (extract-transform-load) pipeline to (a) transform the raw data into events, (b) simulate the event stream, and (c) process the event stream to populate a real-time dashboard.*

## Getting Airport Information

In order to do the time correction, we need to obtain the latitude and longitude of each airport. The BTS has a dataset (*https://oreil.ly/ijlv2*) that contains this information, which we can use to do the lookup. For convenience, I've downloaded the data and made it publicly available at *gs://data-science-on-gcp/edition2/raw/airports.csv*.

Let's examine the data to determine how to get the latitude and longitude of the airports. In Chapter 2, when I needed to explore the flights data to create the first delays model, I loaded the data into BigQuery.

Do we have to import all the data that is shared with us into our BigQuery dataset in order to do exploration? Of course not. We can query BigQuery datasets in other projects without having to make our own copies of the data. In the FROM clause of the

BigQuery query, all that we have to do is to specify the name of the project that the dataset lives in:

```
SELECT
  airline,
  AVG(departure_delay) AS avg_dep_delay
FROM `bigquery-samples.airline_ontime_data.flights`
GROUP BY airline
ORDER by avg_dep_delay DESC
```

What if someone shares a comma-separated values (CSV) file with us, though? Do we have to load the data into BigQuery in order to see what's in the file? No.

BigQuery allows us to query data in Cloud Storage through its *federated query* capabilities. This is the ability of BigQuery to query data that is not stored within the data warehouse product, but instead operate on data sources such as Google Sheets (a spreadsheet on Google Drive) or files on Cloud Storage. Thus, we could leave the files as CSV on Cloud Storage, define a table structure on it, and query the CSV files directly. Recall that we suggested using Cloud Storage if your primary analysis pattern involves working with your data at the level of flat files—this is a way of occasionally applying SQL queries to such datasets.

The first step is to get the schema of these files. Let's look at the first line:

```
gsutil cat gs://data-science-on-gcp/edition2/raw/airports.csv | head -1
```

We get:

```
"AIRPORT_SEQ_ID","AIRPORT_ID","AIRPORT","DISPLAY_AIRPORT_NAME",
"DISPLAY_AIRPORT_CITY_NAME_FULL","AIRPORT_WAC_SEQ_ID2","AIRPORT_WAC",
"AIRPORT_COUNTRY_NAME","AIRPORT_COUNTRY_CODE_ISO","AIRPORT_STATE_NAME",
"AIRPORT_STATE_CODE","AIRPORT_STATE_FIPS","CITY_MARKET_SEQ_ID","CITY_MARKET_ID",
"DISPLAY_CITY_MARKET_NAME_FULL","CITY_MARKET_WAC_SEQ_ID2","CITY_MARKET_WAC",
"LAT_DEGREES","LAT_HEMISPHERE","LAT_MINUTES","LAT_SECONDS","LATITUDE",
"LON_DEGREES","LON_HEMISPHERE","LON_MINUTES","LON_SECONDS","LONGITUDE",
"UTC_LOCAL_TIME_VARIATION","AIRPORT_START_DATE","AIRPORT_THRU_DATE",
"AIRPORT_IS_CLOSED","AIRPORT_IS_LATEST"
```

Use this header to write a BigQuery schema string of the format (specify STRING for any column you are not sure about, since you can always CAST it to the appropriate format when querying the data):

```
AIRPORT_SEQ_ID:INTEGER,AIRPORT_ID:STRING,AIRPORT:STRING, ...
```

Alternately, if you have a similar dataset lying around, start from its schema and edit it:

```
bq show --format=prettyjson dsongcp.sometable > starter.json
```

Once we have the schema of the GCS files, we can make a table definition for the federated source:[2]

```
bq mk --external_table_definition= \
./airport_schema.json@CSV=gs://data-science-on-gcp/edition2/raw/airports.csv \
dsongcp.airports_gcs
```

If you visit the BigQuery web console now, you should see a new table listed in the dsongcp dataset (reload the page if necessary). This is a federated data source in that its storage remains the CSV file on Cloud Storage. Yet you can query it just like any other BigQuery table:

```
SELECT
AIRPORT_SEQ_ID, AIRPORT_ID, AIRPORT, DISPLAY_AIRPORT_NAME,
LAT_DEGREES, LAT_HEMISPHERE, LAT_MINUTES, LAT_SECONDS, LATITUDE
FROM dsongcp.airports_gcs
WHERE DISPLAY_AIRPORT_NAME LIKE '%Seattle%'
```

In the preceding query, I am trying to find in the file which airport column and which latitude column I need to use. The result indicates that AIRPORT and LATITUDE are the columns of interest, but that there are several rows corresponding to the airport SEA:

| Row | AIR PORT_ SEQ_ID | AIR PORT_ ID | AIR PORT | DISPLAY_AIR PORT_NAME | LAT_ DEGREES | LAT_ HEMI SPHERE | LAT_ MINUTES | LAT_ SEC ONDS | LATITUDE |
|---|---|---|---|---|---|---|---|---|---|
| 1 | 1247701 | 12477 | JFB | Seattle 1st National.Bank Helipad | 47 | N | 36 | 25 | 47.60694444 |
| 2 | 1474701 | 14747 | SEA | Seattle Inter national | 47 | N | 26 | 50 | 47.44722222 |
| 3 | 1474702 | 14747 | SEA | Seattle/ Tacoma Inter national | 47 | N | 26 | 57 | 47.44916667 |
| 4 | 1474703 | 14747 | SEA | Seattle/ Tacoma Inter national | 47 | N | 27 | 0 | 47.45 |

Fortunately, there is a column that indicates which row is the latest information, so what I need to do is:

```
SELECT
  AIRPORT, LATITUDE, LONGITUDE
FROM dsongcp.airports_gcs
WHERE AIRPORT_IS_LATEST = 1 AND AIRPORT = 'DFW'
```

---

2 See *04_streaming/design/mktbl.sh* for the actual syntax; we've made adjustments here for printing purposes.

Don't get carried away by federated queries, though. The most appropriate uses of federated sources involve frequently changing, relatively small datasets that need to be joined with large datasets in BigQuery native tables. Because the columnar storage in BigQuery is so fundamental to its performance, we will load most data into Big-Query's native format.

## Sharing Data

Now that we have the *airports.csv* in Cloud Storage and the airports' dataset in Big-Query, it is quite likely that our colleagues will want to use this data too. Let's share it with them—one of the benefits of bringing your data to the cloud (and more specifi-cally into a data warehouse) is to allow the mashing of datasets across organizational boundaries. So, unless you have a clear reason not to do so, like security precautions, try to make your data widely accessible.

Costs of querying are borne by the person submitting the query to the BigQuery engine, so you don't need to worry that you are incurring additional costs for your division by doing this. It is possible to make a GCS bucket "requester-pays" to get the same sort of billing separation for data in Cloud Storage.

### Sharing a Cloud Storage dataset

To share some data in Cloud Storage, use `gsutil`:

```
gsutil -m acl ch -r -u abc@xyz.com:R gs://$BUCKET/data
```

In the preceding command, the `-m` indicates multithreaded mode, the `-r` provides access recursively starting with the top-level directory specified, and the `-u` indicates that this is a user being granted read (`:R`) access.

We could provide read access to the entire organization or a Google Group using `-g`:

```
gsutil -m acl ch -r -g xyz.com:R gs://$BUCKET/data
```

### Sharing a BigQuery dataset

BigQuery sharing can happen at the granularity of a column, a table, or a dataset. None of our BigQuery tables hold personally identifiable or confidential information. Therefore, there is no compelling access-control reason to control the sharing of flight information at a column or table level. So, we can share the `dsongcp` dataset that was created in Chapter 2, and we can make everyone in the organization working on this project a `bigquery.user` so that they can carry out queries on this dataset. You can do this from the BigQuery web console from the dataset menu.

In some cases, you might find that your dataset or table contains certain columns that have personally identifying or confidential information. You might need to restrict access to those columns while leaving the remainder of the table accessible to a wider audience.[3] Whenever you need to provide access to a subset of a table in BigQuery (whether it is specific columns or specific rows), you can use views. Put the table itself in a dataset that is accessible to a very small set of users. Then, create a view on this table that will pull out the relevant columns and rows and save this view in a separate dataset that has wider accessibility. Your users will query only this view, and because the personally identifying or confidential information is not even present in the view, the chances of inadvertent leakage are lowered.

Another way to restrict access at the level of a BigQuery table (*https://oreil.ly/JfQLH*) is to use Cloud IAM. To control access at the level of a column, you'd use policy tags (*https://oreil.ly/788TL*) and Data Catalog.

### Dataplex and Analytics Hub

Once you get into the habit of sharing data widely, governance can become problematic. It is better if you can administer data across Cloud Storage in a consistent manner and track lineage, etc. That's what Dataplex is for.

It can be rather cumbersome to share tables and datasets one at a time with one user or one group at a time. To implement sharing at scale and get statistics on how people are using the data you have shared, use Analytics Hub.

## Time Correction

Correcting times reported in local time to UTC is not a simple endeavor. There are several steps:

- Local time depends on, well, the location. The flight data that we have records only the name of the airport (e.g., ALB for Albany). We, therefore, need to obtain the latitude and longitude given an airport code. The BTS has a dataset that contains this information, which we can use to do the lookup.

- Given a latitude/longitude pair, we need to look up the time zone from a map of global time zones (*https://oreil.ly/khmoN*). For example, given the latitude and longitude of the airport in Albany, we would need to get back America/New_York. There are several web services that do this, but the Python package timezone finder (*https://oreil.ly/BVjVn*) is a more efficient option because it works completely offline. The drawback is that this package does not handle oceanic areas

---

3 Or make a copy or view of the table with anonymized column values—we cover safeguarding personally identifiable information in Chapter 7 and in the Appendix.

and some historical time zone changes,[4] but that's a trade-off that we can make for now.

- The time zone offset (from Greenwich Mean Time [GMT/UTC]) at a location changes during the year due to daylight savings corrections. In New York, for example, it is six hours in summer and five hours in winter behind UTC. Given the time zone (`America/New_York`), therefore, we also need the local departure date and time (say Jan. 13, 2015, 2:08 p.m.) in order to find the corresponding time zone offset. The Python package `pytz` provides this capability by using the underlying operating system.

The problem of ambiguous times still remains—every instant between 01:00 and 02:00 local time occurs twice on the day that the clock switches from daylight savings time (summer time) to standard time (winter time). So, if our dataset has a flight arriving at 01:30, we need to make a choice of what time that represents. In a real-world situation, you would look at the typical duration of the flight and choose the one that is more likely. For the purposes of this book, I'll always assume the winter time (i.e., `is_dst` is `False`) on the dubious grounds that it is the standard time zone for that location.

The complexity of these steps should, I hope, convince you to follow best practices when storing time.

---

### Best Practices When Storing Time

Always try to store two columns for every timestamp:

1. The timestamp in UTC so that you can merge data from across the world if necessary.
2. The currently active time zone offset so that you can carry out analysis that requires the local time. For example, is there a spike associated with traffic between 5 p.m. and 6 p.m. local time?

---

4 For example, the time zone of Sevastopol changed in 2014 from Eastern European Time (UTC+2) to Moscow Time (UTC+4) after the annexation of Crimea by the Russian Federation.

## Apache Beam/Cloud Dataflow

The canonical way to build data pipelines on Google Cloud Platform is to use Cloud Dataflow. Cloud Dataflow is an externalization of technologies called Flume (*https://oreil.ly/Ai2qC*) and MillWheel (*https://oreil.ly/K9m2s*) that have been in widespread use at Google for several years. It employs a programming model that handles both batch and streaming data in a uniform manner, thus providing the ability to use the same codebase both for batch and continuous stream processing. The code itself is written in Apache Beam (*http://beam.apache.org*), either in Java, Python, or Go,[5] and it is portable in the sense that it can be executed on multiple execution environments, including Apache Flink (*https://oreil.ly/hBexq*) and Apache Spark (*https://oreil.ly/gF8lQ*). On GCP, Cloud Dataflow provides a fully managed (serverless) service that is capable of executing Beam pipelines. Resources are allocated on demand, and they autoscale so as to achieve both minimal latency and high resource utilization.

Beam programming involves building a pipeline (a series of data transformations) that is submitted to a runner. The runner will build a graph and then stream data through it. Each input dataset comes from a source and each output dataset is sent to a sink. Figure 4-3 illustrates the Beam pipeline that we are about to build.

Compare the steps in Figure 4-2 with the block diagram of the ETL (extract-transform-load) pipeline in Figure 4-3. Let's build the data pipeline piece by piece.

---

5 The Java API is much more mature and performant, but Python is easier and more concise. In this book, we will use Python.

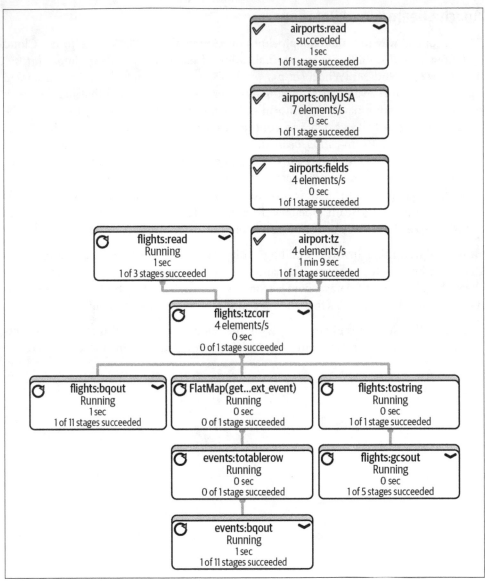

*Figure 4-3. The Dataflow pipeline that we are about to build.*

## Parsing Airports Data

You can download information about the location of airports (*https://oreil.ly/k5SWh*) from the BTS website. I selected all of the fields, downloaded the CSV file to my local hard drive, extracted it, and compressed it with `gzip`. The gzipped airports file is available in the GitHub repository for this book (*https://oreil.ly/AKsBs*).

In order to use Apache Beam from Cloud Shell, we need to install it (*https://oreil.ly/ FP3CO*) into our Python environment. Go ahead and install the time zone packages also at this time:[6]

```
virtualenv ~/beam_env
source ~/beam_env/bin/activate
python3 -m pip install --upgrade \
            timezonefinder pytz \
            'apache-beam[gcp]'
```

The Read transform in the Beam pipeline that follows reads in the airports file line by line:[7]

```
with beam.Pipeline('DirectRunner') as pipeline:
    airports = (pipeline
        | beam.io.ReadFromText('airports.csv.gz')
        | beam.Map(lambda line: next(csv.reader([line])))
        | beam.Map(lambda fields: (fields[0], (fields[21], fields[26])))
    )
```

---

## Apache Beam Python Syntax

The Apache Beam code may look nothing like any Python you have seen before. Let's break it down.

The first line creates a Beam pipeline that will be executed on the local machine ("DirectRunner"):

```
with beam.Pipeline('DirectRunner') as pipeline:
    # some code here
```

Next, all the lines within the with block are executed. However, those lines of code only create the execution graph. Conceptually, you can think of it as the pipeline getting compiled. It is only when the graph corresponding to the full with block has been created that the pipeline is executed.

Let's look at the lines of code within the with block. These consist of data transformation methods executed one after the other, with the output of one transform being fed in as the input to the next transform. For example, these two lines:

```
    beam.io.ReadFromText('airports.csv.gz')
| beam.Map(lambda line: next(csv.reader([line])))
```

---

[6] If you are using an ephemeral shell like Cloud Shell, you will have to run the activate line every time you start a new session. This will load up the virtual environment (*https://oreil.ly/gul4e*) that you were using earlier. This way, you will not need to reinstall the Python packages every time.

[7] This code is in *04_streaming/transform/df01.py* of the GitHub repository of this book.

mean that the file *airports.csv.gz* should be read. `ReadFromText` reads the input file line-by-line. Each line is then sent to the `Map` transform. The pipe symbol (|) is what says that the output of `ReadFromText` has to be sent in as the input to `Map`. You might be familiar with this idiomatic use of the pipe symbol in the Linux command line.

The `Map` transform applies some user-specified function to the data. What function are we applying? We could have written:

```
| beam.Map(parse_line)
```

and defined the function `parse_line` as follows:

```
def parse_line(line):
    return next(csv.reader([line]))
```

But doing this would have involved writing a whole bunch of small functions. The lambda syntax in Python allows us to define a function in-line without giving the function a name:

```
| lambda line: some_code_with(line))
```

The last strange thing might be the function body itself:

```
next(csv.reader([line]))
```

We are invoking the `reader()` function in the Python module called `csv` and passing it an array of lines. The array here has only one item (`[line]`). The `reader()` will give us back an iterator to an array of parsed rows. When we call `next()` in Python, we are asking the iterator to get us the next item. By calling `next()`, therefore, we get the first parsed row.

This is all quite terse, but quite idiomatic. Pick up a Python book if any of this syntax was new to you.

For example, suppose that one of the input lines read out of the text file source is the following:

```
1000401,10004,"04A","Lik Mining Camp","Lik, AK",101,1,"United
States","US","Alaska","AK","02",3000401,30004,"Lik,
AK",101,1,68,"N",5,0,68.08333333,163,"W",10,0,-163.16666667,"",2007-07-01,,0,1,
```

The first `Map` takes this line and passes it to a CSV reader that parses it (taking into account fields like `Lik, AK` that have commas in them) and pulls out the fields as a list of strings. These fields are then passed to the next transform. The second `Map` takes the fields as input and outputs a tuple of the form (the extracted fields are shown in bold in the previous example):

```
(1000401, (68.08333333,-163.16666667))
```

The first number is the unique airport code (we use this, rather than the airport's three-letter code, because airport locations can change over time), and the next two numbers are the latitude/longitude pair for the airport's location. The variable `air ports`, which is the result of these three transformations, is not a simple in-memory list of these tuples. Instead, it is an immutable collection, termed a `PCollection`, that you can take out-of-memory and distribute.

We can write the contents of the `PCollection` to a text file to verify that the pipeline is behaving correctly:

```
(airports
    | beam.Map(lambda airport_data: '{},{}'.format(airport_data[0], ',' \
        .join(airport_data[1])) )
    | beam.io.WriteToText('extracted_airports')
)
```

Try this out: the code, in *04_streaming/transform/df01.py*, is just a Python program that you can run from the command line. First, install the Apache Beam package if you haven't yet done so and then run the program *df01.py* while you are in the directory containing the GitHub repository of this book:

```
cd 04_streaming/simulate
./install_packages.sh
python3 ./df01.py
```

This runs the code in *df01.py* locally. Later, we will change the pipeline line to:

```
with beam.Pipeline('DataflowRunner') as pipeline:
```

and get to run the pipeline on the Google Cloud Platform using the Cloud Dataflow service. With that change, simply running the Python program launches the data pipeline on multiple workers in the cloud. As with many distributed systems, the output of Cloud Dataflow is potentially sharded to one or more files. You will get a file whose name begins with "extracted_airports" (mine was *extracted_airports-00000- of-00001*), a few of whose lines might look something like this:

```
1000101,58.10944444,-152.90666667
1000301,65.54805556,-161.07166667
```

The columns are `AIRPORT_SEQ_ID`, `LATITUDE`, and `LONGITUDE`—the order of the rows you get depends on which of the parallel workers finished first, so it could be different.

## Adding Time Zone Information

Let's now change the code to determine the time zone corresponding to a latitude/ longitude pair. In our pipeline, rather than simply emitting the latitude/longitude pair, we emit a list of three items: latitude, longitude, and time zone:

```
airports = (pipeline
    | beam.Read(beam.io.ReadFromText('airports.csv.gz'))
    | beam.Map(lambda line: next(csv.reader([line])))
```

```
    | beam.Map(lambda fields: (fields[0], addtimezone(fields[21], fields[26])))
)
```

The `lambda` keyword in Python sets up an anonymous function. In the case of the first use of `lambda` in the preceding snippet, that method takes one parameter (`line`) and returns the stuff following the colon. We can determine the time zone by using the `timezonefinder` package:[8]

```
def addtimezone(lat, lon):
    import timezonefinder
    tf = timezonefinder.TimezoneFinder()
    lat = float(lat)
    lon = float(lon)
    return (lat, lon, tf.timezone_at(lng=lon, lat=lat))
```

The location of the import statement in the preceding example might look strange (most Python imports tend to be at the top of the file), but this import-within-the-function pattern is recommended by Cloud Dataflow so that,[9] when we submit it to the cloud, pickling of the main session doesn't end up pickling imported packages also.[10]

For now, though, we are going to run this (*df02.py*) locally. This will take a while because the time zone computation involves a large number of polygon intersection checks and because we are running locally, not (yet!) distributed in the cloud. So, let's speed it up by adding a filter to reduce the number of airport locations we have to look up:

```
    | beam.io.ReadFromText('airports.csv.gz')
    | beam.Filter(lambda line: "United States" in line
                  and line[-2:] == '1,')
```

The BTS flight delay data is only for US domestic flights, so we don't need the time zones of airports outside the United States. The reason for the second check is that airport locations change over time, but we are interested only in the current location of the airport. For example, here are the airport locations for ORD (or Chicago):

```
1393001,...,"ORD",...,41.97805556,...,-87.90611111,...,1950-01-01,2011-06-30,0,0,
1393002,...,"ORD",...,41.98166667,...,-87.90666667,...,2011-07-01,2013-09-30,0,0,
1393003,...,"ORD",...,41.97944444,...,-87.90750000,...,2013-10-01,2015-09-30,0,0,
1393004,...,"ORD",...,41.97722222,...,-87.90805556,...,2015-10-01,,0,1,
```

---

8  This code is in *04_streaming/transform/df02.py* of the GitHub repository of this book.

9  See the answer to the question "How do I handle `NameErrors`?" in the Google documentation (*https://oreil.ly/bqoB2*).

10  Saving Python objects is called pickling (*https://oreil.ly/2kQpa*).

The first row captures the location of Chicago's airport between 1950 and June 30, 2011.[11] The second row is valid from July 1, 2011, to September 30, 2013. The last row, however, is the current location and this is marked by the last column (the AIR PORT_IS_LATEST field) being 1.

That's not the only line we are interested in, however! Flights before 2015-10-01 will report the ID of the second to last row. We could add a check for this, but this looks rather dicey for a slight bit of optimization. So, I'll remove that last check, so that we have only:

```
| beam.io.ReadFromText('airports.csv.gz')
| beam.Filter(lambda line: "United States" in line)
```

Once I do this and run *df02.py*, the extracted information for the airports looks like this:

```
1672301,62.03611111,-151.45222222,America/Anchorage
1672401,43.87722222,-73.41305556,America/New_York
1672501,40.75722222,-119.21277778,America/Los_Angeles
```

The last column in the extracted information has the time zone, which was determined from the latitude and longitude of each airport.

## Converting Times to UTC

Now that we have the time zone for each airport, we are ready to tackle converting the times in the flights data to UTC. At the time that we are developing the program, we'd prefer not to process all the months we have in BigQuery—waiting for the query each time we run the program will be annoying. Instead, we will create a small sample of the flights data in BigQuery against which to develop our code:[12]

```
SELECT *
FROM dsongcp.flights
WHERE RAND() < 0.001
```

This returns about 6,000 rows. We can use the BigQuery web UI to save these results as a JavaScript Object Notation (JSON) file. However, I prefer to script things out:[13]

---

11 Chicago's airport didn't pack up and move on June 30. Most likely, a new terminal or runway was opened at that time, and this changed the location of the centroid of the airport's aerial extent. Notice that the change is just 0.0036 in latitude degrees. At Chicago's latitude, this translates to about 400 meters.

12 Normally, the recommended way to sample a BigQuery table is to do SELECT * FROM dsongcp.flights WHERE TABLESAMPLE SYSTEM (0.001) because table sampling isn't cached, so we will get different results each time. However, at the time of writing, table sampling works only on tables and flights is a View. Besides, in our current use case, we don't care whether or not we get different samples each time we run the query. That's why I'm using rand().

13 See the file *04_streaming/transform/bqsample.sh*.

```
bq query --destination_table dsongcp.flights_sample \
  --replace --nouse_legacy_sql \
  'SELECT * FROM dsongcp.flights WHERE RAND() < 0.001'

bq extract --destination_format=NEWLINE_DELIMITED_JSON \
  dsongcp.flights_sample  \
  gs://${BUCKET}/flights/ch4/flights_sample.json

gsutil cp gs://${BUCKET}/flights/ch4/flights_sample.json
```

This creates a file named *flight_sample.json*, a row of which looks similar to this:

```
{"FL_DATE":"2015-04-28","UNIQUE_CARRIER":"EV","ORIGIN_AIRPORT_SEQ_ID":"1013503",
"ORIGIN":"ABE","DEST_AIRPORT_SEQ_ID":"1039705","DEST":"ATL",
"CRS_DEP_TIME":"1600","DEP_TIME":"1555","DEP_DELAY":-5,"TAXI_OUT":7,
"WHEELS_OFF":"1602","WHEELS_ON":"1747","TAXI_IN":4,"CRS_ARR_TIME":"1809",
"ARR_TIME":"1751","ARR_DELAY":-18,"CANCELLED":false,"DIVERTED":false,
"DISTANCE":"692.00"}
```

Reading the flights data starts out similar to reading the airports data:[14]

```
flights = (pipeline
  | 'flights:read' >> beam.io.ReadFromText('flights_sample.json')
  | 'flights:parse' >> beam.Map(lambda line: json.loads(line))
```

This is the same code as when we read the *airports.csv.gz* file, except that I am also giving a name (`flights:read`) to this transform step and using a JSON parser instead of a CSV parser. Note the syntax here:

```
  | 'name-of-step' >> transform_function()
```

The next step, though, is different because it involves two `PCollections`. We need to join the flights data with the airports data to find the time zone corresponding to each flight. To do that, we make the airports `PCollection` a "side input." Side inputs in Beam are like views into the original `PCollection`, and are either lists or dicts (dictionaries). In this case, we will create a dict that maps airport ID to information about the airports:

```
flights = (pipeline
  |'flights:read' >> beam.io.ReadFromText('flights_sample.json')
  | 'flights:parse' >> beam.Map(lambda line: json.loads(line))
  |'flights:tzcorr' >> beam.FlatMap(tz_correct,
                                    beam.pvalue.AsDict(airports))
)
```

---

14  This code is in *04_streaming/transform/df03.py* of the GitHub repository of this book.

---

The fact that the PCollection has to be a Python list or a Python dict means that side inputs have to be small enough to fit into memory. If you need to join two large PCollections that will not fit into memory, use a CoGroupByKey (*https://oreil.ly/Kiz6x*).

The FlatMap() method calls out to a method tz_correct(), which takes the parsed content of a line from *flights_sample.json* (containing a single flight's information) and a Python dictionary (containing all the airports' time zone information):

```
def tz_correct(fields, airport_timezones):
    try:
        # convert all times to UTC
        # ORIGIN_AIRPORT_SEQ_ID is the name of JSON attribute
        dep_airport_id = fields["ORIGIN_AIRPORT_SEQ_ID"]
        arr_airport_id = fields["DEST_AIRPORT_SEQ_ID"]
        # airport_id is the key to airport_timezones dict
        # and the value is a tuple (lat, lon, timezone)
        dep_timezone = airport_timezones[dep_airport_id][2]
        arr_timezone = airport_timezones[arr_airport_id][2]

        for f in ["CRS_DEP_TIME", "DEP_TIME", "WHEELS_OFF"]:
            fields[f] = as_utc(fields["FL_DATE"], fields[f], dep_timezone)
        for f in ["WHEELS_ON", "CRS_ARR_TIME", "ARR_TIME"]:
            fields[f] = as_utc(fields["FL_DATE"], fields[f], arr_timezone)

        yield json.dumps(fields)
    except KeyError as e:
        logging.exception(" Ignoring " + line +
                          " because airport is not known")
```

Why FlatMap() instead of Map to call tz_correct()? A Map is a 1-to-1 relation between input and output, whereas a FlatMap() can return 0–N outputs per input. The way it does this is with a Python generator function (i.e., the yield keyword—think of the yield as a return that returns one item at a time until there is no more data to return). Using FlatMap here allows us to ignore any flight information corresponding to unknown airports—even though this doesn't happen in the historical data we are processing, a little bit of defensive programming doesn't hurt.

The tz_correct() code gets the departure airport ID from the flight's data and then looks up the time zone for that airport ID from the airport's data. After it has the time zone, it calls out to the method as_utc() to convert each of the datetimes reported in that airport's time zone to UTC:

```
def as_utc(date, hhmm, tzone):
    try:
        if len(hhmm) > 0 and tzone is not None:
            import datetime, pytz
            loc_tz = pytz.timezone(tzone)
            loc_dt = loc_tz.localize(datetime.datetime.strptime(date,'%Y-%m-%d'),
```

```
            is_dst=False)
        loc_dt += datetime.timedelta(hours=int(hhmm[:2]),
                                     minutes=int(hhmm[2:]))
        utc_dt = loc_dt.astimezone(pytz.utc)
        return utc_dt.strftime('%Y-%m-%d %H:%M:%S')
    else:
        return '' # empty string corresponds to canceled flights
except ValueError as e:
    print('{} {} {}'.format(date, hhmm, tzone))
    raise e
```

As before, you can run this locally. To do that, run `df03.py`. A line that originally (in the raw data) looked like:

```
{"FL_DATE":"2015-11-05","UNIQUE_CARRIER":"DL","ORIGIN_AIRPORT_SEQ_ID":"1013503",
"ORIGIN":"ABE","DEST_AIRPORT_SEQ_ID":"1039705","DEST":"ATL",
"CRS_DEP_TIME":"0600","DEP_TIME":"0556","DEP_DELAY":-4,"TAXI_OUT":12,
"WHEELS_OFF":"0608","WHEELS_ON":"0749","TAXI_IN":10,"CRS_ARR_TIME":"0818",
"ARR_TIME":"0759","ARR_DELAY":-19,"CANCELLED":false,
"DIVERTED":false,"DISTANCE":"692.00"}
```

now becomes:

```
{"FL_DATE": "2015-11-05", "UNIQUE_CARRIER": "DL",
"ORIGIN_AIRPORT_SEQ_ID": "1013503", "ORIGIN": "ABE",
"DEST_AIRPORT_SEQ_ID": "1039705", "DEST": "ATL",
"CRS_DEP_TIME": "2015-11-05 11:00:00", "DEP_TIME": "2015-11-05 10:56:00",
"DEP_DELAY": -4, "TAXI_OUT": 12, "WHEELS_OFF": "2015-11-05 11:08:00",
"WHEELS_ON": "2015-11-05 12:49:00", "TAXI_IN": 10,
"CRS_ARR_TIME": "2015-11-05 13:18:00", "ARR_TIME": "2015-11-05 12:59:00",
"ARR_DELAY": -19, "CANCELLED": false, "DIVERTED": false, "DISTANCE": "692.00"}
```

All the times have been converted to UTC. For example, the 0759 time of arrival in Atlanta has been converted to UTC to become 12:59:00.

## Correcting Dates

Look carefully at the following line involving a flight from Honolulu (HNL) to Dallas–Fort Worth (DFW). Do you notice anything odd?

```
{"FL_DATE": "2015-03-06", "UNIQUE_CARRIER": "AA",
"ORIGIN_AIRPORT_SEQ_ID": "1217302", "ORIGIN": "HNL",
"DEST_AIRPORT_SEQ_ID": "1129803", "DEST": "DFW",
"CRS_DEP_TIME": "2015-03-07 05:30:00", "DEP_TIME": "2015-03-07 05:22:00",
"DEP_DELAY": -8, "TAXI_OUT": 40, "WHEELS_OFF": "2015-03-07 06:02:00",
"WHEELS_ON": "2015-03-06 12:32:00", "TAXI_IN": 7,
"CRS_ARR_TIME": "2015-03-06 12:54:00", "ARR_TIME": "2015-03-06 12:39:00",
"ARR_DELAY": -15, "CANCELLED": false, "DIVERTED": false, "DISTANCE": "3784.00"}
```

Examine the departure time in Honolulu and the arrival time in Dallas—the flight is arriving the day before it departed! That's because the flight date (2015-03-06) is the date of departure in local time. Add in a time difference between airports, and it is quite possible that it is not the date of arrival. We'll look for these situations and add 24 hours if necessary. This is, of course, quite a hack (have I already mentioned that times ought to be stored in UTC?!):

```python
def add_24h_if_before(arrtime, deptime):
    import datetime
    if len(arrtime) > 0 and len(deptime) > 0 and arrtime < deptime:
        adt = datetime.datetime.strptime(arrtime, '%Y-%m-%d %H:%M:%S')
        adt += datetime.timedelta(hours=24)
        return adt.strftime('%Y-%m-%d %H:%M:%S')
    else:
        return arrtime
```

The 24-hour hack is called just before the yield in `tz_correct`.[15] Now that we have new data about the airports, it is probably wise to add it to our dataset. Also, as remarked earlier, we want to keep track of the time zone offset from UTC because some types of analysis might require knowledge of the local time. Thus, the new `tz_correct` code becomes the following:

```python
def tz_correct(line, airport_timezones):
    fields = json.loads(line)
    try:
        # convert all times to UTC
        dep_airport_id = fields["ORIGIN_AIRPORT_SEQ_ID"]
        arr_airport_id = fields["DEST_AIRPORT_SEQ_ID"]
        dep_timezone = airport_timezones[dep_airport_id][2]
        arr_timezone = airport_timezones[arr_airport_id][2]

        for f in ["CRS_DEP_TIME", "DEP_TIME", "WHEELS_OFF"]:
            fields[f], deptz = as_utc(fields["FL_DATE"], fields[f], dep_timezone)
        for f in ["WHEELS_ON", "CRS_ARR_TIME", "ARR_TIME"]:
            fields[f], arrtz = as_utc(fields["FL_DATE"], fields[f], arr_timezone)

        for f in ["WHEELS_OFF", "WHEELS_ON", "CRS_ARR_TIME", "ARR_TIME"]:
            fields[f] = add_24h_if_before(fields[f], fields["DEP_TIME"])

        fields["DEP_AIRPORT_TZOFFSET"] = deptz
        fields["ARR_AIRPORT_TZOFFSET"] = arrtz
        yield json.dumps(fields)
    except KeyError as e:
        logging.exception(" Ignoring " + line + " because airport is not known")
```

When I run *df04.py*, which has these changes applied to it, the flight from Honolulu to Dallas becomes:

```
{"FL_DATE": "2015-03-06", "UNIQUE_CARRIER": "AA",
 "ORIGIN_AIRPORT_SEQ_ID": "1217302", "ORIGIN": "HNL",
 "DEST_AIRPORT_SEQ_ID": "1129803", "DEST": "DFW",
```

---

15 This code is in *04_streaming/transform/df04.py* of the GitHub repository of this book.

```
"CRS_DEP_TIME": "2015-03-07 05:30:00", "DEP_TIME": "2015-03-07 05:22:00",
"DEP_DELAY": -8, "TAXI_OUT": 40, "WHEELS_OFF": "2015-03-07 06:02:00",
"WHEELS_ON": "2015-03-07 12:32:00", "TAXI_IN": 7,
"CRS_ARR_TIME": "2015-03-07 12:54:00", "ARR_TIME": "2015-03-07 12:39:00",
"ARR_DELAY": -15, "CANCELLED": false, "DIVERTED": false, "DISTANCE": "3784.00",
"DEP_AIRPORT_TZOFFSET": -36000.0, "ARR_AIRPORT_TZOFFSET": -21600.0}
```

As you can see, the dates have now been corrected (see the bolded parts).

## Creating Events

After we have our time-corrected data, we can move on to creating events to publish into Pub/Sub. For now, we'll limit ourselves to just the departed and arrived messages—we can rerun the pipeline to create the additional events if and when our modeling efforts begin to use other events:

```
def get_next_event(fields):
    if len(fields["DEP_TIME"]) > 0:
        event = dict(fields)  # copy
        event["EVENT_TYPE"] = "departed"
        event["EVENT_TIME"] = fields["DEP_TIME"]
        for f in ["TAXI_OUT", "WHEELS_OFF", "WHEELS_ON",
                  "TAXI_IN", "ARR_TIME", "ARR_DELAY", "DISTANCE"]:
            event.pop(f, None)  # not knowable at departure time
        yield event
    if len(fields["ARR_TIME"]) > 0:
        event = dict(fields)
        event["EVENT_TYPE"] = "arrived"
        event["EVENT_TIME"] = fields["ARR_TIME"]
        yield event
```

Essentially, we pick up the departure time and create a departed event at that time after making sure to remove the fields (such as arrival delay) we cannot know at the departure time. Similarly, we use the arrival time to create an arrived event, as shown in Figure 4-4.

In the pipeline, the event creation code is called on the flights PCollection after the conversion to UTC has happened:

```
flights = (pipeline
  |'flights:read' >> beam.io.ReadFromText('flights_sample.json')
  |'flights:tzcorr' >> beam.FlatMap(tz_correct,
                        beam.pvalue.AsDict(airports))
)
events = flights | beam.FlatMap(get_next_event)
```

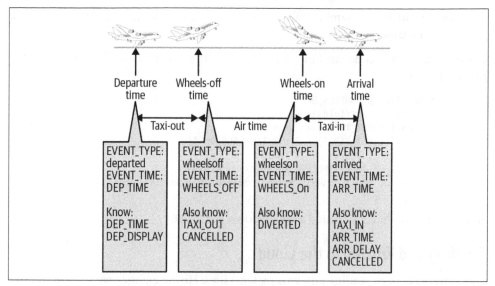

*Figure 4-4. Events, when they are published, and some of the fields present in those events.*

If we now run the pipeline,[16] we will see two events for each flight:

```
{"FL_DATE": "2015-04-28", "UNIQUE_CARRIER": "EV",
"ORIGIN_AIRPORT_SEQ_ID": "1013503", "ORIGIN": "ABE",
"DEST_AIRPORT_SEQ_ID": "1039705", "DEST": "ATL",
"CRS_DEP_TIME": "2015-04-28 20:00:00", "DEP_TIME": "2015-04-28 19:55:00",
"DEP_DELAY": -5, "CRS_ARR_TIME": "2015-04-28 22:09:00", "CANCELLED": false,
"DIVERTED": false, "DEP_AIRPORT_TZOFFSET": -14400.0,
"ARR_AIRPORT_TZOFFSET": -14400.0, "EVENT_TYPE": "departed",
"EVENT_TIME": "2015-04-28 19:55:00"}
{"FL_DATE": "2015-04-28", "UNIQUE_CARRIER": "EV",
"ORIGIN_AIRPORT_SEQ_ID": "1013503", "ORIGIN": "ABE",
"DEST_AIRPORT_SEQ_ID": "1039705", "DEST": "ATL",
"CRS_DEP_TIME": "2015-04-28 20:00:00", "DEP_TIME": "2015-04-28 19:55:00",
"DEP_DELAY": -5, "TAXI_OUT": 7, "WHEELS_OFF": "2015-04-28 20:02:00",
"WHEELS_ON": "2015-04-28 21:47:00", "TAXI_IN": 4,
"CRS_ARR_TIME": "2015-04-28 22:09:00", "ARR_TIME": "2015-04-28 21:51:00",
"ARR_DELAY": -18, "CANCELLED": false, "DIVERTED": false, "DISTANCE": "692.00",
"DEP_AIRPORT_TZOFFSET": -14400.0, "ARR_AIRPORT_TZOFFSET": -14400.0,
"EVENT_TYPE": "arrived", "EVENT_TIME": "2015-04-28 21:51:00"}
```

The first event is a `departed` event and is to be published at the departure time, while the second event is an `arrived` event and is to be published at the arrival time. The

---

16  This code is in *04_streaming/transform/df05.py* of the GitHub repository of this book.

departed event has a number of missing fields corresponding to data that is not known at that time.

Once we have this code working, let's add a third event that will be sent when the plane takes off:

```
if len(fields["WHEELS_OFF"]) > 0:
    event = dict(fields)  # copy
    event["EVENT_TYPE"] = "wheelsoff"
    event["EVENT_TIME"] = fields["WHEELS_OFF"]
    for f in ["WHEELS_ON", "TAXI_IN",
                "ARR_TIME", "ARR_DELAY", "DISTANCE"]:
        event.pop(f, None)  # not knowable at departure time
    yield event
```

At this point, we haven't created a wheelsdown event yet.

# Reading and Writing to the Cloud

So far, we have been reading and writing local files. However, once we start to run our code in production, in a serverless environment, the concept of a local drive no longer makes sense. We have to read and write from Cloud Storage. Also, because this is structured data, it is preferable to read and write to BigQuery—recall that we loaded our full dataset into BigQuery in Chapter 2. Now, we'd like to put the transformed (time-corrected) data there as well.

Fortunately, all this involves is changing the source or the sink. The rest of the pipeline stays the same. For example, in the previous section (see *04_streaming/transform/df05.py*), we read the *airports.csv.gz* as:

```
| 'airports:read' >> beam.io.ReadFromText('airports.csv.gz')
```

Now, in order to read the equivalent file from Cloud Storage, we change the corresponding code in *04_streaming/transform/df06.py* to be:

```
airports_filename = 'gs://{}/flights/airports/airports.csv.gz'.format(
                        bucket)
...
| 'airports:read' >> beam.io.ReadFromText(airports_filename)
```

Of course, we'll have to make sure to upload the file to Cloud Storage and make it readable by whoever is going to run this code. Having the data file be available in our GitHub repository was not going to scale anyway—Cloud Storage (or BigQuery) is the right place for data.

In *df05.py*, I had to read a local file that contained the JSON export of a smart part of the dataset and use a JSON parser to obtain a dict:

```
| 'flights:read' >> beam.io.ReadFromText('flights_sample.json')
| 'flights:parse' >> beam.Map(lambda line: json.loads(line))
```

In *df06.py*, the corresponding code becomes simpler because the BigQuery reader returns a dict where the column names of the result set are the keys:

```
'flights:read' >> beam.io.ReadFromBigQuery(
    query='SELECT * FROM dsongcp.flights WHERE rand() < 0.001',
    use_standard_sql=True)
```

Of course when we run it for real, we'll change the query to remove the sampling (rand() < 0.001) so that we can process the entire dataset.

Similarly, where before we wrote to a local file using:

```
| 'flights:tostring' >> beam.Map(lambda fields: json.dumps(fields))
| 'flights:out' >> beam.io.textio.WriteToText('all_flights')
```

we'll change the code to write to Cloud Storage using:

```
flights_output = 'gs://{}/flights/tzcorr/all_flights'.format(bucket)
...
| 'flights:tostring' >> beam.Map(lambda fields: json.dumps(fields))
| 'flights:gcsout' >> beam.io.textio.WriteToText(flights_output)
```

We can write the same data to a BigQuery table also:

```
flights_schema = \
    'FL_DATE:date,UNIQUE_CARRIER:string,...CANCELLED:boolean'
...
| 'flights:bqout' >> beam.io.WriteToBigQuery(
    'dsongcp.flights_tzcorr', schema=flights_schema,
    write_disposition=beam.io.BigQueryDisposition.WRITE_TRUNCATE,
    create_disposition=beam.io.BigQueryDisposition.CREATE_IF_NEEDED
    )
```

Note that we need to provide a schema when writing to BigQuery, and specify what to do if the table already exists (we ask for the table to be truncated and contents replaced) and if the table doesn't already exist (we ask for the table to be created).

We can try running this code, but the pipeline will require a few extra parameters. So where we used to have:

```
with beam.Pipeline('DirectRunner') as pipeline:
```

we now need:

```
argv = [
    '--project={0}'.format(project),
    '--staging_location=gs://{0}/flights/staging/'.format(bucket),
    '--temp_location=gs://{0}/flights/temp/'.format(bucket),
    '--runner=DirectRunner'
]
with beam.Pipeline(argv=argv) as pipeline:
```

The reason is that when we read from BigQuery, we are providing a query:

```
'flights:read' >> beam.io.ReadFromBigQuery(
       query='SELECT * FROM dsongcp.flights WHERE rand() < 0.001',
       use_standard_sql=True)
```

So, we need to provide the project that needs to be billed. In addition, and this is an implementation detail, some temporary data needs to be staged and cached in Cloud Storage, and we need to provide the pipeline a place to store this temporary data—we will never be sure which operations will require staging or caching, so it's a good idea to always specify a scratch location in Cloud Storage for this purpose.

We can run *df06.py* and then check that new tables are created in BigQuery. So far, we have been running the code locally, either on your laptop or in Cloud Shell.

Next, let's look at how to run this in Cloud Dataflow, which is the GCP managed service for running Apache Beam pipelines.

## Running the Pipeline in the Cloud

That last run took a few minutes on the local virtual machine (VM), and we were processing only a thousand lines! Let's change the code (see *df07.py*) to process all the rows in the BigQuery view:

```
'flights:read' >> beam.io.ReadFromBigQuery(
       query='SELECT * FROM dsongcp.flights',
       use_standard_sql=True)
```

Now that we have much more data, we need to distribute the work, and to do that, we will change the runner from DirectRunner (which runs locally) to DataflowRunner (which lobs the job off to the cloud and scales it out):

```
argv = [
   '--project={0}'.format(project),
   '--job_name=ch04timecorr',
   '--save_main_session',
   '--staging_location=gs://{0}/flights/staging/'.format(bucket),
   '--temp_location=gs://{0}/flights/temp/'.format(bucket),
   '--setup_file=./setup.py',
   '--max_num_workers=8',
   '--region={}'.format(region),
   '--runner=DataflowRunner'
]

pipeline = beam.Pipeline(argv=argv)
```

Notice that there are a few extra parameters now:

- The job name provides the name by which this job will be listed in the GCP console. This is so that we can troubleshoot the job if necessary.

- We ask the Dataflow submission code to save our main session. This is needed whenever we have global variables in our Python program.

---

- The file *setup.py* should list the Python packages that we needed to install (time zonefinder and pytz) as we went along—Cloud Dataflow will need to install these packages on the Compute Engine instances that it launches behind the scenes:

```
REQUIRED_PACKAGES = [
    'timezonefinder',
    'pytz'
]
```

- By default, Dataflow autoscales the number of workers based on throughput—the more lines we have in our input data files, the more workers we need. This is called Horizontal Autoscaling (*https://oreil.ly/htqWw*). To turn off autoscaling, we can specify --autoscaling_algorithm=NONE, and to constrain it somewhat, we can specify the maximum number of workers.

- We specify the region in which the Dataflow pipeline needs to run.

- The runner is no longer DirectRunner (which runs locally). It is now Dataflow Runner.

Running the Python program submits the job to the cloud. Cloud Dataflow autoscales each step of the pipeline based on throughput, and streams the events data into BigQuery (see Figure 4-3). You can monitor the running job on the Cloud Platform Console in the Cloud Dataflow section.

Even as the events data is being written out, we can query it by browsing to the Big-Query console and typing the following:

```
SELECT
  ORIGIN,
  DEP_TIME,
  DEST,
  ARR_TIME,
  ARR_DELAY,
  EVENT_TIME,
  EVENT_TYPE
FROM
  dsongcp.flights_simevents
WHERE
  (DEP_DELAY > 15 and ORIGIN = 'SEA') or
  (ARR_DELAY > 15 and DEST = 'SEA')
ORDER BY EVENT_TIME ASC
LIMIT
  5
```

This returns:

| Row | ORI GIN | DEP_TIME | DEST | ARR_TIME | ARR_DELAY | EVENT_TIME | EVENT_TYPE |
|-----|---------|----------|------|----------|-----------|------------|------------|
| 1 | SEA | 2015-01-01 08:21:00 UTC | IAD | null | null | 2015-01-01 08:21:00 UTC | departed |
| 2 | SEA | 2015-01-01 08:21:00 UTC | IAD | null | null | 2015-01-01 08:38:00 UTC | wheelsoff |
| 3 | SEA | 2015-01-01 08:21:00 UTC | IAD | 2015-01-01 12:48:00 UTC | 22.0 | 2015-01-01 12:48:00 UTC | arrived |
| 4 | KOA | 2015-01-01 10:11:00 UTC | SEA | 2015-01-01 15:45:00 UTC | 40.0 | 2015-01-01 15:45:00 UTC | arrived |
| 5 | SEA | 2015-01-01 16:43:00 UTC | PSP | null | null | 2015-01-01 16:43:00 UTC | departed |

As expected, we see three events for the SEA-IAD flight, one at departure, the next at wheelsoff, and the third at arrival. The arrival delay is known only at arrival.

BigQuery is a columnar database, so a query that selects all fields:

```
SELECT
  *
FROM
  dsongcp.flights_simevents
ORDER BY EVENT_TIME ASC
```

will be inefficient. However, we do need all of the event data in order to send out event notifications. Therefore, we traded off storage for speed by adding an extra column called EVENT_DATA to our BigQuery table and populated it in our Dataflow pipeline as follows:

```
def create_event_row(fields):
    featdict = dict(fields)  # copy
    featdict['EVENT_DATA'] = json.dumps(fields)
    return featdict
```

Then, our query to pull the events could simply be as follows:

```
SELECT
  EVENT_TYPE,
  EVENT_TIME,
  EVENT_DATA
FROM
  dsongcp.flights_simevents
WHERE
  EVENT_TIME >= TIMESTAMP('2015-05-01 00:00:00 UTC')
  AND EVENT_TIME < TIMESTAMP('2015-05-03 00:00:00 UTC')
ORDER BY
  EVENT_TIME ASC
```

```
LIMIT
  2
```

The result looks like this:

| Row | EVENT_TYPE | EVENT_TIME | EVENT_DATA |
|-----|-----------|-----------|------------|
| 1 | wheelsoff | 2015-05-01 00:00:00 UTC | {"FL_DATE": "2015-04-30", "UNIQUE_CARRIER": "DL", "ORIGIN_AIRPORT_SEQ_ID": "1295302", "ORIGIN": "LGA", "DEST_AIRPORT_SEQ_ID": "1330303", "DEST": "MIA", "CRS_DEP_TIME": "2015-04-30T23:29:00", "DEP_TIME": "2015-04-30T23:35:00", "DEP_DELAY": 6.0, "TAXI_OUT": 25.0, "WHEELS_OFF": "2015-05-01T00:00:00", "CRS_ARR_TIME": "2015-05-01T02:53:00", "CANCELLED": false, "DIVER TED": false, "DEP_AIRPORT_TZOFFSET": -14400.0, "ARR_AIRPORT_TZOFFSET": -14400.0, "EVENT_TYPE": "wheelsoff", "EVENT_TIME": "2015-05-01T00:00:00"} |
| 2 | departed | 2015-05-01 00:00:00 UTC | {"FL_DATE": "2015-04-30", "UNIQUE_CARRIER": "DL", "ORIGIN_AIRPORT_SEQ_ID": "1295302", "ORIGIN": "LGA", "DEST_AIRPORT_SEQ_ID": "1320402", "DEST": "MCO", "CRS_DEP_TIME": "2015-04-30T23:55:00", "DEP_TIME": "2015-05-01T00:00:00", "DEP_DELAY": 5.0, "CRS_ARR_TIME": "2015-05-01T02:45:00", "CANCEL LED": false, "DIVERTED": false, "DEP_AIRPORT_TZOFF SET": -14400.0, "ARR_AIRPORT_TZOFFSET": -14400.0, "EVENT_TYPE": "departed", "EVENT_TIME": "2015-05-01T00:00:00"} |

This table will serve as the source of our events; it is from such a query that we will simulate streaming flight data.

# Publishing an Event Stream to Cloud Pub/Sub

Now that we have the source events from the raw flight data, we are ready to simulate the stream. Streaming data in Google Cloud Platform is typically published to Cloud Pub/Sub, a serverless real-time messaging service. Cloud Pub/Sub provides reliable delivery and can scale to more than a million messages per second. Unless you are using Cloud Pub/Sub Lite (*https://oreil.ly/1G8PI*) (which is a single-zone service that is built for low-cost operation), Pub/Sub stores copies of messages in multiple zones to provide "at least once" guaranteed delivery to subscribers, and there can be many simultaneous subscribers.

Our simulator will read from the events table in BigQuery (populated in the previous section) and publish messages to Cloud Pub/Sub. Essentially, we will walk through the flight event records, getting the notification time from each, and simulate publishing those events as they happen.

# Speed-Up Factor

However, we'll also use a mapping between the event notification time (arrival or departure time based on event) and the current system time. Why? Because it is inefficient to always simulate the flight events at real-time speeds. Instead, we might want to run through a day of flight data in an hour (as long as the code that processes these events can handle the increased data rate). At other times, we may be running our event-processing code in a debugging environment that is slower and so we might want to slow down the simulation. I will refer to this ratio between the actual time and simulation time as the *speed-up factor*—the speed-up factor will be greater than 1 if we want the simulation to be faster than real time and less than 1 if we want it to be slower than real time.

Based on the speed-up factor, we'll have to do a linear transformation of the event time to system time. If the speed-up factor is 1, a 60-minute difference between the start of the simulation in event time and the current record's timestamp should be encountered 60 minutes after the start of the simulation. If the speed-up factor is 60, a 60-minute difference in event time translates to a 1-minute difference in system time, and so the record should be published a minute later. If the event time clock is ahead of the system clock, we sleep for the necessary amount of time so as to allow the simulation to catch up.

The simulation consists of four steps (see also Figure 4-5):

- Run the query to get the set of flight event records to publish.
- Iterate through the query results.
- Accumulate events to publish as a batch.
- Publish accumulated events and sleep as necessary.

Even though this is an ETL pipeline, the need to process records in strict sequential order and sleep in between makes this ETL pipeline a poor fit for Cloud Dataflow. Instead, we'll implement this as a pure Python program. The problem with this choice is that the simulation code is not fault tolerant—if the simulation fails, it will not automatically restart and definitely will not start from the last successfully notified event.

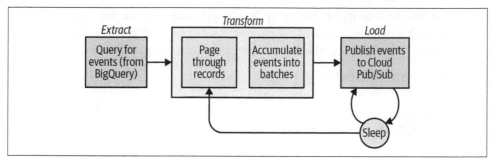

*Figure 4-5. The four steps of simulation.*

The simulation code that we are writing is only for quick experimentation with streaming data. Hence, I will not take the extra effort needed to make it fault-tolerant. If we had to do so, we could make the simulation fault-tolerant by starting from a BigQuery query that is bounded in terms of a time range with the start of that time range automatically inferred from the last-notified record in Cloud Pub/Sub. Then, we could launch the simulation script from a Docker container and use Cloud Run or Google Kubernetes Engine to automatically restart the simulation if the simulation code fails.

## Get Records to Publish

The BigQuery query is parameterized by the start and end time of the simulation and can be invoked through the Google Cloud API for Python (see *04_streaming/simulate/simulate.py* in the GitHub repository):

```
    bqclient = bq.Client(args.project)
    querystr = """
SELECT
  EVENT_TYPE,
  EVENT_TIME AS NOTIFY_TIME,
  EVENT_DATA
FROM
  dsongcp.flights_simevents
WHERE
  EVENT_TIME >= TIMESTAMP('{}')
  AND EVENT_TIME < TIMESTAMP('{}')
ORDER BY
  EVENT_TIME ASC
"""
    rows = bqclient.query(querystr.format(args.startTime,
                                          args.endTime))
```

This, however, is a bad idea. Do you see why?

It's because we are getting the start time and end time from the command line of the simulation script and directly passing it into BigQuery. This is called *SQL injection*, which can lead to security problems.[17] A better approach is to use *parameterized queries*—the BigQuery query contains the parameters marked as @startTime, etc., and the Python query function takes the definitions via the job configuration parameter:

```
    bqclient = bq.Client(args.project)
    querystr = """
SELECT
  EVENT_TYPE,
  EVENT_TIME AS NOTIFY_TIME,
  EVENT_DATA
FROM
  dsongcp.flights_simevents
WHERE
  EVENT_TIME >= @startTime
  AND EVENT_TIME < @endTime
ORDER BY
  EVENT_TIME ASC
"""
    job_config = bq.QueryJobConfig(
        query_parameters=[
            bq.ScalarQueryParameter("startTime", "TIMESTAMP", args.startTime),
            bq.ScalarQueryParameter("endTime", "TIMESTAMP", args.endTime),
        ]
    )
    rows = bqclient.query(querystr, job_config=job_config)
```

The query function returns an object (called rows in the preceding snippet) that we can iterate through:

```
    for row in rows:
      # do something
```

What do we need to do for each of the rows? We'll need to iterate through the records, build a batch of events, and publish each batch. Let's see how each of these steps is done.

## How Many Topics?

As we walk through the query results, we need to publish events to Cloud Pub/Sub. We have three choices in terms of the architecture:

- We could publish all the events to a single topic. However, this can be wasteful of network bandwidth if we have a subscriber that is interested only in the wheels off event. Such a subscriber will have to parse the incoming event, decode the EVENT_TYPE file in the JSON, and discard events in which they are not interested.

---

17 It opens a door to someone passing in queries that could, for example, delete a table. This XKCD cartoon (*https://xkcd.com/327*) is famous for highlighting the issue.

- We could publish all the events to a single topic, but add attributes to each message. For example, to publish an event with two attributes `event_type` and `carrier`, we'd do:

```
publisher.publish(topic, event_data,
                  event_type='departed', carrier='AA')
```

Then, the subscriber could ask for server-side filtering (*https://oreil.ly/KBXKj*) based on an attribute or combination of attributes when creating the subscription:

```
subscriber.create_subscription(request={..., "filter":
  "attributes.carrier='AS' AND attributes.event_type='arrived'"})
```

- Create a separate topic per event type (i.e., an `arrived` topic, a `departed` topic, and a `wheelsoff` topic).

Option 1 is the simplest, and should be your default choice unless you will have many subscribers that are interested only in subsets of the event stream. If you will have subscribers that are interested in subsets of the event stream, choose between Options 2 and 3.

Option 2 adds software complexity. Option 3 adds infrastructure complexity. I suggest choosing Option 3 when you have only one attribute, and that attribute has only a handful of options. This limits infrastructure complexity while keeping publisher and subscriber code simple. Choose Option 2 when you have many attributes each with many possible values because Option 3 in such a scenario will lead to an explosion in the number of topics.

## Iterating Through Records

We will choose to have a separate topic per event type (i.e., an `arrived` topic, a `departed` topic, and a `wheelsoff` topic), so we create three topics:[18]

```
for event_type in ['wheelsoff', 'arrived', 'departed']:
  topics[event_type] = publisher.topic_path(args.project, event_type)
  try:
    publisher.get_topic(topic=topics[event_type])
    logging.info("Already exists: {}".format(topics[event_type]))
  except:
    logging.info("Creating {}".format(topics[event_type]))
    publisher.create_topic(name=topics[event_type])
```

After creating the topics, we call the `notify()` method passing along the rows read from BigQuery:

---

18 See *04_streaming/simulate/simulate.py* in the GitHub repository.

```
# notify about each row in the dataset
programStartTime = datetime.datetime.utcnow()
simStartTime = datetime.datetime.strptime(args.startTime,
                        TIME_FORMAT).replace(tzinfo=pytz.UTC)
notify(publisher, topics, rows, simStartTime,
        programStartTime, args.speedFactor)
```

## Building a Batch of Events

The notify() method consists of accumulating the rows into batches, publishing a batch, and sleeping until it is time to publish the next batch:

```
def notify(publisher, topics, rows, simStartTime, programStart, speedFactor):
    # sleep computation
    def compute_sleep_secs(notify_time):
        time_elapsed = (datetime.datetime.utcnow() -
                            programStart).seconds
        sim_time_elapsed = (notify_time - simStartTime).seconds / speedFactor
        to_sleep_secs = sim_time_elapsed - time_elapsed
        return to_sleep_secs

    tonotify = {}
    for key in topics:
        tonotify[key] = list()

    for row in rows:
        event, notify_time, event_data = row

        # how much time should we sleep?
        if compute_sleep_secs(notify_time) > 1:
            # notify the accumulated tonotify
            publish(publisher, topics, tonotify, notify_time)
            for key in topics:
                tonotify[key] = list()

            # recompute sleep, since notification takes a while
            to_sleep_secs = compute_sleep_secs(notify_time)
            if to_sleep_secs > 0:
                logging.info('Sleeping {} seconds'.format(to_sleep_secs))
                time.sleep(to_sleep_secs)

        tonotify[event].append(event_data)
    # left-over records; notify again
    publish(publisher, topics, tonotify, notify_time)
```

There are a few points to be made here. First is that we work completely in UTC so that the time difference computations make sense. Second, we always compute whether to sleep by looking at the time difference since the start of the simulation. If we simply keep moving a pointer forward, errors in time will accumulate. Finally, note that we check whether the sleep time is more than a second the first time, so as to give records time to accumulate. If, when you run the program, you do not see any sleep, your speed-up factor is too high for the capability of the machine running the simulation code and the network between that machine and Google Cloud Platform. Slow down the simulation, get a larger machine, or run it behind the Google firewall (such as in Cloud Shell or on a Compute Engine instance).

## Publishing a Batch of Events

The notify() method that we saw in the previous code example has accumulated the events in between sleep calls. Even though it appears that we are publishing one event at a time, the publisher actually maintains a separate batch for each topic:

```
def publish(publisher, topics, allevents):
    for key in topics:  # 'departed', 'arrived', etc.
        topic = topics[key]
        events = allevents[key]
        logging.info('Publishing {} {} events'.format(len(events), key))
        for event_data in events:
            publisher.publish(topic, event_data.encode())
```

Note that Cloud Pub/Sub does not guarantee the order in which messages will be delivered, especially if the subscriber lets a huge backlog build up. Out-of-order messages will happen, and downstream subscribers will need to deal with them. Cloud Pub/Sub guarantees "at least once" delivery and will resend the message if the subscriber does not acknowledge a message in time. I will use Cloud Dataflow to ingest from Cloud Pub/Sub, and Cloud Dataflow deals with both these issues (out-of-order and duplication) transparently.

We can try out the simulation by typing the following:

```
python3 simulate.py --startTime '2015-05-01 00:00:00 UTC' \
    --endTime '2015-05-04 00:00:00 UTC' --speedFactor=60
```

This will simulate three days of flight data (the end time is exclusive) at 60 times real-time speed and stream the events into three topics on Cloud Pub/Sub.[19] Because the simulation starts off from a BigQuery query, it is quite straightforward to limit the simulated events to just a single airport or to airports within a latitude/longitude bounding box.

In this section, we looked at how to produce an event stream and publish those events in real time. Throughout this book, we can use this simulator and these topics for experimenting with how to consume streaming data and carry out real-time analytics.

---

[19] At 60 times real-time speed, the 3 days of flight data will take over an hour to complete. Hopefully, that's enough time to complete the rest of the chapter. If not, just restart the simulator. If you get done early, hit Ctrl-C to stop the simulator.

# Real-Time Stream Processing

Now that we have a source of streaming data that includes location information, let's look at how to build a real-time dashboard. Figure 4-6 presents the reference architecture for many solutions on Google Cloud Platform.[20]

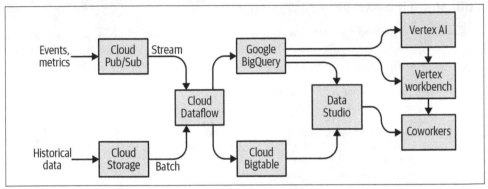

*Figure 4-6. Reference architecture for data processing on Google Cloud Platform.*

In the previous section, we set up a real-time stream of events into Cloud Pub/Sub that we can aggregate in Cloud Dataflow and write to BigQuery. Data Studio can connect to BigQuery and provide a real-time, interactive dashboard. Let's get started.

## Streaming in Dataflow

When we carried out the time correction of the raw flight data, we were working off a complete BigQuery flights table, processing them in Cloud Dataflow, and writing the events table into BigQuery. Processing a finite, bounded input dataset is called *batch processing*.

Here, though, we need to process events in Cloud Pub/Sub that are streaming in. The dataset is *unbounded*. Processing an unbounded set of data is called *stream processing*. Fortunately, the code to do stream processing in Apache Beam is identical to the code to do batch processing.

We could simply receive the events from Cloud Pub/Sub similarly to how we read data from a CSV file:[21]

```
topic_name = "projects/{}/topics/arrived".format(project)
events = (pipeline
         | 'read' >> beam.io.ReadFromPubSub(topic=topic_name)
```

---

20 For an example, see the reference architecture (*https://oreil.ly/j86HQ*) to analyze games on mobile devices.

21 See *04_streaming/realtime/avg01.py* in the GitHub repository.

```
        | 'parse' >> beam.Map(lambda s: json.loads(s))
        )
```

The only change we have to do is to turn on the streaming flag in the Dataflow options:

```
argv = [
        ...
        '--streaming',
    ]
```

We can stream the read-in events to BigQuery using code similar to what we used in batch processing:

```
schema = 'FL_DATE:date,...,EVENT_TYPE:string,EVENT_TIME:timestamp'
(events
        | 'bqout' >> beam.io.WriteToBigQuery(
                'dsongcp.streaming_events', schema=schema,
                create_disposition=beam.io.BigQueryDisposition.CREATE_IF_NEEDED
            )
)
```

In the preceding code, we subscribe to a topic in Cloud Pub/Sub and begin reading from it. As each message streams in, we parse the message, convert it to a TableRow in BigQuery, and then write it out. Indeed, if this is all we need, we can simply use the Google-provided Dataflow template that goes from Pub/Sub to BigQuery (*https:// oreil.ly/7hz4x*).

But let's say that we want to read both the arrived events and the departed events and write them to the same BigQuery table. We can do that quite simply in Beam:

```
events = {}
for event_name in ['arrived', 'departed']:
  topic_name = "projects/{}/topics/{}".format(project, event_name)
  events[event_name] = (pipeline
    | 'read:{}'.format(event_name) >>
            beam.io.ReadFromPubSub(topic=topic_name)
    | 'parse:{}'.format(event_name) >> beam.Map(
            lambda s: json.loads(s))
  )

all_events = (events['arrived'], events['departed']) | beam.Flatten()
```

*Flattening* the two sets of events concatenates them into a single collection. We then write out all_events to BigQuery.

To try this code out, we need to run the simulator we wrote in the previous section so that the simulator can publish events to the Pub/Sub topics. To start the simulation, start the Python simulator that we developed in the previous section:

```
python simulate.py --startTime '2015-05-01 00:00:00 UTC'
--endTime '2015-05-04 00:00:00 UTC'  --speedFactor 30
```

The simulator will send events from May 1, 2015, to May 3, 2015, at 30 times real-time speed, so that an hour of data is sent to Cloud Pub/Sub in two minutes. You can do this from Cloud Shell or from your local laptop. (If necessary, run `install_pack ages.sh` to install the necessary Python packages and `gcloud auth application-default login` to give the application the necessary credentials to execute queries.)

In another terminal, start *avg01.py* to read the stream of events and write them out to BigQuery. We can then query the dataset in BigQuery even as the events are streaming in. The BigQuery UI may not even show this streaming table yet, but it can be queried:

```
SELECT * FROM dsongcp.streaming_events
ORDER BY EVENT_TIME DESC
LIMIT 5
```

## Windowing a Pipeline

Although we could do just a straight data transfer, I'd like to do more. When I populate a real-time dashboard of flight delays, I'd like the information to be aggregated over a reasonable interval—for example, I want a moving average of flight delays and the total number of flights over the past 60 minutes at every airport. So, rather than simply take the input received from Cloud Pub/Sub and stream it out to BigQuery, I'd like to carry out time-windowed analytics on the data as I'm receiving it and write those analytics to BigQuery.[22] Cloud Dataflow can help us do this.

While we may be averaging over 60 minutes, how often should we compute this 60-minute average? It might be advantageous, for example, to use a sliding window and compute this 60-minute average every five minutes.

## Streaming Aggregation

The key difference between batch aggregation and streaming aggregation is the unbounded nature of the data in stream processing. What does an operation like "max" mean when the data is unbounded? After all, whatever our maximum at this point in time, a large value could come along in the stream at a later point.

A key concept when aggregating streaming data is that of a window that becomes the scope for all aggregations. Here, we apply a time-based sliding window on the pipeline. From now on, all grouping, aggregation, and so on is within that time window and there is a separate maximum, average, etc. in each time window:

---

22 If you wanted to write the raw data that is received to BigQuery, you could do that, too, of course—that is what is shown in the previous code snippet. In this section, I assume that we need only the aggregate statistics over the past hour.

```
stats = (all_events
    | 'byairport' >> beam.Map(by_airport)
    | 'window' >> beam.WindowInto(
                beam.window.SlidingWindows(60 * 60, 5 * 60))
    | 'group' >> beam.GroupByKey()
    | 'stats' >> beam.Map(lambda x: compute_stats(x[0], x[1]))
)
```

Let's walk through the preceding code snippet carefully.

The first thing we do is to take all the events and apply the `by_airport` transformation to the events:

```
    | 'byairport' >> beam.Map(by_airport)
```

What this does is to pull out the origin airport for departed events and destination airport for arrival events:

```
def by_airport(event):
    if event['EVENT_TYPE'] == 'departed':
        return event['ORIGIN'], event
    else:
        return event['DEST'], event
```

Next, we apply a sliding window to the event stream. The window is of 60 minutes duration, applied every 5 minutes:

```
    | 'window' >> beam.WindowInto(
                beam.window.SlidingWindows(60 * 60, 5 * 60))
```

Then, we apply a GroupByKey:

```
    | 'group' >> beam.GroupByKey()
```

What's the key?

In the `by_airport` function mentioned previously, we made the airport the key and the entire event object the value. So, the `GroupByKey` groups events by airport.

But the `GroupByKey` is not just by airport. Because we have already applied a sliding window, there is a separate group created for each time window. So, each group now consists of 60 minutes of flight events that arrived or departed at a specific airport.

It is on these groups that we call the `compute_stats` function in the last `Map` of the snippet:

```
    | 'stats' >> beam.Map(lambda x: compute_stats(x[0], x[1]))
```

The `compute_stats` function takes the airport and list of events at that airport, and then computes some statistics:

```
def compute_stats(airport, events):
    arrived = [event['ARR_DELAY'] for event in events
                    if event['EVENT_TYPE'] == 'arrived']
```

```
avg_arr_delay = float(np.mean(arrived)) \
            if len(arrived) > 0 else None

departed = [event['DEP_DELAY'] for event in events
            if event['EVENT_TYPE'] == 'departed']
avg_dep_delay = float(np.mean(departed)) \
            if len(departed) > 0 else None

num_flights = len(events)
start_time = min([event['EVENT_TIME'] for event in events])
latest_time = max([event['EVENT_TIME'] for event in events])

return {
    'AIRPORT': airport,
    'AVG_ARR_DELAY': avg_arr_delay,
    'AVG_DEP_DELAY': avg_dep_delay,
    'NUM_FLIGHTS': num_flights,
    'START_TIME': start_time,
    'END_TIME': latest_time
}
```

In the preceding code, we pull out the arrived events and compute the average arrival delay. Similarly, we compute the average departure delay on the departed events. We also compute the number of flights in the time window at this airport and return all these statistics.

The statistics are then written out to BigQuery using code that should look familiar by now:

```
stats_schema = ','.join(
    ['AIRPORT:string,AVG_ARR_DELAY:float,AVG_DEP_DELAY:float',
     'NUM_FLIGHTS:int64,START_TIME:timestamp,END_TIME:timestamp'])
(stats
    | 'bqout' >> beam.io.WriteToBigQuery(
            'dsongcp.streaming_delays', schema=stats_schema,
        create_disposition=beam.io.BigQueryDisposition.CREATE_IF_NEEDED
            )
)
```

As with the previous section, we can start the simulator, and then start *avg02.py*. When I did this, the resulting aggregations were getting produced every 5 minutes, but within each 5 minute period, the events being notified about covered a 150 minute range (because the 30x simulation processes 150 minutes of data in 5 minutes).

The stream processing engine was applying the sliding windows based on the time on a wall clock. We, however, want it to apply the window based on the timestamp within the images.

How do we do that?

## Using Event Timestamps

We have to add an attribute at the time we publish the events (in *simulate.py*):

```
publisher.publish(topic, event_data.encode(), EventTimeStamp=timestamp)
```

Then, in our Beam pipeline, when read from Pub/Sub, we should tell the pipeline to disregard the publish time in Pub/Sub and use this attribute of the message as the timestamp instead:

```
| 'read:{}'.format(event_name) >> beam.io.ReadFromPubSub(
        topic=topic_name, timestamp_attribute='EventTimeStamp')
```

With this change, when I run the query:

```
SELECT * FROM dsongcp.streaming_delays
WHERE AIRPORT = 'ATL'
ORDER BY END_TIME DESC
```

I get rows approximately 5 minutes apart as expected:

| Row | AIR PORT | AVG_ARR_DELAY | AVG_DEP_DELAY | NUM_FLIGHTS | START_TIME | END_TIME |
|-----|----------|---------------|---------------|-------------|------------|----------|
| 1 | ATL | 35.72222222222222 | 13.666666666666666 | 48 | 2015-05-01 02:24:00 UTC | 2015-05-01 03:21:00 UTC |
| 2 | ATL | 35.25 | 8.717948717948717 | 59 | 2015-05-01 02:15:00 UTC | 2015-05-01 03:12:00 UTC |
| 3 | ATL | 38.666666666666664 | 9.882352941176471 | 52 | 2015-05-01 02:19:00 UTC | 2015-05-01 03:12:00 UTC |
| 4 | ATL | 38.473684210526315 | 5.916666666666667 | 55 | 2015-05-01 02:15:00 UTC | 2015-05-01 03:08:00 UTC |
| 5 | ATL | 35.111111111111114 | 5.53125 | 50 | 2015-05-01 02:15:00 UTC | 2015-05-01 03:03:00 UTC |

The reported times are not exactly 5 minutes apart because the reported times correspond to the earliest/latest flight in Atlanta within the time window. Note also that the length of the time window is approximately an hour.

It is likely, however, that Cloud Shell or your local laptop will struggle to keep up with the event stream. We need to be executing this pipeline in Dataflow in a serverless way.

## Executing the Stream Processing

To run the Beam pipeline in Cloud Dataflow, all I have to do is to change the runner (see *avg03.py* in the GitHub repository):

```
argv = [
        '--project={0}'.format(project),
        '--job_name=ch04avgdelay',
        '--streaming',
    ...
        '--runner=DataflowRunner'
    ]
```

Before we start this pipeline, though, it is a good idea to delete the rows already written to the BigQuery table by *avg02.py* in the previous section. The easiest way to do this is to run the following SQL DML command to *truncate* the table:

```
TRUNCATE TABLE dsongcp.streaming_delays
```

Running *avg03.py* will launch off a Dataflow job. If you now browse to the Cloud Platform console, to the Cloud Dataflow section, you will see that a new streaming job has started and that the pipeline looks like that shown in Figure 4-7.

The pipeline processes flight events as they stream into Pub/Sub, aggregates them into time windows, and streams the resulting statistics into BigQuery.

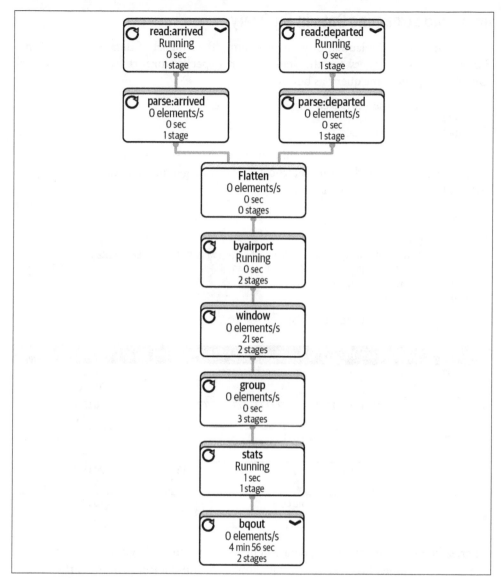

*Figure 4-7. The streaming pipeline to compute delay statistics in real time at each airport.*

## Analyzing Streaming Data in BigQuery

Two minutes after the launch of your program,[23] the first set of data will make it into BigQuery. You can query for the statistics for a specific airport from the BigQuery console using the same query as before:

```
SELECT * FROM dsongcp.streaming_delays
WHERE AIRPORT = 'ATL'
ORDER BY END_TIME DESC
```

The cool thing is that we can do this querying even as the data is streaming! How would we get the latest data for all airports? We could get all the data for each airport, order it by time, and take the latest:

```
SELECT
    AIRPORT,
    ARRAY_AGG(
        STRUCT(AVG_ARR_DELAY, AVG_DEP_DELAY, NUM_FLIGHTS, END_TIME)
        ORDER BY END_TIME DESC LIMIT 1) AS a
FROM dsongcp.streaming_delays d
GROUP BY AIRPORT
```

The results look something like this:

| Row | AIRPORT | a.AVG_ARR_DELAY | a.AVG_DEP_DELAY | a.NUM_FLIGHTS | a.END_TIME |
|-----|---------|-----------------|-----------------|---------------|------------|
| 1 | BUR | -6.8 | -5.666666666666667 | 8 | 2015-05-01 03:26:00 UTC |
| 2 | HNL | 17.11111111111111 | -3.7777777777777777 | 18 | 2015-05-01 03:46:00 UTC |
| 3 | CVG | -7.75 | null | 4 | 2015-05-01 03:48:00 UTC |
| 4 | PHL | 5.636363636363637 | 16.5 | 13 | 2015-05-01 03:48:00 UTC |
| 5 | IND | 40.6 | null | 5 | 2015-05-01 03:45:00 UTC |

Queries like these on streaming data will be useful when we begin to build our dashboard. For example, the first query will allow us to build a time series chart of delays at a specific airport. The second query will allow us to build a map of average delays across the country.

---

[23] Recall that we are computing aggregates over 60 minutes every 5 minutes. Cloud Dataflow treats the first "full" window as happening 65 minutes into the simulation. Because we are simulating at 30 times speed, this is two minutes on your clock.

# Real-Time Dashboard

Now that we have streaming data in BigQuery and a way to analyze it as it is stream-ing in, we can create a dashboard that shows departure and arrival delays in context. Two maps can help explain our contingency table–based model to end users: current arrival delays across the country and current departure delays across the country.

To pull the data to populate these charts, we need to add a BigQuery data source in Data Studio. Although Data Studio supports specifying the query directly in the user interface, it is much better to create a view in BigQuery and use that view as a data source in Data Studio. BigQuery views have a few advantages over queries that you type into Data Studio: they tend to be reusable across reports and visualization tools, there is only one place to change if an error is detected, and BigQuery views map bet-ter to access privileges (Cloud Identity and Access Management roles) based on the columns they need to access.

Here is the query that I used to create the view:

```
CREATE OR REPLACE VIEW dsongcp.airport_delays AS
WITH delays AS (
    SELECT d.*, a.LATITUDE, a.LONGITUDE
    FROM dsongcp.streaming_delays d
    JOIN dsongcp.airports a USING(AIRPORT)
    WHERE a.AIRPORT_IS_LATEST = 1
)

SELECT
    AIRPORT,
    CONCAT(LATITUDE, ',', LONGITUDE) AS LOCATION,
    ARRAY_AGG(
        STRUCT(AVG_ARR_DELAY, AVG_DEP_DELAY, NUM_FLIGHTS, END_TIME)
        ORDER BY END_TIME DESC LIMIT 1) AS a
FROM delays
GROUP BY AIRPORT, LONGITUDE, LATITUDE
```

This is slightly different from the second query in the previous section in that it also adds the location of the airport by joining against the airports table.

Having saved the view in BigQuery, we can create a data source for the view in Data Studio, just as we did in the previous chapter:

- Visit *https://datastudio.google.com*.
- Create a BigQuery data source, point it to the `airport_delays` view, and connect to it.
- Change the location field from Text to a Geo | Latitude, Longitude, then click Create Report.
- Add a Geo Chart to the report.

- Specify the location field as the geo dimension (see Figure 4-8).
- Specify average departure delay as the dimension and United States as the zoom level.
- Change the style so that the color bar includes all areas.
- Repeat for the arrival delay.

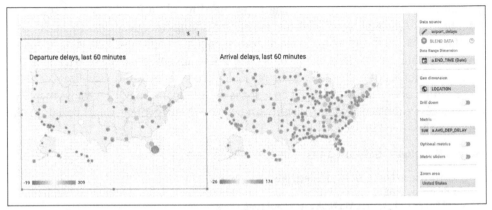

*Figure 4-8. Dashboard of latest flight data from across the United States.*

It is worth reflecting on what we did in this section. We processed streaming data in Cloud Dataflow, creating 60-minute moving averages that we streamed into Big-Query. We then created a view in BigQuery that would show the latest data for each airport, even as it was streaming in. We connected that to a dashboard in Data Studio. Every time the dashboard is refreshed, it pulls new data from the view, which in turn dynamically reflects the latest data in BigQuery.

# Summary

In this chapter, we discussed how to build a real-time analysis pipeline to carry out streaming analytics and populate real-time dashboards. In this book, we are using a dataset that is not available in real time. Therefore, we simulated the creation of a real-time feed so that I could demonstrate how to build a streaming ingest pipeline. Building the simulation also gives us a handy test tool—no longer do we need to wait for an interesting event to happen. We can simply play back a recorded event!

In the process of building out the simulation, we realized that time handling in the original dataset was problematic. Therefore, we improved the handling of time in the original data and created a new dataset with UTC timestamps and local offsets. This is the dataset that we will use going forward.

We also looked at the reference architecture for handling streaming data in Google Cloud Platform. First, receive your data in Cloud Pub/Sub so that the messages can be received asynchronously. Process the Cloud Pub/Sub messages in Cloud Dataflow, computing aggregations on the data as needed, and stream either the raw data or aggregate data (or both) to BigQuery. We worked with all three Google Cloud products (Cloud Pub/Sub, Cloud Dataflow, and BigQuery) using the Google Cloud client libraries in Python. However, in none of these cases did we ever need to create a virtual machine ourselves—these are all serverless and autoscaled offerings. We thus were able to concentrate on writing code, letting the platform manage the rest.

# Suggested Resources

The Apache Beam website has interactive coding exercises (*https://oreil.ly/nBsvI*), called Katas, that provide an excellent hands-on way to learn streaming concepts and how to implement them using Beam.

Dataflow templates are prewritten Apache Beam pipelines that are handy for data migration. In the chapter, we mentioned the Dataflow template for ingesting data from Pub/Sub into BigQuery. Dataflow templates also exist for non-Google sources. For example, there is a Dataflow connector from SAP HANA to BigQuery, as described in the 2017 Google blog post "Using Apache Beam and Cloud Dataflow to Integrate SAP HANA and BigQuery" (*https://oreil.ly/l6XNl*) by Babu Prasad Elumalai and Mark Shalda. That particular connector is written in Java.

This tutorial walks you through the process of creating your own Dataflow template (*https://oreil.ly/CBg0O*). Any Dataflow pipeline can be made into a template for easy sharing and convenient launch.

In this 2021 article, "Processing Billions of Events in Real Time at Twitter," Twitter engineers Lu Zhang and Chukwudiuto Malife describe how Twitter processes 400 billion events (*https://oreil.ly/bQEke*) in real time using Dataflow.

# CHAPTER 5

# Interactive Data Exploration with Vertex AI Workbench

In every major field of study, there is usually a towering figure who did much of the seminal work and blazed the trail for what that particular discipline would evolve into. Classical physics has Newton, relativity has Einstein, game theory has John Nash, and so on. When it comes to computational statistics (the field of study that develops computationally efficient methods for carrying out statistical operations), the towering figure is John W. Tukey. At Bell Labs, he collaborated with John von Neumann on early computer designs soon after World War II—famously, Tukey was responsible for coining the word *bit*. Later, at Princeton (where he founded its statistics department), Tukey collaborated with James Cooley to develop the fast Fourier transform, one of the first examples of using divide-and-conquer to address a formidable computational challenge.

While Tukey was responsible for many "hard science" mathematical and engineering innovations, some of his most enduring work is about the distinctly softer side of science. Unsatisfied that most of statistics overemphasized confirmatory data analysis (i.e., statistical hypothesis testing such as paired *t*-tests),[1] Tukey developed a variety of approaches to do what he termed *exploratory data analysis* (EDA)[2] and many practical statistical approximations. It was Tukey who developed the box plot, jack-knifing, range test, median-median regression, and so on and gave these eminently practical methods a solid mathematical grounding by motivating them in the context of simple conceptual models that are applicable to a wide variety of datasets. In this chapter, we follow Tukey's approach of carrying out exploratory data analysis to identify

---

1 See this Wikipedia article (*https://oreil.ly/62pYc*) for an excellent overview of statistical hypotheses testing.

2 John Tukey. *Exploratory Data Analysis*. Addison-Wesley, 1977.

important variables, discover underlying structure, develop parsimonious models, and use those models to identify unusual patterns and values.

 All of the code snippets in this chapter are available in the folder *05_bqnotebook* of the book's GitHub repository (*https://github.com/ GoogleCloudPlatform/data-science-on-gcp*). See the *README.md* file in that directory for instructions on how to do the steps described in this chapter.

# Exploratory Data Analysis

Ever since Tukey introduced the world to the value of EDA in 1977, the traditional first step for any data scientist has been to analyze raw data by using a variety of graphical techniques. This is not a fixed set of methods or plots; rather, it's an approach meant to develop insight into a dataset and enable the development of robust statistical models. Specifically, as a data scientist, you should do the following:

- Test any underlying assumptions, such as that a particular value will always be present or will always lie within a certain range. For example, as discussed in Chapter 2, the distribution of the distance between any pair of airports might help verify whether the distance is the same across the dataset or whether it reflects the actual flight distance.

- Use intuition and logic to identify important variables. Verify that these variables are, indeed, important as expected. For example, plotting the relationship between departure delay and arrival delay might validate assumptions about the recording of these variables.

- Discover underlying structures in the data (i.e., relationships between important variables and situations such as the data falling into specific statistical regimes). It might be useful to examine whether the season (summer versus winter) has an impact on how often flight delays can be made up.

- Develop a parsimonious model—a simple model with explanatory power, that you can use to hypothesize about what reasonable values in the data look like. If there is a simple relationship between departure delay and arrival delay, values of either delay that are far off the trendline might warrant further examination.

- Detect outliers, anomalies, and other inexplicable data values. This depends on having that parsimonious model. Thus, further examination of outliers from the simple trend between departure and arrival delays might lead to the discovery that such values off the trendline correspond to rerouted flights.

- Discover any potential overarching data quality problems such as the issues we found in Chapter 3 with time being recorded without being UTC.

To carry out exploratory data analysis, it is necessary to load the data in a form that makes interactive analysis possible. In this chapter, we load data into Google Big-Query, explore the data in Vertex AI Workbench, carry out quality control based on what we discover about the dataset, build a new model, and evaluate the model to ensure that it is better than the model we built in Chapter 4. As we go about loading the data and exploring it and move on to building models and evaluating them, we'll discuss a variety of considerations that come up, from security to pricing.

Both exploratory data analysis and the dashboard creation discussed in Chapter 3 involve the creation of graphics. However, the steps differ in two ways—in terms of the purpose and in terms of the audience. The aim of dashboard creation is to crowd-source insight into the working of models from end users and is, therefore, primarily about presenting an explanation of the models to end users. In Chapter 3, I recom-mended doing it very early in your development cycle, but that advice was more about Agile development and getting feedback early than about statistical rigor.[3] The aim of EDA is for you, the data engineer, to develop insights about the data before you delve into developing sophisticated models. The audience for EDA is typically other members of your team and yourself, not end users. In some cases, especially if you uncover strange artifacts in the data, the audience could be the data engineering team that produces the dataset you are working with. For example, when we discov-ered the problem that the times were being reported in local time, with no UTC off-sets, we could have relayed that information back to the US Bureau of Transportation Statistics (BTS).[4] In any case, the assumption is that the audience for an EDA graphic is statistically sophisticated. Although you probably would not include a violin plot in a dashboard meant for end users,[5] you would have no compunctions about using it in an EDA chart that is meant for data scientists.

Doing exploratory data analysis on large datasets poses a few challenges. To test that a particular value will always be present, for example, you would need to check every row of a tabular dataset, and if that dataset is many millions of rows, these tests can take hours. An interactive ability to quickly explore large datasets is indispensable. On Google Cloud Platform, BigQuery provides the ability to run Cloud SQL queries on unindexed datasets (i.e., your raw data) in a matter of seconds even if the datasets

---

3 James Shore. *The Art of Agile Development*, 2nd ed. With Diana Larsen, Gitte Klitgaard, and Shane Warden. O'Reilly Media, 2021.

4 I did confirm with the BTS via email that the times in the dataset were, indeed, in the local time zone of the corresponding airport. The BTS being a government agency that was making the data freely available, I didn't broach the matter of them producing a separate dataset with UTC timestamps. In a contractual relationship with a vendor, however, this is the type of change you might request as a result of EDA.

5 A violin plot is a way of visualizing probability density functions. See the seaborn documentation (*https://oreil.ly/BT3nv*) for examples of violin plots.

are in the terabyte scale. Therefore, in this chapter, we load the flight data into BigQuery.

## Anscombe's Quartet

The statistician Francis Anscombe illustrated that graphs are essential to good statistical analysis using a very powerful example. All four of the datasets shown in Figure 5-1 have the same mean, variance, linear fit, and correlation (to two decimal places) but are obviously quite different from one another.

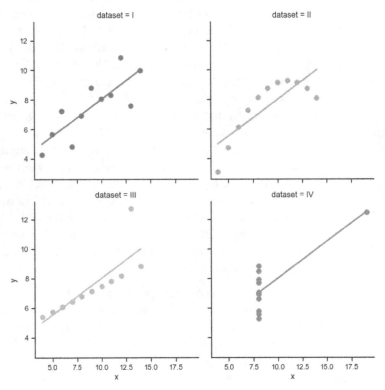

*Figure 5-1. Ansombe's Quartet. Figure from "Graphs in Statistical Analysis" by Francis Anscombe in* American Statistician *27, no. 1 (1973): 17–21 as recreated in the seaborn documentation.*

Anscombe used the quartet to emphasize that summary statistics are not a substitute for graphic data—it's particularly important to graph outliers to develop a holistic understanding of the data.

Identifying outliers and underlying structure typically involves using univariate and bivariate plots.[6] The graphs themselves can be created using Python plotting libraries—I use a mixture of *Matplotlib* (*https://matplotlib.org*) and *seaborn* (*http:// seaborn.pydata.org*) to do this. The networking overhead of moving data between storage and the graphics engine can become prohibitive if I carry out data exploration on my laptop—for exploration of large datasets to be interactive, we need to bring the analytics closer to the data. Therefore, we will want to use a cloud computer (not my laptop) to carry out graph generation. Generating graphics on a cloud computer poses a display challenge because the graphs are being generated on a Compute Engine instance that is *headless*—that is, it has no input or output devices. A Compute Engine instance has no keyboard, mouse, or monitor, and frequently has no graphics card.[7] Such a machine is accessed purely through a network connection. Fortunately, desktop programs and interactive read–eval–print loops (REPLs) are no longer necessary to create visualizations. Instead, notebook servers such as Jupyter (*https://jupyter.org*) have become the standard way that data scientists create graphs and disseminate executable reports. On Google Cloud Platform, Vertex AI Workbench provides a fully managed way to run Jupyter notebooks that connect to Google Cloud Platform services.

## Exploration with SQL

Let's start in the BigQuery console by exploring the time-corrected dataset that we created in BigQuery in Chapter 4:

```
SELECT
    ORIGIN,
    AVG(DEP_DELAY) AS dep_delay,
    AVG(ARR_DELAY) AS arr_delay,
    COUNT(ARR_DELAY) AS num_flights
  FROM
    dsongcp.flights_tzcorr
  GROUP BY
    ORIGIN
```

---

6 A *univariate graph* is a graph of just one variable. For example, we might plot the histogram of arrival delays. A *bivariate graph* is a graph of two variables. For example, we might plot the median taxi-out time by airport.

7 Special general purpose graphics processing unit (GPU) instances exist (*https://oreil.ly/oeNQp*) that are used for high-performance computing applications, but for generating the graphs in this chapter, CPU instances are sufficient.

The result consists of 322 airports (the order you get might be different):

| Row | ORIGIN | dep_delay | arr_delay | num_flights |
|---|---|---|---|---|
| 1 | OTZ | 5.209103840682787 | 6.562952243125903 | 691 |
| 2 | HPN | 11.782807151007983 | 9.087898089171965 | 7850 |
| 3 | SJU | 9.8362379921783 | 2.506036485508635 | 26257 |
| 4 | ANC | 3.2497373643048966 | -0.4801384732734849 | 17043 |
| 5 | CVG | 8.826792206581548 | 5.244408048666357 | 21370 |

Let's look at just the major airports, which we can define as airports that have on average more than 10 flights a day. To do this we can filter by airports that have a sufficient number of flights:

```
WITH all_airports AS (
  SELECT
    ORIGIN,
    AVG(DEP_DELAY) AS dep_delay,
    AVG(ARR_DELAY) AS arr_delay,
    COUNT(ARR_DELAY) AS num_flights
  FROM
    dsongcp.flights_tzcorr
  GROUP BY
    ORIGIN
)

SELECT * FROM all_airports WHERE num_flights > 3650
ORDER BY dep_delay DESC
```

We are thresholding the number of flights at 3,650 because there are 365 days in the dataset. The result, when I did it, was:

| Row | ORIGIN | dep_delay | arr_delay | num_flights |
|---|---|---|---|---|
| 1 | ORD | 13.305085522847 | 7.596119952650316 | 304120 |
| 2 | EWR | 13.182294215975096 | 3.9227994696288535 | 107849 |
| 3 | BWI | 12.893989460498512 | 6.768316724436742 | 92320 |
| 4 | LGA | 12.764120915158792 | 5.043357442317552 | 103281 |
| 5 | IAD | 12.23048266485387 | 4.505307971508886 | 36643 |

It makes sense that airports that serve major American cities experience the worst departure delays (ORD serves Chicago, EWR and LGA serve New York City, and BWI and IAD serve Washington, DC).

What if we restrict this analysis to January, reducing the number of flights threshold to 310 since there are 31 days in January?

```
WITH all_airports AS (
  SELECT
```

```
    ORIGIN,
    AVG(DEP_DELAY) AS dep_delay,
    AVG(ARR_DELAY) AS arr_delay,
    COUNT(ARR_DELAY) AS num_flights
FROM
    dsongcp.flights_tzcorr
WHERE EXTRACT(MONTH FROM FL_DATE) = 1
GROUP BY
    ORIGIN
)

SELECT * FROM all_airports WHERE num_flights > 310
ORDER BY dep_delay DESC
```

Now, we get a somewhat stranger set of airports:

| Row | ORIGIN | dep_delay | arr_delay | num_flights |
|-----|--------|-----------|-----------|-------------|
| 1 | ASE | 20.86779661016949 | 16.988095238095244 | 588 |
| 2 | ORD | 19.96205128205124 | 17.016131923283723 | 22316 |
| 3 | JAC | 18.787172011661802 | 16.096209912536445 | 343 |
| 4 | SBN | 18.491891891891886 | 16.326975476839234 | 367 |
| 5 | FAT | 18.12554744525547 | 17.63823529411766 | 680 |

I don't recognize four of the five airports on this list, and I'm a rather frequent traveler. A short Google Search later, I learned that ASE is a ski resort (Aspen, Colorado) as is JAC (Jackson Hole, Wyoming). This makes sense—ski resorts are open only in winter, have to load up bulky baggage, and probably suffer more weather-related delays.

Using the average delay to characterize airports is not ideal, though. What if most flights to Aspen were actually on time but a few highly delayed flights (perhaps flights delayed by several hours) are skewing the average? I'd like to see a distribution function of the values of arrival and departure delays. BigQuery itself cannot help us with graphs—instead, we need to tie the BigQuery backend to a graphical, interactive exploration tool. Data scientists tend to use Jupyter Notebooks for EDA, so I'll use Vertex AI Workbench, which offers fully managed Jupyter Notebooks.

## Reading a Query Explanation

Before I move on to Notebooks, though, we want to see if there are any red flags regarding query performance on our table in BigQuery. In the BigQuery console, there is a tab (next to Results) labeled "Execution details." Figure 5-2 shows the explanation of the January query.

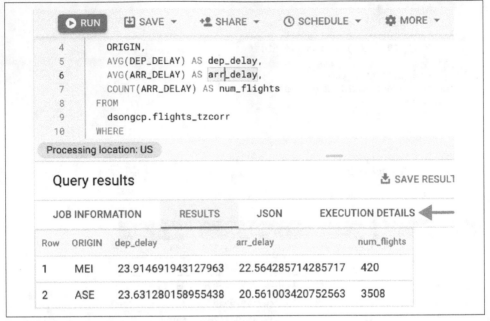

```
     4        ORIGIN,
     5        AVG(DEP_DELAY) AS dep_delay,
     6        AVG(ARR_DELAY) AS arr_delay,
     7        COUNT(ARR_DELAY) AS num_flights
     8      FROM
     9        dsongcp.flights_tzcorr
    10      WHERE
```

Processing location: US

## Query results                                                    ⬇ SAVE RESULT

JOB INFORMATION        RESULTS        JSON        EXECUTION DETAILS ◀━━━

| Row | ORIGIN | dep_delay | arr_delay | num_flights |
|-----|--------|-----------|-----------|-------------|
| 1 | MEI | 23.914691943127963 | 22.564285714285717 | 420 |
| 2 | ASE | 23.631280158955438 | 20.561003420752563 | 3508 |

*Figure 5-2. The explanation of a query in BigQuery.*

Our query has been executed in three stages. Expand each of the stages to see their details:

- The first stage (see Figure 5-3) pulls the origin, departure delay, arrival delay, and date for each flight and filters the result by looking at the month. Then, it groups them by origin, computes averages on each shard of data, and writes them to __stage00_output. __stage00_output is organized by the hash of the ORIGIN.

- The second stage (see Figure 5-4) reads the fields organized by ORIGIN, computes the average delays and count (but starting from the SHARD averages), and filters the result to ensure that the count is greater than 310. Note that the query has been optimized a bit—my WHERE clause was actually outside the WITH statement, but it has been moved here so as to minimize the amount of data written out to __stage01_output.

- The third stage (see Figure 5-5) simply sorts the rows by departure delay and writes to the output.

| S00: Input | | Avg: | | | | | Input: | 5,819,079 |
|---|---|---|---|---|---|---|---|---|
| | ^ | | 5 ms | 44 ms | 196 ms | 5 ms | | |
| | | Max: | | | | | Output: | 936 |
| | | | 11 ms | 47 ms | 212 ms | 5 ms | | |

| READ | $2:ORIGIN, $3:DEP_DELAY, $4:ARR_DELAY, $1:FL_DATE |
|---|---|
| | FROM dsongcp.flights_tzcorr |
| | WHERE equal(extract($1, 2), 1) |
| AGGREGATE | GROUP BY $30 := $2 |
| | $20 := SHARD_AVG($3) |
| | $21 := SHARD_AVG($4) |
| | $22 := COUNT($4) |
| WRITE | $30, $20, $21, $22 |
| | TO __stage00_output |
| | BY HASH($30) |

*Figure 5-3. The first stage.*

| S01: Aggregate+ | | Avg: | | | | | Input: | 936 |
|---|---|---|---|---|---|---|---|---|
| | ^ | | 1 ms | 0 ms | 3 ms | 1 ms | | |
| | | Max: | | | | | Output: | 135 |
| | | | 1 ms | 0 ms | 3 ms | 1 ms | | |

| READ | $30, $20, $21, $22 |
|---|---|
| | FROM __stage00_output |
| FILTER | greater($12, 310) |
| AGGREGATE | GROUP BY $40 := $30 |
| | $10 := ROOT_AVG($20) |
| | $11 := ROOT_AVG($21) |
| | $12 := SUM_OF_COUNTS($22) |
| WRITE | $40, $10, $11, $12 |
| | TO __stage01_output |

*Figure 5-4. The second stage.*

| S02: Output | | Avg: | | | | | Input: | 135 |
|---|---|---|---|---|---|---|---|---|
| | ^ | | 2 ms | 0 ms | 6 ms | 23 ms | | |
| | | Max: | | | | | Output: | 135 |
| | | | 2 ms | 0 ms | 6 ms | 23 ms | | |

| READ | $40, $10, $11, $12 |
|---|---|
| | FROM __stage01_output |
| SORT | $10 DESC |
| WRITE | $50, $51, $52, $53 |
| | TO __stage02_output |

*Figure 5-5. The third stage.*

Based on the preceding second-stage optimization, is it possible to write the query itself in a better way? Yes, by using the HAVING keyword:

```
SELECT
  ORIGIN,
  AVG(DEP_DELAY) AS dep_delay,
  AVG(ARR_DELAY) AS arr_delay,
  COUNT(ARR_DELAY) AS num_flights
FROM
  dsongcp.flights_tzcorr
WHERE EXTRACT(MONTH FROM FL_DATE) = 1
GROUP BY
  ORIGIN
HAVING num_flights > 310
ORDER BY dep_delay DESC
```

In the rest of this chapter, I will use this form of the query that avoids the WITH statement. By using the HAVING keyword, we are not relying on the query optimizer to minimize the amount of data written to __stage01_output.

What do the times in the graphics mean? Each stage (see Figure 5-6) is broken into four steps: wait, read, compute, and write. The average and maximum time spent in each of these steps by the BigQuery workers is reported. So, in another example shown in Figure 5-6, BigQuery spends an average of 353 milliseconds (37 + 115 + 195 + 6) in this stage. A worker could spend as much as 608 milliseconds (49 + 308 + 242 + 9) in it, though.

*Figure 5-6. Average and maximum time spent by BigQuery workers by steps. Each part of each stage in the query explanation is depicted by a color bar that represents the fraction of time spent in that part.*

The length of the bar is the time taken by the most time-consuming step in the stage—so the length of the bar corresponds to 308 ms and the color in each bar is the fraction of that time spent in this step. In other words, the bars are all normalized to the time taken by the longest step (wait, read, compute, or write). A large difference between the average and the maximum (as in the read step of Figure 5-6) indicates a skew—there are some workers who are doing a lot more work than others. Sometimes, it is inherent to the query, but at other times, it might be possible to rework the storage or partitions to reduce such skew.[8]

The wait time is the time spent waiting for the necessary compute resources to become available—a very high value here indicates a job that could not be immediately scheduled on the cluster. A high wait time could occur if you are using the Big-Query flat-rate plan and someone else in your organization is already consuming all of the paid-for capacity. The solution would be to run your job at a different time, make your job smaller, or negotiate with the group that is using the available resources. The read step reads the data required at this stage from the table or from the output of the previous stage. A high value of read time indicates that you might consider reworking the query so that most of the data is read in the initial stages. The compute step carries out the computation required—if you run into high values here, consider whether you can carry out some of the operations in postprocessing or if you could omit the use of user-defined functions (UDFs).[9] The write step writes to temporary storage or to the response and is mainly a function of the amount of data being written out in each stage—optimization of this step typically involves moving filtering options to occur in the innermost query (or earliest stage), although as we saw earlier, the BigQuery optimizer can do some of this automatically.

For all three stages in our query, the read step is what takes the most amount of time, indicating that our query is I/O bound and that the basic cost of reading the data is what dominates the query. It is clear from the numbers in the input column (6 million to 936 to 135) that we are already doing quite well at funneling the data through and processing most of the data in earlier stages. We also noticed from the explanation that BigQuery has already optimized things by moving the filtering step to the earliest possible stage—there is no way to move it any earlier because it is not possible to filter on the number of flights until that value is computed. On the other hand, if this is a frequent sort of filter, it might be helpful to add a table indicating the traffic at each airport and join with this table instead of computing the aggregate each time. It might also be possible to achieve an approximation to this by adding a column indicating some characteristic (such as the population) of the metropolitan area that each airport serves. For now, without any idea of the kinds of airports that the typical user of this dataset will be interested in, there is little to be done. We are determined to process all the data, and processing all the data requires time spent reading that data.

---

8 Reducing the skew is not just about reducing the time taken by the workers who have a lot to do. You should also see if you can rework the query to combine the work carried out by the underworked workers, so that you have fewer workers overall.

9 BigQuery supports UDFs in JavaScript, but the excessive use of UDFs can slow down your query, and certain UDFs can be high-compute queries (*https://oreil.ly/NnsNW*).

If we don't need statistics from all the data, we could consider sampling the data and computing our statistics on that sample instead.

## Exploratory Data Analysis in Vertex AI Workbench

Data scientists have moved en masse to using notebooks because notebooks greatly streamline the workflow of developing, visualizing, collaborating, and publishing in science.[10] The contrast between the user experience of a Jupyter Notebook and the way exploratory data analysis was carried out a few years ago is stark. Take, for example, Figure 5-7, which appears in one of my papers about different ways to track storms in weather radar images (*https://oreil.ly/6pcZF*). Just this single graphic required wrangling multiple languages (C++, R, Java), concepts (distributed programming, statistics), data formats (CSV, PNG, LaTeX, PDF), and collaboration mechanisms (FTP, email)![11] Today, I'd do it all in a Jupyter Notebook with the big data analysis carried out in BigQuery or Dataflow.

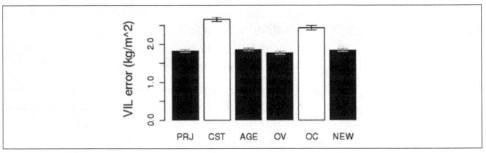

*Figure 5-7. Graph created using a complex workflow.*

---

10 Jupyter Notebooks are a realization of the *literate programming* concept envisioned by Donald Knuth in 1984. By allowing data scientists to interweave statistical and business logic in code and the output of that code within a literate statistical programming paradigm, notebooks foster replicability and reuse.

11 If you are interested in the gory details: Figure 5-7 was created by running the methods in question (PRJ, CST, etc.) on a large dataset of weather radar imagery and computing various evaluation metrics (VIL error in the graphic). For performance reasons, this was done in C++. The metric for each pair of images was written out to a text file (a different text file for each method), and it is the aggregates of those metrics that are reported in Figure 5-7. The text files had to be wrangled from the cluster of machines on which they were written out, combined by key (the method used to track storms), and then aggregated. This code, essentially a MapReduce operation, was written in Java. The resulting aggregate files were read by an R program that ranked the methods, determined the appropriate shading, and wrote out an image file in PNG format. These PNG images were incorporated into a LaTeX report, and a compiler run to create a shareable document in PDF from the LaTeX and PNG sources. It was this PDF of the paper that we could disseminate to interested colleagues. If the colleague then suggested a change, we'd go through the process all over again. The ordering of the programs—C++, followed by Java, followed by R, followed by LaTeX, followed by attaching the PDF to an email —was nontrivial, and there were times when we skipped something in between, resulting in incorrect graphics or text that didn't match the graphs.

---

# Jupyter Notebooks

JupyterLab (*https://jupyter.org*) is open source software that provides an interactive scientific computing experience in a variety of languages, including Python, R, Julia, and Scala. The key unit of work is a Jupyter Notebook, which is a document that contains code, visualizations, and explanatory text. The code in the document is executed on and served from a web server that runs JupyterLab.

A key issue with notebooks is how to manage the web servers that serve them. Running the notebook server on our laptop will work, but is not ideal. Instead, we want the notebook server to run on a cloud machine for the following reasons:

- Because the code is executed on the notebook server, we want the notebook server to be able to handle bigger datasets. It is easier to get a more powerful machine on the public cloud than it is to upgrade one's laptop. You can simplify managing the provisioning of notebook servers by running them on demand in the public cloud. This way, we can stop the machines when we leave for the day, instead of paying for machines even when we are not at work.

- Data science workloads such as machine learning require heavy, repetitive computation—typically, we scale up such workloads using GPUs. However, GPUs are expensive and become superseded by better hardware rather quickly. Ideally, you want to be able to add/remove GPUs on demand from these machines, rather than pay for GPUs all the time that we are using notebooks.

- A common pattern is to develop on small datasets and basic hardware and then, once we have the code working, to execute the code on large datasets on a more powerful machine. This ability to change the infrastructure is possible on the public cloud.

- We might even schedule the execution of these jobs periodically, or in response to an event such as the arrival of new data.

Once we say that we are going to run notebooks ephemerally on hardware that depends on the computations that we are doing, lifecycle management becomes quite important. Vertex AI Workbench on Google Cloud gives us a fully managed notebook experience.

To start a fully managed notebook in Google Cloud, visit the GCP web console, navigate to Vertex AI Workbench, and choose the tab for a Google-managed notebook. Then, create a notebook with the name dsongcp-ch5. Look at the Advanced settings and note that it's possible to add a GPU if we want (see Figure 5-8). Note also there is a default time period after which the notebook server will automatically shut down. We can always restart it by opening the notebook from the GCP console.

Vertex AI Workbench provides a hosted version of JupyterLab on Google Cloud; it knows how to authenticate against Google Cloud so as to provide easy access to

Cloud Storage, BigQuery, Cloud Dataflow, Vertex AI Training, and so on. A few minutes after you launch a managed notebook, the console shows you a JupyterLab link. When you are done using the Notebooks instance, you can manually delete the instance from the web console. You can also stop the instance when you are not using it—you won't be charged for the CPU resources, which are the bulk of the cost, although resources like disks will continue to be charged for. As shown in Figure 5-8, this shutdown can be made to happen automatically after an idle time period that you specify.

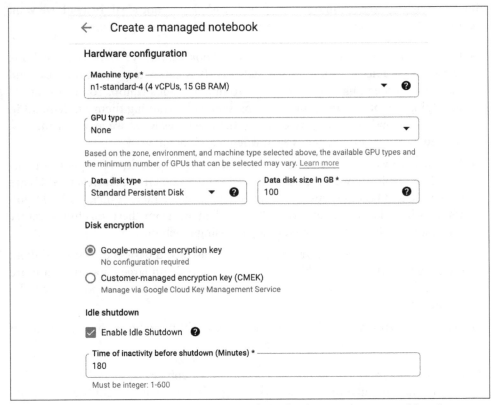

*Figure 5-8. Options when creating a managed notebook in Vertex AI Workbench.*

## Creating a Notebook

After you have launched the Notebooks instance and navigated to JupyterLab, you can create a new Python notebook from the launcher menu that it starts up with. Alternately, navigate to the folder in which you want this notebook to appear and select File > New Notebook.

A notebook contains two key types of cells: a *markdown* cell is a cell with text content,[12] whereas a *code* cell has source code. When you run a markdown cell, the cell contents are formatted nicely, whereas when you run a code cell, the notebook displays the output of *print* statements from that cell.

For example, suppose that you type into a notebook the contents of Figure 5-9 (with the first cell a markdown cell, and the second cell a Python cell).

You can run the cell your cursor is in by clicking Run (or use the keyboard shortcut Ctrl/Cmd + Shift + Enter). You could also run all cells by clicking "Run all cells." When you click this, the cells are evaluated, and the results rendered.

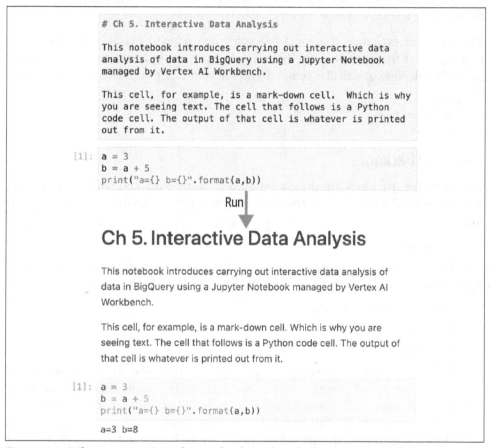

*Figure 5-9. What you type into the notebook (top) and what is rendered (bottom).*

---

12 The *README.md* files in the repository are another example of markdown files. Markdown is ubiquitous enough that it is worth learning the key syntax from a cheat sheet (*https://oreil.ly/QTXnS*).

Note that the markdown has been converted into a visual document, the Python code has been evaluated, and the resulting output printed out.

## Jupyter Commands

You can `git clone` the repository for this book within the notebook environment by typing:

```
!git clone https://github.com/GoogleCloudPlatform/data-science-on-gcp
```

You could have also used the git icon in Vertex AI Workbench or run the preceding command from a terminal. Regardless of how you interact with git, get into the habit of practicing source-code control on changed notebooks.

The use of the exclamation point (when you type `!git` into a code cell) is an indication to Jupyter that the line is not Python code, but is instead a shell command. If you have multiple lines of a shell command, you can start a cell with `%%bash`, for example:

```
%%bash
wget tensorflow ...
pip install ...
```

## Installing Packages

Which Python packages are already installed in Notebooks, and which ones will we have to install? One way to check which packages are installed is to type the following:

```
%pip freeze
```

This lists the Python packages installed. Another option is to add in imports for packages and see if they work. Let's do that with packages that I know that we'll need:

```
import matplotlib.pyplot as plt
import seaborn as sb
import pandas as pd
import numpy as np
```

*NumPy* is the canonical numerical Python library that provides efficient ways of working with arrays of numbers. *Pandas* is an extremely popular data analysis library that provides a way to do operations such as group by and filter on in-memory dataframes. *Matplotlib* is a Matlab-inspired module to create graphs in Python. *seaborn* provides extra graphics capabilities built on top of the basic functionality provided by Matplotlib. All these are open source packages that are installed in Vertex AI Workbench by default.

Had I needed a package that was not already installed, I could have installed it using `pip`. For example, to install the `pytz` package that we used in Chapter 4, execute this code within a cell:

---

```
%pip install pytz
```

Often, you will need to restart the Python kernel for the new package to be picked up (you can do this using the Restart Kernel button on the notebook ribbon user interface).

## Jupyter Magic for Google Cloud

When we used %%bash in the previous section, we were using a Jupyter *magic*, a syntactic element that marks what follows as special.[13] This is how Jupyter can support multiple interpreters or engines. Jupyter knows what language a cell is in by looking at the magic at its beginning. For example, try typing the following into a code cell:

```
%%html
This cell will print out a <b> HTML </b> string.
```

You should see the HTML rendering of that string being printed out on evaluation, as depicted in Figure 5-10.

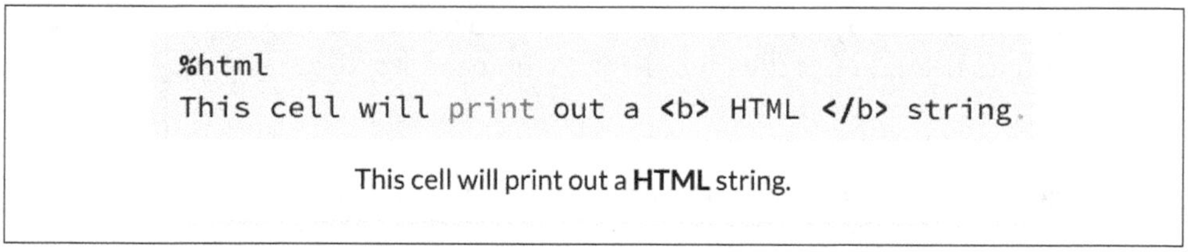

```
%html
This cell will print out a <b> HTML </b> string.

This cell will print out a HTML string.
```

*Figure 5-10. Jupyter magic for HTML rendering.*

Jupyter magics provide a mechanism to run a wide variety of languages and ways to add some more. The BigQuery Python package has added a few magics to make the interaction with Google Cloud Platform convenient.

For example, you can run a query on your BigQuery table using the %%bigquery magic environment that comes with Vertex AI Workbench:

```
%%bigquery
SELECT
  COUNTIF(arr_delay >= 15)/COUNT(arr_delay) AS frac_delayed
FROM dsongcp.flights_tzcorr
```

If you get the fraction of flights that are delayed, as shown in Figure 5-11, all is well.

If not, look at the error message and carry out appropriate remedial actions. You might need to authenticate yourself, set the project you are working in, or change permissions on the BigQuery table.

---

13 Magics use a syntax element that is not valid in the underlying language. In the case of notebooks in Python, this is the % symbol.

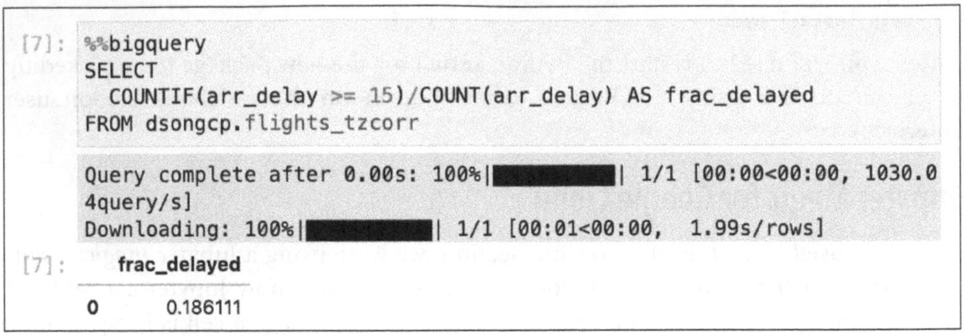

```
[7]: %%bigquery
SELECT
  COUNTIF(arr_delay >= 15)/COUNT(arr_delay) AS frac_delayed
FROM dsongcp.flights_tzcorr

Query complete after 0.00s: 100%|███████████| 1/1 [00:00<00:00, 1030.0
4query/s]
Downloading: 100%|██████████| 1/1 [00:01<00:00,  1.99s/rows]

[7]:    frac_delayed

    0      0.186111
```

*Figure 5-11. The %%bigquery magic environment that comes with Vertex AI Workbench.*

The fact that we refer to %%bigquery as a Jupyter magic should indicate that this is not pure Python—you can execute this only within a notebook environment. The magic, however, is simply a wrapper function for Python code.[14] If there is a piece of code that you'd ultimately want to run outside a notebook (perhaps as part of a scheduled script), it's better to use the underlying Python and not the magic pragma:[15]

```
sql = """
SELECT
  COUNTIF(arr_delay >= 15)/COUNT(arr_delay) AS frac_delayed
FROM dsongcp.flights_tzcorr
"""
from google.cloud import bigquery
bq = bigquery.Client()
df = bq.query(sql).to_dataframe()
print(df)
```

One way to use the underlying Python is to use the google.cloud.bigquery package —this allows us to use code independent of the notebook environment. This is, of course, the same bigquery package in the Cloud Client Library that we used in Chapters 2 and 4. The client library includes interconnections between BigQuery results and NumPy/Pandas to simplify the creation of graphics.

# Exploring Arrival Delays

Now that we have a notebook up and running, let's use it to do exploratory analysis of arrival delays because this is the variable we want to be able to predict.

---

14 See GitHub (*https://oreil.ly/YCxiW*) for the Python code being wrapped.

15 See *05_bqnotebook/exploration.ipynb* in the GitHub repository.

---

## Basic Statistics

To pull the arrival delays corresponding to the model created in Chapter 3 (i.e., of the arrival delay for flights that depart more than 10 minutes late), we can do the following:

```
%%bigquery df
SELECT ARR_DELAY, DEP_DELAY
FROM dsongcp.flights_tzcorr
WHERE DEP_DELAY >= 10
```

This code uses the `%%bigquery` magic to run the SQL statement and stores the result set into a Pandas dataframe named df. Recall that in Chapter 4, we did this using the Google Cloud Platform API.

After we have the dataframe, getting fundamental statistics about the two columns returned by the query is as simple as this:

```
df.describe()
```

This gives us the mean, standard deviation, minimum, maximum, and quartiles of the arrival and departure delays given that departure delay is more than 10 minutes, as illustrated in Figure 5-12 (see the `WHERE` clause of the query):

| [12]: | df.describe() | | |
|---|---|---|---|
| [12]: | | **ARR_DELAY** | **DEP_DELAY** |
| | **count** | 1.286778e+06 | 1.294778e+06 |
| | **mean** | 4.611797e+01 | 5.094516e+01 |
| | **std** | 6.360700e+01 | 6.151423e+01 |
| | **min** | -7.800000e+01 | 1.000000e+01 |
| | **25%** | 1.100000e+01 | 1.700000e+01 |
| | **50%** | 2.700000e+01 | 3.000000e+01 |
| | **75%** | 5.900000e+01 | 6.100000e+01 |
| | **max** | 1.971000e+03 | 1.988000e+03 |

*Figure 5-12. Getting the fundamental statistics of a Pandas dataframe.*

## Plotting Distributions

Beyond just the statistical capabilities of Pandas, we can also pass the Pandas dataframes and underlying NumPy arrays to plotting libraries like *seaborn*. For example, to plot a violin plot of our decision surface from Chapter 3 (i.e., of the arrival delay for flights that depart more than 10 minutes late), we can do the following:

```
sns.set_style("whitegrid")
ax = sns.violinplot(data=df, x='ARR_DELAY', inner='box', orient='h')
ax.axes.set_xlim(-50, 300);
```

This produces the graph shown in Figure 5-13.

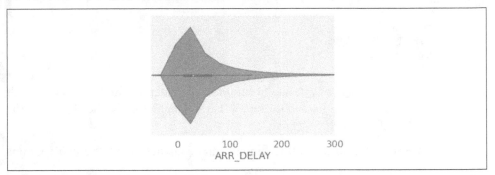

*Figure 5-13. Violin plot of arrival delay.*

A violin plot is a *kernel density plot;*[16] that is, it is an estimate of the probability distribution function (PDF).[17] We see that, even though the distribution peaks around 10 minutes (which is the mode), deviations around this peak are skewed toward larger delays than smaller ones. Importantly, we also notice that there is only one peak—the distribution is not, for example, bimodal.

Let's compare the violin plot for flights that depart more than 10 minutes late with the violin plot for flights that depart less than 10 minutes late and zoom in on the x-axis close to our 15-minute threshold. First, we pull all of the delays using the following:

```
%%bigquery df
SELECT ARR_DELAY, DEP_DELAY
FROM dsongcp.flights_tzcorr
```

In this query, I have dropped the WHERE clause. Instead, we will rely on Pandas to do the thresholding. I can now create a new column in the Pandas dataframe that is either True or False depending on whether the flight departed less than 10 minutes late:

```
df['ontime'] = df['DEP_DELAY'] < 10
```

We can graph this new Pandas dataframe using *seaborn:*

---

16 A kernel density plot (*https://oreil.ly/za47l*) is just a smoothed histogram—the challenge lies in figuring out how to smooth the histogram while balancing interpretability against the loss of information. Here, I'm just letting *seaborn* use its default settings for the smoothing bandwidth.

17 See the discussion of the PDF in Chapter 1.

---

```
ax = sns.violinplot(data=df, x='ARR_DELAY', y='ontime',
                    inner='box', orient='h')
ax.set_xlim(-50, 200)
```

The difference between the previous violin plot and this one is the inclusion of the ontime column. This results in a violin plot (see Figure 5-14) that illustrates how different flights that depart 10 minutes late are from flights that depart early.

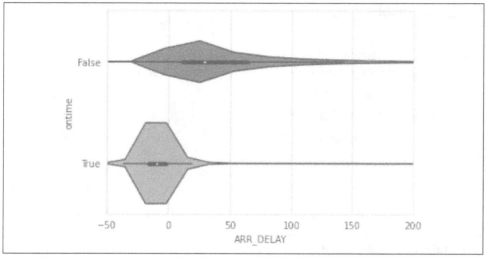

*Figure 5-14. Difference between violin plots of all late flights (top) versus on-time flights (bottom).*

> The angular peak of the top violin plot indicates that the *seaborn* default smoothing was too coarse. You can fix this by passing in a gridsize parameter:
>
> ```
> ax = sns.violinplot(data=df, x='ARR_DELAY', y='ontime',
> inner='box', orient='h', gridsize=1000)
> ```
>
> But doing so will make the computation take much longer. The notebook (*https://oreil.ly/CmzHa*) in the GitHub repository shows what the result looks like with greater smoothing.

As we discussed in Chapter 3, it is clear that the 10-minute threshold separates the dataset into two separate statistical regimes, so that the typical arrival delay for flights that depart more than 10 minutes late is skewed toward much higher values than for flights that depart more on time. We can see this in Figure 5-14, both from the shape of the violin plot and from the box plot that forms its center. Note how centered the on-time flights are versus the box plot (the dark line in the center) for delayed flights.[18]

However, the extremely long, skinny tail of the violin plot is a red flag—it is an indication that the dataset might pose modeling challenges. Let's investigate what is going on.

## Quality Control

We can continue writing queries in the notebook, but doing so on the BigQuery console gives me immediate feedback on syntax and logic errors. So, I switch over to the BigQuery console (*https://oreil.ly/cgJIR*) and type in my first query:

```
SELECT
  AVG(ARR_DELAY) AS arrival_delay
FROM
  dsongcp.flights_tzcorr
GROUP BY
  DEP_DELAY
ORDER BY
  DEP_DELAY
```

This should give me the average arrival delay associated with every value of departure delay (which, in this dataset, is stored as an integer number of minutes). I got back more than one thousand rows. Are there really more than one thousand unique values of DEP_DELAY? What's going on?

### Oddball values

To look at this further, let's add more elements to my initial query:

```
SELECT
  DEP_DELAY,
  AVG(ARR_DELAY) AS arrival_delay,
  COUNT(ARR_DELAY) AS numflights
FROM
  dsongcp.flights_tzcorr
GROUP BY
  DEP_DELAY
ORDER BY
  DEP_DELAY
```

The resulting table explains what's going on. The first few rows have only a few flights each:

---

18 I created this second, zoomed-in violin plot by adding `ax.set_xlim(-50, 50)`.

| Row | DEP_DELAY | arrival_delay | numflights |
|-----|-----------|---------------|------------|
| 1 | null | null | 0 |
| 2 | -82.0 | -80.0 | 1 |
| 3 | -68.0 | -87.0 | 1 |
| 4 | -61.0 | -77.0 | 1 |
| 5 | -56.0 | -26.0 | 1 |

However, departure delay values of a few minutes have hundreds of thousands of flights:

| | | | |
|-----|-----|----------------------|--------|
| 56 | 0.0 | -5.100334305600409 | 328442 |
| 57 | 1.0 | -4.188285855693881 | 159619 |
| 58 | 2.0 | -3.2246696399075128 | 121080 |
| 59 | 3.0 | -2.1957821784079146 | 104177 |
| 60 | 4.0 | -1.2101860730716607 | 92813 |

Oddball values that are such a small proportion of the data can probably be ignored. Moreover, if the flight does really leave 82 minutes early, I'm quite sure that you won't be on the flight, and if you are, you know that you will make the meeting. There is no reason to complicate our statistical modeling with such odd values.

### Outlier removal: Big data is different

How can you remove such outliers? There are two ways to filter the data: one would be based on the departure delay variable itself, keeping only values that met a condition such as this:

```
WHERE dep_delay > -15
```

A second method would be to filter the data based on the number of flights:

```
WHERE numflights > 300
```

The second method—using a quality-control filter that is based on removing data for which we have insufficient examples—is preferable.

This is an important point that gets at the key difference between statistics on "normal" datasets and statistics on big data. Although I agree that the term *big data* has become completely hyped, people who claim that big data is just data are missing a key point—the fundamental approach to problems becomes different when datasets grow sufficiently large. The way we detect outliers is just one such example.

For a dataset that numbers in the hundreds to thousands of examples, you would filter the dataset and remove values outside, say, $\mu \pm 3\sigma$ (where $\mu$ is the mean and $\sigma$ the standard deviation).[19] We can find out what the range would be by running a Big-Query query on the table:

```
SELECT
   AVG(DEP_DELAY) - 3*STDDEV(DEP_DELAY) AS filtermin,
   AVG(DEP_DELAY) + 3*STDDEV(DEP_DELAY) AS filtermax
FROM
   dsongcp.flights_tzcorr
```

This yields the range $[-102, 121]$ minutes so that the WHERE clause would become as follows:

```
WHERE dep_delay BETWEEN -102 AND 121
```

Of course, a filter that retains values in the range $\mu \pm 3\sigma$ is based on an implicit assumption that the distribution of departure delays is Gaussian. We can avoid such an assumption by using percentiles, perhaps by omitting the top and bottom 5% of values:

```
SELECT
   APPROX_QUANTILES(DEP_DELAY, 20)
FROM
   dsongcp.flights_tzcorr
```

This would lead us to retain values in the range $[-9, 66]$. Regardless of how we find the range, though, the range is based on an assumption that unusually high and low values are outliers.

On datasets that number in the hundreds of thousands to millions of examples, thresholding your input data based on value is dangerous because you can very well be throwing out valuable nuance—if there are sufficient examples of a delay of 150 minutes, it is worth modeling such a value regardless of how far off the mean it is. Customer satisfaction and "long-tail" business strategies might hinge on our systems coping well with usually small or large values. There is, therefore, a world of difference between filtering our data using:

```
WHERE dep_delay > -15
```

versus filtering it using:

```
WHERE numflights > 370
```

The first method imposes a threshold on the input data and is viable only if we are sure that a departure delay of less than $-15$ minutes is absurd. The second method, on the other hand, is based on how often certain values are observed—the larger our dataset grows, the less unusual any particular value becomes.

---

19 In a Gaussian distribution, 99.7% of values lie within three standard deviations of the mean. It's a handy way to identify outliers.

The term *outlier* is, therefore, somewhat of a misnomer when it comes to big data. An outlier implies a range within which values are kept, with outliers being values that lie outside that range. Here, we are keeping data that meets a criterion involving frequency of occurrence—any value is acceptable as long as it occurs often enough in our data.[20]

---

## How Far Can You Trust Quality Flags in Datasets?

Many datasets include metadata about their data quality. These might even be on a row-by-row basis. Should you discard any rows whose quality is marked as being bad?

The quality flags that you find in many datasets are themselves highly suspect. Many of them are set with no basis on a holistic understanding of the environment ("the instrument was left unshielded") but simply based on statistical analysis of the data values. The statistical techniques used are often carried over from the days of small datasets. So, if you can do your own analysis based on frequency of occurrence, you should.

Of course, if you don't have time to examine the data, the quality flag in the dataset is better than nothing. Take it into consideration! However, the way to take it into consideration is to treat it as one more input to your model and not to discard the supposedly bad values.

In our flights dataset, we will trust flags such as whether the flight was canceled or diverted (those reflect an understanding of the environment) but carry out our own statistical analysis of values such as departure delay based on occurrence frequency.

---

### Filtering data on occurrence frequency

To filter the dataset based on frequency of occurrence, we first need to compute the frequency of occurrence and then threshold the data based on it. We can accomplish this by using a HAVING clause:

```
SELECT
  DEP_DELAY,
  AVG(ARR_DELAY) AS arrival_delay,
  STDDEV(ARR_DELAY) AS stddev_arrival_delay,
  COUNT(ARR_DELAY) AS numflights
FROM
  dsongcp.flights_tzcorr
GROUP BY
```

---

[20] In this dataset, floating-point numbers have already been discretized. For example, arrival delays have been rounded to the nearest minute. If this is not the case, you will have to discretize continuous data before computing the frequency of occurrence.

```
            DEP_DELAY
    HAVING
        numflights > 370
    ORDER BY
        DEP_DELAY
```

Why threshold the number of flights at 370? This number derives from a guideline called the *three-sigma rule*,[21] which is traditionally the range within which we consider "nearly all values"[22] to lie. If we assume (for now; we'll verify it soon) that at any departure delay, arrival delays are normally distributed, we can talk about things that are true for "almost every flight" if our population size is large enough. Because 99.73% of values in a Gaussian distribution lie within the three-sigma bounds, filtering our dataset so that we have at least $1 / (1 - 0.9973) = 370$ examples of each input value is a rule of thumb that achieves this.[23]

How different would the results be if we were to choose a different threshold? We can look at the number of flights that are removed by different quality-control thresholds by looking at the slope of a linear model between arrival delay and departure delay using this query:

```
CREATE TEMPORARY FUNCTION linear_fit(NUM_TOTAL INT64, THRESH INT64)
RETURNS STRUCT<thresh INT64, num_removed INT64, lm FLOAT64>
AS ((
    SELECT AS STRUCT
        THRESH,
        (NUM_TOTAL - SUM(numflights)) AS num_removed,
        AVG(arrival_delay * numflights) / AVG(dep_delay * numflights) AS lm
    FROM
    (
        SELECT
            DEP_DELAY,
            AVG(ARR_DELAY) AS arrival_delay,
            STDDEV(ARR_DELAY) AS stddev_arrival_delay,
            COUNT(ARR_DELAY) AS numflights
        FROM
```

---

21  For a normal distribution (at each departure delay, the number of flights is in the hundreds to thousands, so usual statistical thinking applies), 68.27% of values lie in the $\mu \pm \sigma$ range, 95.45% of values lie in the $\mu \pm 2\sigma$ range, and 99.73% of values lie in the $\mu \pm 3\sigma$ range. That last range is termed the three-sigma rule. For more information, see the Encyclopedia of Mathematics entry (*https://oreil.ly/Da4Xp*) for the three-sigma rule.

22  Traditions, of course, are different in different fields and often depend on how much data you can reasonably collect in that field. In business statistics, this three-sigma rule is quite common. In the social sciences and in medicine, two-sigma is the typical significance threshold. Meanwhile, when the Higgs boson discovery announcement was made, the significance threshold to classify it as a true discovery and not just a statistical artifact was five-sigma or 1 in 3.5 million (see the blog at *Scientific American* (*https://oreil.ly/zDo6O*)).

23  It might appear fishy that this number is independent of the size of the dataset, but if you think about it, this rule of thumb has to be such that we are less likely to discard outliers the more data we have. The larger the dataset, the more likely it is that there will be 370 instances of any particular condition. Corner cases on small datasets will have enough company on very large datasets.

---

```
                dsongcp.flights_tzcorr
            GROUP BY
                DEP_DELAY
        )
      WHERE numflights > THRESH
  ))
  ;
```

Running this function for various different thresholds on `numflights` (see *exploration.ipynb* in the GitHub repository), we get the following results:

| Row | stats.thresh | stats.num_removed | stats.lm |
|-----|--------------|-------------------|----------|
| 1 | 1000 | 175873 | 0.25 |
| 2 | 500 | 143801 | 0.34 |
| 3 | 370 (three-sigma rule) | 135518 | 0.36 |
| 4 | 300 | 129835 | 0.38 |
| 5 | 200 | 123640 | 0.40 |
| 6 | 100 | 115471 | 0.43 |
| 7 | 22 (two-sigma rule) | 108247 | 0.45 |
| 8 | 10 | 106958 | 0.46 |
| 9 | 5 | 106319 | 0.46 |

As you can see, the slope varies extremely slowly as we remove fewer and fewer flights by decreasing the threshold. Thus, the differences in the model created for thresholds of 300, 370, or 500 are quite minor. However, that model is quite different from that created if the threshold were 5 or 10. The order of magnitude of the threshold matters, but perhaps not the exact value.

## Arrival Delay Conditioned on Departure Delay

Now that we have a query that cleans up oddball values of departure delay from the dataset, we can take the query over to the Jupyter Notebook to continue our exploratory analysis and to develop a model to help us make a decision on whether to cancel our meeting.

In Chapter 3, we built a simple model based on simply thresholding the departure delay. Here, however, we see that there are many flights for each value of departure delay. Given a certain departure delay, what arrival delays are likely?

### Distribution of arrival delays

I simply copy and paste from the BigQuery console to the notebook and give the Pandas dataframe a name, as shown here:

```
%%bigquery depdelay
SELECT
```

```
        DEP_DELAY,
        AVG(ARR_DELAY) AS arrival_delay,
        STDDEV(ARR_DELAY) AS stddev_arrival_delay,
        COUNT(ARR_DELAY) AS numflights
FROM
        dsongcp.flights_tzcorr
GROUP BY
        DEP_DELAY
HAVING numflights > 370
ORDER BY DEP_DELAY
```

We can display the first five rows of the dataframe using [:5]:

```
depdelay[:5]
```

The result is:

| Row | DEP_DELAY | arrival_delay | stddev_arrival_delay | numflights |
|---|---|---|---|---|
| 1 | -23.0 | -23.888646288209607 | 11.432163250582196 | 458 |
| 2 | -22.0 | -23.22748815165877 | 12.590133374822704 | 633 |
| 3 | -21.0 | -22.29978118161926 | 11.558312559289162 | 914 |
| 4 | -20.0 | -21.40782122905028 | 12.066489232808147 | 1432 |
| 5 | -19.0 | -20.430769230769243 | 11.910133697086701 | 1950 |

Let's plot this data to see what insight we can get. Even though we have been using *seaborn* so far, Pandas itself has plotting functions built in:

```
ax = depdelay.plot(kind='line', x='DEP_DELAY',
                y='arrival_delay', yerr='stddev_arrival_delay')
```

This yields the plot shown in Figure 5-15.

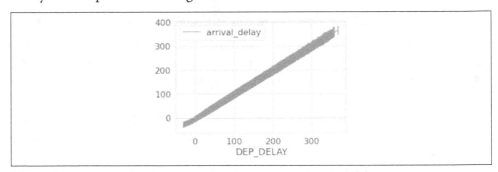

*Figure 5-15. Relationship between departure delay and arrival delay.*

It certainly does appear as if the relationship between departure delay and arrival delay is quite linear. The width of the standard deviation of the arrival delay is also pretty constant, on the order of 10 minutes.

### Applying a probabilistic decision threshold

Recall from Chapter 1 that our decision criteria are 15 minutes and 30%. If the plane is more than 30% likely to be delayed (on arrival) by more than 15 minutes, we want to send a text message asking to postpone the meeting. At what departure delay does this happen?

By computing the standard deviation of the arrival delays corresponding to each departure delay, we implicitly assumed that arrival delays are normally distributed. For now, let's continue with that assumption. I can examine a complementary cumulative distribution table (*https://oreil.ly/JEb7T*) and find where 0.3 happens. From the table, this happens at Z = 0.52.

Let's now go back to Jupyter to plug this number into our dataset:

```
Z_30 = 0.52
depdelay['arr_delay_30'] = (Z_30 * depdelay['stddev_arrival_delay']) \
            + depdelay['arrival_delay']
ax = plt.axes()
depdelay.plot(kind='line', x='DEP_DELAY', y='arr_delay_30',
            ax=ax, ylim=(0,30), xlim=(0,30), legend=False)
ax.set_xlabel('Departure Delay (minutes)')
ax.set_ylabel('> 30% prob of this Arrival Delay (minutes)');

x = np.arange(0, 30)
y = np.ones_like(x) * 15
ax.plot(x, y, 'r');
```

The plotting code yields the plot depicted in Figure 5-16.

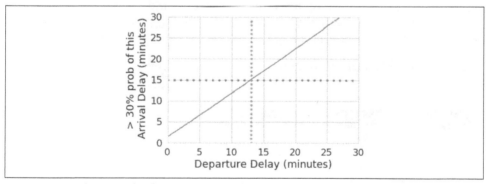

*Figure 5-16. Choosing the departure delay threshold that results in a 30% probability of an arrival delay of < 15 minutes.*

Looking up the x-axis value corresponding to the decision threshold of 15 minutes (see dotted lines in Figure 5-16). It appears that our decision criteria translate to a departure delay of 13 minutes. If the departure delay is 13 minutes or more, the aircraft is more than 30% likely to be delayed by 15 minutes or more.

### Empirical probability distribution function

The analysis in the previous section used the number 0.52, which assumes that the distribution of flights at each departure delay is normally distributed. What if we drop that assumption? We then will need to empirically determine the 30% likelihood at each departure delay. Happily, we do have at least 370 flights at each departure delay (the joys of working with large datasets!), so we can simply compute the 30th percentile for each departure delay.

We can compute the 30th percentile in BigQuery by discretizing the arrival delays corresponding to each departure delay into 100 bins and picking the arrival delay that corresponds to the 70th bin:

```
SELECT
    DEP_DELAY,
    APPROX_QUANTILES(ARR_DELAY, 101)[OFFSET(70)] AS arrival_delay_30th,
    COUNT(ARR_DELAY) AS numflights
FROM
    dsongcp.flights_tzcorr
GROUP BY
    DEP_DELAY
HAVING numflights > 370
ORDER BY DEP_DELAY
```

The function APPROX_QUANTILES() takes the ARR_DELAY and divides it into N + 1 bins (here we specified N = 101).[24] The first bin is the approximate minimum, the last bin the approximate maximum, and the rest of the bins are what we'd traditionally consider the bins. Hence, the 70th percentile is the 71st element of the result. The [ ] syntax finds the nth element of that array—OFFSET(70) will provide the 71st element because OFFSET is zero-based.[25] Why 70 and not 30? Because we want the arrival delay that could happen with 30% likelihood and this implies the larger value.

The results of this query provide the empirical 30th percentile threshold for every departure delay:

| Row | DEP_DELAY | arrival_delay_30th | numflights |
|-----|-----------|--------------------|------------|
| 1 | -23.0 | -20.0 | 458 |
| 2 | -22.0 | -19.0 | 633 |
| ... | | | |
| 39 | 15.0 | 14.0 | 38835 |

---

24 This function computes the approximate quantiles (*https://oreil.ly/qIksk*) because computing the exact quantiles on large datasets, especially of floating-point values, can be very expensive in terms of space. Instead, most big data databases use some variant of Greenwald and Khanna's algorithm (*https://oreil.ly/4BuOU*) to compute approximate quantiles.

25 Had I used ORDINAL instead of OFFSET, it would have been 1-based.

| Row | DEP_DELAY | arrival_delay_30th | numflights |
|-----|-----------|--------------------|------------|
| 40  | 16.0      | 15.0               | 35771      |
| 41  | 17.0      | 16.0               | 33964      |
| ... |           |                    |            |

Plugging the query back into the Jupyter Notebook, we can avoid the Z-lookup and Z-score calculation associated with Gaussian distributions. We get the chart shown in Figure 5-17.

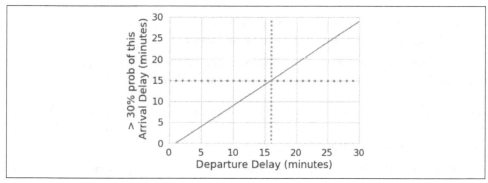

Figure 5-17. *Departure delay threshold that results in a 30% likelihood of an arrival delay of < 15 min.*

## The answer is…

From the chart in Figure 5-16, our decision threshold, without the assumption of normal distribution, is 16 minutes. If a flight is delayed by more than 16 minutes, there is a greater than 30% likelihood that the flight will arrive more than 15 minutes late.

Recall that the aforementioned threshold is conditioned on rather conservative assumptions—you are going to cancel the meeting if there is more than 30% likelihood of being late by 15 minutes. What if you are a bit more audacious in your business dealings, or if this particular customer will not be annoyed by a few minutes' wait? What if you won't cancel the meeting unless there is a greater than 70% chance of being late by 15 minutes? The good thing is that it is easy enough to come up with a different decision threshold for different people and different scenarios out of the same basic framework.

Another thing to notice is that the addition of the actual departure delay in minutes has allowed us to make a better decision than going with just the contingency table. Using just the contingency table, we would cancel meetings whenever flights were just 10 minutes late. Using the actual departure delay and a probabilistic decision framework, we were able to avoid canceling our meeting unless flights were delayed by 16 minutes or more.

# Evaluating the Model

But how good is this advice? How many times will my advice to cancel or not cancel the meeting be the correct one? Had you asked me that question, I would have hemmed and hawed—I don't know how accurate the threshold is because we have no independent sample. Let's address that now—as our models become more sophisticated, an independent sample will be increasingly required.

There are two broad approaches to finding an independent sample:

- Collect new data. For example, we could go back to BTS and download 2016 data and evaluate the recommendation on that dataset.

- Split the 2015 data into two parts. Create the model on the first part (called the *training set*), and evaluate it on the second part (called the *test set*).

The second approach is more common because datasets tend to be finite. In the interest of being practical here, let's do the same thing even though, in this instance, we could go back and get more data.[26]

When splitting the data, we must be careful. We want to ensure that both parts are representative of the full dataset (and have similar relationships to what you are predicting), but at the same time we want to make sure that the testing data is independent of the training data. To understand what this means, let's take a few reasonable splits and talk about why they won't work.

## Random Shuffling

We might split the data by randomly shuffling all the rows in the dataset and then choosing the first 70% as the training set, and the remaining 30% as the test set. In BigQuery, you could do that using the RAND() function:

```
SELECT
  ORIGIN, DEST,
  DEP_DELAY,
  ARR_DELAY
FROM
  dsongcp.flights_tzcorr
WHERE
  RAND() < 0.7
```

The RAND() function returns a value between 0 and 1, so approximately 70% of the rows in the dataset will be selected by this query. However, there are several problems with using this sampling method for machine learning:

---

26 By the time we get to Chapter 10, I will have based so many decisions on 2015–2018 data that I will get 2019 data to act as a truly independent test set.

- It is not nearly as easy to get the 30% of the rows that were not selected to be in the training set to use as the test dataset.

- The RAND() function returns different things each time it is run, so if you run the query again, you will get a different 70% of rows. In this book, we are experimenting with different machine learning models, and this will play havoc with comparisons between models if each model is evaluated on a different test set.

- The order of rows in a BigQuery result set is not guaranteed—it is essentially the order in which different workers return their results. So, even if you could set a random seed to make RAND() repeatable, you'll still not get repeatable results. You'd have to add an ORDER BY clause to explicitly sort the data (on an ID field, a field that is unique for each row) before doing the RAND(). This is not always going to be possible.

Further, on this particular dataset, random shuffling is problematic for another reason. Flights on the same day are probably subject to the same weather and traffic factors. Thus, the rows in the training set and test sets will not be independent if we simply shuffle the data. This consideration is relevant only for this particular dataset—shuffling the data and taking the first 70% will work for other datasets that don't have this interrow dependence, as long as you have an id field.

We could split the data such that Jan–Sep 2015 is training data and Oct–Dec is testing data. But what if delays can be made up in summer but not in winter? This split fails the representativeness test. Neither the training dataset nor the test dataset will be representative of the entire year if we split the dataset by months.

## Splitting by Date

The approach that we will take is to find all the unique days in the dataset, shuffle them, and use 70% of these days as the training set and the remainder as the test set. For repeatability, I will store this division as a table in BigQuery.

The first step is to get all the unique days in the dataset:

```
SELECT
  DISTINCT(FL_DATE) AS FL_DATE
FROM
  dsongcp.flights_tzcorr
ORDER BY
  FL_DATE
```

The next step is to select a random 70% of these to be our training days:

```
SELECT
  FL_DATE,
  IF(ABS(MOD(FARM_FINGERPRINT(CAST(FL_DATE AS STRING)), 100)) < 70,
    'True', 'False') AS is_train_day
```

```
FROM (
  SELECT
    DISTINCT(FL_DATE) AS FL_DATE
  FROM
    dsongcp.flights_tzcorr)
ORDER BY
  FL_DATE
```

In the preceding query, the hash value of each of the unique days from the inner query is computed using the FarmHash library and the is_train_day field is set to True if the last two digits of this hash value are less than 70:[27]

| Row | FL_DATE | is_train_day |
|-----|------------|-------|
| 1 | 2015-01-01 | True |
| 2 | 2015-01-02 | False |
| 3 | 2015-01-03 | False |
| 4 | 2015-01-04 | True |
| 5 | 2015-01-05 | True |

The final step is to save this result as a table in BigQuery:

```
CREATE OR REPLACE TABLE dsongcp.trainday AS
  . . .
```

We can join with this table whenever we want to pull out training rows. For your convenience, the preceding query is in the GitHub repository in the file *trainday.txt*, so you can simply do:

```
cat trainday.txt | bq query --nouse_legacy_sql
```

In some chapters, we won't be using BigQuery. Just in case we aren't using BigQuery, I will also export the table as a CSV file—we can do this on the web console, but we can also script it:

```
bq extract dsongcp.trainday gs://${BUCKET}/flights/trainday.csv
```

## Training and Testing

Now, I can go back and edit my original query to carry out the percentile using only data from my training days. To do that, I will change this string in my original query:

```
FROM
    dsongcp.flights_tzcorr
```

to:

---

27 See the Google Open Source Blog (*https://oreil.ly/3KDFA*) for a description and GitHub (*https://oreil.ly/r9x0I*) for the code.

```
FROM
    dsongcp.flights_tzcorr
JOIN dsongcp.trainday USING(FL_DATE)
WHERE is_train_day = 'True'
```

Now, the percentile is computed out only on days for which is_train_day is True.

The code to create the plot remains the same. On running it, the threshold (the x-axis value of the intersection point) remains consistent, as depicted in Figure 5-18.

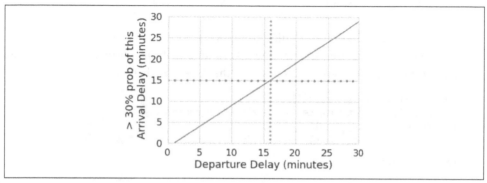

*Figure 5-18. The departure delay threshold remains consistent with earlier methods.*

This is gratifying because we get the same answer—16 minutes—after creating the empirical probabilistic model on just the training data.

Let's formally evaluate how well our recommendation of 16 minutes does in terms of predicting an arrival delay of 15 minutes or more. To do that, we have to find the number of times that we would have wrongly canceled a meeting or missed a meeting. We can compute these numbers using this query on days that are not training days:

```
SELECT
  SUM(IF(DEP_DELAY < 16
      AND arr_delay < 15, 1, 0)) AS correct_nocancel,
  SUM(IF(DEP_DELAY < 16
      AND arr_delay >= 15, 1, 0)) AS wrong_nocancel,
  SUM(IF(DEP_DELAY >= 16
      AND arr_delay < 15, 1, 0)) AS wrong_cancel,
  SUM(IF(DEP_DELAY >= 16
      AND arr_delay >= 15, 1, 0)) AS correct_cancel
FROM (
  SELECT
    DEP_DELAY,
    ARR_DELAY
  FROM
    dsongcp.flights_tzcorr
  JOIN dsongcp.trainday USING(FL_DATE)
  WHERE is_train_day = 'False'
)
```

Note that unlike when I was computing the decision threshold, I am not removing outliers (i.e., thresholding on 370 flights at a specific departure delay) when evaluating the model—outlier removal is part of my training process, and the evaluation needs to be independent of that. The second point to note is that this query is run on days that are not in the training dataset. Running this query in BigQuery, I get:

| Row | correct_nocancel | wrong_nocancel | wrong_cancel | correct_cancel |
|-----|------------------|----------------|--------------|----------------|
| 1   | 1259740          | 66081          | 52827        | 217669         |

We will cancel meetings corresponding to a total of 52,827 + 217,669 or around 270k flights. What fraction of the time are these recommendations correct? We can do the computation in the notebook (assuming that the dataframe is named eval):

```
print(eval['correct_nocancel'] /
      (eval['correct_nocancel'] + eval['wrong_nocancel']))
print(eval['correct_cancel'] /
      (eval['correct_cancel'] + eval['wrong_cancel']))
```

Figure 5-19 presents the results.

```
[36]:  print(df_eval['correct_nocancel'] /
             (df_eval['correct_nocancel'] + df_eval['wrong_nocancel']))
       print(df_eval['correct_cancel'] /
             (df_eval['correct_cancel'] + df_eval['wrong_cancel']))

       0    0.947403
       dtype: float64
       0    0.8187
       dtype: float64
```

*Figure 5-19. Computing accuracy on independent test dataset.*

It turns out when I recommend that you not cancel your meeting, I will be correct 95% of the time, and when I recommend that you cancel your meeting, I will be correct 82% of the time.

Why is this not 70%? Because the populations are different. In creating the model, we found the 70th percentile of arrival delay given a specific departure delay. In evaluating the model, we looked at the dataset of all flights. One's a marginal distribution, and the other's the full one. Another way to think about this is that the 95% figure is padded by all the departure delays of more than 20 minutes when canceling the meeting is an easy call.

We could evaluate right at the decision boundary by changing our scoring function:

```
SELECT
  SUM(IF(DEP_DELAY = 15
      AND arr_delay < 15, 1, 0)) AS correct_nocancel,
```

```
    SUM(IF(DEP_DELAY = 15
        AND arr_delay >= 15, 1, 0)) AS wrong_nocancel,
    SUM(IF(DEP_DELAY = 16
        AND arr_delay < 15, 1, 0)) AS wrong_cancel,
    SUM(IF(DEP_DELAY = 16
        AND arr_delay >= 15, 1, 0)) AS correct_cancel
...
```

If we do that, evaluating only at departure delays of 15 and 16 minutes, the contingency table and ratios look like those in Figure 5-20.

```
%%bigquery eval
SELECT
  SUM(IF(DEP_DELAY = 15
      AND arr_delay < 15, 1, 0)) AS correct_nocancel,
  SUM(IF(DEP_DELAY = 15
      AND arr_delay >= 15, 1, 0)) AS wrong_nocancel,
  SUM(IF(DEP_DELAY = 16
      AND arr_delay < 15, 1, 0)) AS wrong_cancel,
  SUM(IF(DEP_DELAY = 16
      AND arr_delay >= 15, 1, 0)) AS correct_cancel
FROM (
  SELECT
    DEP_DELAY,
    ARR_DELAY
  FROM
    dsongcp.flights_tzcorr
  JOIN dsongcp.trainday USING(FL_DATE)
  WHERE is_train_day = 'False'
)
```

```
Query complete after 0.00s: 100%|██████████| 3/3 [00:00<00:00, 1313.46query/s]
Downloading: 100%|██████████| 1/1 [00:00<00:00,  1.06rows/s]
```

```
eval.head()
```

|   | correct_nocancel | wrong_nocancel | wrong_cancel | correct_cancel |
|---|---|---|---|---|
| 0 | 7684 | 2935 | 6787 | 2942 |

```
print(eval['correct_nocancel'] / (eval['correct_nocancel'] + eval['wrong_nocancel']))
print(eval['correct_cancel'] / (eval['correct_cancel'] + eval['wrong_cancel']))
```

```
0    0.723609
dtype: float64
0    0.302395
dtype: float64
```

Figure 5-20. Evaluating only at marginal decisions.

As expected, we are correct to not cancel the meeting 72% of the time, close to our target of 70%. We chose the departure delay threshold of 16 minutes on the training dataset because we expected to be 70% correct in not canceling if we do so, and now we've proved on an independent dataset that this is the case. This model achieves the 70% correctness measure that was our target but does so by canceling fewer flights than the contingency table–based model of Chapter 3.

# Summary

In this chapter, we began to carry out exploratory data analysis. To be able to interactively analyze our large dataset, we loaded the data into BigQuery, which gave us the ability to carry out queries on millions of rows in a matter of seconds. We required sophisticated statistical plotting capabilities, and we obtained that by using a Jupyter Notebook in the form of Vertex AI Workbench.

In terms of the model itself, we were able to use nonparametric estimation of the 30th percentile of arrival delays, at each departure delay, to pick the departure delay threshold. We discovered that doing this allows us to cancel fewer meetings while attaining the same target correctness. We evaluated our decision threshold on an independent set of flights by dividing our dataset into two parts—a training set and a testing set—based on randomly partitioning the distinct days that comprise our dataset.

# Suggested Resources

To learn how to carry out EDA using Python libraries like Matplotlib, NumPy, and Pandas, read the O'Reilly Media book *Hands-On Exploratory Data Analysis with Python* by Suresh Kumar Mukhiya and Usman Ahmed. For a more theoretically grounded introduction to the topic, consider taking the online course on EDA (*https://oreil.ly/Swjj0*) from Johns Hopkins.

Peruse and work through the gallery of *seaborn* plots (*https://oreil.ly/XkazV*) so that you are familiar with the different ways of visualizing data that are available.

While Jupyter is great for EDA, it is not a great environment for developing standalone Python programs. Ultimately, you will want to refactor your notebook code into functions and move them into a Python package. At that point, use a proper integrated development environment like PyCharm (*https://oreil.ly/1vWEK*) or Visual Studio Code (*https://oreil.ly/teQf4*). This is exactly what we will do in this book. To learn this workflow, read this 2018 article by Florian Wilhelm, "Working Efficiently with JupyterLab Notebooks" (*https://oreil.ly/xjevC*). You don't need to install Jupyter because Vertex AI Workbench manages that for you, but the rest of Florian's advice applies.

# CHAPTER 6

# Bayesian Classifier with Apache Spark on Cloud Dataproc

Having become accustomed to running queries in BigQuery where there were no clusters to manage, I'm dreading going back to configuring and managing Hadoop clusters. But I did promise you a tour of data science on the cloud, and in many companies, Hadoop plays an important role in that.

In this chapter, we tackle the next stage of our data science problem, by creating a Bayes model to predict the likely arrival delay of a flight. We will do this through an integrated workflow that involves BigQuery and Spark SQL.

All of the code snippets in this chapter are available in the folder *06_dataproc* of the book's GitHub repository (*https://github.com/GoogleCloudPlatform/data-science-on-gcp*). See the *README.md* file in that directory for instructions on how to do the steps described in this chapter.

## MapReduce and the Hadoop Ecosystem

MapReduce was described in a paper by Jeff Dean and Sanjay Ghemawat (*https://oreil.ly/oMGK8*) as a way to process large datasets on a cluster of machines. They showed that many real-world tasks can be decomposed into a sequence of two types of functions: `map` functions that process key-value pairs to generate intermediate key-value pairs, and `reduce` functions that merge all the intermediate values associated with the same key. A flexible and general-purpose framework can run programs that are written following this MapReduce model on a cluster of commodity machines. Such a MapReduce framework will take care of many of the details that make writing distributed system applications so difficult—the framework, for example, will partition the input data appropriately, schedule running the program across a set of machines, and handle job or machine failures.

## How MapReduce Works

Imagine that you have a large set of documents and you want to compute word frequencies on that dataset. Before MapReduce, this was an extremely difficult problem. One approach you might take would be to scale up—that is, to get an extremely large, powerful machine.[1] The machine will hold the current word frequency table in memory, and every time a word is encountered in the document, this word frequency table will be updated. Here it is in pseudocode:

```
wordcount(Document[] docs):
    wordfrequency = {}
    for each document d in docs:
        for each word w in d:
            wordfrequency[w] += 1
    return wordfrequency
```

We can make this a multithreaded solution by having each thread work on a separate document, sharing the word frequency table between the threads, and updating this in a thread-safe manner. You will at some point, though, run into a dataset that is beyond the capabilities of a single machine. At that point, you will want to scale out, by dividing the documents among a cluster of machines. Each machine on the cluster then processes a fraction of the complete document collection. The programmer implements two methods, map and reduce:

```
map(String docname, String content):
    for each word w in content:
        emitIntermediate(w, 1)

reduce(String word, Iterator<int> intermediate_values):
    int result = 0;
    for each v in intermediate_values:
        result += v;
    emit(result);
```

The framework manages the orchestration of the maps and reduces and interposes a group-by-key in between (i.e., it's the framework that makes these calls—not the programmer):

```
wordcount(Document[] docs):
    for each doc in docs:
        map(doc.name, doc.content)
    group-by-key(key-value-pairs)
```

---

1 In Chapter 2, we discussed scaling up, scaling out, and data in situ from the perspective of data center technologies. This background is useful to have here.

```
for each key in key-values:
    reduce(key, intermediate_values)
```

To improve speed in an environment in which network bisection bandwidth (see Chapter 2) is low,[2] the documents are stored on local drives attached to the compute instance. The map operations are then scheduled by the MapReduce infrastructure in such a way that each map operation runs on a compute instance that already has the data it needs (this assumes that the data has been presharded on the cluster), as shown in Figure 6-1.

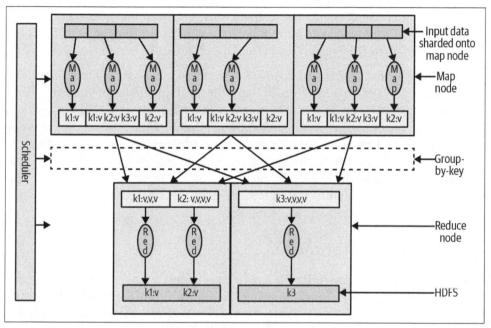

*Figure 6-1. MapReduce is an algorithm for distributed processing of datasets in which the data are presharded onto compute instances such that each map operation can access the data it needs using a local filesystem call.*

As the diagram indicates, there can be multiple map and reduce jobs assigned to a single machine. The key capability that the MapReduce framework provides is the orchestration and massive group-by-key after the map tasks complete and before the reduce jobs can begin.

---

2 See Slide 6 of Dean and Ghemawat's original presentation (*https://oreil.ly/8EOyd*)—the MapReduce architecture they proposed assumes that the cluster has limited bisection bandwidth and local, rather slow drives.

## Apache Hadoop

When Dean and Ghemawat published the MapReduce paper, they did not make Google's MapReduce implementation open source.[3] Hadoop (*https://oreil.ly/Ozqzy*) is open source software that was created from parts of Apache Nutch (*https://oreil.ly/Q2UnK*), an open source web crawler created by Doug Cutting based on a couple of Google papers. Cutting modeled the distributed file system in his crawler on Google's descriptions of the Google File System (*https://oreil.ly/3bx4I*) (a predecessor of the Colossus filesystem (*https://oreil.ly/lFUq0*) that is in use within Google Cloud Platform today) and the data processing framework on Dean and Ghemawat's MapReduce paper. These two parts were then factored out into Hadoop in 2006 as the Hadoop Distributed File System (HDFS) and the MapReduce engine.

Hadoop today is managed by the Apache Software Foundation. It is a framework that runs applications using the MapReduce algorithm, enabling these applications to process data in parallel on a cluster of commodity machines. Apache Hadoop provides Java libraries necessary to write MapReduce applications (i.e., the `map` and `reduce` methods) that will be run by the framework. In addition, it provides a scheduler, called YARN, and a distributed file system (HDFS). To run a job on Hadoop, the programmer submits a job by specifying the location of the input and output files (typically, these will be in HDFS) and uploading a set of Java classes that provide the implementation of the `map` and `reduce` methods.

# Google Cloud Dataproc

Normally, the first step in writing Hadoop jobs is to get a Hadoop installation going. This involves setting up a cluster, installing Hadoop on it, and configuring the cluster so that the machines all know about one another and can communicate with one another in a secure manner. Then, you'd start the YARN and MapReduce processes and finally be ready to write some Hadoop programs.

On Google Cloud, Google Cloud Dataproc (*https://oreil.ly/Z8d48*) makes it convenient to spin up a Hadoop cluster that is capable of running MapReduce, Pig, Hive, Presto, and Spark.

If you are using Spark, Dataproc offers a fully managed, serverless Spark environment—you can simply submit a Spark program and Dataproc will execute it. In this way, Dataproc is to Apache Spark what Dataflow is to Apache Beam. In fact, Dataproc and Dataflow share backend services. At the time I'm writing this chapter (December 2021), this serverless execution environment in Dataproc supports only

---

3 Now, research papers from Google are often accompanied by open source implementations—Kubernetes, Apache Beam, TensorFlow, and Inception are examples.

Spark, although there are plans to expand it to other frameworks commonly used in Hadoop clusters.

Even if you are not using Spark, Dataproc will still reduce the toil associated with running Hadoop workloads in several ways:

- Dataproc ties into Cloud identity and access management (IAM), Cloud Logging, etc., so that you don't have to manage security or logging on a cluster-by-cluster basis.

- It is autoscaling and will shrink or grow to accommodate your workloads, so you don't have to manage and provision machines yourself.

- It reads directly off Cloud Storage, so you don't have to manage the storage yourself.

- It offers a metadata service so that, even if you run clusters only for the duration of the job, Hive jobs can have persistent metadata.

We can create a fully configured Dataproc cluster by using the following single gcloud command:[4]

```
gcloud dataproc clusters create ch6cluster \
  --enable-component-gateway \
  --region us-central1 --zone us-central1-a \
  --master-machine-type n1-standard-4 \
  --master-boot-disk-size 500 --num-workers 2 \
  --worker-machine-type n1-standard-4 \
  --worker-boot-disk-size 500 --image-version 2.0 \
  --properties dataproc:dataproc.personal-auth.user=$EMAIL \
  --optional-components JUPYTER --project $PROJECT \
  --scopes https://www.googleapis.com/auth/cloud-platform
```

A minute or so later, the Cloud Dataproc cluster is created, all ready to go. The `--num-workers`, `--worker-machine-type`, and `--master-machine-type` parameters specify the hardware configuration of the cluster. The `scopes` parameter indicates what Cloud IAM roles this cluster's service account should have. For example, to create a cluster that will run programs that will need to administer Cloud Bigtable and invoke BigQuery queries, you could specify the scope as follows:

```
--scopes=https://www.googleapis.com/auth/bigtable.admin,bigquery
```

Here, I'm allowing the cluster to work with all Google Cloud Platform products. Cloud Dataproc allows you to specify an image version, so that any work you carry out is repeatable. Leave out `--image-version` to use the latest stable version. The

---

4 As discussed in Chapter 3, the gcloud command makes a REST API call, so this can be done programmatically. You could also use the Google Cloud Platform web console. This command is available in the GitHub repository as *05_dataproc/create_cluster.sh*.

`--enable-component-gateway` parameter creates readily accessible, but secure, https proxy endpoints for various services running on the cluster. Besides the standard Hadoop services, we also want Jupyter, and so we specify it as an optional component. If your data (that will be processed by the cluster) is in a single-region bucket on Google Cloud Storage, you should create your cluster in that same zone to take advantage of the high bisection bandwidth within a Google data center; that's what the `--zone` specification does.

Although the cluster creation command supports a `--bucket` option to specify the location of a staging bucket to store such things as configuration and control files, best practice is to allow Cloud Dataproc to determine its own staging bucket. This allows you to keep your data separate from the staging information needed for the cluster to carry out its tasks. Cloud Dataproc will create a separate bucket in each geographic region, choose an appropriate bucket based on the zone in which your cluster resides, and reuse such Cloud Dataproc–created staging buckets between cluster create requests if possible.[5]

Because we specified `--enable-component-gateway`, we can verify that Hadoop is running by visiting the Cloud Dataproc section of the Google Cloud Platform web console and accessing the HDFS NameNode web interface (from the Web Interfaces section of the cluster details). You should be able to see the list of data nodes.

 If you want to use Secure Shell (SSH) to connect to the cluster, you can, but you'd have to give the master node an external IP in order to do so. This is generally not a good idea. Instead, interact with the cluster through the available web interfaces. Later in this chapter, I'll show you how to install software on startup so that you don't need to SSH into the cluster to install software.

## Need for Higher-Level Tools

The word count example is embarrassingly parallel, and therefore trivial to implement in terms of a single map and a single reduce operation. However, it is nontrivial to cast more complex data processing algorithms into sequences of map and reduce operations. Higher-level solutions are called for, and as different organizations implemented add-ons to the basic Hadoop framework and made these additions available as open source, the Hadoop ecosystem was born.

Apache Pig (*http://pig.apache.org*) provided one of the first ways to simplify the writing of MapReduce programs to run on Hadoop. Apache Pig requires you to write

---

5 To find the name of the staging bucket created by Cloud Dataproc, run `gcloud dataproc clusters describe`.

code in a language called *Pig Latin*; these programs are then converted to sequences of MapReduce programs, and these MapReduce programs are executed on Apache Hadoop. Because Pig Latin (sometimes just referred to as Pig) comes with a command-line interpreter, it is very conducive to interactive creation of programs meant for large datasets. At the same time, it is possible to save the interactive commands and execute the script on demand. This provides a way to achieve both embarrassingly parallel data analysis and data flow sequences consisting of multiple interrelated data transformations. Pig can optimize the execution of MapReduce sequences, thus allowing the programmer to express tasks naturally without worrying about efficiency.

Apache Hive (*https://hive.apache.org*) provides a mechanism to project structure onto data that is already in distributed storage. With the structure (essentially a table schema) projected onto the data, it is possible to query, update, and manage the dataset using SQL. Typical interactions with Hive use a command-line tool or a Java Database Connectivity (JDBC) driver.

Pig and Hive both rely on the distributed storage system to store intermediate results. Apache Spark (*http://spark.apache.org*), on the other hand, takes advantage of in-memory processing and a variety of other optimizations. Because many data pipelines start with large, out-of-memory data, but quickly aggregate it to something that can be fit into memory, Spark can provide dramatic speedups when compared to Pig and as well as speedups for Spark SQL when compared to Hive.[6] In addition, because Spark (like Pig and BigQuery) optimizes the directed acyclic graph (DAG) of successive processing stages, it can provide gains over handwritten Hadoop operations. With the growing popularity of Spark, a variety of machine learning, data mining, and streaming packages have been written for it. Hence, in this chapter, we focus on Spark solutions. Cloud Dataproc, though, provides an execution environment for Hadoop jobs regardless of the abstraction level (i.e., whether you submit jobs in Hadoop, Pig, Hive, or Spark). All these software packages are installed by default on Cloud Dataproc.

## Jobs, Not Clusters

We will look at how to submit jobs to the Cloud Dataproc clusters shortly, but after you are done with the cluster, delete it by using the following:

```
gcloud dataproc clusters delete ch6cluster
```

You can even set the cluster up so that it is automatically deleted if it's idle for a specific time duration.

---

6 Hive has been sped up in recent years through the use of a new application framework (Tez (*https://oreil.ly/zHGQP*)) and a variety of optimizations for long-lived queries (*https://oreil.ly/T8n0V*).

This is not the typical Hadoop workflow—if you are used to an on-premises Hadoop installation, you might have set up the cluster a few months ago and it has remained up since then. The better practice on Google Cloud Platform, however, is to delete the cluster after you are done. The reasons are twofold. First, it typically takes less than two minutes to start a cluster. Because cluster creation is fast and can be automated, it is wasteful to keep unused clusters around—you are paying for the cluster regardless of whether you are running anything useful on them. Second, one reason that on-premises Hadoop clusters are kept always on is because the data is stored on HDFS. Although you can use HDFS in Cloud Dataproc (recall that we looked at HDFS NameNode to get the status of the Hadoop cluster), it is not recommended. Instead, it is better to keep your data on Google Cloud Storage and directly read from Cloud Storage in your MapReduce jobs—the original MapReduce practice of assigning map processes to nodes that already have the necessary data came about in an environment in which network bisection speeds were low. On the Google Cloud Platform, for which network bisection speeds are on the order of a petabit per second, the best practice has changed. Instead of sharding your data onto HDFS, keep your data on Cloud Storage and read the data into an ephemeral cluster, as demonstrated in Figure 6-2.

Because of the high network speed that prevails within the Google data center, reading from Cloud Storage is competitive with HDFS in terms of speed for sustained reads of large files (the typical Hadoop use case). If your use case involves frequently reading small files, reading from Cloud Storage could be slower than reading from HDFS. However, even in this scenario, you can counteract this lower speed by simply creating more compute nodes—because storage and compute are separate, you are not limited to the number of nodes that happen to have the data. Because Hadoop clusters tend to be underutilized, you will often save money by creating an ephemeral cluster many times the size of an always-on cluster with an HDFS filesystem. Getting the job done quickly with a lot more machines and deleting the cluster when you are done is often the more frugal option (you should measure this on your particular workflow, of course, and estimate the cost of different scenarios).[7] This method of operating with short-lived clusters is also quite conducive to the use of preemptible instances (*https://oreil.ly/8gF35*)—you can create a cluster with a given number of standard instances and many more preemptible instances, thus getting a lower cost for the full workload.

---

7 For a tool to estimate costs quickly, go to the Google Cloud Pricing Calculator (*https://oreil.ly/osWqs*).

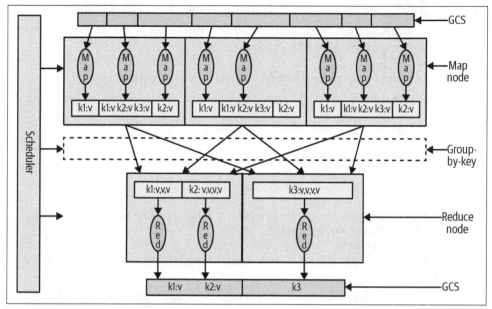

*Figure 6-2. Because network bisection speeds on Google Cloud are on the order of a petabit per second, best practice is to keep your data on Cloud Storage and simply spin up short-lived compute nodes to perform the map operations. These nodes will read the data across the network. In other words, there is no need to preshard the data.*

## Preinstalling Software

Creating and deleting clusters on demand is fine if you want a plain, vanilla Hadoop cluster, but what if you need to install specific software on the individual nodes?

There are two approaches. One is to create your own custom Docker images and ask Dataproc to use those:

```
gcloud dataproc clusters create --image=...
```

You can create these images starting from an existing Dataproc base image and adding any other packages you require in your Dockerfile.

The second option is to use *initialization actions*. These are simply startup executables, stored on Cloud Storage, that will be run on the nodes of the cluster. For example, suppose that we want a specific Python package:

- Create a script to carry out whatever software we want preinstalled:[8]

```
#!/bin/bash

# Things to do on both Master and Worker
apt-get -y update
apt-get install python-dev
apt-get install python-pip
pip install --upgrade google-api-python-client

ROLE=$(/usr/share/google/get_metadata_value attributes/dataproc-role)
if [[ "${ROLE}" == 'Master' ]]; then
  cd home/dataproc
  git clone https://github.com/GoogleCloudPlatform/data-science-on-gcp
fi
```

Now, when the cluster is created, the specified packages will exist on all the nodes and the GitHub repository will exist on the Master node.

- Save the script on Cloud Storage:

```
#!/bin/bash
BUCKET=cloud-training-demos-ml
ZONE=us-central1-a
INSTALL=gs://$BUCKET/flights/dataproc/install_on_cluster.sh

# upload install file
gsutil cp install_on_cluster.sh $INSTALL
```

- Supply the script to the cluster creation command:[9]

```
gcloud dataproc clusters create \
    --num-workers=2 \
    ...
    --initialization-actions=$INSTALL \
    ch6cluster
```

Some components, like Jupyter, are already available for installation in Cloud Dataproc. For Jupyter, we could get away with just specifying it as one of the `--optional-components` to be installed.

---

8 One efficient use of initialization actions is to preinstall all the third-party libraries you might need, so that they don't have to be submitted with the job. This script is *06_dataproc/install_on_cluster.sh*.

9 This script is in the GitHub repository of this book as *06_dataproc/create_cluster.sh*.

# Quantization Using Spark SQL

So far, we have used only one variable in our dataset—the departure delay—to make our predictions of the arrival delay of a flight. However, we know that the distance the aircraft needs to fly must have some effect on the ability of the pilot to make up for delays en route. The longer the flight, the more likely it is that small delays in departure can be made up in flight. So, let's build a statistical model that uses two variables—the departure delay and the distance to be traveled.

One way to do this is to put each flight into one of several bins, as shown in Table 6-1.

*Table 6-1. Quantizing distance and departure delay to carry out Bayesian classification over two variables*

|  | < 10 min | 10–12 min | 12–15 min | > 15 min |
|---|---|---|---|---|
| < 100 miles | For example:<br><br>• Arrival Delay $\geq$ 15 min: 150 flights<br>• Arrival Delay < 15 min: 850 flights<br>• 85% of flights have arrival delay < 15 minutes | | | |
| 100–500 miles | | | | |
| > 500 miles | | | | |

For each bin, I can look at the number of flights within the bin that have an arrival delay of more than 15 minutes and the number of flights with an arrival delay of less than 15 minutes, and then determine which category is higher. The majority vote then becomes our prediction for that entire bin. Because our threshold for decisions is 70% (recall that we want to cancel the meeting if there is a 30% likelihood that the flight will be late), we'll recommend canceling the meeting for flights that fall into a bin if the fraction of arrival delays of less than 15 minutes is less than 0.7. This method is called *Bayesian classification*, and the statistical model is simple enough that we can build it from scratch with a few lines of code.

The probability that the flight will be late given that the distance $x_0$ is 120 miles and the departure delay $x_1$ is 8 minutes is called the *conditional probability*,[10] written as $P(C_{late} \mid x_0, x_1)$. Within each bin, we are calculating the conditional probability $P(C_{ontime} \mid x_0, x_1)$ and $P(C_{late} \mid x_0, x_1)$ where $(x_0, x_1)$ is the pair of predictor variables (mileage and departure delay) and $C_k$ is one of two classes depending on the value of the arrival delay of the flight. Because the probability of a specific value of a continuous variable is zero, we need to estimate the probability over an interval, and, in this case, the intervals are given by the bins. Thus, to estimate $P(C_{ontime} \mid x_0, x_1)$,

---

[10] For a good, intuitive introduction to conditional probability, see Statistics How To (*https://oreil.ly/gwqcb*).

we find the bin that $(x_0, x_1)$ falls into and use that as the estimate of $P(C_{ontime})$. If this is less than 70%, our decision will be to cancel the meeting.

Of all the ways of estimating a conditional probability, the way we are doing it—by divvying up the dataset based on the values of the variables—is the easiest, but it will work only if we have large enough populations in each of the bins. This method of directly computing the probability tables works with two variables, but will it work with 20 variables? How likely is it that there will be enough flights for which the departure airport is TUL, the distance is about 350 miles, the departure delay is about 10 minutes, the taxi-out time is about 4 minutes, and the hour of day that the flight departs is around 7 a.m?

As the number of variables increases, we will need more sophisticated methods in order to estimate the conditional probability. A scalable approach that we can employ if the predictor variables are independent is a method called *Naive Bayes*. In the Naive Bayes approach, we compute the probability tables by taking each variable in isolation (i.e., computing $P(C_{ontime} \mid x_0)$ and $P(C_{ontime} \mid x_1)$ separately) and then multiplying them to come up with $P(C_k \mid x_i)$.[11] However, for just two variables, for a dataset this big, we can get away with binning the data and directly estimating the conditional probability.

## JupyterLab on Cloud Dataproc

Developing the Bayesian classification from scratch requires being able to interactively carry out development. Although we could spin up a Cloud Dataproc cluster, connect to it via SSH, and do development on the Spark read–eval–print loop (REPL), it would be better to use JupyterLab and get a notebook experience similar to how we worked with BigQuery in Chapter 5.

Among the web interfaces that we enabled with `--enable-component-gateway` was that for JupyterLab. Hence, we can connect to it similar to the way we connected to the HDFS NameNode, from the Google Cloud web console, in the Web Interfaces part of the cluster details section.

In Jupyter, use the File Browser on the left to navigate to */home/dataproc* on the local disk and open the notebook *06_dataproc/quantization.ipynb* in the clone of the course repository that you find there.

---

11 The exact calculation involves dividing by a scaling factor so that the outcome is the probability. See the Wikipedia entry on the Naive Bayes classifier (*https://oreil.ly/4BdyQ*) for more details on the mathematics.

---

# Independence Check Using BigQuery

Before we can get to computing the proportion of delayed flights in each bin, we need to decide how to quantize the delay and distance. What we do not want are bins with very few flights—in such cases, statistical estimates will be problematic. In fact, if we could somehow spread the data somewhat evenly between bins (using *quantization*), it would be ideal.

For simplicity, we would like to choose the quantization thresholds for distance and for departure delay separately, but we can do this only if they are relatively independent. Let's verify that this is the case. Cloud Dataproc is integrated with the managed services on Google Cloud Platform, so even though we have our own Hadoop cluster, we can still call out to BigQuery from the notebook that is running on Cloud Dataproc. Using BigQuery, Pandas, and seaborn as we did in Chapter 5, here's what the query looks like:

```
sql = """
SELECT DISTANCE, DEP_DELAY
FROM dsongcp.flights_tzcorr
WHERE RAND() < 0.001 AND dep_delay > -20
    AND dep_delay < 30 AND distance < 2000
"""
df = bq.query(sql).to_dataframe()sns.set_style("whitegrid")
g = sns.jointplot(x=df['DISTANCE'], y=df['DEP_DELAY'], kind="hex",
                  height=10, joint_kws={'gridsize':20})
```

The query samples the full dataset, pulling in 1/1,000 of the flights' distance and departure delay fields (that lie within reasonable ranges) into a Pandas dataframe. This sampled dataset is sent to the seaborn plotting package and a hexbin plot is created. The resulting graph is shown in Figure 6-3.

Each hexagon of a hexagonal bin plot is colored based on the number of flights in that bin, with darker hexagons indicating more flights. It is clear that at any distance, a wide variety of departure delays is possible and for any departure delay, a wide variety of distances is possible. The distribution of distances and departure delays in turn is similar across the board. There is no obvious trend between the two variables—in Figure 6-3, note that the Pearson correlation coefficient is 0.07. This indicates that we can treat the two variables as independent.

The distribution plots at the top and right of the center panel of the graph show how the distance and departure delay values are distributed. This will affect the technique that we can use to carry out quantization. Note that the distance is distributed relatively uniformly until about 1,000 miles, beyond which the number of flights begins to taper off. The departure delay, on the other hand, has a long tail and is clustered around −5 minutes. We might be able to use equispaced bins for the distance variable (at least in the 0- to 1,000-mile range), but for the departure delay variable, our bin size must be adaptive to the distribution of flights. In particular, our bin size must be wide in the tail areas and relatively narrow where there are lots of points.

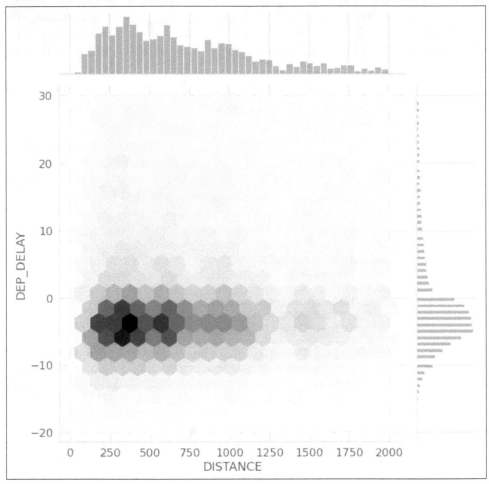

*Figure 6-3. The hexbin plot shows the joint distribution of departure delay and the distance flown. You can use such a plot to verify whether the fields in question are independent.*

There is one issue with the hexbin plot in Figure 6-3: we have used data that we are not allowed to use. Recall that our model must be developed using only the training data. While we used it only for some light exploration, it is better to be systematic about excluding days that will be part of our evaluation dataset from all model development. To do that, we need to join with the `traindays` table and retain only days for which `is_train_day` is `True`. We could do that in BigQuery, but even though Cloud Dataproc is integrated with other Google Cloud Platform services, invoking BigQuery from a Hadoop cluster feels like a cop-out. So, let's try to recreate the same plot as before, but this time using Spark SQL, and this time using only the training data.

## Spark SQL in JupyterLab

A Spark session can be created by typing the following into a code cell:

```
from pyspark.sql import SparkSession
spark = SparkSession \
    .builder \
    .appName("Bayes classification using Spark") \
    .getOrCreate()
```

With the spark variable in hand, we can read in the time-corrected JavaScript Object Notation (JSON) files that we wrote to Google Cloud Storage in Chapter 4:

```
inputs = 'gs://{}/flights/tzcorr/all_flights-*'.format(BUCKET))
flights = spark.read.json(inputs)
```

Even though we do want to ultimately read all the flights and create our model from all of the data, we will find that development goes faster if we read a fraction of the dataset. So, let's change the input from all_flights-* to all_flights-00000-*:

```
inputs = 'gs://{}/flights/tzcorr/all_flights-00000-*'.format(BUCKET))
```

Because I had 26 JSON files, doing this change means that I will be processing just the first file, and we will notice an increase in speed of 26 times during development. Of course, we should not draw any conclusions from processing such a small sample other than that the code works as intended.[12] After the code has been developed on 4% of the data, we'll change the string so as to process all the data and increase the cluster size so that this is also done in a timely manner. Doing development on a small sample on a small cluster ensures that we are not underutilizing a huge cluster of machines while we are developing the code.

With the flights dataframe created as shown previously, we can employ SQL on the dataframe by creating a temporary view (it is available only within this Spark session):

```
flights.createOrReplaceTempView('flights')
```

---

12 Just as an example, the Google Cloud Dataflow job that wrote out this code could have ordered the JSON file by date, and in that case, this file will contain only the first 14 days of the year.

Now, we can employ SQL to query the `flights` view, for example by doing this:

```
results = spark.sql('SELECT COUNT(*) FROM flights WHERE dep_delay >
-20 AND distance < 2000')
results.show()
```

On my development subset, this yields the following result:

```
+--------+
|count(1)|
+--------+
|  59665 |
+--------+
```

This is just about right to comfortably fit in memory, but even if it were somewhat larger I dare not go any smaller than 2%–3% of the data, even in development.

To create the `traindays` dataframe, we can follow the same steps, but for a CSV file this time:

```
traindays = spark.read \
    .option("header", "true") \
    .option("inferSchema", "true") \
    .csv('gs://{}/flights/trainday.csv'.format(BUCKET))
traindays.createOrReplaceTempView('traindays')
```

A quick check illustrates that `traindays` has been read, and the column names and types are correct:

```
results = spark.sql('SELECT * FROM traindays')
results.head(5)
```

This yields the following:

```
[Row(FL_DATE='2015-01-01', is_train_day=True),
 Row(FL_DATE='2015-01-02', is_train_day=False),
 Row(FL_DATE='2015-01-03', is_train_day=False),
 Row(FL_DATE='2015-01-04', is_train_day=True),
 Row(FL_DATE='2015-01-05', is_train_day=True)]
```

To restrict the `flights` dataframe to contain only training days, we can do a SQL join:

```
statement = """
SELECT
  f.FL_DATE AS date,
  CAST(distance AS FLOAT) AS distance,
  dep_delay,
  IF(arr_delay < 15, 1, 0) AS ontime
FROM flights f
JOIN traindays t
ON f.FL_DATE == t.FL_DATE
WHERE
  t.is_train_day AND
  f.dep_delay IS NOT NULL
ORDER BY
```

```
    f.dep_delay DESC
  """
  flights = spark.sql(statement)
```

Now, we can use the `flights` dataframe for the hexbin plots after clipping the x-axis and y-axis to reasonable limits:

```
df = flights[(flights['distance'] < 2000) & \
    (flights['dep_delay'] > -20) & \
    (flights['dep_delay'] < 30)]
```

When we drew the hexbin plot in the previous section, we sampled the data to 1/1,000, but that was because we were passing in a Pandas dataframe to seaborn. This sampling was done so that the Pandas dataframe would fit into memory. However, whereas a Pandas dataframe must fit into memory, a Spark dataframe does not. As of this writing (i.e., December 2021), though, there is no way to directly plot a Spark dataframe either—you must convert it to a Pandas dataframe; therefore, we will still need to sample it, at least when we are processing the full dataset.

Because there are about 50,000 rows on 1/25 of the data, we expect the full dataset to have about 6 million rows. Let's sample this down to about 100,000 records, which would be about 0.02 of the dataset:

```
pdf = df.sample(False, 0.02, 20).toPandas()
g = sns.jointplot(x=pdf['distance'], y=pdf['dep_delay'], kind="hex",
                height=10, joint_kws={'gridsize':20})
```

This yields a hexbin plot that is not very different from the one we ended up with in the previous section. The conclusion—that we need to create adaptive-width bins for quantization—still applies. Just to be sure, though, this is the point at which I'd repeat the analysis on the entire dataset to ensure our deductions are correct had I done only the Spark analysis. However, we did do it on the entire dataset in BigQuery, so let's move on to creating adaptive bins.

## Histogram Equalization

To choose the quantization thresholds for the departure delay and the distance in an adaptive way (wider thresholds in the tails and narrower thresholds where there are a lot of flights), we will adopt a technique from image processing called *histogram equalization*.[13]

---

13 For examples of histogram equalization applied to improve the contrast of images, go to OpenCV.org (*https://oreil.ly/IhYKh*).

Low-contrast digital images have histograms of their pixel values distributed such that most of the pixels lie in a narrow range. Take, for example, the photograph in Figure 6-4.[14]

*Figure 6-4. Original photograph of the pyramids of Giza used to demonstrate histogram equalization.*

As depicted in Figure 6-5, the histogram of pixel values in the Pyramids image is clustered around two points: the dark pixels in the shade, and the bright pixels in the sun.

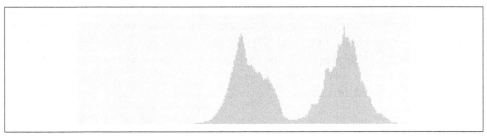

*Figure 6-5. Histogram of pixel values in photograph of the pyramids.*

Let's remap the pixel values such that the full spectrum of values is present in the image, so that the new histogram looks like that shown in Figure 6-6.

---

14 Photograph by the author.

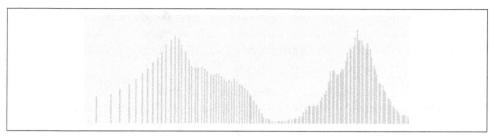

Figure 6-6. Histogram of pixels after remapping the pixels to occupy the full range.

The remapping is of pixel values and has no spatial component. For example, all pixel values of 125 in the old image might be changed to a pixel value of 5 in the new image regardless of where they are in terms of horizontal and vertical position. Figure 6-7 presents the remapped image.

Figure 6-7. Note that after the histogram equalization, the contrast in the image is enhanced.

What we implicitly did was to remap the pixel values, such that each section of the spectrum from black to white now has approximately the same number of pixels (whereas previously they were all in the gray middle). Histogram equalization has helped to enhance the contrast in the image and bring out finer details. Look, for example, at the difference in the rendering of the sand in front of the pyramid or of the detail of the midsection of Khafre's pyramid (the tall one in the middle).[15]

How is this relevant to what we want to do? We are also looking to remap values when we seek to find quantization intervals. In the image case, the output had the

---

15 Not the tallest, though. Khufu's pyramid (the tall pyramid in the forefront) is taller and larger, but has been completely stripped of its alabaster topping and is situated on slightly lower ground.

same range as the input. But in our flight example, we'd like to remap a distance value of 422 miles to a quantized value of perhaps 3. As in histogram equalization, we want the bin values to be uniformly distributed. We can, therefore, apply the same technique as is employed in the image processing filter to achieve this.

What we want to do is to divide the spectrum of distance values into, say, five bins. The first bin will contain all values in $[0, d_0)$, the second will contain values in $[d_0, d_1]$, and so on, until the last bin contains values in $[d_4, \infty)$. Histogram equalization requires that $d_0$, $d_1$, and so on be such that the number of flights in each bin is approximately equal—that is, for the data to be uniformly distributed after quantization. As in the example photograph of the pyramids, it won't be perfectly uniform because the input values are also discrete. However, the goal is to get as close to an equalized histogram as possible.

With histogram equalization, at any specific departure delay, the number of flights at each distance and delay bin should remain large enough that our conclusions are statistically valid. Assuming independence and 6 million total flights, if we divvy up the data into 100 bins (10 bins per variable), we will have about 60,000 flights in each bin. That's probably still okay, but let's be safe and divvy up the data into just five bins each. Divvying up the data into five bins implies a probability range of 0, 0.2, ..., 0.8 or five probabilistic thresholds:

```
np.arange(0, 1.0, 0.2)
```

Finding thresholds that make the two quantized variables uniformly distributed is quite straightforward using the approximate quantiles method discussed in Chapter 5. There is an approxQuantile() method available on the Spark dataframe also:

```
distthresh = flights.approxQuantile('distance',
                    list(np.arange(0, 1.0, 0.2)), 0.02)
delaythresh = flights.approxQuantile('dep_delay',
                    list(np.arange(0, 1.0, 0.2)), 0.02)
```

On the development dataset, here's what the distance thresholds turn out to be:

```
[130.0, 370.0, 621.0, 1009.0]
```

The zeroth percentile is essentially the minimum. The next ones are the 25th percentile, median, and 75th percentile. In order to have have all bin boundaries, we can tack on infinity at the end:

```
distthresh[-1] = float('inf')
```

Other than setting the policy (histogram equalization), we don't need to be in the business of choosing distance thresholds. This automation is important because it allows us to dynamically update thresholds if necessary on the most recent data,[16] taking care to use the same set of thresholds in prediction as was used in training.

We can similarly quantize the departure delay thresholds into equal boundaries, and we get:

```
[-22.0, -5.0, -3.0, 0.0, inf]
```

Unfortunately, this variable is not as well-behaved as the distance—more than 75% of flights depart on-time or early, so the really interesting delayed departures are all hidden in the last bin. This is going to be a problem that we will fix shortly.

# Bayesian Classification

Now that we have the quantization thresholds, what we need to do is find out the recommendation (whether to cancel the meeting) for each bin based on whether 70% of flights in that bin are on time or not.

## Bayes in Each Bin

We can find the flights that belong to the $m$th distance bin and $n$th delay bin by slicing the full set of flights:

```
bdf = flights[(flights['distance'] >= distthresh[m])
            & (flights['distance'] < distthresh[m+1])
            & (flights['dep_delay'] >= delaythresh[n])
            & (flights['dep_delay'] < delaythresh[n+1])]
```

Once we do that, we can compute the fraction of flights that arrive on time for this bin:

```
ontime_frac = (bdf.agg(F.sum('ontime')).collect()[0][0] /
             bdf.agg(F.count('ontime')).collect()[0][0])
```

Looping through the first on-time fractions for the first few bins, we immediately notice a problem:

```
m n ontime_frac
0 0 0.9853403141361257
0 1 0.9847756410256411
0 2 0.9753028890959925
0 3 0.6346045989904655
1 0 0.9721913236929922
1 1 0.9650856389986825
```

---

[16] If, for example, there is a newfangled technological development that enables pilots to make up time in the air better or, more realistically, if new regulations prompt airline schedulers to start padding their flight-time estimates.

```
1 2 0.9711299153807864
1 3 0.5715380684721513
```

The on-time fraction is nearly 100% for all the delay bins except the largest value for n. This makes perfect sense because only the last departure delay bin has any delayed flights.

We'll have to fix this—one way to do so is to hand-select the departure delay bins. Because we already looked at thresholding the departure delay in Chapter 3, we know that the interesting range is between 10 and 20 minutes and that departure delays are reported in integer minutes. So, we simply need to try delay variables of 10, 11, 12, …, 20 minutes.

So, let's change the delay thresholds and look at them in increments of one minute:

```
delaythresh = range(10, 20)
```

To find the delay threshold for each distance threshold where the value is closest to the 0.70 decision boundary (see *quantization.ipynb* in the GitHub repository):

```
df['score'] = abs(df['frac_ontime'] - 0.7)
bayes = (df.sort_values(['score']).groupby('dist_thresh')
        .head(1).sort_values('dist_thresh'))
```

The resulting model is a *lookup table* that consists of a delay threshold for each distance bin:

| Distance bin | delay_thresh |
|---|---|
| [130, 370] | 17 |
| [370, 621] | 13 |
| [621, 1009] | 17 |
| [1009, inf] | 18 |

If the departure delay is greater than the threshold corresponding to how far the flight is, then we will cancel the meeting because we expect the flight to be late. We are finding the delay beyond which we need to cancel flights for each distance and saving just that threshold. This makes it quite easy to productionize the model—just write out the preceding table as a CSV file, perhaps, and ask the developer of the application to apply the appropriate threshold based on the lookup table.

For example, what is the appropriate decision for a flight with a distance of 800 miles that departs 16 minutes late? The flight falls into the [621, 1009] bin. For such flights, we need to cancel the meeting only if the flight departs 17 or more minutes late—a shorter departure delay is something that can be made up en route.

# Evaluating the Model

How well does this model do? To evaluate the model, we have to look at flights that were not used in creating the model. The held-out days are obtained by looking for:

```
t.is_train_day == 'False'
```

We can compute the contingency table values for any given bin using:

```
SELECT
ROUND(SUM(IF(dep_delay < {2:f} AND arr_delay < 15, 1, 0))/COUNT(*), 2)
        AS correct_nocancel,
ROUND(SUM(IF(dep_delay >= {2:f} AND arr_delay < 15, 1, 0))/COUNT(*), 2)
        AS false_positive,
ROUND(SUM(IF(dep_delay < {2:f} AND arr_delay >= 15, 1, 0))/COUNT(*), 2)
        AS false_negative,
ROUND(SUM(IF(dep_delay >={2:f} AND arr_delay >= 15, 1, 0))/COUNT(*), 2)
        AS correct_cancel,
COUNT(*) AS total_flights
FROM flights f
JOIN traindays t
ON f.FL_DATE == t.FL_DATE
WHERE
  t.is_train_day == 'False' AND
  f.distance >= {0:f} AND f.distance < {1:f}
""".format( distthresh[m], distthresh[m+1],
            bayes[
                bayes['dist_thresh'] == distthresh[m]
            ]['delay_thresh'].values[0] )
```

When I did this, I got the results shown in Figure 6-8. We can not put too much stock in this model, though, because it was trained on just 1/25 of the data. Let's fix that next.

| bin | correct_nocancel | false_positive | false_negative | correct_cancel | total_flights |
|---|---|---|---|---|---|
| 130-370 miles | 0.82 | 0.02 | 0.02 | 0.13 | 3131 |

| bin | correct_nocancel | false_positive | false_negative | correct_cancel | total_flights |
|---|---|---|---|---|---|
| 370-621 miles | 0.77 | 0.03 | 0.03 | 0.15 | 3626 |

| bin | correct_nocancel | false_positive | false_negative | correct_cancel | total_flights |
|---|---|---|---|---|---|
| 621-1009 miles | 0.8 | 0.03 | 0.03 | 0.14 | 3782 |

| bin | correct_nocancel | false_positive | false_negative | correct_cancel | total_flights |
|---|---|---|---|---|---|
| 1009-100000 miles | 0.8 | 0.04 | 0.05 | 0.11 | 7624 |

*Figure 6-8. Results of evaluating the Bayes model.*

# Dynamically Resizing Clusters

The thresholds in the previous section have been computed on about 1/25 of the data (recall that our input was only one shard: `all-flights-00000-of-*`). So, we should find the actual thresholds that we will want to use by repeating the processing on all of the training data at hand. To do this in a timely manner, we will also want to increase our cluster size. Fortunately, we don't need to bring down our Cloud Dataproc cluster in order to add more nodes.

Let's add machines to the cluster so that it has 20 workers, 15 of which are *secondary* and so are heavily discounted in price:[17]

```
gcloud dataproc clusters update ch6cluster\
    --num-secondary-workers=15 --num-workers=5 --region=us-central1
```

The secondary machines are preemptible. These machines are provided by Google Cloud Platform at a large (fixed) discount to standard Google Compute Engine instances in return for users' flexibility in allowing the machines to be taken away at very short notice.[18] They are particularly helpful on Hadoop workloads because Hadoop is fault-tolerant and can deal with machine failure—it will simply reschedule those jobs on the machines that remain available. Using preemptible machines on your jobs is a frugal choice—here, the five standard workers are sufficient to finish the task in a reasonable time. However, the availability of 15 more machines means that our task could be completed four times faster and much more inexpensively than if we have only standard machines in our cluster.[19]

We can navigate to the Google Cloud Platform console in a web browser and check that our cluster now has 20 workers, as illustrated in Figure 6-9.

---

17 Trying to increase the number of workers might have you hitting against (soft) quotas on the maximum number of CPUs, drives, or addresses. If you hit any of these soft quotas, request an increase from the Google Cloud Platform console's section on Compute Engine quotas (*https://oreil.ly/NMXtu*). Besides the necessary CPU quota, you may need to ask for an increase in Persistent Disk and In-use IP addresses. Because a Cloud Dataproc cluster is in a single region, these are *regional* quotas. See the documentation on resource quotas in Compute Engine (*https://oreil.ly/3KHNQ*) for details. In Chapter 7, I had to ask for additional CPUs, and the process of getting a quota increased is explained there as well. If you are in an organization where increasing the quota is a bureaucratic process, ask for the larger quota you will need for Chapter 7 now.

18 Less than a minute's notice as of this writing in December 2021.

19 If the preemptible instances cost 20% of a standard machine (as they do as of this writing in December 2021), the 15 extra machines cost us only as much as three standard machines.

---

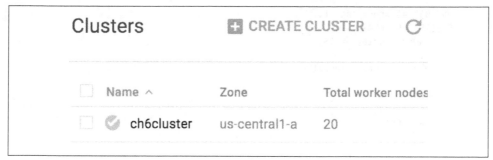

| Clusters | ➕ CREATE CLUSTER | ↻ |
|---|---|---|

| | Name ⌃ | Zone | Total worker nodes |
|---|---|---|---|
| | ✓ ch6cluster | us-central1-a | 20 |

*Figure 6-9. The cluster now has 20 workers.*

Now, go to the JupyterLab Notebook and change the input variable to process the full dataset. Next, in the JupyterLab Notebook, click Kernel > "Restart Kernel and Clear All Outputs" to avoid mistakenly using a value corresponding to the development dataset. Then, click on Run > "Run all Cells."

All the graphs and charts are updated. After we have the results, we can resize the cluster back to something smaller so that we are not wasting cluster resources:

```
gcloud dataproc clusters update ch6cluster\
    --num-secondary-workers=0 --num-workers=2
```

On the full dataset, the lookup table is:

| Distance bin | delay_thresh |
|---|---|
| [31, 328] | 14 |
| [328, 541] | 15 |
| [541, 802] | 15 |
| [802, inf] | 17 |

Note that the thresholds changed (the quantiles are different once we add the remaining 95% of information). The delay threshold also changes quite smoothly as the distance increases. The behavior matches our intuition that we can be tolerant of longer delays on longer flights.

## Comparing to Single Threshold Model

Yes, but is this better than the single, universal threshold that we used in Chapter 5? How well does this new two-variable model perform? We can modify the evaluation BigQuery query from Chapter 5 to add in a distance criterion and supply the appropriate threshold for that distance:

```
SELECT
  SUM(IF(DEP_DELAY = 14
      AND arr_delay < 15,
      1,
```

```
        0)) AS wrong_cancel,
  SUM(IF(DEP_DELAY = 14
    AND arr_delay >= 15,
    1,
    0)) AS correct_cancel
FROM (
  SELECT
    DEP_DELAY,
    ARR_DELAY
  FROM
    dsongcp.flights_tzcorr f
  JOIN
    dsongcp.trainday t
  ON
    f.FL_DATE = t.FL_DATE
  WHERE
    t.is_train_day = 'False'
    AND f.DISTANCE < 328)
```

In this query, 14 minutes is the newly determined threshold for distances under 328 miles and the WHERE clause is now limited to flights over distances of less than 328 miles. The result is:

| Row | wrong_cancel | correct_cancel |
|-----|-------------|----------------|
| 1   | 1244        | 582            |

This indicates that we cancel meetings when it is correct to do so 582 / (582 + 1,244) or 32% of the time—remember that our goal was 30%. Similarly, we can do the other four distance categories. Both with this model and with a model that took into account only the departure delay (as in Chapter 5), we are able to get reliable predictions—canceling meetings when the flight has more than a 30% chance of being delayed.

When we have two models that perform equally well on the primary metric, it is possible that we can see if they differ on a secondary metric that also matters to us. Even if two models have the same reliability (of 30%), a model that allows us to achieve that reliability while canceling fewer meetings would be preferable. Or perhaps there is a certain category of meetings that are more important than others. The more complex model is worthwhile if we end up canceling fewer important meetings or if we can be more fine-grained in our decisions (i.e., change which meetings we cancel). If our secondary metric is the total number of meetings canceled, we can compute the sum of correct_cancel and wrong_cancel over all flights. In the case of using only the departure delay variable, we used a threshold of 16 minutes, and we would have canceled 270k meetings. How about now? Let's look at the total number of flights in the test set that would cause us to cancel our meetings:

```
SELECT
  SUM(IF(DEP_DELAY >= 14 AND DISTANCE < 328, 1, 0)) +
  SUM(IF(DEP_DELAY >= 15 AND DISTANCE >= 328 AND DISTANCE < 541, 1, 0)) +
  SUM(IF(DEP_DELAY >= 15 AND DISTANCE >= 541 AND DISTANCE < 802, 1, 0)) +
  SUM(IF(DEP_DELAY >= 17 AND DISTANCE >= 802, 1, 0))
  AS cancel
FROM (
  SELECT
    DEP_DELAY,
    ARR_DELAY,
    DISTANCE
  FROM
    dsongcp.flights_tzcorr f
  JOIN
    dsongcp.trainday t
  ON
    f.FL_DATE = t.FL_DATE
  WHERE
    t.is_train_day = 'False')
```

This turns out to be 275k. It appears, then, that our simpler univariate model got us pretty much the same results as this more complex model using two variables.[20] However, the decision surfaces are different—in the single-variable threshold, we cancel meetings whenever the flight is delayed by 16 minutes or more. However, when we take into account distance, we cancel more meetings corresponding to shorter flights (threshold is now 14–15 minutes) and cancel fewer meetings corresponding to longer flights (threshold is now 17 minutes). One reason to use this two-variable Bayes model over the one-variable threshold determined empirically is to make such finer-grained decisions. This might or might not be important—it comes down to whether longer flights are typically those corresponding to more important meetings.

Why did we not get an improvement in the number of canceled meetings? Perhaps the round-off in the delay variables (they are rounded off to the nearest minute) has hurt our ability to locate more precise thresholds. Also, maybe the extra variable would have helped if I'd used a more sophisticated model—direct evaluation of conditional probability on relatively coarse-grained quantization bins is a very simple method. In Chapter 7, we explore a more complex approach.

---

20 Occam's razor suggests that we should pick the simpler model whenever its performance is comparable to a more complex model—it costs money and time to collect the data corresponding to additional features and keep them quality-controlled. Famously, although Netflix paid out $1 million to a team that developed a better recommendation algorithm, it also announced that it had no plans (*https://oreil.ly/zDsC9*) to put that algorithm into production because of the combination of additional engineering effort and changes to Netflix's business model. We have to balance this desire for simplicity against the additional expressive power offered by the more complex model. For example, greater granularity might raise interesting questions to get you greater performance later—perhaps we can investigate the reason behind the dip in the second quartile, identify the city pairs driving this degradation, and impose rules that address the scenario.

# Orchestration

So far, in this chapter, we have developed and run the Spark jobs interactively. Once you have done so, you will want to operationalize the job and run it routinely. Although you can productionize a Jupyter Notebook using tools such as Papermill (*https://oreil.ly/t05D8*), I recommend that you convert the code into a Python program that you can execute in a standalone way.

 Although you can just copy-paste the code cells out of a Jupyter Notebook into a Python file, a more systematic way is to convert the Jupyter Notebook to a Python program using a tool called nbconvert (*https://oreil.ly/U50EE*). After that, we can do minor editing to get rid of the display cells (such as plotting the hexbin plots). The Python program corresponding to the Jupyter Notebook that we've developed so far is in the GitHub repository as *bayes_in_spark.py*.

## Submitting a Spark Job

We already have a Dataproc cluster that we have been using during development—our Jupyter Notebook is running on a Dataproc cluster. We can submit our Python program to this cluster from Cloud Shell:

```
gcloud dataproc jobs submit pyspark \
    --cluster ch6cluster --region $REGION \
    bayes_in_spark.py \
    -- \
    --bucket $BUCKET --debug
```

This is the approach you'd take if you have an already running cluster and wish to submit Spark jobs to it. However, this will require ensuring that the cluster has enough resources to handle your job. If you happen to submit your job at the same time as some other team that is already utilizing the cluster, your job might run very slowly. The solution for this problem is to use job-specific clusters.

## Workflow Template

I recommend that you create ephemeral clusters, run jobs on them, and then delete them when you are done. Instead of doing them manually, you can automate it using a *workflow template*:

```
TEMPLATE=ch6eph
MACHINE_TYPE=n1-standard-4
CLUSTER=ch6eph

gcloud dataproc --quiet workflow-templates create $TEMPLATE
```

The first step of the template will be to create a cluster of the appropriate size and set it to be a managed cluster so that it gets deleted once all the steps in the template are complete:

```
gcloud dataproc workflow-templates set-managed-cluster $TEMPLATE \
    --master-machine-type $MACHINE_TYPE \
    --worker-machine-type $MACHINE_TYPE \
    --initialization-actions $STARTUP_SCRIPT \
    --num-preemptible-workers=3 --num-workers 2 \
    --image-version 2.0 \
    --cluster-name $CLUSTER
```

Then, you can add jobs to the template. For example, to run a Pig program, we'd do:

```
gcloud dataproc workflow-templates add-job \
  pig gs://$BUCKET/bayes_final.pig \
  --step-id create-report \
  --workflow-template $TEMPLATE \
  -- --bucket=$BUCKET
```

Finally, instantiate the template to run the jobs and delete the cluster once done:

```
gcloud dataproc workflow-templates instantiate $TEMPLATE
```

One key change that we have to make to our program is to ensure that the output of the Spark program goes to a Cloud Storage location (rather than a local file on disk) because the cluster will be deleted once the job is complete:

```
bayes.to_csv('gs://${BUCKET}/flights/bayes.csv'.format(BUCKET),
              index=False)
```

## Cloud Composer

If your Dataproc job is part of a larger data pipeline, you will typically write the data pipeline in Apache Airflow. Cloud Composer provides a fully managed experience for Airflow on Google Cloud.

Within your Airflow graph, you can launch the workflow template (*https://oreil.ly/tkMHJ*) using an Airflow operator:

```
start_template_job = DataprocInstantiateWorkflowTemplateOperator(
      …
    )
```

Your considerations might change, however, if your company owns a Hadoop cluster on premises. In that case, you will submit Spark jobs to that long-lived cluster and will typically be concerned with ensuring that the cluster is not overloaded.

For the scenario in which you own an on-premises cluster, you might want to consider using a public cloud as a spillover in those situations for which there are more jobs than your cluster can handle. You can achieve this by monitoring YARN jobs and sending such spillover jobs to Cloud Dataproc. Cloud Composer provides the necessary plug-ins to be able to do this, but discussing how to set up such a hybrid system is beyond the scope of this book.

## Autoscaling

When we created the workflow template, we specified the number of workers in the cluster. When we were developing the Spark program, we resized the cluster to add workers when we were ready to create the model on the full dataset. In both scenarios, we have to know what size of cluster we need. This can be difficult for new workloads and for spiky jobs.

On a production system, it is possible to tell Dataproc to *autoscale*—the autoscaler monitors the cluster and, when it sees that the machines are getting maxed out, it adds more workers. When it sees machines on the cluster being idle, it shuts down a few workers. To do this, specify an autoscaling policy when creating the Dataproc cluster:

```
gcloud dataproc clusters create ch6cluster \
    --autoscaling-policy=ch6policy \
    ...
```

The autoscaling policy is specified in a YAML file with the syntax:

```
workerConfig:
  minInstances: 3
  maxInstances: 10
  weight: 1
secondaryWorkerConfig:
  minInstances: 0
  maxInstances: 20
  weight: 1
basicAlgorithm:
  cooldownPeriod: 2m
  yarnConfig:
    scaleUpFactor: 0.05
    scaleDownFactor: 1.0
    scaleUpMinWorkerFraction: 0.0
    scaleDownMinWorkerFraction: 0.0
    gracefulDecommissionTimeout: 1h
```

Note how the range of the number of primary and secondary workers is specified, as is the rate by which workers are scaled up. Once the autoscaling policy is specified, it is registered using gcloud:

```
gcloud dataproc autoscaling-policies import ch6policy \
    --source=filepath/filename.yaml \
    --region=region
```

Then, submit jobs to the cluster as and when you need them to be run:

```
gcloud dataproc jobs submit pyspark \
    --cluster=ch6cluster bayes_final.py \
    -- --bucket=$BUCKET
```

The cluster will be autoscaled based on the resources needed by the job subject to the limits specified in the policy.

## Serverless Spark

However, even autoscaling requires a cluster to be running.

An even better approach would be if we can simply submit a Spark program to a Dataproc service, and the service starts the cluster, runs the job, autoscales it if necessary, and deletes the cluster. We'd like our Spark job to be *serverless*.

To do so, we put the script itself on Cloud Storage:

```
gsutil cp bayes_on_spark.py gs://$BUCKET/
```

and submit the job using `gcloud`:

```
gcloud beta dataproc batches submit pyspark \
    --project=$(gcloud config get-value project) \
    --region=$REGION \
    gs://${BUCKET}/bayes_on_spark.py \
    -- \
    --bucket ${BUCKET} --debug
```

See *submit_serverless.sh* in the GitHub repository for details.

Once we do this, Dataproc takes care of all the infrastructure details. It runs our job and puts the lookup table in Cloud Storage. We can see the status of the job and examine its logs using the GCP console (see Figure 6-10).

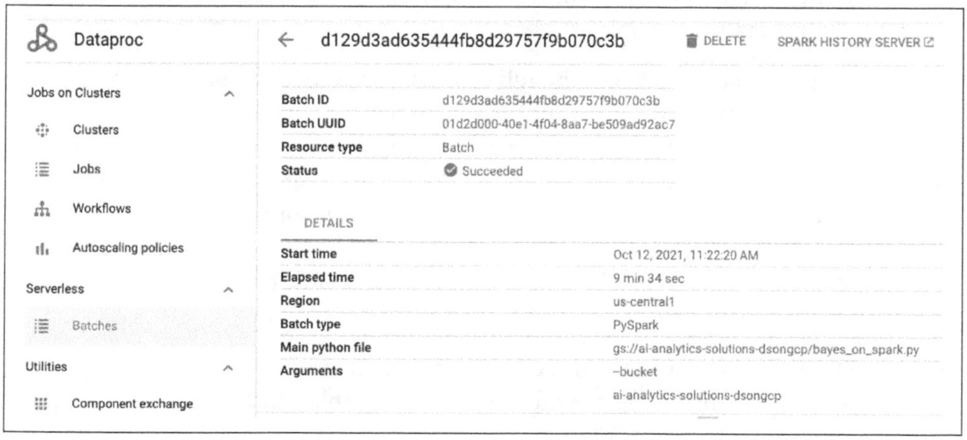

*Figure 6-10. To view the status of the serverless Spark job, visit the Dataproc section of the GCP web console.*

When I did this, I got:

```
dist_thresh,delay_thresh,frac_ontime,score
31.0,14.0,0.6874006359300477,0.012599364069952212
328.0,15.0,0.6958465263550009,0.004153473644999073
544.0,15.0,0.7054307116104869,0.005430711610486916
802.0,17.0,0.6874393150322182,0.012560684967781732
```

This matches the lookup table that we got when we ran the notebook on the full dataset:

| Distance bin | delay_thresh |
|--------------|--------------|
| [31, 328]    | 14           |
| [328, 541]   | 15           |
| [541, 802]   | 15           |
| [802, inf]   | 17           |

Because running the job involves only a single `gcloud` command, it is possible to schedule the Spark program to run every month, or whenever a new month of data is received by updating the Cloud Run and Cloud Scheduler solution that we created in Chapter 2.

# Summary

In this chapter, we explored how to create a two-variable Bayes model to provide insight as to whether to cancel a meeting based on the likely arrival delay of a flight. We quantized the two variables (distance and departure delay), created a conditional probability lookup table, and examined the on-time arrival percentage in each bin. We carried out the quantization using histogram equalization and on-time arrival percentage computations in Spark.

Upon discovering that equalizing the full distribution of departure delays resulted in a very coarse sampling of the decision surface, we chose to go with the highest possible resolution in the crucial range of departure delay.[21] However, to ensure that we would have statistically valid groupings, we also made our quantization thresholds coarser in distance. On doing this, we discovered that the probability of the arrival delay being less than 15 minutes varied rather smoothly. Because of this, our conditional probability lookup reduced to a table of thresholds that could be applied cleanly using IF-THEN rules.

On evaluating the two-variable model, we found that we would be canceling about the same number of meetings as with the single-variable model while retaining the

---

21 One-minute increments in the range (10, 20).

same overall accuracy. We hypothesize that the improvement isn't higher because the departure delay variable has already been rounded off to the nearest minute, limiting the scope of any improvement we can make.

In terms of tooling, we created a three-node Cloud Dataproc cluster for development and resized it on the fly to 20 workers when our code was ready to be run on the full dataset. Cloud Dataproc goes a long way toward making this a low-touch endeavor— we saw that it is possible to create and schedule ephemeral jobs because Dataproc provides a serverless experience for Spark. The reason that Dataproc can create, resize, and delete the clusters for our job is that our data is held not in HDFS, but on Google Cloud Storage. We carried out development in JupyterLab, which gives us an interactive notebook experience. We also found that we were able to integrate Big-Query and Spark SQL into our workflow on the Hadoop cluster.

Finally, we converted the notebook into a Python Spark program that can be run routinely in production. We explored different ways of doing this: submitting the Spark to an already running cluster, creating a Workflow template, using Cloud Composer, and running Spark in a serverless way. Of these, serverless Spark involves the least amount of fiddling around with infrastructure. If you can do serverless, do serverless.

# Suggested Resources

The most common reason that organizations use Dataproc today is that they used to have Hadoop clusters on premises. On-premises Hadoop workloads are typically lifted-and-shifted to Dataproc, optimized to take advantage of cloud computing (for example, using ephemeral clusters), and then modernized over time to BigQuery and Dataflow. This technical guide (*https://oreil.ly/2lcEG*) steps you through the considerations in moving the data, migrating the jobs, and connecting various types of clients and security tools.

One common question is whether to use Dataflow or Dataproc—both these products support data ingest and data processing. The flowchart in Figure 6-11, from the Google Cloud documentation, suggests that this depends on whether you want to use Hadoop tools like Spark.

As the flowchart suggests, the second common reason that organizations use Dataproc is that they wish to have some degree of control over their infrastructure. Perhaps they have tasks that have to be carried out on premises for regulatory reasons. When doing so it is important to adopt best practices (*https://oreil.ly/nOnsX*) for storage, compute, and operations. I would add a third consideration here—Dataflow is much better at streaming than any alternative on Hadoop. My colleague Grace Mollison has collected these flow charts (*https://oreil.ly/nyhmH*) on her website.

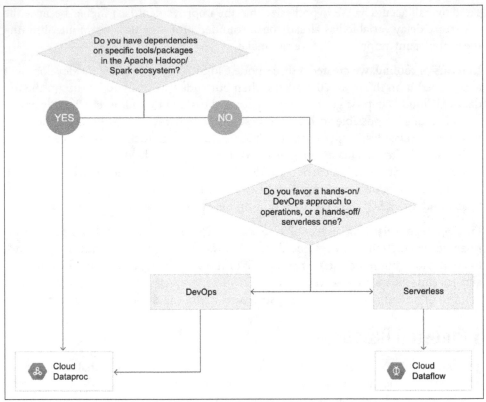

*Figure 6-11. Choosing between Dataproc and Dataflow.*

# CHAPTER 7

# Logistic Regression Using Spark ML

In Chapter 6, we created a model based on two variables—distance and departure delay—to predict the probability that a flight will be more than 15 minutes late. We found that we could get a finer-grained decision if we used a second variable (distance) instead of using just one variable (departure delay).

Why not use all the variables in the dataset? Or at least many more of them? In particular, I'd like to use the TAXI_OUT variable—if it is too high, the flight will be stuck on the runway waiting for the airport tower to allow the plane to take off, and so the flight is likely to be delayed. The Naive Bayes approach in Chapter 6 was quite limiting in terms of being able to incorporate additional variables. As we add variables, we would need to continue slicing the dataset into smaller and smaller bins. We would then find that many of our bins would contain very few samples, resulting in decision surfaces that would not be well behaved. Remember that, after we binned the data by distance, we found that the departure delay decision boundary was quite well behaved—departure delays above a certain threshold were associated with the flight not arriving on time. Our simplification of the Bayesian classification surface to a simple threshold that varied by bin would not have been possible if the decision boundary had been noisier.[1] The more variables we use, the more bins we will have, and this good behavior will begin to break down. This sort of breakdown in good behavior as the number of variables (or *dimensions*) increases is called the *curse of dimensionality*; it affects many statistical and machine learning techniques, not just the quantization-based Bayesian approach of Chapter 6.

---

1 We also put our thumb on the scale a little. Recall that we quantized the distance variable quite coarsely. Had we quantized distance into many more bins, there would have been fewer flights in each bin.

---

All of the code snippets in this chapter are available in the folder *07_sparkml* of the GitHub repository (*https://github.com/Google CloudPlatform/data-science-on-gcp*). See the *README.md* file in that directory for instructions on how to do the steps described in this chapter.

# Logistic Regression

One way to address the breakdown in behavior as the number of variables increases is to change the approach from that of directly evaluating the probability based on the input dataset. Instead, we could attempt to fit a smooth function on the variables in the dataset (a multidimensional space) to the probability of a flight arriving late (a single-dimensional space) and use the value of that function as the estimate of the probability. In other words, we could try to find a function f, such that:

$$P(Y) \approx f\left(x_0, x_1, \ldots, x_{n-1}\right)$$

In our case, $x_0$ could be the departure delay, $x_1$ the taxi-out time, $x_2$ the distance, and so on. Each row will have different values for the x's and represent different flights. The idea is that we have a function that will take these x's and somehow transform them to provide a good estimate of the probability that the flight corresponding to that row's input variables is on time.

## How Logistic Regression Works

One of the simplest transformations of a multidimensional space to a single-dimensional one is to compute a weighted sum of the input variables, as demonstrated here:

$$L = w_0 x_0 + w_1 x_1 + \ldots + w_{n-1} x_{n-1} + b$$

The w's (called the weights) and the constant b (called the intercept) are constants, but we don't initially know what they are. We need to find "good" values of the w's and b such that the weighted sum for any row closely approximates either 1 (when the flight is on time) or 0 (when the flight is late). Because this process of finding good values is averaged over a large dataset, the value L is the prediction that flights with a specific departure delay, taxi-out time, and so on will arrive on time. If that number is 0.8, we would like it to be that 80% of such flights would arrive on time and 20% would be late. In other words, rather than L being simply 1 or 0, we'd like it to be the probability that the flight will arrive on time.

There is a problem, though. The preceding weighted sum cannot function as a probability. This is because the linear combination (L) can take any value, whereas a
probability will need to lie between 0 and 1. One common solution for this problem
is to transform the linear combination using the *logistic* function:

$$P(Y) = \frac{1}{1 + e^{-L}}$$

Fitting a logistic function of a linear combination of variables to binary outcomes
(i.e., finding "good" values for the w's and b such that the estimated P(Y) are close to
the actual recorded outcome of the flight being on time) is called *logistic regression*.

In machine learning, the original linear combination, L, which lies between $-\infty$ and
$\infty$, is called the *logit*. You can see that if the logit adds up to $\infty$, $e^{-L}$ will be 0 and so,
P(Y) will be 1. If the original linear combination adds up to $-\infty$, then $e^{-L}$ will be $\infty$ and
so, P(Y) will be 0. Therefore, Y could be an event such as the flight arriving on time
and P(Y), the probability of that event happening. Because of the transformation, P(Y)
will lie between 0 and 1 as required for anything to be a probability.

If P(Y) is the probability, the logit, L, is given by the following:

$$\log_e \frac{P(Y)}{1 - P(Y)}$$

The *odds* is the ratio of the probability of the event happening, P(Y), to the probability of the event not happening, $1 - P(Y)$. Therefore, the logit can also be interpreted as
the log-odds where the base of the logarithm is e.

Figure 7-1 depicts the relationship between the logit, the probability, and the odds.

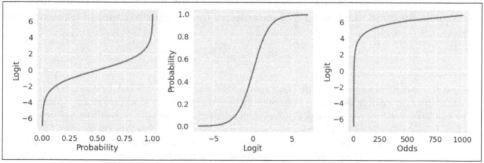

*Figure 7-1. The relationships among the probability, the logit, and the odds.*

Spend some time looking at the graphs in Figure 7-1 and gaining an intuitive understanding for what the relationships mean. For example, see if you can answer this set of questions (feel free to sketch out the curves as you do your reasoning):[2]

- At equal odds (i.e., the flight is as likely to be late as not), what is the logit? How about if the odds are predominantly in favor of a flight being on time?

- At what probability does the logit function change most rapidly?

- Where is the gradient (rate of change) of the logit function slowest?

- Which logit change, from 2 to 3 or from 2 to 1, will result in a greater change in probability?

- How does the value of the intercept, b, affect the answer to Question 4?

- Suppose the intercept is zero. If all the input variables double, what happens to the logit?

- If the logit value doubles, what happens to the probability? How does this depend on the original value of the logit?

- What logit value does it take to provide a probability of 0.95? How about 0.995?

- How extreme do the input variables have to be to attain probabilities that are close to zero or one?

Many practical considerations in classification problems in machine learning derive from this set of relationships. So, as simple as these curves are, it is important that you understand their implications.

The name *logistic regression* is a little confusing—regression is normally a way of fitting a real-valued number, whereas classification is a way of fitting to a categorical outcome. Here, we fit the observed variables (the x's) to a logit (which is real-valued) —this is the regression that is being referred to in the name. However, we then use the logistic function that has no free parameters (no weights to tune) to transform the

---

2 Answers (but don't take my word for it): (1) At equal odds, the probability is ½ and the logit is zero. If the odds are predominantly in favor of the flight being on time, the probability of on-time arrival is nearly 1.0 and the logit has a very large positive value. (2) The logit function changes fastest at probabilities near zero and one. (3) The gradient of the logit function is slowest near a probability of ½. (4) The change from 2 to 1 will result in a greater change in probability. Near probabilities of zero and one, larger logit changes are required to have the same impact on probability. As you get nearer to a probability of ½, smaller logit changes suffice. (5) The intercept directly impacts the value of the logit, so it moves the first curve upwards or downwards. (6) The logit doubles. (7) If the original probability is near zero or one, doubling of the logit has negligible impact (look at what happens if the logit changes from 4 to 8, for example). If the original probability is between about 0.3 and 0.7, the relationship is quite linear: doubling of the logit ends up causing a proportional increase in probability. (8) About 3, and about 5. (9) Doubling of the logit value at 0.95 is required to reach 0.995. Lots of "energy" in the input variables is required to move the probability needle at the extremes.

real-valued number to a probability. Overall, therefore, logistic regression functions as a classification method.

## Spark ML Library

Given a multivariable dataset, Spark has the ability to carry out logistic regression and give us the optimal weight for each variable. Spark's logistic regression module will give us the w's and b if we show it a bunch of x's and the corresponding Y's. The logistic regression module is part of Apache Spark's machine learning library, MLlib, which you can program against in Java, Scala, Python, or R. Spark MLlib (colloquially known as Spark ML) includes implementations of many canonical machine learning algorithms: decision trees, random forests, alternating least squares, k-means clustering, association rules, support vector machines, and so on. Spark can execute on a Hadoop cluster; thus, it can scale to large datasets.

The problem we are solving—to find a set of weights that optimizes model predictions based on known outcomes—is an instance of a *supervised* learning problem. In supervised learning problems, the actual answers, called *labels*, need to be known for some dataset. As illustrated in Figure 7-2, first you ask the machine (here, Spark) to learn (the w's) from data (the x's) that has labels (the Y's). This is called *training*.

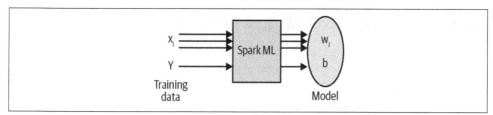

*Figure 7-2. In supervised learning, the machine (here, Spark) learns a set of parameters (the w's and b's) from training data that consists of inputs (x's) and their corresponding labels (Y's).*

The learned set of weights, along with the original equation (the logistic function of a linear combination of x's), is called a *model*. After you have learned a model from the training data, you can save it to a file. Then, whenever you want to make a prediction for a new flight, you can re-create the model from that file, pass in the x's in the same order, and compute the logistic function and obtain the estimate P(Y). This process, called *prediction*, might be carried out in real time in response to a request that includes the input variables, whereas the training of the model might happen less frequently, as shown in Figure 7-3.

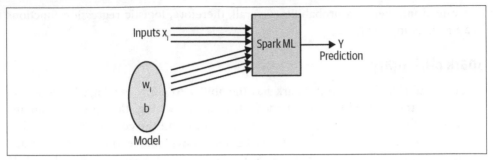

*Figure 7-3. You can use the learned set of weights to predict the value of Y for new data (x's).*

Of course, the prediction can be carried outside of Spark—all that we'd need to do is compute the weighted sum of the inputs and the intercept, and then compute the logistic function of the weighted sum. In general, though, you should seek to use the same libraries for prediction as you use for training. This helps to mitigate *training-serving skew*, the situation that we talked about in Chapter 2 in which the input variables in prediction are subtly different from those used in training and which leads to poorly performing models.

## Getting Started with Spark Machine Learning

To run Spark conveniently, I will continue to use the Cloud Dataproc cluster that I launched in the previous chapter. In case you deleted it, start a new one using:

```
cd 06_dataproc
./create_cluster.sh bucketname region
```

Even though we are going to develop the logistic regression code in a Jupyter Notebook, we should keep in mind that our end goal is to run the machine jobs routinely. To achieve that goal, it is important to keep a notebook with the final machine learning workflow and export this notebook into a standalone program. You can submit the standalone program to the cluster whenever the machine learning needs to be repeated on new datasets.

As in Chapter 6, we open the notebook from the Web Interfaces section of the Google Cloud console. Within the notebook, we start out creating a `SparkContext` variable `sc` and the `SparkSession` variable `spark`:[3]

```
from pyspark.sql import SparkSession
from pyspark import SparkContext
sc = SparkContext('local', 'logistic')
spark = SparkSession \
```

---

3 See *logistic_regression.ipynb* in the GitHub repository for this book.

```
    .builder \
    .appName("Logistic regression w/ Spark ML") \
    .getOrCreate()
```

After we do this, any line that works in the interactive shell will also work when launched from the notebook *logistic_regression.ipynb* or the script *logistic.py*. The application name (`logistic`) will show up in logs when the script is run.

# Spark Logistic Regression

The logistic regression implementation, `L-BFGS`, is in *pyspark.mllib* and is named for the initials of the independent inventors (Broyden, Fletcher, Goldfarb, and Shanno)[4] of a popular, iterative, fast-converging optimization algorithm. The L-BFGS algorithm is used by Spark to find the weights that minimize the *logistic loss* function:

$$\Sigma log\left(1 + e^{-yL}\right)$$

over the training dataset, where y, the training label, is either −1 or 1 and L is the logit computed from the input variables, the weights, and the intercept.

So, let's begin by adding `import` lines for the Python classes that we'll need:

```
from pyspark.mllib.classification import LogisticRegressionWithLBFGS
from pyspark.mllib.regression import LabeledPoint
```

Knowing the details of the logistic formulation and loss function used by Spark is important. This is because different machine learning libraries use equivalent (but not identical) versions of these formulae. For example, another common approach taken by machine learning frameworks is to minimize the *cross-entropy*:

$$\Sigma - ylogP(Y) - (1 - y) \log (1 - P(Y)))$$

Here, y is the training label, and P(Y) is the probabilistic output of the model. In that case, the training label will need to be 0 or 1. I won't go through the math, but even though the two loss functions look very different, minimizing the logistic loss and minimizing the cross-entropy loss turn out to be equivalent.

Rather confusingly, the Spark documentation notes that "a binary label y is denoted as either +1 (positive) or −1 (negative), which is convenient for the formulation. However, the negative label is represented by 0 in *spark.mllib* instead of −1, to be consistent with multiclass labeling."[5] In other words, Spark ML uses the logistic loss

---

4 The *L* stands for low-memory—this is a limited-memory variant of the BFGS algorithm.

5 See the section on loss functions in the Spark documentation (*https://oreil.ly/W3JDv*).

function, but requires that the labels we provide be 0 or 1. There really is no substitute for reading the documentation!

To summarize, the preprocessing that you might need to do to your input data depends on the formulation of the loss function employed by the machine learning framework you are using. Suppose that we decide to do this:

y = 0 if arrival delay ≥ 15 minutes

y = 1 if arrival delay < 15 minutes

Because we have mapped on-time flights to 1, the machine learning algorithm (after training) will predict the probability that the flight is on time.

## Creating a Training Dataset

First, let's read in the list of training days. To do that, we need to read *trainday.csv* from Cloud Storage, remembering that the comma-separated value (CSV) file has a header that will help with inferring its schema:

```
traindays = spark.read \
    .option("header", "true") \
    .csv('gs://{}/flights/trainday.csv'.format(BUCKET))
```

For convenience, I'll make this a Spark SQL view, as well:

```
traindays.createOrReplaceTempView('traindays')
```

We can print the first few lines of this file:

```
spark.sql("SELECT * from traindays LIMIT 5").show()
```

This obtains the following eminently reasonable result:

```
+----------+------------+
|   FL_DATE|is_train_day|
+----------+------------+
|2015-01-01|        True|
|2015-01-02|       False|
|2015-01-03|       False|
|2015-01-04|        True|
|2015-01-05|        True|
+----------+------------+
```

While we're developing the code (on my minimal Hadoop cluster that is running Jupyter), it would be easier to read only a small part of the dataset. Hence, we define the inputs variable to be just one of the shards:

```
inputs = 'gs://{}/flights/tzcorr/all_flights-00000-*'.format(BUCKET)
```

After we have developed all of the code, we can change the inputs to the full dataset:

```
#inputs = 'gs://{}/flights/tzcorr/all_flights-*'.format(BUCKET)  # FULL
```

For now, though, let's leave the latter line commented out. We can read in the flights dataset as we did in Chapter 6:

```
flights = spark.read.json(inputs)
flights.createOrReplaceTempView('flights')
```

Training will need to be carried out on the flights that were on days for which is_train_day is True:

```
trainquery = """
SELECT
  f.*
FROM flights fJOIN traindays t
ON f.FL_DATE == t.FL_DATE
WHERE
  t.is_train_day == 'True'
"""
traindata = spark.sql(trainquery)
```

### Dealing with corner cases

Let's verify that `traindata` does contain the data we need. We can look at the first few (here, the first two) rows of the dataframe using the following:

```
traindata.head(2)
```

The result seems quite reasonable:

```
[Row(ARR_AIRPORT_LAT=33.43416667, ARR_AIRPORT_LON=-112.01166667,
ARR_AIRPORT_TZOFFSET=-25200.0, ARR_DELAY=-16.0, ARR_TIME='2015-07-28T18:20:00',
CANCELLED=False, CRS_ARR_TIME='2015-07-28T18:36:00',
CRS_DEP_TIME='2015-07-28T17:05:00', DEP_AIRPORT_LAT=33.9425,
DEP_AIRPORT_LON=-118.40805556, DEP_AIRPORT_TZOFFSET=-25200.0, DEP_DELAY=-3.0,
DEP_TIME='2015-07-28T17:02:00', DEST='PHX', DEST_AIRPORT_SEQ_ID='1410702',
DISTANCE='370.00', DIVERTED=False, FL_DATE='2015-07-28', ORIGIN='LAX',
ORIGIN_AIRPORT_SEQ_ID='1289203', TAXI_IN=6.0, TAXI_OUT=14.0,
UNIQUE_CARRIER='AA', WHEELS_OFF='2015-07-28T17:16:00',
WHEELS_ON='2015-07-28T18:14:00'),
```

Date fields are dates, and airport codes are reasonable, as are the latitudes and longitudes. But eyeballing is no substitute for truly verifying that all of the values exist.

So, let's restrict the query to fields we want:

```
SELECT
  DEP_DELAY, TAXI_OUT, ARR_DELAY, DISTANCE
FROM flights f
...
```

Knowing that the four variables we are interested in are all floats, we can ask Spark to compute simple statistics over the full dataset:

```
traindata.describe().show()
```

The describe() method computes column-by-column statistics, and the show() method causes those statistics to be printed. We now get the following:[6]

```
+-------+----------+---------+---------+---------+
|summary| DEP_DELAY| TAXI_OUT| ARR_DELAY| DISTANCE|
+-------+----------+---------+---------+---------+
|  count|    259692|   259434|    258706|   275062|
|   mean|    13.178|  16.9658|    9.7319| 802.3747|
| stddev|   41.8886|  10.9363|   45.0384|  592.254|
|    min|     -61.0|      1.0|     -77.0|     31.0|
|    max|    1587.0|    225.0|    1627.0|   4983.0|
+-------+----------+---------+---------+---------+
```

Notice anything odd?

Notice the count statistic. There are 275,062 DISTANCE values, but only 259,692 DEP_DELAY values, and even fewer TAXI_OUT values. What is going on? This is the sort of thing that you will need to chase down to find the root cause. In this case, the reason has to do with flights that are scheduled but never leave the gate and flights that depart the gate but never take off. Similarly, there are flights that take off (and have a TAXI_OUT value) but are diverted and do not have an ARR_DELAY. In the data, these are denoted by NULL, and Spark's describe() method doesn't count NULLs.

We don't want to use canceled and diverted flights for training either. One way to tighten up the selection of our training dataset would be to simply remove NULLs, as shown here:

```
trainquery = """
SELECT
  DEP_DELAY, TAXI_OUT, ARR_DELAY, DISTANCE
FROM flights f
JOIN traindays t
ON f.FL_DATE == t.FL_DATE
WHERE
  t.is_train_day == 'True' AND
  f.dep_delay IS NOT NULL AND
  f.arr_delay IS NOT NULL
"""

traindata = spark.sql(trainquery)
traindata.describe().show()
```

Running this gets us a consistent value of the count across all the columns:

```
|summary| DEP_DELAY| TAXI_OUT| ARR_DELAY| DISTANCE|
|  count|    258706|   258706|    258706|   258706|
```

---

6 Your results might be different because the actual flight records held in your first shard (recall that the input is all_flights-00000-*) are possibly different.

---

However, I strongly encourage you not to do this. Removing NULLs is merely fixing the symptom of the problem. What we really want to do is to address the root cause. In this case, you'd do that by removing flights that have been canceled or diverted, and fortunately, we do have this information in the data. So, we can change the query to be the following:

```
trainquery = """
SELECT
  DEP_DELAY, TAXI_OUT, ARR_DELAY, DISTANCE
FROM flights f
JOIN traindays t
ON f.FL_DATE == t.FL_DATE
WHERE
  t.is_train_day == 'True' AND
  f.CANCELLED == 'False' AND
  f.DIVERTED == 'False'
"""

traindata = spark.sql(trainquery)
traindata.describe().show()
```

This, too, yields the same counts as when we threw away the NULLs, thereby demonstrating that our diagnosis of the problem was correct.

Discovering corner cases and problems with an input dataset at the time we begin training a machine learning model is quite common. In this case, I knew this problem was coming and was careful to select the CANCELLED and DIVERTED columns to be part of my input dataset (in Chapter 2). In real life, you will need to spend quite a bit of time troubleshooting this, potentially adding new logging operations to your ingest code to uncover the reason that underlies a simple problem. What you should not do is to simply throw away bad values.

> Bad values (like NULL) are usually a symptom of a problem. Investigate the issue. Don't simply discard bad values.

### Creating training examples

Now that we have the training data, we can look at the documentation for LogisticRegressionModel to determine the format of its input. The documentation indicates that each row of the training data needs to be transformed to a Labeled Point whose documentation in turn indicates that its constructor requires a label and an array of features, all of which need to be floating-point numbers.

Let's create a method that will convert each data point of our dataframe into a *training example* (an example is a combination of the input features and the true answer):

```
def to_example(raw_data_point):
   return LabeledPoint(
              float(raw_data_point['ARR_DELAY'] < 15), # on-time?
              [
                  raw_data_point['DEP_DELAY'],
                  raw_data_point['TAXI_OUT'],
                  raw_data_point['DISTANCE'],
              ])
```

Note that we have created a label and an array of features. Here, the features consist of three numeric fields that we pass in as-is. It is good practice to create a separate method that takes the raw data and constructs a training example because this allows us to fold in other operations as well. For example, we can begin to do preprocessing of the feature values, and having a method to construct training examples allows us to reuse the code between training and evaluation.

After we have a way to convert each raw data point into a training example, we need to apply this method to the entire training dataset. We can do this by mapping the dataset row by row:

```
examples = traindata.map(to_example)
```

## Training the Model

Now that we have a dataframe in the requisite format, we can ask Spark to fit the training dataset to the labels:

```
lrmodel = LogisticRegressionWithLBFGS.train(examples, intercept=True)
```

We'd have specified `intercept = False` if we believed that when all x = 0, the prediction needed to be 0. We have no reason to expect this, so we ask the model to find a value for the intercept.

When the `train()` method completes, the `lrmodel` will have the weights and intercept, and we can print them out:

```
print lrmodel.weights,lrmodel.intercept
```

This yields the following:[7]

```
[-0.164,-0.132,0.000294] 5.1579
```

The `weights` is an array, one for each variable. These numbers, plus the formula for logistic regression, are enough to set up code for the model in any language we choose. Remember that in our labeled points, 0 indicated late arrivals and 1 indicated

---

7 Because of random seeds used in the optimization process, and different data in shards, your results will be different.

on-time arrivals. So, applying these weights to the departure delay, taxi-out time, and flight distance of a flight will yield the probability that the flight will be on time.

In this case, it appears that the departure delay has a weight of –0.164. The negative sign indicates that the higher the departure delay, the lower the probability that the flight will be on time (which sounds about right). On the other hand, the sign on the distance is positive, indicating that higher distances are associated with more on-time behavior. Even though we are able to look at the weights and reason with them on this dataset, such reasoning will begin to break down if the variables are not independent. If you have highly correlated input variables, the magnitudes and signs of the weights are very hard to interpret.

Let's try out a prediction:

```
lrmodel.predict([6.0,12.0,594.0])
```

The result is 1—that is, the flight will be on time when the departure delay is 6 minutes, the taxi-out time is 12 minutes, and the flight is for 594 miles. Let's change the departure delay from 6 minutes to 36 minutes:

```
lrmodel.predict([36.0,12.0,594.0])
```

The result now is 0—the flight won't arrive on time.

But wait a minute. We want the output to be a probability, not 0 or 1 (the final label). To do that, we can remove the implicit threshold of 0.5:

```
lrmodel.clearThreshold()
```

With the thresholding removed, we get probabilities. The probability of arriving late increases as the departure delay increases.

By keeping two of the variables constant, it is possible to study how the probability varies as a function of one of the variables. For example, at a departure delay of 20 minutes and a taxi-out time of 10 minutes, this is how the distance affects the probability that the flight is on time:

```
dist = np.arange(10, 2000, 10)
prob = [lrmodel.predict([20, 10, d]) for d in dist]
plt.plot(dist, prob)
```

Figure 7-4 shows the plot.

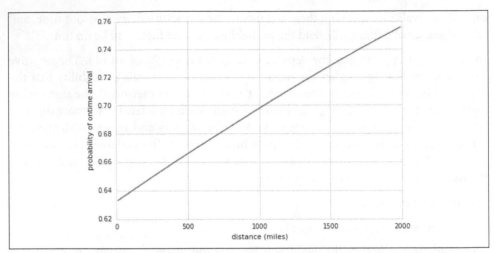

*Figure 7-4. How the distance of the flight affects the probability of on-time arrival. According to our model, longer flights tend to have higher likelihoods of arriving on time, but the effect (0.63 to 0.76) is rather minor.*

As you can see, the effect is relatively minor. The probability increases from about 0.63 to about 0.76 as the distance changes from a very short hop to a cross-continental flight. On the other hand, if we hold the taxi-out time and distance constant and examine the dependence on departure delay, we see a more dramatic impact (see Figure 7-5):

```
delay = np.arange(-20, 60, 1)
prob = [lrmodel.predict([d, 10, 500]) for d in delay]
ax = plt.plot(delay, prob)
```

Although the probabilities are useful to be able to plot the behavior of the model in different scenarios, we do want a specific decision threshold. Recall that we want to cancel the meeting if the probability of the flight arriving on time is less than 70%. So, we can change the decision threshold:

```
lrmodel.setThreshold(0.7)
```

Now, the predictions are 0 or 1, with the probability threshold set at 0.7.

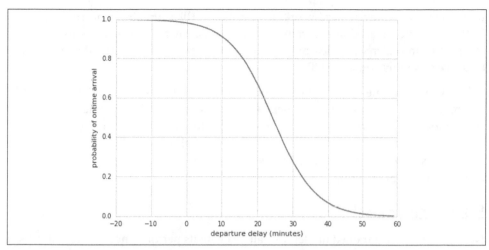

*Figure 7-5. How the departure delay of the flight affects the probability of on-time arrival. The effect of the departure delay is rather dramatic.*

## Predicting Using the Model

Now that we have a trained model, we can save it to Cloud Storage and retrieve it whenever we need to make a prediction. To save the model, we provide a location on Cloud Storage:

```
MODEL_FILE='gs://' + BUCKET + '/flights/sparkmloutput/model'
lrmodel.save(sc, MODEL_FILE)
```

To retrieve the model, we load it from the same location:

```
from pyspark.mllib.classification import LogisticRegressionModel
lrmodel = LogisticRegressionModel.load(sc, MODEL_FILE)
lrmodel.setThreshold(0.7)
```

Note that we must take care to set the decision threshold; it is not part of the model.

Now, we can use the `lrmodel` variable to carry out predictions:

```
print lrmodel.predict([36.0,12.0,594.0])
```

Obviously, this code could be embedded into a Python web application to create a prediction web service or API.

A key point to realize is that whereas model training in Spark is distributed and requires a cluster, model prediction is a pretty straightforward mathematical computation. Model training is a batch operation that requires the ability to scale out to multiple processors, but online prediction requires fast computation on a single processor. When the machine learning model is relatively small (as in our logistic regression workflow),[8] hardware optimizations (like graphics processing units [GPUs]) are not needed in the training stage. Thus, when choosing how to resize the cluster to run our machine learning training job over the full dataset, it is more cost-effective to simply add more CPUs.

When would you need GPUs in machine learning? GPUs are potentially needed in the prediction stage for small models. GPUs become useful in prediction even for small models if the system needs to provide for low latency and a high number of queries per second (QPS). Of course, had we been training a deep learning model for image classification with hundreds of layers, GPUs would have been called for both in training and in prediction.

## Evaluating a Model

Now that we have a trained model, we can evaluate its performance on the test days, a set of days that were not used in training (we created this test dataset in Chapter 5). To do that, we change the query to pull out the test days:

```
testquery = trainquery.replace(\
        "t.is_train_day == 'True'","t.is_train_day == 'False'")
print testquery
```

Here is the resulting query:

```
SELECT
  DEP_DELAY, TAXI_OUT, ARR_DELAY, DISTANCE
FROM flights f
JOIN traindays t
ON f.FL_DATE == t.FL_DATEWHERE
  t.is_train_day == 'False' AND
  f.CANCELLED == 'False' AND
  f.DIVERTED == 'False'
```

We then carry out the same ML pipeline as we did during training:

```
testdata = spark.sql(testquery)
examples = testdata.map(to_example)
```

Note that we are able to reuse the function to_example to go from the raw data to the training examples.

As soon as we have the dataframe examples, we can have the model predict the label given the set of features for each row:

```
labelpred = examples.map(lambda p: \
            (p.label, lrmodel.predict(p.features)))
```

---

8 Very large deep neural networks, such as those used for image classification, are another story. Such models can have hundreds of layers, each with hundreds of weights. Here, we have three weights—four if you count the intercept.

The `map` function applies the `predict` method to each row of features and creates a dataframe that contains the true label and the model prediction for each row.

To evaluate the performance of the model, we first find out how many flights we will need to cancel and how accurate we are in terms of flights we cancel and flights we don't cancel:

```
def eval(labelpred):
    cancel = labelpred.filter(lambda (label, pred): pred == 1)
    nocancel = labelpred.filter(lambda (label, pred): pred == 0)
    corr_cancel = cancel.filter(lambda (label, pred): \
                                       label == pred).count()
    corr_nocancel = nocancel.filter(lambda (label, pred): \
                                       label == pred).count()
    return {'total_cancel': cancel.count(), \
            'correct_cancel': float(corr_cancel)/cancel.count(), \
            'total_noncancel': nocancel.count(), \
            'correct_noncancel': float(corr_nocancel)/nocancel.count()\
           }
```

Here's what the resulting statistics turn out to be:

```
{'correct_cancel': 0.7917474551623849, 'total_noncancel': 115949,
 'correct_noncancel': 0.9571363271783284, 'total_cancel': 33008}
```

As discussed in Chapter 5, the reason the correctness percentages are not 70% is because the 70% threshold is on the marginal distribution—the accuracy percentages here are computed on the total distribution and so are padded by the easy decisions. However, let's go back and modify the evaluation function to explicitly print out statistics around the decision threshold—this is important to ensure that we are, indeed, making a probabilistic decision.

We should clear the threshold so that the model returns probabilities and then carry out the evaluation twice: once on the full dataset, and next on only those flights that fall near the decision threshold of 0.7:

```
lrmodel.clearThreshold() # so it returns probabilities
labelpred = examples.map(lambda p: \
                         (p.label, lrmodel.predict(p.features)))
print eval(labelpred)
# keep only those examples near the decision threshold
labelpred = labelpred.filter(lambda (label, pred):\
                         pred > 0.65 and pred < 0.75)
print eval(labelpred)
```

Of course, we must change the evaluation code to work with probabilities instead of with categorical predictions. The four variables now become as follows:

```
cancel = labelpred.filter(lambda (label, pred): pred < 0.7)
nocancel = labelpred.filter(lambda (label, pred): pred >= 0.7)
corr_cancel = cancel.filter(lambda (label, pred): \
                            label == int(pred >= 0.7)).count()
```

```
corr_nocancel = nocancel.filter(lambda (label, pred): \
                      label == int(pred >= 0.7)).count()
```

When run, the first set of results remains the same, and the second set of results now yields this:

```
{'correct_cancel': 0.30886504799548276, 'total_noncancel': 2224,
 'correct_noncancel': 0.7383093525179856, 'total_cancel': 1771}
```

Note that we are correct about 74% of the time in our decision to go ahead with a meeting (our target was 70%). Although useful to verify that the code is working as intended, the actual results are meaningless because we are not running on the entire dataset, just one shard of it. Therefore, the final step is to export the code from the notebook, remove the various show() and plot() functions, and create a submittable script.[9]

We can submit the script to the Cloud Dataproc cluster from a laptop with the Cloud SDK installed, from Cloud Shell, or from the Cloud Dataproc section of the Google Cloud Platform web console (*https://oreil.ly/JF3wn*). Before we submit the script, we need to resize the cluster, so that we can process the entire dataset on a larger cluster than the one on which we did development. So, what we need to do is to increase the size of the cluster, submit the script, and decrease the size of the cluster after the script is done. Alternatively, we can use an autoscaling Dataproc cluster or serverless Spark as discussed in Chapter 6.[10]

Running *logistic.py* on a more powerful cluster, we create a model and then evaluate it on the test days. We obtain these results from the logs:

```
All flights: {'total_cancel': 291895, 'correct_cancel': 0.8122920913342127,
 'total_noncancel': 1304422, 'correct_noncancel': 0.9642401002129679}
```

Looking at these overall results, notice that we are canceling about 292k meetings. We are accurate 96.4% of the time we don't cancel a meeting and 81.2% of the time when we decide to cancel. Remember that we canceled 275k meetings when using the Bayesian classifier in Chapter 6 and were correct 83% of the time that we decided to cancel. Based on our secondary criterion, the Naive Bayes approach in Chapter 6 with only two variables is better than the logistic regression approach in this chapter with three variables! There is, in machine learning, no substitute for experimentation to see what works.

How about the results on the marginal distribution (i.e., on flights for which our probability is near 0.7)? These, too, are in the logs. They indicate that we are, indeed, making an appropriately probabilistic decision—our decision to go ahead with a meeting is correct 73% of the time:

---

9 See *logistic.py* in *07_sparkml*.

10 The script *submit_spark.sh* in *07_sparkml* uses the serverless Spark approach.

```
Flights near decision threshold: {'total_cancel': 15084,
 'correct_cancel': 0.3325377883850438, 'total_noncancel': 18441,
 'correct_noncancel': 0.7279431701100808}
```

A close examination of the preceding numbers indicates what is going on—we are correct to cancel 33% of the time while in Chapter 6, we were correct to cancel only 30% of the time. This extra 3% allows us to cancel more meetings. It is clear, then, that simply looking at the number of meetings we cancel is not a good secondary criterion of model performance. Instead, we will find a different criterion by comparing the performance of the model against ideal performance across all thresholds. We will do that in the next section.

# Feature Engineering

Still, it is unclear whether we really needed all three variables in the logistic regression model. Any variable you include in a machine learning model brings with it an increased danger of overfitting. Known as the principle of parsimony (*https://oreil.ly/F5VF3*) (often referred to as Occam's razor),[11] the idea is that it is preferable to use a simpler model to a more complex model that has similar accuracy—the fewer variables we have in our model, the better it is.

One manifestation of the principle of parsimony is that there are practical considerations involved with every new variable in a machine learning model. A hand-coded system of rules can deal with the presence or absence of values (for example, if the variable in question was not collected) for specific variables relatively easily—simply write a new rule to handle the case. On the other hand, machine learning models require the presence of enough data when that variable value is absent. Thus, a machine learning model will often be unusable if all of its variable values are not present in the data. Even if a variable value is present in some new data, it might be defined differently or computed differently, and we might have to go through an expensive retraining effort in order to use it. Thus, extra variables pose issues around the applicability of a machine learning model to new situations. We should attempt to use as few variables as possible.

## Experimental Framework

It is also unclear whether the three variables we chose are the ones that matter most. Perhaps we could use more variables from the dataset besides the three we are using. In machine learning terminology, the inputs to the model are called *features*. The features could be different from the raw input variables because the input variables could be transformed in some way before being provided to the model. The process

---

11 William of Ockham (later spelled Occam), who was a friar in medieval England, actually wrote "*Pluralitas non est ponenda sine necessitate*," which translates to "Entities should not be multiplied unnecessarily."

of designing the transforms that are carried out on the raw input variables is called *feature engineering*.

To test whether a feature provides value to the model, we need to build an experimental framework. We could begin with one feature (departure delay, for example) and test whether the incorporation of a new feature (perhaps the distance) improves model performance. If it does, we keep it and try out one more feature. If not, we discard it and try the next feature on our list. This way, we get to select a subset of features and ensure that they do matter. Another approach is to train a model with all possible features, remove a feature, and retrain. If performance doesn't go down, leave the feature out. At the end, as before, we will be left with a subset of features that matter. The second approach is preferable because it allows us to capture interactions—perhaps a feature by itself doesn't matter, but its presence alongside another is powerful. Choosing the set of features through a systematic process is called *feature selection*.

For both feature engineering and feature selection, it is important to devise an experimental framework to test out our hypotheses as to whether a feature is needed. On which dataset should we evaluate whether a feature is important? We cannot evaluate how much it improves accuracy on the training dataset itself because the model might be fitting noise in the training data. Instead, we need an independent dataset in order to carry out feature selection. However, we cannot use the test dataset because if we use the test dataset in our model creation process, it is no longer independent and cannot be used as a good indicator of model performance. Therefore, we will split the training dataset itself into two parts—one part will be used for training, whereas the other will be held out and used to evaluate different models.

Figure 7-6 shows what our experimentation framework is going to look like.

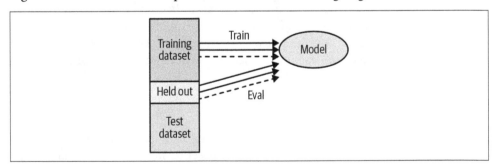

*Figure 7-6. We often split a dataset into three parts. The training dataset is used to tune the weights of a model, and the held-out dataset is used to evaluate the impact of model changes, such as feature selection. The independent test dataset is used only to gauge the performance of the final, selected model.*

First, we break the full dataset into two parts and keep one part of it for the final evaluation of models (we did this in Chapter 6 when we created the `traindays` dataset). This part is called the test dataset and is what we have been using for end-of-chapter evaluations. However, when we are creating several models and need to choose among them, we cannot use the test dataset. Therefore, we will split our original training dataset itself into two parts. We'll retain the larger part of it for actual training and use the held-out portion to evaluate the model. In Figure 7-6, for example, we are deciding whether to use the third input variable. We do this based on whether that feature improves model performance enough.

### Choosing a metric

What metric should we evaluate in order to choose between two models? *Not* the number of canceled flights! It is easy to game metrics computed from the contingency table because it is possible to change the probability threshold to get a wide range of accuracy, precision, or recall metrics.[12] A contingency table–based metric is a good way to understand the performance of a model, but not to choose between two models unless care is taken to ensure that the measure is not tunable by changing the threshold. One way to do this would be to, for example, compare precision at a fixed recall rate, but you should do this only if that fixed recall is meaningful. In our problem, however, it is the probability that is meaningful, not the precision or recall.

Hence, it is not possible to fix either of them, and we are left comparing two pairs of numbers.

Another way to avoid the problem that the metric can be gamed is to use a measure that uses the full distribution of probabilities that are output by the model. When carrying out feature selection or any other form of hyperparameter tuning, we could use a measure such as the logistic loss or cross-entropy that conveys this full distribution. As a simpler, more intuitive measure that nevertheless uses the full distribution of probabilities, let's use the root mean squared error (RMSE) between the true labels and the probabilistic predictions:

```
totsqe = labelpred.map(
        lambda data: (data[0] - data[1]) * (data[0] - data[1])
).sum()
rmse = np.sqrt(totsqe / float(cancel.count() + nocancel.count()))
```

---

12 The Machine Learning Crash Course from Google has a good explanation of these metrics (*https://oreil.ly/ NgJyo*). Remember that we need to threshold the probabilistic output of the model to get the entries in the contingency table. A correct cancel, for example, is the situation that the flight arrived more than 15 minutes late and the predicted probability of on-time arrival was less than 0.7. The metrics evaluated on the contingency table are extremely sensitive to this choice of threshold. Different models will be different at thresholds of 0.65, 0.68, or 0.70, especially for models whose performance is quite comparable. If, for example, we want the overall correct cancel percentage to be 80%, we can change the threshold to get this. We can also change the threshold to get an overall correct cancel percentage of 20% if that is what we desire.

What is "enough" of an improvement when it comes to RMSE? There are no hard-and-fast rules. We need the model performance to improve enough to outweigh the drawbacks involved with additional inputs and the loss of agility and model runtime speed that additional input features entail. Here, I will choose to use 0.5% as my threshold. If the model performance, based on some metric we decide upon, isn't reduced by at least 0.5% by removing a variable, I won't use the extra variable.

## Creating the held-out dataset

Because the held-out dataset is going to be used only for model evaluation and only within Spark, we do not need to create the held-out dataset the same way we created the test dataset in Chapter 5. For example, we do not need to store the held-out days as a separate dataset that can be read from multiple frameworks.[13] However, the principle of repeatability still applies—every time we run our Spark program, we should get the same set of held-out days. Otherwise, it will not be possible to compare the performance of different models (because evaluation metrics depend on the dataset on which they are evaluated).

After I read the `traindays` dataset, I will add in a new temporary column called `hold out` that will be initialized from a random array:[14]

```
from pyspark.sql.functions import rand
SEED = 13
traindays = traindays.withColumn("holdout", rand(SEED) > 0.8)  # 20%
traindays.createOrReplaceTempView('traindays')
```

I am passing in a seed so that I get the exact same array (and hence the same set of held-out days) every time I run this Spark code.

The first few rows of the `traindays` table are now as follows:

```
Row(FL_DATE=u'2015-01-01', is_train_day=u'True', holdout=False),
Row(FL_DATE=u'2015-01-02', is_train_day=u'False', holdout=True),
Row(FL_DATE=u'2015-01-03', is_train_day=u'False', holdout=False),
Row(FL_DATE=u'2015-01-04', is_train_day=u'True', holdout=False),
Row(FL_DATE=u'2015-01-05', is_train_day=u'True', holdout=True),
```

Note that we have both `is_train_day` and `holdout`—obviously, we are not going to be holding out any *test* data, so the query to pull training samples is as follows:

```
SELECT
    *
```

---

13 Recall that we stored the training versus test days both as a BigQuery table and as a CSV file on Cloud Storage. We had to save the `traindays` dataset to persistent storage because otherwise we would have run into the problem of different hash function implementations in Spark, Pig, and Tensorflow. There would have been no way to evaluate model performance on the same dataset.

14 See *experimentation.ipynb* and *experiment.py* in *07_sparkml*.

```
FROM flights f
JOIN traindays t
ON f.FL_DATE == t.FL_DATE
WHERE
    t.is_train_day == 'True' AND
    t.holdout == False AND
    f.CANCELLED == 'False' AND
    f.DIVERTED == 'False'
```

After we have trained the model, we evaluate it not on the test data as before, but on the held-out data:

```
evalquery = trainquery.replace("t.holdout == False",
                               "t.holdout == True")
```

After we have developed this code, we can export it out of the notebook into a stand-alone script so that it can be submitted conveniently.

# Feature Selection

Let's use this experimental framework and the held-out dataset to decide whether all three input variables are important. As explained earlier, we will remove one variable at a time and check the RMSE on the evaluation dataset. Conveniently, this involves changing only the to_example() method from:

```
def to_example(raw_data_point):
    features = [
            fields['DEP_DELAY'],
            fields['DISTANCE'],
            fields['TAXI_OUT'],
        ]
    return LabeledPoint(
            float(fields['ARR_DELAY'] < 15), #ontime
            features)
```

to:

```
def to_example(raw_data_point):
    features = [
            # fields['DEP_DELAY'],
            fields['DISTANCE'],
            fields['TAXI_OUT'],
        ]
    return LabeledPoint(
            float(fields['ARR_DELAY'] < 15), #ontime
            features)
```

## Creating a large cluster

In the last chapter, running the logistic regression program script with serverless Spark took 15 minutes. Of this, nearly two minutes were for the cluster to start and an additional three minutes for it to autoscale to a sufficient size.

We are going to run many variations of this job, and because we don't quite know what possibilities we want to try, we want jobs that start immediately and finish quickly. Saving five minutes by having an already sized cluster ready to go will speed up our experimentation by 33% for our use case.

Therefore, let's create a cluster consisting of 50 machines that have 8 vCPUs each:[15]

```
#!/bin/bash
gcloud dataproc clusters create ch7cluster \
   --enable-component-gateway \
   --region ${REGION} --zone ${REGION}-a \
   --master-machine-type n1-standard-4 \
   --master-boot-disk-size 500 \
   --num-workers 30 --num-secondary-workers 20 \
   --worker-machine-type n1-standard-8 \
   --worker-boot-disk-size 500 \
   --project $PROJECT \
   --scopes https://www.googleapis.com/auth/cloud-platform
```

Unfortunately, when I tried it, the script immediately exited with an error:

```
ERROR: (gcloud.dataproc.clusters.create) INVALID_ARGUMENT:
Insufficient 'CPUS' quota. Requested 404.0, available 67.0.
```

I didn't have the necessary quota—I needed 404 CPUs, but had only 67 available.

### Increasing quota

The number of CPUs that I'm allowed to use in a region is an example of a *soft quota*. Soft quotas are meant to guard against human error and billing surprises. They are quite easy to change.

To increase my quota, I visited the Quotas page on the GCP web console (*https://oreil.ly/g7N4s*) and found the Compute Engine CPUs quota for the region I am interested in:

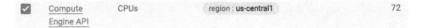

My quota is 72, but I must already be using 5, which is why the error indicated that only 67 are available.

I then clicked on "Edit quotas," requested 500, and explained why:

---

15 See *create_large_cluster.sh*.

## Compute Engine API

Quota: CPUs - us-central1

Current limit: 72

Enter a new quota limit. Your request will be sent to your service provider for approval. ❓

New limit *

500

Request description *

Needed to demonstrate experimentation in Spark.

Your description will be sent to your service provider and is used to evaluate your request. It's useful to include the intent of the quota usage, future growth plans, region or zone spread, and any additional requirements or dependencies.

DONE

Amazingly enough, the approval for my quota increase arrived in my email inbox within a minute of my requesting it. However, the email asked me to wait 15 minutes for the quota increase to get propagated throughout.

Once the quotas page showed that my quota increase had gone through, I was able to rerun the cluster creation command successfully.

### Autoscale up and down

A 400-CPU machine cluster feels a bit dangerous, though—what if we forget and leave it running for months on end? Let's add an autoscaling policy to this cluster (we could have done it when creating the cluster too, but creating the cluster first and then adding the autoscaling policy allows us to verify that we have the quota to go as high as needed).

First, I create a policy file:

```
workerConfig:
  minInstances: 2
  maxInstances: 30
secondaryWorkerConfig:
  maxInstances: 20
basicAlgorithm:
  cooldownPeriod: 15m
  yarnConfig:
    scaleUpFactor: 0.05
    scaleDownFactor: 1.0
    gracefulDecommissionTimeout: 1h
```

Then, I update the policy of the cluster that I just created:

```
gcloud dataproc autoscaling-policies import experiment-policy \
  --source=autoscale.yaml --region=$REGION

gcloud dataproc clusters update ch7cluster \
  --autoscaling-policy=experiment-policy --region=$REGION
```

The difference between this and serverless Spark is that once this cluster is started, we can simply submit jobs to it. There is no need to wait for the cluster to start at the beginning of each experiment. At the same time, the cluster will remain at the auto-scaled size, and as long as we submit the next job to it within 15 minutes, we can continue using the machines already spun up. After an hour of no activity, the cluster is decommissioned.

Yes, this is all a bit hacky. BigQuery and its near-instantaneous spin-up, autoscaling, and spin-down are so much nicer! Still, we are in Spark world here, and this is pretty flexible for being in Spark world.

When you're using a large cluster and submitting jobs one after the other, it is a good idea to monitor the Hadoop nodes to ensure that all the machines are available and that jobs are being spread over the entire cluster. You can access the monitoring details from the Dataproc section of the GCP web console. You should see an uptick in CPU usage during the regression part of the code and use of all 50 node managers as demonstrated in Figure 7-7.

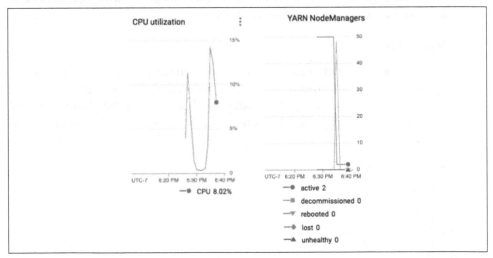

*Figure 7-7. Monitor the CPU usage and use of all the nodes during the regression phase to ensure that all the machines are being used effectively.*

In my case, monitoring revealed that simply increasing the number of workers didn't actually spread out the processing to all the nodes. This is because Spark estimates the number of partitions based on the raw input data size (here just a few gigabytes), so that estimate is probably too low for our 50-worker cluster. Hence, I modified the reading code to add in an explicit repartitioning step:

```
traindata = spark.sql(trainquery).repartition(1000)
```

And similarly, when reading the evaluation data:

```
evaldata = spark.sql(evalquery).repartition(1000)
```

After this bit of optimization, I am able to run an experiment in about 10 minutes, as I expected, by backing out the startup and upscaling time from the serverless Spark runtime. The longer the experiment, the less of a benefit all this fine tuning provides. We are better off leaving it to serverless Spark.

### Removing features

Now that we have a faster way of running the job, we can carry out our experiment of removing one variable at a time (i.e., in Experiment 3, we use DEP_DELAY and TAXI_OUT as input features):

| Experiment # | Variables | RMSE | Percent increase in RMSE |
| --- | --- | --- | --- |
| 1 | DEP_DELAY<br>DISTANCE<br>TAXI_OUT | 0.205 | N/A |
| 2 | Remove DEP_DELAY | 0.361 | 76% |
| 3 | Remove DISTANCE | 0.207 | 1% |
| 4 | Remove TAXI_OUT | 0.227 | 11% |

It is clear that some variables are dramatically more important than others, but also that all three variables do carry information and you should not discard them. Contrary to my assumption in Chapter 6, the distance has the least amount of impact—had I known this earlier, Chapter 6 might have involved Bayesian selection of departure delay and taxi-out time!

## Feature Transformations

In the previous section, we carried out feature selection to determine that the distance variable was the least important of the variables included in the model. However, there is another possibility why including the distance variable did not affect the RMSE greatly—it could be that the distance variable ranges over a wider range (thousands of miles), whereas the time intervals range to only a few minutes. Therefore, the distance variable might be overpowering the other variables—assuming that both variables are given equal weights, the impact of the distance variable will be magnified 1,000-fold over that of the time interval. In an effort to reduce the impact of distance on both the sum and the gradient, the optimization process might move the distance weight to 0. And thus, the distance might end up not playing much of a role.

This is less likely in the case of logistic regression because it is a linear model, and gradients in linear models can be scaled more effectively. However, having all the variables have similar magnitudes will become important as our models become more complex.

## Scaling

Another reason we'd like to scale all the input values so that they all have similar (and small) magnitudes is that the initial, random weights in optimization routines are often set to be in the range −1 to 1, and this is where the optimizer starts to search. Thus, starting with all the variables having less than unit magnitude can help the optimizer converge more efficiently and effectively. Following are common choices for scaling functions:

- To map the minimum value of the variable to −1 and the maximum to 1. This involves scanning the dataset to find the minimum and maximum within each column—Spark has a class called `AbsScaler` that will do this for us (but it requires an extra pass through the data). However, the choices of the minimum and maximum need not be exact, so we can use the data exploration that we carried out in previous chapters to do an approximate scaling. As long as we scale the variables the same way during training and during prediction (for example, if we scale linearly such that a distance of 30 maps to −1.0 and a distance of 6,000 maps to 1.0 both in training and during prediction), the precise minimum and maximum don't matter.

- To map the mean of the variable within the column to 0 and values one standard deviation away to −1 or 1. The tails of the distribution will map to quite large values, but such values will also be rarer. This serves to emphasize unusual values while linearly scaling the common ones.

Let's use Option 1, which is to do linear scaling between an approximate minimum and maximum. Let's assume that departure delays are in the range (−30, 30), distance in the range (0, 2,000), and taxi-out times in the range (0, 20). These are approximate, but quite reasonable, and using these reasonable values helps us to avoid being overly affected by outliers in the data.[16] To map these ranges to (−1, 1), this is the transformation we would carry out on the input variables inside the `to_example()` function that converts a row into a training example:

```
def to_example(raw_data_point):
  return LabeledPoint(\
```

---

16 This presupposes that you have done exploratory data analysis, and understand your data. If you don't know what a reasonable range is, then you could use the 5th and 95th percentiles of the column values in the training data.

```
            float(raw_data_point['ARR_DELAY'] < 15), #ontime \
        [ \
            raw_data_point['DEP_DELAY'] / 30, \
            (raw_data_point['DISTANCE'] / 1000) - 1, \
            (raw_data_point['TAXI_OUT'] / 10) - 1, \
        ])
```

After making these changes to scale the three variables, and running the experiment again, I see that the RMSE is unaffected—scaling doesn't make a difference:

| Experiment # | Variables | RMSE | Percent improvement |
|---|---|---|---|
| 1 (values from experiment #1 repeated for convenience) | Raw values of DEP_DELAY DISTANCE TAXI_OUT | 0.20537 | N/A |
| 5 | Scaled values of the three variables | 0.20537 | 0 |

## Clipping

Another possible preprocessing that we could carry out is called *clipping*. Values that are beyond what we would consider reasonable are clamped to the bounds. For example, we could treat distances of more than 2,000 miles as 2,000 miles, and departure delays of more than 30 minutes as 30 minutes. This allows the optimization algorithm to focus on the part of the data where the majority of the data lies, and not be pulled off the global minimum by outliers. Also, some error metrics can be susceptible to outliers, so it is worth doing one more experiment after clipping the input variables.

Adding clipping to scaled variables is straightforward:

```
def to_example(raw_data_point):
  def clip(x):
    if x < -1:
        return -1
    if x > 1:
        return 1
    return x
  return LabeledPoint(\
            float(raw_data_point['ARR_DELAY'] < 15), #ontime \
        [ \
            clip(raw_data_point['DEP_DELAY'] / 30), \
            clip((raw_data_point['DISTANCE'] / 1000) - 1), \
            clip((raw_data_point['TAXI_OUT'] / 10) - 1), \
        ])
```

Carrying out the experiment on clipped variables, and adding in the RMSE to the table, we see these results:

| Experiment # | Transform | RMSE | Percent improvement | Keep transform? |
|---|---|---|---|---|
| 1 (repeated for convenience) | Raw values of DEP_DELAY DISTANCE TAXI_OUT | 0.20537 | N/A | N/A |
| 6 | Scaled | 0.20537 | None | No |
| 7 | Clipped | 0.20538 | Negative | No |

It turns out that neither scaling nor clipping matters for this algorithm (logistic regression) in this framework (Spark ML). In general, though, experimenting with different preprocessing transforms should be part of your workflow. It could have a dramatic impact.

## Feature Creation

So far, we have tried out the three numeric predictors in our dataset. Why did I pick only the numeric fields in the dataset? Because the logistic regression model is, at heart, just a weighted sum. We can quite easily multiply and add numeric values (actually not all numeric values but those that are continuous),[17] but what does it mean to use a timestamp such as 2015-03-13-11:00:00 as an input variable to the logistic regression model?

We cannot simply convert such a timestamp to a numeric quantity, such as the day number within the year, and then add it to the model. One rule of thumb is that to use a value as input to a model, you should have at least 5 to 10 instances of that value appearing in the data. Columns that are too specific to a particular row or handful of rows can cause the model to become *overfit*—an overfit model is one that will perform extremely well on the training dataset (essentially, it will memorize exactly what happened at each historical timestamp—for example, that flights in the Midwest were delayed on May 11, 2015) but then not work well on new data. It won't work well on new data because the timestamps in that data (such as May 11, 2018) will not have been observed.[18]

Therefore, we need to do smarter things with attributes such as timestamps so that they are both relevant to the problem and not too specific. We could, for example, use the hour of day as an attribute in the model. The hour of day might matter—most airports become busy in the early morning and early evening because many flights

---

17 For example, you cannot add and multiply employee ID numbers even if they are numeric. Employee ID numbers are not continuous.

18 The reason that we stratify our dataset into training and validation is to catch nonobvious instances of overfitting. If the training loss is very low, but the validation error is high, it is likely that the model has overfit. It is then up to you to diagnose the reason!

are scheduled around the daily work schedules of business travelers. In addition, delays accumulate over the day because an aircraft that is delayed in arriving is also delayed on takeoff.

Suppose that we extract the hour of day from the timestamp. Given a timestamp such as 2015-03-13-11:00:00, what is the hour? It's 11, of course, but the 11 is in the time zone corresponding to the UTC time zone. On the other hand, we care about the time zone at the American airport because many airports are busier early in the morning and late in the evening. This is one instance for which it is local time that matters. Thus, to extract the hour of day, we will need to correct by the time zone offset and then extract the hour of day. The *feature* hour of day is computed from two input variables—the departure time and the time zone offset.

It is worth pausing here and clarifying that I am making a distinction between the words *input* and *feature*—the timestamp is the input, the hour of day is the feature. What the client application provides when it wants a prediction is the input, but what the ML model is trained on is the feature. The feature could be (as in the case of scaling of input variables) a transformation of an input variable. In other cases, as with the hour of day, it could be a combination of multiple input variables. The to_exam ple() method is the method that converts inputs (raw_data_point) to *examples* (where each example is a tuple of features and a label). Different machine learning APIs will ask for inputs, features, or examples, and it is good to be clear on what exactly the three terms mean.

Given a departure timestamp and a time zone offset,[19] we can compute the hour in local time using the time-handling code we discussed in Chapter 4:

```
def to_example(raw_data_point):
  def get_local_hour(timestamp, correction):
      import datetime
      TIME_FORMAT = '%Y-%m-%dT%H:%M:%S'
      t = datetime.datetime.strptime(timestamp, TIME_FORMAT)
      d = datetime.timedelta(seconds=correction)
      t = t + d
      return t.hour
  return LabeledPoint(\
            float(raw_data_point['ARR_DELAY'] < 15), #ontime \
            [ \
              raw_data_point['DEP_DELAY'], \
              raw_data_point['TAXI_OUT'], \
              get_local_hour(raw_data_point['DEP_TIME'], \
                    raw_data_point['DEP_AIRPORT_TZOFFSET'])
            ])
```

---

19 The time zone offset is a float, and must be added to the schema as such.

There is one potential problem with treating the hour of day as a straightforward number. Hour 22 and hour 2 are only 4 hours apart, and it would be good to capture this somehow. An elegant way to work with periodic variables in machine learning is to convert them to two features—sin(theta) and cos(theta), where theta in this case would be the angle of the hour hand in a 24-hour clock:[20]

```python
def to_example(raw_data_point):
  def get_local_hour(timestamp, correction):
      import datetime
      TIME_FORMAT = '%Y-%m-%dT%H:%M:%S'
      t = datetime.datetime.strptime(timestamp, TIME_FORMAT)
      d = datetime.timedelta(seconds=correction)
      t = t + d
      theta = np.radians(360 * t.hour / 24.0)
      return [np.sin(theta), np.cos(theta)]

  features = [ \
                  raw_data_point['DEP_DELAY'], \
                  raw_data_point['TAXI_OUT'], \
              ]
  features.extend(get_local_hour(raw_data_point['DEP_TIME'],
                          raw_data_point['DEP_AIRPORT_TZOFFSET']))
  return LabeledPoint(\
              float(raw_data_point['ARR_DELAY'] < 15), #ontime \
              features)
```

This encoding of a periodic variable using the sin and cos makes it two features. These two features capture the information present in the periodic variable, but do not distort the distance between two values.

Another approach would be to *bucketize* the hour. For example, we could group hours 20 to 23 and hours 0 to 5 as "night," hours 6 to 9 as "morning," and so on. Obviously, bucketizing takes advantage of what human experts know about the problem. We suspect that the behavior of flight delays changes depending on the time of day—long taxi-out times during busy hours are probably built into the scheduled arrival time, but a plane that experiences a long taxi-out because the towing vehicle broke down and had to be replaced will almost definitely arrive late. Hence, our bucketizing of the hour of day relies on our intuition of what the busy hours at an airport are:

```python
def get_category(hour):
  if hour < 6 or hour > 20:
    return [1, 0, 0]  # night
  if hour < 10:
    return [0, 1, 0] # morning
  if hour < 17:
```

---

[20] The distribution of hours in the dataset, we assume, follows the Fisher–von Mises distribution, which describes points distributed on an n-dimensional sphere. If n = 2, this reduces to points on a unit circle. An hour hand is just that.

```
        return [0, 0, 1] # mid-day
    else:
        return [0, 0, 0] # evening
def get_local_hour(timestamp, correction):
    ...
    return get_category(t.hour)
```

You might find two things odd about the preceding snippet:

- We are returning binary numbers, for example [1, 0, 0]. The first number in the triplet captures whether the hour is at night or not. The second captures whether it is in the morning or not. In essence, we convert the hour variable which is numeric and continuous into four independent variables, each of which is 1 or 0.

- But we don't have four binary numbers, one for each class. We have only three! Note that the vector corresponding to the last category is [0, 0, 0] and not [0, 0, 0, 1], as you might have expected. This is because we don't want the four features to always add up to one—that would make them linearly dependent. This trick of dropping the last column keeps the values independent. Assuming that we have N categories, bucketizing will make the hour variable into N − 1 features.

How do we know which of these methods—the raw value, the sin/cos trick, or bucketizing—works best for the hour of day? We don't, so we need to run an experiment and choose (note that we are using the departure delay, distance, and taxi-out, and now adding a new variable to see if it helps):

| Experiment # | Transform | RMSE |
|---|---|---|
| 1 (repeated for convenience) | Without hour | 0.20537 |
| 8 | raw hour | 0.20536 |
| 9 | sin(theta) cos(theta) | 0.20535 |
| 10 | bucketize | 0.20538 |

The fact that we aren't able to reduce the RMSE by adding the hour information suggests that the hour of day is already adequately captured by the scheduling rules used by the airlines. It can be tempting to simply throw away the hour information, but we should follow our systematic process of keeping all our variables and then discarding one variable at a time—it is possible that the hour of day doesn't matter now, but it might after we include some other variables. So, for now, let's pick one of the possibilities arbitrarily—I will use the bucketed hour as the way to create a feature from the timestamp. Of course, I could have created additional features from the timestamp input variable—day of week, season, and so on.

Spark ML supports a rich set of feature transforms (*https://oreil.ly/P3gSM*)—it is a good idea to go through that list and learn the types of variables for which they are meant. Knowing the tools available to you is a prerequisite to be able to call on them when appropriate. If this is the first time you are encountering machine learning, you might be surprised by how much we are relying on our experimental framework. Running experiments like this, though, is the unglamorous work that lies behind most machine learning applications. Although my approach in this chapter has required careful record keeping, a better way would be if our machine learning framework would provide structure around experiments, not just single training operations. Spark ML provides this functionality (*https://oreil.ly/3XSXz*) via the `Cross Validator` tool, but even that still requires quite a bit of scaffolding.

There is another problem, though. The runtime increased from 10 minutes to 15 minutes with the addition of the hour variable. This doesn't bode well—we have a lot more features we want to try to include.

## Categorical Variables

How about using the airport code as a predictor? What we are doing when using the airport code as a predictor is that we are asking the ML algorithm to learn the idiosyncrasies of each airport. I remember, for example, sitting on the taxiway at New York's LaGuardia airport for nearly 45 minutes and then being surprised when the flight arrived in Dallas a few minutes ahead of schedule! Apparently, a 45-minute taxi-out time in New York is quite common and nothing to be worried about.

To use timestamp information, we extracted a numeric part of the timestamp—the hour—and used it in our model. We tried using it in raw form, as a periodic variable, and as a bucketized set of categories. We cannot use that approach here because there is no numeric component to the letters DFW or LGA. So how can we use the airport code as an input to our model?

The trick here is to realize that bucketizing the hour was a special case of making the variable categorical. A more bludgeon-like, but often effective, approach is to do *one-hot encoding*. Essentially, the hour variable is made into 24 features. The 11th feature is 1.0 and the rest of the features 0.0 when the hour is 11, for example. One-hot encoding is the standard way to deal with *categorical* features (i.e., features for which there is no concept of magnitude or ranking between different values of the variable). [21] This is the way we'll need to encode the departure airport if we were minded to include it in our model—we'd essentially have one feature per airport, so that the DFW feature would be 1, and the rest of the features 0 for flights that departed from DFW.

---

21 It is not the case that all strings are categorical and all numeric columns are continuous. To use my previous example, an employee ID might be numeric but is categorical. On the other hand, student grades (A+, A, A–, B+, B, etc.) are strings but can easily be translated to a continuous variable.

---

Unlike bucketing hours, though, we need to find all the possible airport codes (called the *vocabulary*) and assign a specific binary column to them. For example, we might need to assign DFW to the 143rd column. Fortunately, we don't need to write the code. One-hot encoding is available as a prebuilt feature transformation in Spark; we can add a new column of vectors to the `traindata` dataframe using this code:

```python
def add_categorical(df):
    from pyspark.ml.feature import OneHotEncoder, StringIndexer
    indexer = StringIndexer(inputCol='ORIGIN',
                            outputCot='origin_index')
    index_model = indexer.fit(df)  # ❶
    indexed = index_model.transform(df)  # ❷
    encoder = OneHotEncoder(inputCol='origin_index',
                            outputCot='origin_onehot')
    return encoder.transform(indexed) # ❸
traindata = add_categorical(traindata)
```

❶ Create an index from origin airport codes (e.g., DFW) to an origin index (e.g., 143).

❷ Transform the dataset so that all flights with `ORIGIN=DFW` have `ori gin_index=143`.

❸ One-hot encode the index into a binary vector that is used as input to training.

During evaluation, the same change needs to be made to the dataset, except that the index model will need to be reused from training (so that DFW continues to map to 143). In other words, we need to save the `index_model` and carry out the last three lines before prediction. So we modify the `add_categorical()` method to:[22]

```python
index_model = 0
def add_categorical(df, train=False):
    from pyspark.ml.feature import OneHotEncoder, StringIndexer
    if train:
        indexer = StringIndexer(inputCol='ORIGIN',
                                outputCol='origin_index')
        index_model = indexer.fit(df)
    indexed = index_model.transform(df)
    encoder = OneHotEncoder(inputCol='origin_index',
                            outputCol='origin_onehot')
    return encoder.transform(indexed)
traindata = add_categorical(traindata, train=True)
...
evaldata = add_categorical(evaldata)
```

---

22 See *experiment.py*.

This is bookkeeping to which we need to pay careful attention because doing this sort of thing incorrectly will result in training–serving skew. Spark provides a `Pipeline` mechanism to help you record which operations you carried out on the dataset so that you can repeat them when evaluating, but it introduces yet another level of abstraction into an already complex topic.

During prediction, things become even more complicated. No longer is it simply a matter of calling `lrmodel.predict()`. Instead, you will need to first construct a dataframe out of your raw input data, apply these transforms, and finally invoke the actual model.

All this is academic, however. If you are wondering why there was no RMSE stated after I added the one-hot encoded airports, it's because my program ran out of resources. Adding the airport variable completely overwhelmed the cluster. I got memory errors and disk swapping:

```
WARN org.apache.spark.storage.memory.MemoryStore: Not enough space to cache
rdd_46_403 in memory! (computed 5.6 MiB so far)
```

I put the program out of its misery after about an hour.

The problem is the large quantity of input features one-hot encoding creates. Because there are about 300 distinct airports in our dataset,[23] the airport variable will now become about 300 separate features. The `flights` dataset is about 21 million rows with the training data being about 65% of it, or about 14 million rows, and we used only one categorical column with about 300 unique values. Yet, this brought down the machines. Real-world business datasets are larger. The "small clicks" Criteo ads data used in a Kaggle competition and demonstrated in Vertex AI, for example, is 45 million rows (the full ads dataset contains four billion rows). Nearly all of its columns are categorical, and some of them have thousands of unique values.

## Repeatable, Real Time

In the previous section, we discussed that one-hot encoding leads to a large quantity of input features. One way of reducing the explosion of input features caused by one-hot encoding is to carry out dimensionality reduction. The idea is to pass in the one-hot encoded set and ask the machine learning algorithm itself to come up with weights to combine these columns into, say, four features that are used downstream in the model. This is called creating an *embedding*. This embedding model itself will be part of the full model, and so the embedding weights can be discovered at the same time. We look at creating embeddings in Chapter 10, when we discuss TensorFlow.

---

[23] You can check, as I did, by running `SELECT DISTINCT(ORIGIN) FROM dsongcp.tzcorr` on the BigQuery console.

One of the side effects of having complex library code to carry out feature transformations is that it adds a dependency on the program that makes the predictions. That program needs to run Spark in order to carry out the one-hot encoding correctly—an extremely difficult situation if the program that actually makes the predictions runs on mobile phones or outside of your company's firewall. Building a realistic machine learning pipeline with Spark, as we have seen, requires a fair bit of tooling and framework building.[24] It is easy to get started, but difficult to productionize. One way to ensure repeatability is to store the necessary transformations in the model itself.

BigQuery ML, which we will cover in Chapter 8, addresses the scalability issue. Vertex AI, which we use in Chapter 10, resolves this problem by being able to deploy an autoscaling, low-latency prediction model that is accessed via a REST API.

Finally, we could improve the way we use taxi-out times. Flight arrival times are scheduled based on the average taxi-out time experienced at the departure airport at that specific hour. For example, at peak hours in New York's JFK airport, taxi-out times on the order of an hour are quite common, so airlines take that into account when publishing their flight schedules. It is only when the taxi-out time exceeds the average that we ought to be worried. To augment the training dataset with an aggregate feature that is computed in real time like this, we will need the same code that processes batch data to also process streaming data in real time. One way to do this is to use Apache Beam. We do this in Chapter 11.

## Summary

In this chapter, we took our first foray into machine learning using Apache Spark. Spark ML is an intuitive, easy-to-use package, and running Spark on Cloud Dataproc gives us the ability to quickly build machine learning models on moderately sized datasets.

We created a dataset using Spark SQL and discovered that there were problems with missing values for some of the columns. Rather than simply remove the missing data, though, we found the root cause to be canceled or diverted flights and removed such flights from the dataset. We employed logistic regression, a machine learning model that provides probabilistic outputs, to predict the probability that the flight will be on time. Setting the probability threshold at 0.70 allows us to make a decision as to whether to cancel a scheduled meeting that depends on us arriving at the airport within 15 minutes of the scheduled arrival time.

We carried out feature selection and feature engineering and explored categorical features. To choose the features systematically, we devised an experimental framework in

---

24 One approach (*https://oreil.ly/bliID*) is to convert the Spark ML model to ONNX and then use ONNX runtime for serving.

which the training dataset itself was broken into two parts and the second part used to decide whether to keep the feature or transformation in question. We also discovered some pain points when building a production machine learning system on large datasets in Spark. Primarily, these had to do with the ability to deal with scale, of carrying out more complex models, of getting low-latency predictions outside of the development framework, and of being able to use features computed in real-time windows.

## Suggested Resources

I am hesitant to recommend too many resources here. Ultimately, Spark is not the best framework for machine learning. You are better off using XGBoost, Pytorch, or TensorFlow in Vertex AI.

If you are planning to use Spark MLlib, read the concise yet complete documentation (*https://oreil.ly/gSbx1*) from start to finish. Definitely try out pipelines and different types of models, but before you make your decision, make sure to compare against more modern alternatives.

Spark pipelines do not have all the capabilities such as metadata tracking that one expects out of a proper pipelines framework. A better approach to operationalize Spark MLlib is to use Vertex AI Pipelines and have it delegate to Dataproc, as described in the 2021 Medium blog post "Sparkling Vertex AI Pipelines" by Ivan Nardini (*https://oreil.ly/TkcyY*). Even though we will cover Vertex Pipelines in the context of TensorFlow in Chapter 10, Vertex AI Pipelines works on any containerized code.

While you can use Spark for basic regression, classification, and recommendation problems, it is not capable of doing advanced machine learning. A better approach is to use Spark for data preparation, but use distributed TensorFlow for machine learning. This is the approach that was used at Yahoo (*https://oreil.ly/tRNFm*), where they ran both Spark and TensorFlow on the same Hadoop cluster. Avoid having to install and manage TensorFlow yourself by delegating TensorFlow training tasks to Vertex AI. See the 2017 blog post "Using Apache Spark with TensorFlow on Google Cloud Platform" (*https://oreil.ly/Mjv5V*) by Bill Prin and Neeraj Kashyap for more details.

# CHAPTER 8

# Machine Learning with BigQuery ML

BigQuery is a serverless, highly scalable data warehouse. Amazingly enough, it is also an excellent machine learning platform. This combination is very convenient since you can do machine learning without having to extract data out of the data warehouse. If your organization has a lot of privacy-sensitive or confidential data, not having extracts of data floating around in people's projects is important for security. The auditability that BigQuery provides out of the box means that you know exactly who created the model and which data was used in which model.

Given the scalability, power, ease-of-use, and security of BigQuery ML, I recommend using it, rather than Spark, for the first machine learning model you should build when working with tabular data. In fact, as you will see in this chapter, you can get best-in-class accuracy, explainability, and prediction capabilities using BigQuery ML. Because of its connections to Vertex AI, it can be your production machine learning framework also.

 All of the code snippets in this chapter are available in the folder *08_bqml* of the book's GitHub repository (*https://github.com/Google CloudPlatform/data-science-on-gcp*). See the *README.md* file in that directory for instructions on how to do the steps described in this chapter.

## Logistic Regression

Let's start where we left off in Chapter 7—recall that we trained a logistic regression model, added the airport code, and overwhelmed Spark in the process. So, let's start by replicating the last working model that we had. We trained the logistic regression model on three features: departure delay, taxi-out time, and distance.

The first step in BigQuery ML is to create the training dataset. We want the three features and the label, so let's use SQL to craft the dataset just the way we want it:

```
SELECT
  IF(arr_delay < 15, 'ontime', 'late') AS ontime,
  dep_delay,
  taxi_out,
  distance,
FROM dsongcp.flights_tzcorr f
WHERE
  f.CANCELLED = False AND
  f.DIVERTED = False
LIMIT 5
```

The SELECT statement pulls the required fields, taking care to not train on flights that were canceled or diverted. The result consists of the four columns we care about:

| Row | ontime | dep_delay | taxi_out | distance |
|-----|--------|-----------|----------|----------|
| 1 | ontime | -5.0 | 10.0 | 399.0 |
| 2 | late | 33.0 | 13.0 | 1046.0 |
| 3 | ontime | -3.0 | 8.0 | 95.0 |
| 4 | ontime | 5.0 | 9.0 | 201.0 |
| 5 | ontime | -4.0 | 5.0 | 204.0 |

Creating a logistic regression model in BigQuery ML is as simple as running the following query:[1]

```
CREATE OR REPLACE MODEL dsongcp.arr_delay_lm
OPTIONS(input_label_cols=['ontime'],
        model_type='logistic_reg')AS
SELECT
  IF(arr_delay < 15, 'ontime', 'late') AS ontime,
  dep_delay,
  taxi_out,
  distance,
FROM dsongcp.flights_tzcorr f
WHERE
  f.CANCELLED = False AND
  f.DIVERTED = False
```

We are creating a logistic regression model where the label column is called ontime, and the remaining columns will be used as input features to the model. BigQuery ML will take care of splitting the data (randomly) and carrying out evaluation on the withheld dataset.

---

1 See *bqml_logistic.ipynb* in the GitHub repository of this book. You can run this in Vertex Workbench.

The resulting model parameters will be stored in a BigQuery model object called arr_delay_lm in the dataset dsongcp.

## Presplit Data

In Chapter 5, we discussed why we don't want to randomly split the flight data—we need to avoid having correlated flights on the same day split between training and test datasets. That's why we presplit the data and created a table that specifies which days should be used for training and which days for evaluation.

We can explicitly tell BigQuery ML to use one of our columns in the training dataset to split the data. Let's add that column to our SELECT statement as a Boolean value by joining the flight data against the table of prespecified training days:

```
SELECT
  IF(arr_delay < 15, 'ontime', 'late') AS ontime,
  dep_delay,
  taxi_out,
  distance,
  IF(is_train_day = 'True', False, True) AS is_eval_day
FROM dsongcp.flights_tzcorr f
JOIN dsongcp.trainday t
ON f.FL_DATE = t.FL_DATE
WHERE
  f.CANCELLED = False AND
  f.DIVERTED = False
LIMIT 5
```

It returns:

| Row | ontime | dep_delay | taxi_out | distance | is_eval_day |
|-----|--------|-----------|----------|----------|-------------|
| 1 | ontime | -5.0 | 10.0 | 399.0 | true |
| 2 | late | 33.0 | 13.0 | 1046.0 | false |
| 3 | ontime | -3.0 | 8.0 | 95.0 | false |
| 4 | ontime | 5.0 | 9.0 | 201.0 | true |
| 5 | ontime | -4.0 | 5.0 | 204.0 | false |

The fifth column can now be used to tell BigQuery which rows to withhold for evaluation, i.e., when this column is *TRUE* the corresponding row is reserved for evaluation and not used for training. This involves specifying a custom data split method:

```
CREATE OR REPLACE MODEL dsongcp.arr_delay_lm
OPTIONS(input_label_cols=['ontime'],
        model_type='logistic_reg',
        data_split_method='custom',
        data_split_col='is_eval_day')
AS
```

```
SELECT
  IF(arr_delay < 15, 'ontime', 'late') AS ontime,
  dep_delay,
  taxi_out,
  distance,
  IF(is_train_day = 'True', False, True) AS is_eval_day
...
```

## Interrogating the Model

When we run the preceding query, BigQuery trains a logistic regression model and puts the weights into the model arr_delay_lm. We can obtain the training error (called the loss) as the model is being trained, or even afterwards by querying the result of the special function ML.TRAINING_INFO:

```
SELECT * FROM ML.TRAINING_INFO(MODEL dsongcp.arr_delay_lm)
```

This retrieves the loss on the training dataset and on the evaluation dataset iteration-by-iteration:

| training_run | iteration | loss | eval_loss | learning_rate | duration_ms |
|---|---|---|---|---|---|
| 0 | 19 | 0.000003 | 0.000004 | 104857.6 | 3306 |
| 0 | 18 | 0.000007 | 0.000007 | 52428.8 | 3350 |
| 0 | 17 | 0.000013 | 0.000012 | 26214.4 | 2941 |
| 0 | 16 | 0.000027 | 0.000020 | 13107.2 | 2921 |

We can obtain the weights themselves by calling ML.WEIGHTS:

```
SELECT * FROM ML.WEIGHTS(MODEL dsongcp.arr_delay_lm)
```

Because logistic regression is a linear model, we get one weight for each input, plus an intercept term:

| processed_input | weight |
|---|---|
| dep_delay | -0.132984 |
| taxi_out | -0.121715 |
| distance | 0.000223 |
| __INTERCEPT__ | 4.762572 |

However, there is usually no point to getting just the weights. Instead, what we want is the predicted value for some set of inputs. To carry out prediction, we could directly call ML.PREDICT:

```
SELECT * FROM ML.PREDICT(MODEL dsongcp.arr_delay_lm,
                    (
SELECT 12.0 AS dep_delay, 14.0 AS taxi_out, 1231 AS distance
                    ))
```

While we can use `ML.PREDICT` to actually carry out predictions, the predictions will be subject to the typical BigQuery latency of a second or so. So, `ML.PREDICT` is typically used for batch predictions over large datasets. For online prediction (i.e., exposing the prediction service to a microservice using REST), we can extract the model as a TensorFlow model and deploy it into Vertex AI.

## Evaluating the Model

We can look at the model evaluation by going to the BigQuery Evaluation tab and moving the threshold slider bar as close to 0.7 as possible (see Figure 8-1).

Alternatively, we can evaluate the model by calling `ML.EVALUATE` in SQL. BigQuery will evaluate the model on the withheld data (where `is_train_day` is False), but use a threshold of 0.5:

```
SELECT *
FROM ML.EVALUATE(MODEL dsongcp.arr_delay_lm)
```

Unfortunately, in order to change the threshold to 0.7, we have to also explicitly provide the data to evaluate over. So we do:

```
SELECT *
FROM ML.EVALUATE(MODEL dsongcp.arr_delay_lm,
                    (

SELECT
  IF(arr_delay < 15, 'ontime', 'late') AS ontime,
  dep_delay,
  taxi_out,
  distance
FROM dsongcp.flights_tzcorr f
JOIN dsongcp.trainday t
ON f.FL_DATE = t.FL_DATE
WHERE
  f.CANCELLED = False AND
  f.DIVERTED = False AND
    is_train_day = 'False'

                    ),
                    STRUCT(0.7 AS threshold))
```

The resulting evaluation statistics are:

| precision | recall | accuracy | f1_score | log_loss | roc_auc |
|-----------|--------|----------|----------|----------|---------|
| 0.964337 | 0.956535 | 0.935174 | 0.96042 | 0.167233 | 0.956248 |

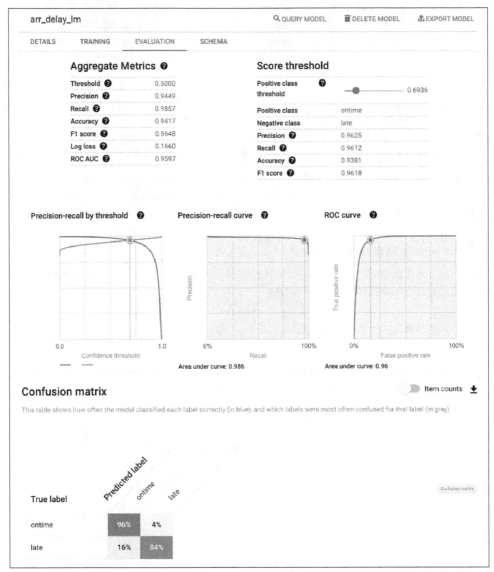

Figure 8-1. Model Evaluation tab in the BigQuery console.

The precision is how often the model is right when it reports a flight as being on time, while the recall is the fraction of on-time flights correctly classified. The receiver operating characteristic (ROC) is a threshold-independent measure of classifier performance.

We can use `ML.PREDICT` to actually carry out predictions in case we want to compute some other metric. For example, the root mean squared error (RMSE) can be computed as:

```
WITH predictions AS (
SELECT
  *
FROM ML.PREDICT(MODEL dsongcp.arr_delay_lm,
      ... )


SELECT
   SQRT(SUM((IF(ontime = 'ontime', 1, 0) - p.prob) *
            (IF(ontime = 'ontime', 1, 0) - p.prob))
                /COUNT(*)) AS rmse
FROM predictions, UNNEST(predicted_ontime_probs) p
WHERE p.label = 'ontime'
```

The preceding query pulls out the probability field from the predictions (it's an array, one for each category, hence the `UNNEST`) and uses it to compute the RMSE. The resulting RMSE was 0.2131.

Note that we cannot compare this number 0.2131 against the RMSE numbers from the previous chapter because they are computed on different datasets. In Spark, we did not compute the RMSE on the independent evaluation dataset because it would have been too slow to load in two datasets, one for training and the other for evaluation.

## Scale and Simplicity

We ended Chapter 7 by saying that the Spark model could not handle the addition of a categorical variable corresponding to an airport because one-hot encoding the airport results in hundreds of new features. To showcase the scalability of BigQuery, let's add *two* such fields, the origin and destination airport:

```
CREATE OR REPLACE MODEL dsongcp.arr_delay_airports_lm
OPTIONS(input_label_cols=['ontime'],
        model_type='logistic_reg',
        data_split_method='custom',
        data_split_col='is_eval_day') AS
SELECT
  IF(arr_delay < 15, 'ontime', 'late') AS ontime,
  dep_delay,
  taxi_out,
  distance,
  origin,
  dest,
```

```
    IF(is_train_day = 'True', False, True) AS is_eval_day
FROM dsongcp.flights_tzcorr f
JOIN dsongcp.trainday t
ON f.FL_DATE = t.FL_DATE
WHERE
  f.CANCELLED = False AND
  f.DIVERTED = False
```

The model that includes the airport information has an RMSE of 0.2098, which is an improvement over the original model.

BigQuery handles the airport fields without any issues. Had I not tried this in Spark and failed, I wouldn't even have known that including the airport as an input is a challenging undertaking. Notice also that including the airport field didn't require me to do any of the careful handling of one-hot variables and vocabularies that we needed in Spark. With the help of BigQuery, using a categorical variable was as transparent and straightforward as using a numeric variable.

The scale and simplicity of BigQuery ML make it one of my favorite products in Google Cloud.

# Nonlinear Machine Learning

What's the point of a scalable, simple machine learning service if it limits you to just linear models? Fortunately, BigQuery ML is not limited to just linear regression and classification models. You can train deep neural networks, forecast time series, and create recommender systems. You can also use gradient boosted trees.

## XGBoost

When it comes to classification models on structured data, one of the best performing techniques is XGBoost (see sidebar). To use this method instead of logistic regression, all that we have to do is to change the model_type in the CREATE MODEL statement:[2]

```
CREATE OR REPLACE MODEL dsongcp.arr_delay_airports_xgboost
OPTIONS(input_label_cols=['ontime'],
        model_type='boosted_tree_classifier',
        data_split_method='custom',
        data_split_col='is_eval_day')
AS

SELECT
  IF(arr_delay < 15, 'ontime', 'late') AS ontime,
  dep_delay,
```

---

2 The code for this section is in *bqml_nonlinear.ipynb*.

---

```
    taxi_out,
    distance,
    origin,
    dest,
    IF(is_train_day = 'True', False, True) AS is_eval_day
FROM dsongcp.flights_tzcorr f
JOIN dsongcp.trainday t
ON f.FL_DATE = t.FL_DATE
WHERE
    f.CANCELLED = False AND
    f.DIVERTED = False
```

That's it! No other changes are needed. Ten minutes later, we have a shiny new ML model. The underlying model is now much more complex, but we can use it in the same way that we used the linear model—by calling `ML.EVALUATE` and `ML.PREDICT`.

---

## What Is XGBoost?

XGBoost (*https://oreil.ly/jmQLH*) is a gradient boosting algorithm that creates an ensemble of decision trees. That's quite a word salad, so let's unpack it a bit.

A *decision tree* is a set of if-then statements. For example, the rule: if the departure delay is 10 minutes or more, then if the distance is 1,000 miles or more, whether the flight will be on time can be represented as part of a decision tree (see Figure 8-2).

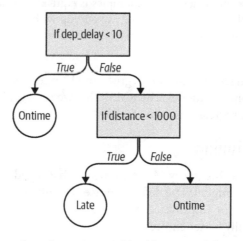

*Figure 8-2. Decision tree based on two variables (departure delay and distance).*

The preceding decision tree consists of three such if-then rules, one for each of the leaves of the tree:

- If the departure delay is less than 10 minutes, the flight will be on time.

- If the departure delay is 10 minutes or more, then if the distance is less than 1,000 miles, the flight will be late.

- If the departure delay is 10 minutes or more, then if the distance is 1,000 miles or more, the flight will be on time.

A machine learning algorithm tunes the variables (`dep_delay`, `distance`) and thresholds (10 and 1,000) for the decision tree based on the data. The more if-then statements there are, the greater the *depth* of the tree.

It is possible to create multiple such trees by choosing different variables and thresholds. Thus, it is possible to create an *ensemble of decision trees*. We can then average the result of all these trees to come up with a final output. Why is this useful? Because some decision trees might be especially useful for nighttime flights, other decision trees may be very accurate for flights from New York, and so on. Getting a fuller picture of what various decision trees would say for a given flight can give us more opinions and the possibility of a more accurate decision in the end.

Can we employ a strategy in choosing the trees that form this ensemble? Yes. One approach is called *boosting*. The idea is to choose a tree and find the examples that the tree classifies incorrectly. The next decision tree is then trained so that it does better on the misclassified examples—we can do this by artificially boosting their importance.

Mathematically, boosting misclassified examples is equivalent to weighting the gradient associated with those examples. Hence, we end up with a gradient boosting algorithm that creates an ensemble of decision trees: XGBoost.

The training takes longer than logistic regression (12 minutes rather than 6 minutes) because it's a more complex model. The RMSE that we now get is 0.2072, an improvement over the logistic regression score of 0.2098.

## Hyperparameter Tuning

One of the reasons that BigQuery ML is so nice is that it hides a lot of the knobs or *hyperparameters* of the model. The default choices usually work pretty well, but there is usually some room for improvement if we are willing to expend compute cycles searching for potentially better choices.

There are two hyperparameters that I'm particularly interested in exploring:

- BigQuery reduces the impact of outliers by imposing a penalty on large weight values. This is called *L2 regularization*, and the intuition underlying the technique is as follows: when you have a very complex model with lots and lots of free parameters ("weights") and you have an outlier, the model can force the outlier to have the correct label by twisting and warping the optimization space in the vicinity of the outlier. This twisting and warping leads to large weight values (the mathematics behind this gets a little hairy, so let's take this on trust). By imposing a penalty on large weights, the model avoids getting drawn into this trap. However, the relative amount of L2 regularization that works is highly dependent on the dataset and how significant and prevalent these outliers are. BigQuery uses a default value of 1.0, but that is by no means the authoritative value. I'd like to try out values between 0.5 and 3.0. Maybe some other L2 value will work better.

- Boosted trees work by creating an ensemble of weak learners. Each of the decision trees in the ensemble is pretty bad by itself, but when you average all these weak learners in a special way (called boosting), the ensemble turns out to be better than any single tree. But how weak can each individual tree be? Can we have just two IF-THEN rules? Or should we allow 10? By default, BigQuery uses a maximum tree depth of 6. This is by no means an authoritative value that works on all problems. I'd like to try out values between 2 and 10.

We can do a grid search of the hyperparameter space. If we try L2 regularization values between 0.5 and 3.0 in increments of 0.1 and tree depths between 2 and 10 in increments of 1, we'd need to try out $25 \times 8 = 200$ possible values. At 10 minutes a training run, that's 2,000 minutes or 1.4 days. Even though I could parallelize these somewhat, I don't have that kind of patience.

Fortunately, there's a better way that employs Bayesian methods to choose the optimization path. We can specify a budget (five trials, for example) and have a Vertex AI optimizer called Vizier do the selection of the five most promising possibilities. To do this, instead of specifying a single value for the L2_reg and max_tree_depth, we specify a range of values:

```
CREATE OR REPLACE MODEL dsongcp.arr_delay_airports_xgh
OPTIONS(input_label_cols=['ontime'],
        model_type='boosted_tree_classifier',
        num_trials=5,
        l2_reg=hparam_range(0.5, 3.0),
        max_tree_depth=hparam_range(2, 10),
        data_split_method='custom',
        data_split_col='is_eval_day')
```

However, there is a small hitch. When BigQuery does hyperparameter tuning, what independent dataset should it test out the models on? It cannot use the nontraining-days dataset because that is meant for final testing. So, we need to change the SELECT statement slightly:

```
SELECT
  IF(arr_delay < 15, 'ontime', 'late') AS ontime,
  dep_delay,
  taxi_out,
  distance,
  origin,
```

```
        dest,
        IF(is_train_day = 'True',
            IF(RAND() < 0.8, 'TRAIN', 'EVAL'),
            'TEST') AS is_eval_day
    FROM dsongcp.flights_tzcorr f
    JOIN dsongcp.trainday t
    ON f.FL_DATE = t.FL_DATE
    WHERE
        f.CANCELLED = False AND
        f.DIVERTED = False
```

The is_eval_day column used to be a Boolean column. Now, it is a string with three possible values: TRAIN, EVAL, and TEST. The old training dataset has been broken into TRAIN and EVAL datasets, and the old withheld data is now called the TEST dataset—the TEST dataset is the one that consists of days where is_train_day is not True.

Once the hyperparameter job is complete (it will take a couple of hours), we can query for the trials that were run:

```
SELECT
    hyperparameters.l2_reg,
    hyperparameters.max_tree_depth,
    eval_loss
FROM ML.TRIAL_INFO(MODEL dsongcp.arr_delay_airports_xgh)
ORDER BY eval_loss ASC LIMIT 3
```

This returns:

| Row | l2_reg | max_tree_depth | eval_loss |
|-----|--------|----------------|-----------|
| 1 | 2.5 | 10 | 0.152403 |
| 2 | 1.8827838728344135 | 8 | 0.154935 |
| 3 | 2.9999853271420043 | 6 | 0.156696 |

We learn that the lowest evaluation loss is for a tree depth of 10 and L2 regularization of 2.5. This can now be our final model.

The RMSE that we now get is 0.2043, an improvement over the score of 0.2072 that we got with the default values. It is noteworthy that this improvement is more than the improvement (0.2098 to 0.2072) we got when we replaced the logistic regression with XGBoost.

## Vertex AI AutoML Tables

The fact that doing hyperparameter tuning gave us a large improvement gives me a bit of pause. Is XGBoost really the best model? These days, deep neural networks (DNNs) do well, even on structured data. Should I not be trying them? If I use deep neural networks, how many layers and nodes do I need? Do I really want to do hyperparameter tuning of the DNN also?

---

Instead of trying out a variety of models and hyperparameter tuning each model type, I can call out to Vertex AI's AutoML service from BigQuery. This, too, is as simple as changing the model type in the SQL command:

```
CREATE OR REPLACE MODEL dsongcp.arr_delay_airports_automl
OPTIONS(input_label_cols=['ontime'],
        model_type='automl_classifier')
AS

SELECT
  IF(arr_delay < 15, 'ontime', 'late') AS ontime,
  dep_delay,
  taxi_out,
  distance,
  origin,
  dest
FROM dsongcp.flights_tzcorr f
JOIN dsongcp.trainday t
ON f.FL_DATE = t.FL_DATE
WHERE
  f.CANCELLED = False AND
  f.DIVERTED = False AND
  is_train_day = 'True'
```

Unfortunately, at the time of writing, AutoML as invoked from BigQuery ML doesn't support a custom data split method, so I had to go with the default random split.[3] This training now takes longer. Considerably longer, over an hour.

Computing the evaluation also takes longer (12 minutes), whereas it was nearly instantaneous with XGBoost. Although the result is heartening—I got an RMSE of 0.1998—it is not really comparable because I was not able to use a custom split method.

The experiments so far are summarized in Table 8-1.

*Table 8-1. BigQuery ML experiments*

| Method | RMSE |
|---|---|
| Logistic regression | 0.2131 |
| Add origin, destination airport | 0.2098 |
| XGBoost | 0.2072 |
| XGBoost with hparam (10, 2.5) | 0.2043 |
| AutoML tables | 0.1998 (note: not comparable) |

---

3 AutoML supports a custom data split method. We'll use it in Chapter 9. It's AutoML as invoked in SQL through BigQuery ML that doesn't.

While hyperparameter tuning and AutoML were tempting, this was not a good time to do them. I should have waited because I have more ideas about features that I can bring in to improve the model. More data beats a better model, and so I should exhaust the data before I try more sophisticated models.

AutoML can be the final step after we have determined what features to use. I jumped the gun a bit. Sorry. Let's go back to the main program.

# Time Window Features

One of the data ideas I have is that we could improve the way we use taxi-out times.

I remember a flight from New York to Dallas. My flight sat on the runway at New York's LGA airport for nearly an hour before finally taking off. Yet, it arrived early in Dallas! At peak hours, taxi-out times on the order of an hour are quite common in New York area airports. So, airlines take that into account when publishing their flight schedules. It is only when the taxi-out time exceeds the average of the airport that we ought to be worried.

## Taxi-Out Time

My one anecdote does not make the average taxi-out time an important factor. Let's validate my intuition from the data.

Does taxi-out time vary by airport? Is the same value of taxi-out associated with late arrivals in one airport, but with on-time arrivals in another? To check, we can compute the average taxi-out for all airports that start with the letter D (this should give us a small, but random sample):[4]

```
%%bigquery txout

SELECT
  ORIGIN,
  IF (arr_delay < 15, True, False) AS is_on_time,
  AVG(taxi_out) AS taxi_out
FROM dsongcp.flights_tzcorr
WHERE SUBSTR(ORIGIN, 1, 1) = 'D'
GROUP BY ORIGIN, is_on_time
```

The BigQuery magic in the first line of the Vertex AI Workbench notebook ensures that the result of the query is stored in the Pandas dataframe called txout. From there, we can plot the data:

```
txout = txout.sort_values(by='ORIGIN')
sns.barplot(data=txout, x='ORIGIN', y='taxi_out', hue='is_on_time');
```

---

4 The code is in the notebook *bqml_timewindow.ipynb*.

The result is shown in Figure 8-3. It is clear that there is a significant difference between late and on-time flights when it comes to the amount of time they spend on the taxiway.

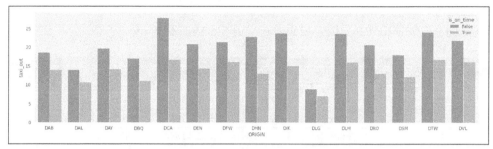

*Figure 8-3. The average taxi-out time associated with late and on-time flights at various airports.*

It's also clear that any threshold we impose on taxi-out delay in our model will vary between airports. At airports like Washington DC (DCA), Denver (DEN), and Dallas (DFW), on-time flights have a 15-minute taxi-out time on average. In smaller airports like DAL (Dallas Love Field) and DBO (Dubbo City), this is more than the average taxi-out time associated with delayed flights.

It seems that the average taxi-out times associated with the airport are worth knowing. We can add it to our training dataset by modifying the SELECT statement used. First, we compute the average taxi-out times by airport:

```
WITH taxiout_by_airport AS (
  SELECT
    ORIGIN, AVG(taxi_out) AS avg_taxi_out
  FROM
    dsongcp.flights_tzcorr
  GROUP BY ORIGIN
)
```

Then, we join the original data against the average taxi-out times using the origin airport:

```
SELECT
  IF(arr_delay < 15, 'ontime', 'late') AS ontime,
  dep_delay,
  taxi_out,
  avg_taxi_out,
  distance,
  origin,
  dest,
  IF(is_train_day = 'True', False, True) AS is_eval_day
FROM dsongcp.flights_tzcorr f
JOIN dsongcp.trainday t
ON f.FL_DATE = t.FL_DATE
```

```
JOIN taxiout_by_airport USING(ORIGIN)
WHERE
  f.CANCELLED = False AND
  f.DIVERTED = False
LIMIT 5
```

The dataset now contains the average taxi-out times in each row:

| Row | ontime | dep_delay | taxi_out | avg_taxi_out | dis tance | ori gin | dest | is_eval_day |
|-----|--------|-----------|----------|--------------|-----------|---------|------|-------------|
| 1 | ontime | -1.0 | 4.0 | 7.507122507122507 | 548.0 | OTZ | ANC | true |
| 2 | ontime | -8.0 | 13.0 | 16.184090332402953 | 1056.0 | HPN | PBI | false |
| 3 | ontime | -2.0 | 21.0 | 13.344790914960695 | 1046.0 | SJU | FLL | false |
| 4 | late | 91.0 | 15.0 | 16.184090332402953 | 1097.0 | HPN | FLL | false |
| 5 | ontime | -10.0 | 8.0 | 12.900537006770952 | 1192.0 | ANC | ADK | false |

In the third row, the plane departed 2 minutes early and spent 8 minutes longer than usual on the taxiway. Therefore, it took off 6 minutes later than usual. This will surely have an impact on the arrival delay. So, it makes sense that the taxi-out times associated with late and on-time flights are different.

## Compounding Delays

The delays of flights that take off ten minutes apart are correlated. If a couple of runways are unavailable due to prevailing winds, for example, delays will start to compound. Looking at the average departure delay over the previous hour is potentially a good indicator of how well the airport is clearing these delays.

To compute the moving average, we can use the window functionality of SQL:

```
SELECT
  dep_time,
  AVG(dep_delay) OVER time_window AS dep_delay,
  AVG(arr_delay) OVER time_window AS arr_delay
FROM dsongcp.flights_tzcorr
WHERE
  ORIGIN = 'DFW' AND FL_DATE = '2015-03-02'
WINDOW time_window AS (ORDER BY UNIX_SECONDS(dep_time)
                      RANGE BETWEEN 3600 PRECEDING AND 1 PRECEDING)
```

The preceding statement computes the average departure and arrival delays over a time window. The time window is defined in the SQL statement as consisting of the rows 3,600 seconds to 1 second before the current row's departure time. For plotting purposes, I'm limiting the query to flights from Dallas on March 2, 2015. The result is shown in Figure 8-4.

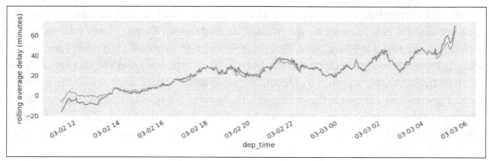

*Figure 8-4. The average departure and arrival delays increased over the course of Mar 2, 2015.*

Adding the rolling average feature to the training dataset involves code similar to the code used for plotting previously, except that we make sure to partition the window by the origin airport (so that the moving average is computed only on flights that depart from the same airport):

```
...
SELECT
  IF(arr_delay < 15, 'ontime', 'late') AS ontime,
  dep_delay,
  AVG(dep_delay) OVER (origin_time_window) AS avg_dep_delay,
  taxi_out,
    ...
FROM dsongcp.flights_tzcorr f
...
WINDOW origin_time_window AS (PARTITION BY ORIGIN
                             ORDER BY UNIX_SECONDS(dep_time)
                             RANGE BETWEEN 3600 PRECEDING AND 1 PRECEDING)
```

## Causality

Adding these two time-based features and training the model with BigQuery defaults, we get an RMSE of 0.2040 compared to the 0.2072 we got without these features. The additional data gives us a boost on par with hyperparameter tuning. And we still have hyperparameter tuning in our back pocket!

However, this is not strictly correct. I cheated a bit. Did you notice where I cheated?

The mischief started with this line:

```
WITH taxiout_by_airport AS (
  SELECT
    ORIGIN, AVG(taxi_out) AS avg_taxi_out
  FROM
    dsongcp.flights_tzcorr
  GROUP BY ORIGIN
)
```

What am I computing the average of? The average taxi-out at each airport over all the training flights? No, I am using the evaluation flights too! Oops. That's relatively easy to fix. I could add a WHERE clause. But there is another problem. Suppose I am evaluating the prediction that happened on May 5, 2015. Am I allowed to use the average delay of flights that happened in December 2015 just because they are in the training data? How would I provide this value in production? Shouldn't the global average be kept up-to-date, so that predictions on May 5, 2015, use the average delay of flights from the start of the dataset until May 2015 (or maybe the average delay of flights that happened in the 12 months preceding May 2015?).

We used the average departure delay at the origin airport. What if we also want to include the average arrival delay at the destination airport? How would we partition the time window? Not based on the time window of the current flight—it hasn't arrived yet! I suppose it is possible to do this in SQL, but it requires greater SQL skills than I have. Also, I don't trust myself to not make causality mistakes like the ones in the previous paragraph.

The moment we start including time-based averages in our ML models, we have to be very careful about causality. In Chapter 11, we'll look at how to compute time-windowed features in a less error-prone way by using a stream analytics system.

# Time Features

Time windows introduce a lot of complexity, but time-based features are quite important for this problem. Is there a simpler approach to incorporate time?

## Departure Hour

What if, instead of computing hourly averages, we use the hour as an input field? If we have sufficiently large data, the model will learn to associate different behavior with different hours. Thus, for example, the model might be able to learn that high taxi-out times are common during rush hour and infer that the flight would still be able to arrive on-time.

But we did try adding the hour as an input in Chapter 7 and found that it didn't improve the performance. Trying out the same action a second time and expecting a different result might seem strange. However, it's not quite the same thing that we are trying. A linear model might not be able to easily differentiate between 5 p.m. in New York and 5 p.m. in a smaller airport. The nonlinear XGBoost model that we are using here has more expressive power and might be able to learn the difference. So, it is worth giving the hour feature another try.

The hour is not the only part of the timestamp that matters. Flights tend to be more delayed on weekdays than on weekends. So, let's also add the day of the week as an input. To do so, we can adapt the query that creates the training dataset to be:[5]

```
SELECT
  IF(arr_delay < 15, 'ontime', 'late') AS ontime,
  dep_delay,
  taxi_out,
  distance,
  origin,
  dest,
  EXTRACT(hour FROM dep_time) AS dep_hour,
  EXTRACT(dayofweek FROM dep_time) AS dep_day,
  IF(is_train_day = 'True', False, True) AS is_eval_day
FROM dsongcp.flights_tzcorr f
JOIN dsongcp.trainday t
ON f.FL_DATE = t.FL_DATE
WHERE
  f.CANCELLED = False AND
  f.DIVERTED = False
```

This creates a dataset that looks like this:

| Row | ontime | dep_delay | taxi_out | distance | origin | dest | dep_hour | dep_day | is_eval_day |
|-----|--------|-----------|----------|----------|--------|------|----------|---------|-------------|
| 1 | ontime | -5.0 | 10.0 | 399.0 | ANC | BET | 3 | 5 | true |
| 2 | late | 33.0 | 13.0 | 1046.0 | FLL | SJU | 14 | 7 | false |
| 3 | ontime | -3.0 | 8.0 | 95.0 | SIT | JNU | 13 | 5 | false |
| 4 | ontime | 5.0 | 9.0 | 201.0 | LIH | OGG | 22 | 6 | true |
| 5 | ontime | -4.0 | 5.0 | 204.0 | BRW | SCC | 4 | 4 | false |

There is a problem with simply extracting features and adding them to the dataset. When we want the prediction for a flight, we will need to provide the departure hour and departure day because that's what the model was trained on (see Figure 8-5). However, it is unclear to a programmer who's coding up the client program how the hour needs to be provided. Should 7 a.m. be 07 or 7? Should this hour be in local time or in UTC? Similarly, should the day of the week be Thu or 5 or 05? What is the first day of the week? All the questions that we successfully resolved in Chapter 4 will again raise their heads.

---

5 The code is in *bqml_timetxf.ipynb*.

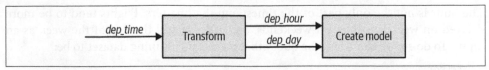

*Figure 8-5. The model is trained with hour and day-of-week as features, but they are not directly present in the input data feed. Instead, they are extracted from the departure timestamp.*

## Transform Clause

Ideally, the machine learning model takes, as input, the timestamp (which is what is present in the datafeed) and internally knows how to transform the departure time into hour and day-of-week. This transformation can be carried out identically both during training and during inference.

The way to specify such transformations in BigQuery ML is to use the TRANSFORM clause:

```
CREATE OR REPLACE MODEL dsongcp.arr_delay_airports_timefeatures
TRANSFORM(
    * EXCEPT(dep_time),
    EXTRACT(hour FROM dep_time) AS dep_hour,
    EXTRACT(dayofweek FROM dep_time) AS dep_day
)
OPTIONS(input_label_cols=['ontime'],
        model_type='boosted_tree_classifier',
        ...)

AS

SELECT
  IF(arr_delay < 15, 'ontime', 'late') AS ontime,
  dep_delay,
  taxi_out,
  distance,
  origin,
  dest,
  dep_time,
  IF(is_train_day = 'True', False, True) AS is_eval_day
...
```

Note that the training dataset (the SELECT statement) has the dep_time column as-is. The TRANSFORM clause pulls in all the columns from the SELECT statement but replaces the dep_time column with two columns extracted from the departure time.

At this time, I will take advantage of the hyperparameter tuning that I have already done and change the L2 regularization and maximum tree depth from their default values to be the value that was best:

```
OPTIONS(input_label_cols=['ontime'],
        model_type='boosted_tree_classifier',
        data_split_method='custom',
        data_split_col='is_eval_day',
        l2_reg=2.5,
        max_tree_depth=10)
```

On training an XGBoost model with these settings, I get a model whose RMSE on the evaluation dataset is 0.2043. This is quite close to the value that we got from using time windows. It's also a lot simpler because there is no need to build real-time infrastructure that computes moving averages. Of course, we don't know whether using time windows will provide an additional improvement. Let's defer this discussion to Chapter 11.

 In large-scale ML, you can get much of the benefit of time-windowed averages by using time features. Time features are a lot simpler from an engineering perspective than real-time pipelines.

## Categorical Variable

Although we got pretty good performance from using the departure hour and day of the week as-is, there is a small problem. By default, BigQuery ML treats all numbers as numeric features and all strings as categorical features. The day of the week as extracted from the timestamp is not a string (e.g., Thursday), but is a number (5). Therefore, BigQuery ML would have treated it as a numeric input. This is usually okay, but it is not the case that Saturday is greater than Monday.

Let's try treating the day of the week as categorical. While we could simply cast the integer into a string, let's try adding a bit of prior knowledge, that days 1 and 7 are weekends:

```
TRANSFORM(
   * EXCEPT(dep_time),
   EXTRACT(hour FROM dep_time) AS dep_hour,
   IF(EXTRACT(dayofweek FROM dep_time) BETWEEN 2 and 6,
      'weekday', 'weekend') AS dep_day
)
```

On training with the day of the week as categorical, we get an RMSE of 0.2042, a very slight improvement over treating it as numeric. We'll stick with this because it is a better representation.

## Feature Cross

There is a difference between 5 p.m. on Friday in New York versus 5 p.m. on Friday in a smaller airport such as Columbus, Ohio. The way to capture this important combination is to concatenate the three fields (hour, day of week, and origin airport) and treat them as a single categorical variable. This is called a *feature cross*, and it can be expressed in BigQuery ML as:

```
TRANSFORM(
    * EXCEPT(dep_time),
    ML.FEATURE_CROSS(STRUCT(
      ML.BUCKETIZE(EXTRACT(hour FROM dep_time),
                   [0, 4, 8, 12, 16, 20]) AS dep_hour,
      IF(EXTRACT(dayofweek FROM dep_time) BETWEEN 2 and 6,
                 'weekday', 'weekend') AS dep_day,
      origin
    )) AS day_hour
)
```

On training with the feature cross, we get an RMSE of 0.2043—the feature cross hasn't helped. This might be because of sparsity—one of the problems with a feature cross is that it greatly increases the number of possible values. There are 24 possible hours, 2 possible values for dep_day (weekday and weekend), and more than 300 values for the origin airport. Because we are combining the possibilities, and treating each unique combination independently, the feature cross results in a categorical variable with $24 \times 2 \times 300$ values. Bucketizing the hour into 6 buckets of 4 hours each helps reduce the number of combinations. Obviously, that wasn't enough. In Chapter 9, we will look at a machine learning concept called embedding that will help with this sparsity problem (see sidebar).

Another thing to consider is that we don't have the hour or day-of-week by itself anymore. Perhaps the feature cross needs to be an additional feature, instead of replacing the individual columns.

The last few changes we have tried have had minimal impact on the performance of the model. At some point, with feature engineering, we hit diminishing returns. So, this seems as good a time as any to stop.

---

## When to Use Low-Code and No-Code Systems

What we observed with sparsity and the need for an embedding is a pretty common scenario in software tools and frameworks—whether the framework is for building mobile applications or user interfaces, websites, or machine learning models.[6]

A *no-code* tool is the easiest to use. Point-and-click and you are done. AutoML on Google Cloud is a no-code system for creating and deploying machine learning models (we will encounter it in Chapter 10). It is completely GUI-driven.

---

6 It is quite likely that the BigQuery ML team will read this and will have added support for embeddings by the time you read this book. The general principle still holds though.

A *low-code* system is one where there is a library or framework that provides common use cases via simple APIs. BigQuery ML is a low-code system. All we need is SQL to do a wide variety of use cases, ranging from regression and classification to time-series forecasting, *k*-means clustering, and product recommenders. Even though we write SQL, BigQuery ML delegates the actual work to C++ code running on BigQuery slots or to TensorFlow code running in Vertex AI. All this is abstracted away from us.

Low-code systems are easier to use than the sophisticated underlying software that actually does the work. At some point, however, you will need a capability that has not been wrapped around by the designer of the low-code or no-code framework. At that point, you will want to directly use the more sophisticated framework. The need for an embedding is when we reached that point with BigQuery ML, but every low-code and no-code tool eventually reaches a breaking point.

When you are choosing tooling for your data science platform, low-code and no-code tools can be tempting, but you should always verify that, if needed, you can drop down to code. Also verify that the code that you then write is portable, can be version-controlled, and uses standard and popular APIs.

Use AutoML and BigQuery ML whenever you can, confident that you can drop down to Vertex AI and TensorFlow if necessary. Don't overcorrect and use only TensorFlow code—you will be sacrificing a lot of productivity if you thumb your nose at low-code and no-code tools.

# Summary

BigQuery ML provides a simple and powerful SQL interface for doing machine learning. We created a classifier model for predicting flight delays using BigQuery ML. We were able to evaluate this model and use it for batch predictions with just SQL.

We then created a more sophisticated model using gradient boosted trees and saw an improvement over the simple logistic regression model we used earlier. The scale and simplicity of BigQuery allowed us to add additional features like airport codes. We saw that the addition of these features resulted in improved performance.

We also saw that we could get a worthwhile performance boost using hyperparameter tuning and AutoML. Because of how time-consuming these two options are, we should be using them at the end of our experimentation process, after we have exhausted all the data improvements.

We experimented with adding time-windowed moving averages. Although the SQL syntax is quite straightforward, the semantics of causality are hard to keep track of. It's better to compute time averages in a stream analytics system—we will do this in Chapter 10.

Considering the difficulty of including time-windowed features, we explored whether directly using different parts of time would be a good alternative. We found that we could match the performance improvement of the time-windowed moving average by including the hour and day of week as input features.

Carrying out transformation like this is hard to keep track of, and so we put all our transformations into the TRANSFORM clause. That way, they are automatically applied to the input data during prediction.

We finally hit diminishing returns with feature engineering, so we stopped.

## Suggested Resources

BigQuery ML is one of my favorite go-to products in Google Cloud. So, I've written a large number of blogs about BigQuery ML features. Here are a few of the superpowers of BigQuery ML that we didn't have time to cover in this chapter:

- Time-series forecasting models. See Lak Lakshmanan, "How To Do Time Series Forecasting in BigQuery" (*https://oreil.ly/7IKFZ*), *Towards Data Science* (blog), March 30, 2020.

- Recommendation models. See Lak Lakshmanan, "Training a Recommendation Model for Google Analytics Data Using BigQuery ML" (*https://oreil.ly/VDsOj*), *Towards Data Science* (blog), April 20, 2020.

- K-means clustering. See Lak Lakshmanan, "How to Use K-Means Clustering in BigQuery ML to Understand and Describe Your Data Better" (*https://oreil.ly/vuBaX*), *Towards Data Science* (blog), April 10, 2019.

- Anomaly detection. See Lak Lakshmanan, "Anomaly Detection in Time Series Data Using BigQuery ML" (*https://oreil.ly/QCe2N*), *Medium* (blog), July 14, 2021.

- Export trained models to Vertex AI for online prediction. See Lak Lakshmanan, "How to Export a BigQuery ML Model and Deploy It for Online Prediction" (*https://oreil.ly/jrG4T*), *Towards Data Science* (blog), May 17, 2020.

- Import trained TensorFlow models for batch prediction. See Lak Lakshmanan, "How to Do Batch Predictions of TensorFlow Models Directly in BigQuery" (*https://oreil.ly/bHsw0*), *Towards Data Science* (blog), April 10, 2019

- Explaining a BigQuery ML model. See Lak Lakshmanan, "Explaining a BigQuery ML Model" (*https://oreil.ly/KRLEE*), *Towards Data Science* (blog), July 29, 2021.

How about specific use cases? Many common use cases in BigQuery ML are often just a web search away:

- Propensity to buy. See Damodar Panigrahi, "How to Build an End-to-End Propensity to Purchase Solution Using BigQuery ML and Kubeflow Pipelines" (*https://oreil.ly/PpYa0*), *Google Cloud - Community* (blog), September 8, 2020.

- E-commerce recommendations. See Polong Lin, "How to Build a Recommendation System on E-Commerce Data Using BigQuery ML" (*https://oreil.ly/UenSu*), *Google Cloud - Community* (blog), July 13, 2020.

- Audience segmentation. See Tai Conley, "How to Build Audience Clusters With Website Data Using BigQuery ML" (*https://oreil.ly/Vwz83*), *Google Cloud - Community* (blog), November 4, 2020.

If there is only one Google Cloud data product you can learn, it should be BigQuery. Fortunately, there is an excellent book on BigQuery by your favorite author, *Google BigQuery: The Definitive Guide* by Valliappa Lakshmanan and Jordan Tigani (O'Reilly).

# CHAPTER 9

# Machine Learning with TensorFlow in Vertex AI

In Chapter 7, we built a machine learning model in Spark but ran into problems when trying to scale it out and make it operational. We were able to address the scalability challenge by using BigQuery ML in Chapter 8, but the operationalization challenges still remain. In addition, although BigQuery ML was scalable, we were not able to build the most expressive ML model possible. Briefly, there are four challenges that we identified:

- One-hot encoding of categorical columns caused an explosion in the size of the dataset because of the increased size of the columns. BigQuery ML was able to handle this, but Spark wasn't.

- Embeddings would have involved special bookkeeping in Spark, and this was not an option in BigQuery ML.

- Putting the model into production requires the machine learning library to be portable to environments beyond the Hadoop cluster or BigQuery data warehouse on which the model is trained.

- Preventing training–serving skew when using a time-windowed aggregate feature requires being able to use the same data preparation code for both historical data (which is batch) and real-time data (which is streaming).

We will solve the fourth problem, of time-windowed aggregates, in Chapter 11 by using Apache Beam and its ability to employ the same code for both batch and stream.

The solution to the first three problems requires a portable machine learning library that is (1) powerful enough to carry out training using accelerators such as GPUs and

Tensor Processing Units (TPUs) in a distributed manner, (2) flexible enough to support the latest machine learning research such as wide-and-deep networks,[1] and (3) portable enough to support both massively parallel prediction on custom application-specific integrated circuits (ASICs) and prediction carried out on handheld devices. TensorFlow (*https://tensorflow.org*), the open source machine learning library developed at Google, meets all these objectives.

If you skipped ahead to this chapter without reading Chapters 7 and 8, please go back and read them. Those two chapters look at logistic regression using Spark and using BigQuery ML, and I introduce a number of machine learning concepts that are essential to understanding this one. In particular, understanding the limitations of the approaches presented in Chapters 7 and 8 will help you to understand the architecture of the TensorFlow/Keras model that we develop here.

 All of the code snippets in this chapter are available in the folder *09_vertexai* of the GitHub repository (*https://github.com/Google CloudPlatform/data-science-on-gcp*). See the *README.md* file in that directory for instructions on how to do the steps described in this chapter.

# Toward More Complex Models

Normally, when you want a computer to do something for you, you need to program the computer to do it by using an explicit set of rules. For example, if you want a computer to look at an image of a screw on a manufacturing line and figure out whether the screw is faulty or not, you need to code up a set of rules: Is the screw bent? Is the screw head broken? Is the screw discolored? With machine learning, you turn the problem around on its head. Instead of coming up with all kinds of logical rules for why a screw might be bad, you show the computer a whole bunch of data. Maybe you show it 5,000 images of good screws and 5,000 images of faulty screws that your (human) operators discarded for one reason or the other. Then, you let the computer learn how to identify a bad screw from a good one. The computer is the "machine" and it's "learning" to make decisions based on data. In this particular case, the "machine" is learning a discriminant function from the manually labeled training data, which separates *good* screws from *bad* screws. This kind of machine learning is called "supervised" because there is a ground truth supplied by an expert—in this analogy, the human quality inspectors function as the supervisors of the machine learning algorithm.

---

1 Heng-Tze Cheng et al., "Wide & Deep Learning for Recommender Systems," arXiv, June 24, 2016. https://arxiv.org/abs/1606.07792.

Our approach in Chapters 6–8 involved machine learning. We took all of the data, chose a model (Bayesian classification in Chapter 6, logistic regression in Chapter 7, and boosted tree classification in Chapter 8), and asked the computer to figure out the parameters in the model (the empirical probabilities in Bayes, the weights in logistic regression, breakpoints in boosted trees). We then could use the "trained" model to make predictions on new data points.

Even plain old linear regression, in this view, can be thought of as machine learning— that is, if the model is effective at capturing the nuances of the data. Many real-world problems are much more complex than can be adequately captured by linear regression or similarly simple models. When people talk of machine learning, they are usually thinking of more complex models with many more parameters.

Tell a statistician about complex models with lots of parameters, and you'll get back a lecture on the dangers of overfitting, of building a model that (instead of capturing the nuances of the problem) is simply fitting observation noise in the data. So, another aspect of machine learning is that you need to counteract the dangers of overfitting when using very complex models by training the model on extremely large and highly representative datasets.[2] Additionally, even though these complex models may be more accurate, the trade-off is that you cannot readily analyze them to retroactively derive logical rules and reasoning. When people think of machine learning, they think of complex models like random forests, support vector machines, and neural networks.

For our problem, we could use random forests, support vector machines, or neural networks, and I suspect that we will get very similar results. This is true of many real-world problems—the biggest return for your effort is going to be in terms of finding additional data to provide to the training model or in devising better input features using the available data. In contrast, changing the machine learning model doesn't provide as much benefit. However, for a specific class of problems—those with extremely dense and highly correlated inputs such as audio and images,[3] deep neural networks begin to shine. In general, you should try to use a linear model if you can and reserve the use of more complex models (deep neural networks, convolutional networks, transformers, recurrent neural networks, etc.) only if the particular problem warrants it. For the flight delay use case, I will use a *wide-and-deep* model that consists of two parts: a wide or linear part for input features that are sparse and a part consisting of deep layers for input features that are continuous.

---

2 If you come from a statistics background, training a machine learning model is the same thing as fitting a statistical model or function to data.

3 In this context, *dense* inputs are those where small differences in numeric values are meaningful—that is, where the inputs are continuous numbers.

To train the model, we will use TensorFlow, an open source software library developed at Google to carry out numerical computation for machine learning research. The guts of the library are written in C++ to permit you to deploy computation to one or more CPUs or GPUs in a desktop or the cloud. Come prediction time, the trained model can be run on CPUs, GPUs, a server that uses Google's custom ASIC chips for machine learning (called Tensor Processing Units or TPUs), or even a mobile device. However, it is not necessary to program in C++ to use TensorFlow because the programming paradigm is to build a data flow graph and then stream data into that graph. It is possible to control the graph creation and streaming from Python without losing the efficiency of C++, or the ability to do GPU and ASIC computations. Nodes in the graph represent mathematical operations (such as the summation and sigmoid function that we used in logistic regression), whereas the graph edges represent the multidimensional data arrays (tensors) communicated between these nodes.

In fact, we could have expressed logistic regression as a simple neural network consisting of a single node and done the training using TensorFlow rather than Spark, as illustrated in Figure 9-1.

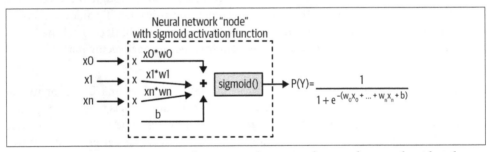

*Figure 9-1. Logistic regression can be expressed as a simple neural network with only one node. The X's are the model inputs (the features) and the W's are the weights of the model.*

For comparison purposes, the first neural network that we will build in this chapter will be precisely this. We will then be able to examine the impact of the additional input features while keeping the model (logistic regression) the same as what was used in Chapter 7.

Having done the comparison, though, we will move on to building a neural network that will have many more nodes and will be distributed in more layers. We'll keep the output node a sigmoid so that the output is restricted to lie in [0,1] but add in intermediate layers and nodes with other activation functions. The number of nodes and layers is something that we must determine via experimentation. At some point, increasing the number of nodes and layers will begin to result in overfitting, and the exact point is dependent on the size of your dataset (both the number of labeled examples and the number of predictor variables), the extent to which the predictor variables do predict the label, and the extent to which the predictors are independent. This problem is hairy enough that there is no real way to know beforehand how big and large you can afford your neural network to be. If your neural network is too small, it won't fit all the nuances of the problem adequately and your training error will be large. Again, you won't know that your neural network is too small unless you try a slightly larger neural network. The relationship is not going to be nice and smooth because there are random seeds involved in all the optimization methods that you will use to find the weights and biases. Because of that, machine learning is going to have to involve many, many runs. The best advice is to try out different numbers of nodes and layers and different activation functions (different ones work better for different problems) and see what works well for your problem. Having a cloud platform that supports this sort of experimentation to be carried out on your complete dataset in a timely manner is very important. When it's time to run our experiment on the full dataset, we will use Vertex AI (*https://oreil.ly/7nHXR*).

Every node in a neural network adds up all the weighted inputs and then applies an *activation function* to the weighted sum. In a classifier, the activation function of the output node is the sigmoid (or s-shaped) function that we saw earlier in logistic regression. For the intermediate layers, we will use Rectified Linear Units (ReLUs)[4] as the activation functions. The ReLU has a linear activation function that is clamped to nonnegative values. Essentially the input of the node is passed through to the output after thresholding it at 0—so if the weighted sum of the inputs is 3, the output is 3, but if the weighted sum of the inputs is −3, the output is 0.

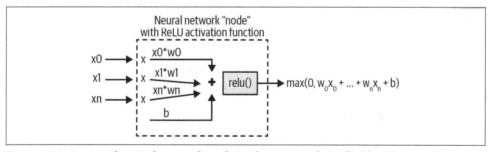

*Figure 9-2. A typical neural network node in the intermediate (hidden) layers of a neural network consists of the weighted sum of its inputs transformed by a nonlinear function.*

---

4 Using ReLU rather than sigmoidal (or tanh) activation functions is a trade-off—the sigmoid activation function saturates between 0 and 1 (see the graphs in Chapter 7), and therefore the output won't blow up. However—and this is where the trade-off comes in—the outputs of neurons with ReLU activation functions can reach really large, positive magnitudes. Some of the theoretical advances in machine learning over the past few years have been on how to initialize and train ReLUs without having the intermediate outputs of the neural network go flying off the handle.

# Preparing BigQuery Data for TensorFlow

There are four approaches that we can take in order to train a TensorFlow model on data that is in BigQuery:

- Use the BigQuery client library to load the data from BigQuery into an in-memory Pandas dataframe. Then, we can use `tf.convert_to_tensor` (*https://oreil.ly/fmseF*) to read the Pandas data frame into TensorFlow. You should use this approach only on datasets that will fit comfortably into memory.

- Use `BigQueryReader` (*https://oreil.ly/XaWF7*) to iterate through a BigQuery table (or a subset of it) into a TensorFlow dataset. The BigQueryReader uses BigQuery's Storage API and is therefore very efficient and can be invoked in parallel if we are doing distributed training. However, the Storage API is not free, and so we will end up paying to read the data each time.[5] Use this for quick experimentation, but this approach can get expensive because training an ML model involves reading data multiple times. Nevertheless, you should use this approach for fast-changing data.

- Export the subset of BigQuery data you need to files on Google Cloud Storage (GCS), and read these files from the ML pipeline.

- Train the model in BigQuery ML using `model_type=dnn_classifier` or `model_type=automl_classifier` and then export the trained model for use in Vertex AI. These model types train a TensorFlow model in Vertex AI. However, you are restricted to the model types supported by BigQuery ML.

I'm going to take the third approach because it is the least expensive option that will work for large datasets and allow me to create a custom TensorFlow model. I will create a temporary table in BigQuery to contain the data we need, export the table to CSV files on Google Cloud Storage, and delete the temporary table (see *flights_model_tf2.ipynb* in the code repository):

```
CREATE OR REPLACE TABLE dsongcp.flights_train_data AS

SELECT
  IF(arr_delay < 15, 1.0, 0.0) AS ontime,
  dep_delay,
  taxi_out,
  distance,
  origin,
  dest,
  EXTRACT(hour FROM dep_time) AS dep_hour,
  IF (EXTRACT(dayofweek FROM dep_time) BETWEEN 2 AND 6, 1, 0) AS is_weekday,
  UNIQUE_CARRIER AS carrier,
```

---

5 As opposed to the approaches in #1 and #3 where we query the data only once.

```
    dep_airport_lat,
    dep_airport_lon,
    arr_airport_lat,
    arr_airport_lon
FROM dsongcp.flights_tzcorr f
JOIN dsongcp.trainday t
ON f.FL_DATE = t.FL_DATE
WHERE
    f.CANCELLED = False AND
    f.DIVERTED = False AND
    is_train_day = 'True'
```

Then, I extract it to a CSV file using:

```
for dataset in "train" "eval" "all"; do
    TABLE=dsongcp.flights_${dataset}_data
    CSV=gs://${BUCKET}/ch9/data/${dataset}.csv
    bq extract --destination_format=CSV $TABLE $CSV
    bq rm -f $TABLE
done
```

Note that my data now includes a few more parameters that I used in the previous chapter. There is one more categorical variable (the airline company, or carrier) and the location of the departure and arrival airports.

Note also that my label is 1.0 if the flight is on time (arrives less than 15 minutes after the scheduled time) and 0.0 if it is not.

## Reading Data into TensorFlow

To read the CSV files from GCS into TensorFlow, we use a method from the `tf.data` package:

```
training_data_uri = 'gs://{}/ch9/data/train*'.format(BUCKET)
dataset = tf.data.experimental.make_csv_dataset(
                training_data_uri, batch_size=5)
```

Let's write a `read_dataset()` function that reads the training data, yielding `batch_size` examples each time, which allows us to stop iterating once a certain number of examples have been read. This is the function that we want:

```
def read_dataset(pattern, batch_size,
                mode, truncate):
```

The reason for the `mode` parameter is that the function needs to behave differently when reading the training versus when reading the evaluation data. During evaluation, we need to read the entire dataset only once. During training, though, we need to read the dataset and pass it through the model several times. In addition, if we are training on multiple workers, we want the workers to see different examples. We can achieve this by calling `shuffle()` with a large enough buffer. Finally, it's efficient to prefetch a batch of data using the CPU while the GPU is busy crunching the data. Putting these concepts together, we have:[6]

```
if mode == tf.estimator.ModeKeys.TRAIN:
  dataset = dataset.shuffle(batch_size*10)
  dataset = dataset.repeat()
dataset = dataset.prefetch(1)
if truncate is not None:
  dataset = dataset.take(truncate)
```

Shuffling the order in which the sharded input data is read each time is important for distributed training. The way distributed training is carried out is that each of the workers is assigned a batch of data to process. The workers compute the gradient on their batch and send it to *parameter servers* that maintain a shared state of the training run.[7] For reasons of fault tolerance, the results from very slow workers might be discarded. If there was a consistently slow worker and the same data was always assigned to the same worker, that data might always be discarded and never used. Therefore, it is important that the same batch of data not be assigned to the same slow worker in each run. Shuffling the data before it gets assigned to each worker helps mitigate this possibility.

The dataset contains all the columns in the CSV file, named according to the header line. The data consists of both features and the label. It's better to separate them to make the later code easier to read. Hence, we'll apply a map() function to the dictionary and return a tuple of features and labels:

```
def features_and_labels(features):
  label = features.pop('ontime')
  return features, label

dataset = dataset.map(features_and_labels)
```

At this point, a batch that is read will consist of a tuple. The first item of the tuple will be a dictionary of features. The second item of the tuple will be a *tensor* of labels. (A tensor is just an array of arbitrary dimensions.) Assuming the batch size is 2, the labels tensor will be of shape (2,) as will each of the feature tensors:

```
[
(OrderedDict([
  ('dep_delay',
    <tf.Tensor: shape=(2,), dtype=int32,
     numpy=array([-11,    9], dtype=int32)>),
  ('taxi_out',
```

---

6 I encourage you to read *Machine Learning Design Patterns* by Valliappa Lakshmanan, Sara Robinson, and Michael Munn (O'Reilly) for many tips on applying ML in real-world scenarios.

7 Mu Li et al., "Scaling Distributed Machine Learning with the Parameter Server," Operating Systems Design and Implementation (OSDI), USENIX (2014): 583–98. https://research.google.com/pubs/pub44634.html.

---

```
    <tf.Tensor: shape=(2,), dtype=int32,
      numpy=array([10, 10], dtype=int32)>),
   ... ,
  ('arr_airport_lon',
     <tf.Tensor: shape=(2,), dtype=float32,
       numpy=array([-149.99806 ,  -72.683334], dtype=float32)>)
]),
<tf.Tensor: shape=(2,), dtype=int32,
  numpy=array([1, 1], dtype=int32)>)
]
```

Every time the TensorFlow model needs a new batch of data, it is a tuple like this that it will get.

Now that we have set up the data pipeline, let's move on to implementing the model itself.

# Training and Evaluation in Keras

Keras is an open source library that simplifies the writing of machine learning models and can work with a variety of backends, including TensorFlow. We first create a Keras model and then call `fit()` on the model to train it, passing it the training dataset. Once the model is trained, we can also call `evaluate()` and `predict()` on the model.

To create a Keras model, we need to specify the inputs, the feature engineering to be performed, the model function, the optimization algorithm, and the evaluation metrics.

## Model Function

In Chapter 7, we built a logistic regression model based on three continuous variables: departure delay, taxi-out time, and distance. We then tried to add one more variable—the origin airport—and because the origin is a categorical variable, it needed to be one-hot encoded. One-hot encoding the origin airport ended up creating more than a hundred new columns, making the model two orders of magnitude more complex. Thus, the addition of this fourth variable caused the Spark ML model to collapse (although BigQuery ML was able to handle this just fine).

Here, let's build a logistic regression model in Keras, but because we do have many more columns now, let's use them all. As discussed earlier in this chapter, logistic regression is simply a linear model with a sigmoidal output node:

```
output = tf.keras.layers.Dense(1,
              activation='sigmoid', name='pred')(inputs)
model = tf.keras.Model(inputs, output)
```

The model contains a single layer that is fully connected (dense) to its inputs, has one output, and has a sigmoid activation function.

But how do we get the input layer?

Recall from Chapter 8 that there is a difference between *inputs* and *features*—a structured data model takes raw data as input, and then creates new features from those inputs. It's these features that are actually used by the model for training. So, what we need is to create features from the inputs and pass those features to the model:

```
inputs = …
features = tf.keras.layers.DenseFeatures(…)(inputs)

output = tf.keras.layers.Dense(1,
            activation='sigmoid', name='pred')(features)
model = tf.keras.Model(inputs, output)
```

This is because we cannot pass the input values as-is into the neural network. We will have to convert all the inputs into a single vector of floating point values. The process of converting the raw inputs into floating point values that are amenable to being input into a machine learning model is called *feature engineering*. In Keras, the raw inputs are Input layers, and the conversion is carried out by feature columns and a special layer called `DenseFeatures`. Let's look at those next.

## Features

We typically create one feature for every column in our tabular data. Keras has support for feature columns, opening up the ability to represent structured data using standard feature engineering techniques like embedding, bucketizing, and feature crosses.

We know that numeric data can be passed in directly to the ML model. So, let's keep the real-valued columns separate from the *sparse* (or string) columns:

```
real = {
    colname : numeric_column(colname)
        for colname in
          (
              'dep_delay,taxi_out,distance,dep_hour,is_weekday,' +
              'dep_airport_lat,dep_airport_lon,' +
              'arr_airport_lat,arr_airport_lon'
          ).split(',')
}
sparse = {
      'carrier': categorical_column_with_vocabulary_list(
                  'carrier',
                  vocabulary_list=(
                  'AS,VX,F9,UA,US,WN,HA,EV,MQ,DL,OO,B6,NK,AA'
                  .split(','))),
      'origin' : categorical_column_with_hash_bucket(
```

```
                  'origin', hash_bucket_size=1000),
    'dest'      : categorical_column_with_hash_bucket(
                  'dest', hash_bucket_size=1000),
}
```

Features that are discrete (and have to be one-hot encoded [see Chapter 7]) are represented by `categorical_column`. The airline carrier can be one of the following strings:

```
AS,VX,F9,UA,US,WN,HA,EV,MQ,DL,OO,B6,NK,AA
```

Thus, it is represented by a sparse column with those specific keys. This is called the *vocabulary* of the column; to find the vocabulary of the carrier codes, I used Big-Query:

```
SELECT
  DISTINCT UNIQUE_CARRIER
FROM
  flights.tzcorr
```

Although I could have done the same thing for the origin and destination airport codes (most likely by saving the airport codes from the BigQuery result set to a file and reading that file from Python), I decided to use a shortcut by mapping the airport codes to hashed buckets; rather than find all the origin airports in the dataset, I ask TensorFlow to create a deterministic hash of the airport code and then discretize the hash number into one thousand buckets (a number larger than the number of unique airports).[8] Provided the hash works as intended, the airports will be uniformly discretized into one thousand bins. For any bucket with only one airport in it, this is equivalent to one-hot encoding. However, there is likely to be some small amount of collision, and so using the hash rather than explicitly specifying the keys will be somewhat worse.

 The hashed feature design pattern also helps when the categorical features have an incomplete vocabulary. This will help if a new airport gets built, for example. See *Machine Learning Design Patterns* by Valliappa Lakshmanan, Sara Robinson, Michael Munn (O'Reilly) for details. Summarized notes from the book are available in a 2021 *Geek Culture* blog post, "Data Representation Design Patterns" (*https://oreil.ly/5THuF*), by Manoj Kumar Patra.

---

8 A *hash function* is a function that maps input values as evenly as possible over its output range. Python has a built-in hash function called `hash()` that returns an integer—it is common to override the `hash()` function in classes to take into account some unique combination of attributes (called the keys) of the object.

## Inputs

All these features come directly from the input file (and will have to be provided by any client that wants a prediction for a flight). Because the Input layers map 1:1 to the input features and their types, rather than repeat the column names, I can create an Input layer for each of these columns, specifying the right data type (either a float or a string):

```
inputs = {
    colname : tf.keras.layers.Input(
        name=colname, shape=(), dtype='float32')
        for colname in real.keys()
}
inputs.update({
    colname : tf.keras.layers.Input(
        name=colname, shape=(), dtype='string')
        for colname in sparse.keys()
})
```

At this point, we have an Input layer for each of the feature columns in the training data file.

The feature columns are applied to the inputs using DenseFeatures, and the resulting features are passed to the subsequent Dense layer:

```
features = tf.keras.layers.DenseFeatures(
    list(sparse) + list(real), name='features')(inputs)

output = tf.keras.layers.Dense(1,
            activation='sigmoid', name='pred')(features)
model = tf.keras.Model(inputs, output)
```

At this point, the model has been created. Let's move on to training the model.

## Training the Keras Model

Once we have created the Keras model, we can call methods such as `fit()`, `evaluate()`, and `predict()` on the model. The distribution strategy will take care of calling the optimizer for the model in a distributed way (i.e., across several accelerators or across machines) to adjust the weights of the model every time a batch of training examples is read.[9]

Before we can train the model, though, we have to *compile* it, specifying the optimizer, the loss metric, and any evaluation metrics that we want to report during training:

---

9 The default option—MirroredStrategy—works for zero or more GPUs on a single machine. Since that's what I'm doing, you will not see the strategy referenced explicitly in the code.

```
model.compile(optimizer='adam',
              loss='binary_crossentropy',
              metrics=['accuracy'])
```

Then, we call `fit()` to train the model, passing in the training dataset and the validation dataset on which to report metrics as the model is being trained:

```
train_dataset = read_dataset('gs://.../train*',
                             train_batch_size)
eval_dataset = read_dataset('gs://.../valid*',
                            eval_batch_size,
                            tf.estimator.ModeKeys.EVAL,
                            num_eval_examples)

history = model.fit(train_dataset,
                    validation_data=eval_dataset,
                    epochs=epochs,
                    steps_per_epoch=steps_per_epoch,
                    validation_steps=10)
```

The history object will contain the training loss and evaluation metrics after each epoch. We can plot it using:

```
for idx, key in enumerate(['loss', 'accuracy']):
    ax = fig.add_subplot(nrows, ncols, idx+1)
    plt.plot(history.history[key])
    plt.plot(history.history['val_{}'.format(key)])
    plt.title('model {}'.format(key))
    plt.ylabel(key)
    plt.xlabel('epoch')
    plt.legend(['train', 'validation'], loc='upper left');
```

In Chapter 7, we discussed the need for a metric that is independent of threshold and captures the full spectrum of probabilities. For comparison purposes, therefore, it would be good to also compute the RMSE. We can do this by adding an evaluation metric to the `model` definition:[10]

```
metrics=['accuracy', rmse]
```

The `rmse()` function is defined as follows:

```
def rmse(y_true, y_pred):
    return tf.sqrt(tf.reduce_mean(tf.square(y_pred - y_true)))
```

---

10 See the full context on GitHub (*https://github.com/GoogleCloudPlatform/data-science-on-gcp/blob/main/10_mlops/model.py*).

## Saving and Exporting

In order for us to be able to deploy the model to serve requests, we need to save it in a format that can be deployed:

```
export_dir = os.path.join(OUTPUT_DIR,
                          'export/flights_{}'.format(
                          time.strftime("%Y%m%d-%H%M%S")))
tf.saved_model.save(model, export_dir)
```

With all the components in place, we are now ready to run the code.

## Deep Neural Network

Making sure that the Vertex AI Workbench notebook that I'm working on has a GPU attached to it, I can now launch off the training job. The model being trained is a simple one, of course—a linear regression model. Even though I've added several new features (carrier, airport locations), the resulting RMSE hasn't budged from when we did linear regression in BigQuery ML. This is not surprising—there is a limit to the expressiveness of linear models. We should try a more complex model.

What happens if we change our model from a linear model to a deep neural network? In Keras, if we want two hidden layers with 64 and 8 nodes, we would insert a couple of Dense layers that have a `relu` activation function:

```
features = tf.keras.layers.DenseFeatures(
    list(sparse) + list(real), name='features')(inputs)
h1 = tf.keras.layers.Dense(
    64, activation='relu', name='pred')(features)h2 = tf.keras.layers.Dense(
    8, activation='relu', name='pred')(h1)
output = tf.keras.layers.Dense(
    1, activation='sigmoid', name='pred')(h2)
model = tf.keras.Model(inputs, output)
model.compile(optimizer='adam',
              loss='binary_crossentropy',
              metrics=['accuracy'])
```

In BigQuery ML, we could achieve this by changing the model type:

```
CREATE OR REPLACE MODEL dsongcp.arr_delay_airports_dnn
OPTIONS(input_label_cols=['ontime'],
        model_type='dnn_classifier',
        hidden_units=[64, 8],
```

The result with a deep neural network is an RMSE of 0.205, which is not a meaningful difference. But let's not give up just yet!

Now that we have more data, TensorFlow/Keras in our tool chest, and the ability to train machine learning models on the larger dataset, why not also improve our machine learning modeling?

# Wide-and-Deep Model in Keras

An influential paper suggests using a hybrid model that the authors call a *wide-and-deep model* on structured data.[11] In the wide-and-deep model, there are two parts. One part directly connects the inputs to the outputs; in other words, it is a linear model. The other part connects the inputs to the outputs via a deep neural network. The modeler places the sparse columns in the linear part of the model, and the real-valued columns in the deep part of the model.

## Representing Air Traffic Corridors

Recall that we have two Python dictionaries of features: one is a dict of real-valued columns, and the other is a dict of sparse columns. Among the real-valued columns are the latitude and longitude of the departure and arrival airports. The precise latitudes themselves should not have much of an impact on a flight being early or late, but rather the general location of the airport and the flight path between pairs of cities do play a part. For example, flights along the West Coast of the United States are rarely delayed, whereas flights that pass through the high-traffic area between Chicago and New York tend to experience a lot of delays. This is true even if the flight in question does not originate in Chicago or New York.

Indeed, the Federal Aviation Administration in the United States manages airplanes in flight in terms of air traffic corridors or areas (see Figure 9-3). We could make the machine learning problem easier for the model if there were a way to provide this human insight directly, instead of expecting it to be learned directly from the raw latitude and longitude data.

---

11 Heng-Tze Cheng et al., "Wide & Deep Learning for Recommender Systems."

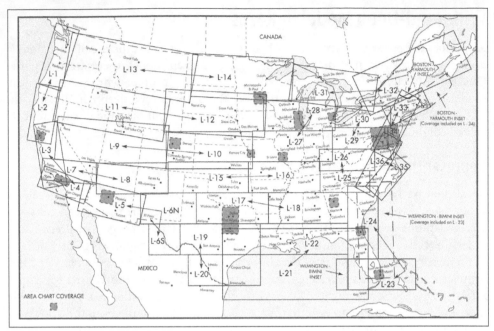

*Figure 9-3. Air traffic in the USA is managed by the US Federal Aviation Administration (FAA) in terms of separate traffic corridors, shown here as boxes. Image courtesy FAA.*

## Bucketing

Real-valued columns whose precision is overkill (thus, likely to cause overfitting) can be discretized and made into categorical columns. For example, if we have a column for the age of the aircraft, we might discretize into just three bins—less than 5 years old, 5 to 20 years old, and more than 20 years old.

Even though we could explicitly program in the air traffic corridors, let's use the discretization shortcut: we can discretize the latitudes and longitudes (the thick arrows in Figure 9-4) and cross the buckets—this will result in breaking up the country into grids and yield the grid point into which a specific latitude and longitude falls.

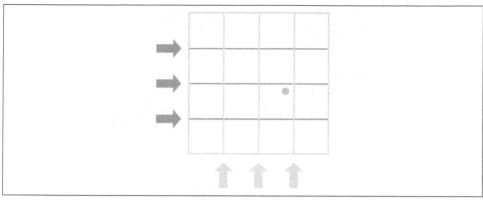

*Figure 9-4. Bucketizing latitude and longitude essentially separates out the space into grid boxes.*

The following code takes the real-valued latitude and longitude columns and discretizes them into nbuckets each:

```
latbuckets = np.linspace(20.0, 50.0, NBUCKETS).tolist()  # USA
lonbuckets = np.linspace(-120.0, -70.0, NBUCKETS).tolist() # USA
disc = {}
disc.update({
        'd_{}'.format(key) : tf.feature_column.bucketized_column(real[key],
   latbuckets)
            for key in ['dep_lat', 'arr_lat']
})
disc.update({
        'd_{}'.format(key) : tf.feature_column.bucketized_column(real[key],
   lonbuckets)
            for key in ['dep_lon', 'arr_lon']
})
```

The dictionary disc at this point contains four discretized columns: d_dep_lat, d_arr_lat, d_dep_lon, and d_arr_lat.

## Feature Crossing

Finally, we apply feature crossing to categorical features that work well in combination. As discussed in Chapter 8, we can think of a feature cross as being an AND condition. If you have a column for colors and another column for sizes, the feature cross of colors and sizes will result in sparse columns for color-size combinations such as red-medium.

We can take the discretized columns corresponding to the lats and lons and cross them to create two sparse columns: one for the box within which the departure lat-lon falls, and another for the box within which the arrival lat-lon falls:

```
sparse['dep_loc'] = tf.feature_column.crossed_column(
        [disc['d_dep_lat'], disc['d_dep_lon']], NBUCKETS*NBUCKETS)
sparse['arr_loc'] = tf.feature_column.crossed_column(
        [disc['d_arr_lat'], disc['d_arr_lon']], NBUCKETS*NBUCKETS)
```

We can also create a feature cross of the pair of departure and arrival grid cells, essentially capturing flights between two boxes. In addition, we can also feature cross the departure and arrival airport codes (e.g., ORD–JFK for flights that leave Chicago's O'Hare airport and arrive at New York's John F. Kennedy airport):[12]

```
sparse['dep_arr'] = tf.feature_column.crossed_column(
        [sparse['dep_loc'], sparse['arr_loc']], NBUCKETS ** 4)
sparse['ori_dest'] = tf.feature_column.crossed_column(
        ['origin', 'dest'], hash_bucket_size=1000)
```

Even though we want to use the sparse columns directly in the linear part of the model, we would also like to perform dimensionality reduction on them and use them in the deep part of the model:

```
embed = {
        'embed_{}'.format(colname) :
            tf.feature_column.embedding_column(col, dimension=10)
                for colname, col in sparse.items()
}
real.update(embed)
```

 An embedding is a learnable data representation that maps high-cardinality data (e.g., there are 300 unique airports) to a low-dimensional space (say, 10 dimensions). Unlike one-hot encoding, which would treat all airports as independent, embeddings allow us to capture similarities between airports. For more on the Embedding Design Pattern, please see (you guessed it) the O'Reilly Media book *Machine Learning Design Patterns*.

## Wide-and-Deep Classifier

With the sparse and real feature columns thus enhanced beyond the raw inputs, we can create a `wide_and_deep_classifier` passing in the linear and deep feature columns separately:

```
def wide_and_deep_classifier(inputs,
    linear_feature_columns, dnn_feature_columns, dnn_hidden_units):
        deep = tf.keras.layers.DenseFeatures(
```

---

12 If we feature cross the airports as categorical variables, what extra information could there be in the categorical variable that is the feature cross between the departure box and the arrival box? Answer: feature crossing the airports gives us the precise airport pair, whereas feature crossing the boxes gives us general neighborhoods. Thus, the latter helps us treat all airports in Alaska or New York City similarly.

```
            dnn_feature_columns, name='deep_inputs')(inputs)
    for layerno, numnodes in enumerate(dnn_hidden_units):
        deep = tf.keras.layers.Dense(numnodes,
            activation='relu', name='dnn_{}'.format(layerno+1))(deep)
    wide = tf.keras.layers.DenseFeatures(
            linear_feature_columns, name='wide_inputs')(inputs)
    both = tf.keras.layers.concatenate([deep, wide], name='both')
    output = tf.keras.layers.Dense(
            1, activation='sigmoid', name='pred')(both)
    model = tf.keras.Model(inputs, output)
    model.compile(optimizer='adam',
                    loss='binary_crossentropy',
                    metrics=['accuracy'])
    return model
```

The model function that results is shown in Figure 9-5.

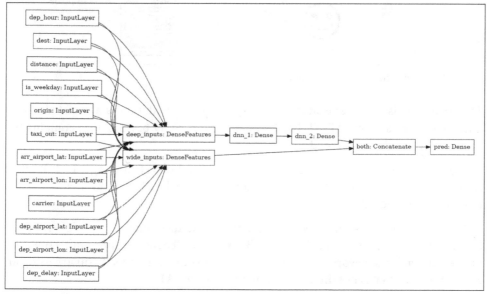

*Figure 9-5. The wide-and-deep Keras model.*

This wide-and-deep model with feature crosses that match human intuition yielded an RMSE of 0.196, which is the best yet.

# Deploying a Trained TensorFlow Model to Vertex AI

Now that we have trained a TensorFlow model and exported it, how do we deploy the model so that any client can get predictions from it? We use Vertex AI, the managed service for training, deploying, monitoring, and orchestrating machine learning models in Google Cloud Platform.

## Concepts

There are a few important concepts here, so refer to Figure 9-6 as we go along. The code snippets are in the notebook *flights_model_tf2.ipynb* in the code repository.

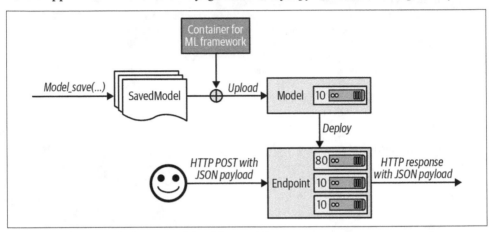

*Figure 9-6. Steps to deploy a model to Vertex AI.*

The basic idea is that clients access an endpoint. Every endpoint is associated with a URL. The clients send a HTTP POST request with a JSON payload that contains the input to the prediction method.

The endpoint contains a number of Vertex AI Model objects among which it splits traffic. Figure 9-6 depicts 80% of traffic going to Model 1, 10% to Model 2, and the remainder to Model 3.

A Vertex AI Model is an object that references models built in a wide variety of frameworks (TensorFlow, PyTorch, XGBoost, etc.). There are pre-built container images for each framework. You can also bring in your containers if you are using an ML framework that is not directly supported by Vertex AI.

The TensorFlow container image looks for SavedModel files, the format that Keras/ TensorFlow 2.0 models are exported into by default when you call `model.save(...)` or `tf.saved_models.save()` from your training code.

Deploying a model involves uploading the model artifacts to Vertex AI, creating an endpoint, and deploying the model to the endpoint.

## Uploading Model

The first step is to upload the saved model files, specifying the pre-built Vertex container (*https://oreil.ly/3zH67*) for your ML framework. Here, I'm using the Tensor-Flow 2.6 container built for serving using CPUs:

```
CONTAINER=us-docker.pkg.dev/vertex-ai/prediction/tf2-cpu.2-6:latest
gcloud ai models upload --region=$REGION \
    --display-name=$MODEL_NAME \
    --container-image-uri=$CONTAINER \
    --artifact-uri=$EXPORT_PATH
```

What's the MODEL_NAME?

I recommend that you use a unique display name for every model (Vertex AI does assign a unique model ID, but it's an opaque number that is not human readable):

| Name | ID |
| --- | --- |
| flights-20211102-064051 | 3935868997391613952 |

An easy way is to append a timestamp to the name that you want to use, so each time you upload a model you have a new name:

```
TIMESTAMP=$(date +%Y%m%d-%H%M%S)
MODEL_NAME=flights-${TIMESTAMP}
```

---

## BigQuery ML Models in Vertex AI

BigQuery supports exporting trained models in TensorFlow SavedModel format. Here's how to export the BigQuery ML model we trained in Chapter 8 into a Saved-Model:

```
EXPORT_PATH=gs://${BUCKET}/bqml_model_export/
bq extract -m dsongcp.arr_delay_lm $EXPORT_PATH
```

Use the EXPORT_PATH as the artifact URI when uploading the model to Vertex AI:

```
CONTAINER=us-docker.pkg.dev/vertex-ai/prediction/tf2-cpu.2-6:latest
gcloud ai models upload --region=$REGION \
    --display-name=$MODEL_NAME \
    --container-image-uri=$CONTAINER \
    --artifact-uri=$EXPORT_PATH
```

Nearly all BigQuery ML models—AutoML, DNN, KMeans, Matrix Factorization, PCA, and linear models—can be exported (*https://oreil.ly/ulXJD*) in TensorFlow SavedModel format.

The exception is that boosted tree models are written out as *.bst* files in XGBoost 0.82 format. Fortunately, Vertex AI also provides pre-built containers for XGBoost. All we have to do is to change the container that is being used from the TensorFlow one to the one for XGBoost 0.82:

```
CONTAINER=us-docker.pkg.dev/vertex-ai/prediction/xgboost-cpu.0-82:latest
```

The rest of the steps remain the same.

---

## Creating Endpoint

We need a unique name for the endpoint as well, but we will not be creating multiple endpoints. Just one. This is because the URL at which the model predictions can be accessed will be based on the endpoint ID. So you want to reuse the endpoint so that you can update models without breaking existing clients. Therefore, there is no need for a timestamp. Just verify that the endpoint doesn't exist before you create it:

```
ENDPOINT_NAME=flights
if [[ $(gcloud ai endpoints list --region=$REGION \
   --format='value(DISPLAY_NAME)' --filter=display_name=${ENDPOINT_NAME}) ]]; then
     echo "Endpoint $ENDPOINT_NAME already exists"
else
    # create model
    echo "Creating Endpoint $ENDPOINT_NAME for $MODEL_NAME"
    gcloud ai endpoints create --region=${REGION} --display-name=${ENDPOINT_NAME}
fi
```

## Deploying Model to Endpoint

Now that we have a model and an endpoint, we can deploy the model to the endpoint:

```
gcloud ai endpoints deploy-model $ENDPOINT_ID \
    --region=$REGION \
    --model=$MODEL_ID \
    --display-name=$MODEL_NAME \
    --machine-type=n1-standard-2 \
    --min-replica-count=1 \
    --max-replica-count=1 \
    --traffic-split=0=100
```

Note how I am making sure to specify the traffic split and the machine type I need (I could add GPUs at this point, but I don't need GPUs to serve predictions for a tabular data model). Because this is the first model, we send 100% of the traffic to this one with:

```
--traffic-split=0=100
```

If we had an older model, we'd specify the relative split between two models. To send 10% of the traffic to this new model and 90% to an older model, we'd do:

```
--traffic-split=0=10,OLD_DEPLOYED_MODEL_ID=90
```

Note that all these commands require the model ID and endpoint ID (not the model name and endpoint name). To get the ID from the name (assuming you are using unique names as I recommended):

```
MODEL_ID=$(gcloud ai models list --region=$REGION \
            --format='value(MODEL_ID)' \
            --filter=display_name=${MODEL_NAME})
ENDPOINT_ID=$(gcloud ai endpoints list --region=$REGION \
```

```
                    --format='value(ENDPOINT_ID)' \
                    --filter=display_name=${ENDPOINT_NAME})
```

If necessary, you can get the ID of the most recently deployed model or endpoint by adding a sort:

```
ENDPOINT_ID=$(gcloud ai endpoints list --region=$REGION \
                    --format='value(ENDPOINT_ID)'\
                    --filter=display_name=${ENDPOINT_NAME} \
                    --sort-by=creationTimeStamp | tail -1)
```

## Invoking the Deployed Model

Here's how client programs can invoke the model that we have deployed. Assume that they have the input data in a JSON file called *example_input.json*:

```
{"instances": [
  {"dep_hour": 2, "is_weekday": 1, "dep_delay": 40, "taxi_out": 17,
   "distance": 41, "carrier": "AS", "dep_airport_lat": 58.42527778,
   "dep_airport_lon": -135.7075, "arr_airport_lat": 58.35472222,
   "arr_airport_lon": -134.57472222, "origin": "GST", "dest": "JNU"},
  {"dep_hour": 22, "is_weekday": 0, "dep_delay": -7, "taxi_out": 7,
   "distance": 201, "carrier": "HA", "dep_airport_lat": 21.97611111,
   "dep_airport_lon": -159.33888889, "arr_airport_lat": 20.89861111,
   "arr_airport_lon": -156.43055556, "origin": "LIH", "dest": "OGG"}
]}
```

They can send an HTTP POST request:

```
curl -X POST\
-H "Authorization: Bearer "$(gcloud auth application-default print-access-token)\
-H "Content-Type: application/json; charset=utf-8"\
-d @example_input.json\
"https://...${PROJECT}/locations/${REGION}/endpoints/${ENDPOINT_ID}:predict"
```

Of course, you need to tell them the region, project, and endpoint ID at which the model is deployed. Many times, it's easier to hide this URL behind a simpler URL that redirects to this. Such a level of indirection also helps with throttling and with charging for each invocation. On Google Cloud, you can do this using Apigee (*https://oreil.ly/cCxSB*).

Clients who send the HTTP POST request will get the result back as JSON:

```
{
  "predictions": [
    [
      0.228779882
    ],
    [
      0.766132474
    ]
  ],
  "deployedModelId": "2339101036930662400",
```

```
    "model": "projects/379218021631/locations/us-central1/models/39358689973916",
    "modelDisplayName": "flights-20211102-064051"
}
```

Of course, it's a REST API, so you can invoke it from pretty much any language. There are also client API libraries available.

Vertex AI provides a fully managed, autoscaling, serverless environment for machine learning models. You get the benefits of paying for any compute resources (such as CPUs or GPUs) only when you are using them. Because the models are containerized, dependency management is taken care of. The endpoints take care of traffic splits, allowing you to do A/B testing in a convenient way.

The benefits go beyond not having to manage infrastructure. Once your model is deployed to Vertex AI, you get a lot of neat capabilities without any additional code— explainability, drift detection, monitoring, etc.

At this point, we have written the model in Python in a Jupyter Notebook and deployed the model using `gcloud` commands that you can run from a Unix shell. This sort of hybrid language and environment is hard to automate.

Much better would be if we could do it all from plain Python programs—following a clean separation of responsibility between model code and operations code will also make the MLOps teams happy. Let's look at how to do that next.

## Summary

In this chapter, we extended the machine learning approach that we started in Chapter 7, but using the TensorFlow library instead of Spark MLlib. Realizing that categorical columns result in an explosion of the dataset features, we used TensorFlow to carry out GPU-accelerated training. Another advantage that TensorFlow provides is that its design allows a computer scientist to go as low-level as they need to, and so many machine learning research innovations are implemented in TensorFlow. As machine learning practitioners, therefore, using TensorFlow allows us to use innovative machine learning research soon after it is published rather than wait for a reimplementation in some other framework. Finally, using TensorFlow allows us to deploy the model rather easily into our data pipelines regardless of where they are run because TensorFlow is portable across a wide variety of hardware platforms.

We trained a logistic regression model on all of the input values and learned that the model was unable to effectively use the new features like airport locations.

We discussed that, intuitively, the nodes in a deep neural network help provide decision hyperplanes, and that successive layers help to combine individual hyperplanes into more complex decision surfaces. Using a deep neural network instead of logistic regression didn't provide any benefit with our inputs, though. However, bringing in human insight in the form of additional features that bucketed some of the continuous features, creating feature crosses, and using a wide-and-deep model yielded a further reduction in the RMSE. We deployed this model and invoked it using REST APIs to do online prediction.

# Suggested Resources

The most important skill in machine learning is being able to formulate the problem in such a way that ML can be successful at solving it. That is the focus of the course "Managing Machine Learning Projects with Google Cloud" (*https://oreil.ly/q2Dme*) by Google Cloud Training on Coursera.

To learn more about being an ML practitioner, check out these books:

- *Hands-On Machine Learning with Scikit-Learn, Keras, and TensorFlow* by Aurélien Géron (O'Reilly).
- *Machine Learning Design Patterns* by Lakshmanan, Robinson, and Munn (O'Reilly).

The Vertex AI samples GitHub repository (*https://oreil.ly/wMNeD*) is a gold mine of examples.

# CHAPTER 10

# Getting Ready for MLOps with Vertex AI

In Chapter 9, we developed a TensorFlow model in a Jupyter Notebook. We were able to train the model, deploy it to an endpoint, and get predictions from it from the notebook environment. While that worked for us during development, it is not a scalable workflow.

Taking a TensorFlow model that you trained in your Jupyter Notebook and deploying the SavedModel to Vertex AI doesn't scale to hundreds of models and large teams. Retraining is going to be difficult because the ops team will have to set up all of the ops and monitoring and scheduling on top of something that is really clunky and totally nonminimal.

In order for a machine learning model to be placed into production, it needs to meet the following requirements:

- The model should be under version control. Source code control systems such as git work much better with text files (such as *.py* files) than with mixtures of text and binaries (which is what *.ipynb* files are).

- The entire process—from dataset creation to training to deployment—has to be driven by code. This is so that it is easy to automatically retrigger a training run using GitHub Actions or GitLab Continuous Integration whenever new changed code is checked in.

- The entire process should be invokable from a single entry point, so that the retraining can be triggered by noncode changes such as the arrival of new data in a Cloud Storage bucket.

- It should be easy to monitor the performance of models and endpoints and take measures to fix some subset of issues that arise without having to modify the model code. For example, if GPUs are getting saturated, it should be easy to add extra resources for training or serving. It should be possible to continuously evaluate the model, and if the distribution of an input feature changes or if the evaluation metric falls below a specific threshold, it should be possible to trigger model retraining.

Together, these criteria go by the name *MLOps*. Google Cloud, in general, and Vertex AI, in particular, provide a number of MLOps capabilities. However, in order to take advantage of these inbuilt capabilities, it is better if we clearly separate out the model code from the ops code and express everything in Python rather than in notebooks.

# Developing and Deploying Using Python

Jupyter Notebooks are great for development, but I strongly recommend against putting those notebooks directly into production, even though Vertex AI will allow you to do this.

What I recommend is that you convert your initial prototyping model code into a Python file and then continue all development in it. Throw away the Jupyter Notebook. The Python files will be what's in your code repository, and will be the maintained codebase from now onwards.

Look at the code in the files *model.py* and *train_on_vertexai.py* in the code repository of this book, and use them to follow along.

---

### Using Local Python Module from JupyterLab

If you throw away the Jupyter Notebook in which you did development, how can you do future ad-hoc work and demos? What I recommend is that you invoke the extracted (and maintained) Python code from a new notebook for future experimentation, ad-hoc data analytics, or demos. For example, supposing you extract the code to a file named *model.py*, you can invoke functions in that file from JupyterLab:

```
import model
trainds = model.read_dataset(...)
```

If you find yourself changing *model.py* as you write code in your new notebook, make sure to add this magic at the top of your notebook:

```
%autoreload
```

This automatically reloads (*https://oreil.ly/bEDD2*) the module whenever you change *model.py* so that you are not running older code.

---

# Writing model.py

I created the file *model.py* by extracting all the Keras model code from the Jupyter Notebook I wrote in the previous section (*flights_model_tf2.ipynb*). Much of the notebook code has been extracted into a function called `train_and_evaluate.py`:

```
def train_and_evaluate(train_data_pattern, eval_data_pattern, test_data_pattern,
                       export_dir, output_dir):
    ...
    train_dataset = read_dataset(train_data_pattern, train_batch_size)
    eval_dataset = read_dataset(eval_data_pattern, eval_batch_size,
                                tf.estimator.ModeKeys.EVAL, num_eval_examples)

    model = create_model()
    history = model.fit(train_dataset,
                        validation_data=eval_dataset,
                        epochs=epochs,
                        steps_per_epoch=steps_per_epoch,
                        callbacks=[cp_callback])
    # export
    logging.info('Exporting to {}'.format(export_dir))
    tf.saved_model.save(model, export_dir)
```

There are three key things to note:

- The data is read from URIs specified by `train_data_pattern`,[1] `eval_data_pattern`, and `test_data_pattern` for training, validation, and test datasets, respectively.

- The model creation code is extracted out to a function called `create_model`.

- The model is written out to `export_dir`, and any other intermediate outputs are written to `output_dir`.

I get the data patterns and output directories in *model.py* using environment variables:

```
OUTPUT_MODEL_DIR = os.getenv("AIP_MODEL_DIR")
TRAIN_DATA_PATTERN = os.getenv("AIP_TRAINING_DATA_URI")
EVAL_DATA_PATTERN = os.getenv("AIP_VALIDATION_DATA_URI")
TEST_DATA_PATTERN = os.getenv("AIP_TEST_DATA_URI")
```

These environment variables form the contract between my code and Vertex AI and are needed in order for all the automagical things to happen.

I will, however, also want to run this code outside Vertex AI (for example, during development). In such a case, the environment variable will not be set, and so the

---

1 *URIs* or Uniform Resource Identifiers are strings that identify information resources on a network. URIs are a broader category than URLs in that we can also use identifiers such as **gs://**....

variables will all be None. I look for that case and set them to values in my development environment:

```
if not OUTPUT_MODEL_DIR:
    OUTPUT_MODEL_DIR = os.path.join(OUTPUT_DIR,
                                    'export/flights_{}'.format(
                                    time.strftime("%Y%m%d-%H%M%S")))
if not TRAIN_DATA_PATTERN:
    TRAIN_DATA_PATTERN = 'gs://{}/ch9/data/train*'.format(BUCKET)
if not EVAL_DATA_PATTERN:
    EVAL_DATA_PATTERN = 'gs://{}/ch9/data/eval*'.format(BUCKET)
```

These files can be very small because they are only for development. Actual production runs will run inside Vertex AI where the environment variables will be set.

Once I finish extracting the code into *model.py*, I make sure it works:

```
python3 model.py  --bucket <bucket-name> --develop
```

I can also run it on the full dataset by dropping the develop flag (I suggest you visit the accompanying code to understand the *model.py* script and its arguments). The results are the same as my Jupyter Notebook, so I can move on to invoking this from a Vertex AI pipeline.

## Writing the Training Pipeline

The training pipeline (See train_on_vertexai.py) needs to do five things in code:

- Load up a managed dataset in Vertex AI.
- Set up training infrastructure to run *model.py*.
- Train the model by invoking functions in *model.py* on the managed dataset.
- Find the endpoint to which to deploy the model.
- Deploy the model to the endpoint.

Let's look at them one by one.

First, I load up a tabular dataset (options exist for image, text, and other datasets, and for tabular data in BigQuery):

```
data_set = aiplatform.TabularDataset.create(
        display_name='data-{}'.format(ENDPOINT_NAME),
        gcs_source=['gs://{}/ch9/data/all.csv'.format(BUCKET)]
)
```

Note that I am passing in *all* of the data. Vertex AI will take care of splitting the data into train, validate, and test datasets and sending it to the training program. By default, the split will be random, whereas we want to split based on the daywise split that we have set up. I'll get back to this.

Second, I create a training job passing in *model.py*, the training container image, and the serving container image:

```
model_display_name = '{}-{}'.format(ENDPOINT_NAME, timestamp)
job = aiplatform.CustomTrainingJob(
        display_name='train-{}'.format(model_display_name),
        script_path="model.py",
        container_uri=train_image,
        requirements=[],  # any extra Python packages
        model_serving_container_image_uri=deploy_image
)
```

Just as we did when we did it with bash scripts, we are assigning a timestamped name to the model.

The third step is to run the job. This involves running *model.py* on the managed dataset on some hardware:

```
model = job.run(
        dataset=data_set,
        model_display_name=model_display_name,
        args=['--bucket', BUCKET],
        replica_count=1,
        machine_type='n1-standard-4',
        accelerator_type=aip.AcceleratorType.NVIDIA_TESLA_T4.name,
        accelerator_count=1
     )
```

I get back a model that I wish to deploy to a preexisting endpoint. To find an existing endpoint or create one, I then do:

```
endpoints = aiplatform.Endpoint.list(
    filter='display_name="{}"'.format(ENDPOINT_NAME),
    order_by='create_time desc',
    project=PROJECT, location=REGION,
)
if len(endpoints) > 0:
    endpoint = endpoints[0]  # most recently created
else:
    endpoint = aiplatform.Endpoint.create(
        display_name=ENDPOINT_NAME, project=PROJECT, location=REGION
    )
```

Finally, I deploy the model to the endpoint using:

```
model.deploy(
        endpoint=endpoint,
        traffic_split={"0": 100},
        machine_type='n1-standard-2',
        min_replica_count=1,
        max_replica_count=1
     )
```

That's it! Now, we have a Python program that we can run anytime we want to retrain and/or deploy the trained model. Of course, the MLOps person will typically not replace the model wholesale, but send only a small fraction of the traffic to the model. They'll probably also set up monitoring and continuous evaluation on the endpoint in Vertex AI. But we've made it easy for them to do that.

We can try out the training pipeline:

```
python3 train_on_vertexai.py --project <project> \
       --bucket <bucket-name> –develop
```

This time, though, the training happens in the managed service. The GCP web console shows me GPU utilization and the job's logs show up in Cloud Logging.

## Predefined Split

By default, Vertex AI does a fractional split of the data (80% to training, 10% each for validation and testing). Here, however, we want to explicitly assign each row to a data split. To do this, we need to add a column to our dataset that controls the split. We can do this when creating the data:

```
CREATE OR REPLACE TABLE dsongcp.flights_all_data AS
SELECT
  IF(arr_delay < 15, 1.0, 0.0) AS ontime,
  dep_delay,
  taxi_out,
  ...
  IF (is_train_day = 'True',
      IF(ABS(MOD(FARM_FINGERPRINT(CAST(f.FL_DATE AS STRING)), 100)) < 60,
                                           'TRAIN', 'VALIDATE'),
      'TEST') AS data_split
FROM dsongcp.flights_tzcorr f
...
```

Basically, there is a column that I'm calling data_split that takes the values TRAIN, VALIDATE, or TEST. So, every row in the managed dataset is assigned to one of these three splits.

Then, when I'm training the job, I specify what the predefined splitting column is:

```
model = job.run(
        dataset=data_set,
        predefined_split_column_name='data_split',
        model_display_name=model_display_name,
```

Vertex AI will take care of the rest, including assigning all the necessary metadata to the models being trained.

## AutoML

What changes should I make in the preceding pipeline if I want to use AutoML instead of my custom training job? Well, I don't need my own *model.py* of course. So, instead of the `CustomTrainingJob`, I'll use AutoML.

Setting and running the training job (Steps 3 and 4 in "Writing the Training Pipeline" on page 338) now become:

```
def train_automl_model(data_set, timestamp):
    # train
    model_display_name = '{}-{}'.format(ENDPOINT_NAME, timestamp)
    job = aiplatform.AutoMLTabularTrainingJob(
        display_name='train-{}'.format(model_display_name),
        optimization_prediction_type='classification'
    )
    model = job.run(
        dataset=data_set,
        target_column='ontime',
        model_display_name=model_display_name,
        budget_milli_node_hours=(300 if develop_mode else 2000),
        disable_early_stopping=False
    )
    return job, model
```

That's the only change! The rest of the pipeline stays the same. Vertex AI provides a unified platform for ML development regardless of the ML technique you use. In fact, we can similarly change the ML framework to PyTorch or to sklearn or XGBoost and, as far as the MLOps people are concerned, there are only minimal changes.

In my *train_on_vertexai.py*, I switch between custom Keras code and AutoML with a command-line parameter.

How well does AutoML do? Does it beat our custom Keras model with the latitude and longitude feature crosses? Unfortunately (see Figure 10-1), AutoML reports precision, recall, area under the curve, and several other metrics. However, it does not report RMSE (as of this writing in January 2022).

Looking at the feature importance graph that is part of the GCP console for AutoML models (see Figure 10-2), it appears that AutoML didn't take much advantage of the latitude and longitude of the airports.

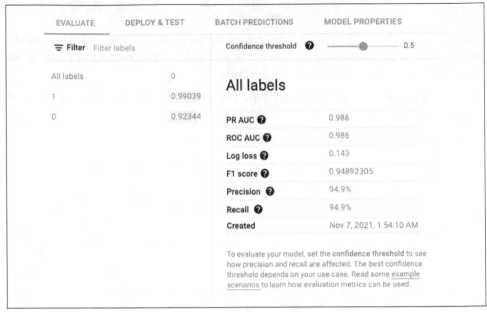

*Figure 10-1. Performance metrics from AutoML do not include RMSE.*

In order to compute custom evaluation metrics, we can ask AutoML to dump the evaluation data and predictions to a table in BigQuery. In order to do so, I added the following to the AutoML job:

```
model = job.run(
        dataset=data_set,
        predefined_split_column_name='data_split',
        target_column='ontime',
        model_display_name=model_display_name,
        budget_milli_node_hours=(300 if develop_mode else 2000),
        disable_early_stopping=False,
        export_evaluated_data_items=True,
        export_evaluated_data_items_bigquery_destination_uri=(
            '{}:dsongcp.ch9_automl_evaluated'.format(PROJECT)),
        export_evaluated_data_items_override_destination=True
    )
```

Now, when I rerun the AutoML training job, a table is created in BigQuery and I can compute the RMSE in SQL:

```
SELECT
  SQRT(SUM(
      (CAST(ontime AS FLOAT64) - predicted_ontime.scores[OFFSET(0)])*
      (CAST(ontime AS FLOAT64) - predicted_ontime.scores[OFFSET(0)])
      )/COUNT(*))
FROM dsongcp.ch9_automl_evaluated
```

The result? AutoML Tables on the dataset achieved an RMSE of 0.199. So, our custom model with the feature crosses is better than AutoML (0.196), but AutoML came really close.

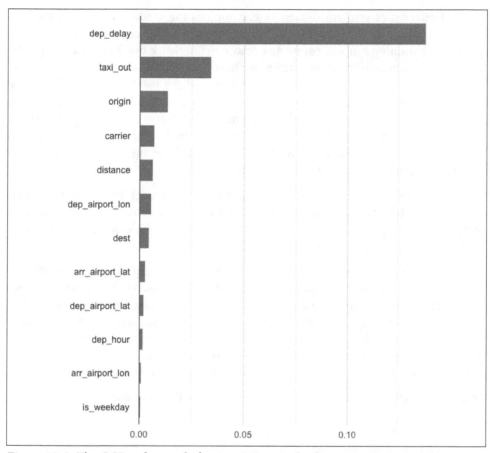

*Figure 10-2. The GCP web console for AutoML provides feature importance.*

# Hyperparameter Tuning

Our custom model is better than AutoML, but could it be even better? There are a number of hyperparameters—learning rate, batch size, number of layers/nodes in the neural network, number of buckets, number of embedding dimensions, etc. that I essentially just guessed.

For example, the number of layers and the number of hidden nodes was essentially arbitrary. As discussed earlier, more layers help the model learn more complex input spaces, but it is difficult to have an intuition about how difficult this particular problem (predicting flight delays) is. However, the choice of model architecture does matter—choosing too few layers will result in a suboptimal classifier, whereas choosing too many layers might result in overfitting. We need to select an appropriate number of layers and nodes.

The optimizer uses gradient descent, but computes the gradients on small batches. We used a batch size of 64, but that choice was arbitrary. The larger the batch size, the quicker the training run will complete because the network overhead scales with the number of batches—with larger batches, we have fewer batches to complete an epoch, and so the training will complete faster. However, if the batch size is too large, the sensitivity of the optimizer to specific data points reduces and hurts the ability of the optimizer to learn the nuances of the problem. Even in terms of efficiency, too large a batch will cause matrix multiplications to spill over from more efficient memory to less efficient memory (such as from a GPU to a CPU or thrashing from RAM to HDD). Thus, the choice of batch size matters.

There are other arbitrary choices that are specific to our model. For example, we discretized the latitude and longitude into five buckets each. What should this number of buckets actually be? Too low a number, and we will lose the discrimination ability; too high a number, and we will begin to overfit.

As a final step in improving the model, we'll carry out an experiment with different choices for these three parameters: number of hidden units, batch size, and number of buckets. Even though we could laboriously carry out these experiments one-by-one, we will use a capability of Vertex AI called Vizier that allows for a nonlinear hyperparameter tuning approach. We'll specify ranges for these three parameters, specify a maximum number of trials we want to try out, and have Vizier carry out a search in hyperparameter space for the best set of parameters.

To add this capability to our Python code, this is what I have to do:

- Parameterize the model in *model.py*.
- Implement a shorter training run.
- Write out metrics during training.
- Implement a hyperparameter tuning pipeline.
- Run the best trial to completion.

Recall that the model training file exists as *model.py* in the code repository of this book and the pipeline orchestrator is *train_on_vertexai.py*. Use the code in the two files to follow along.

## Parameterize Model

The first step is to make the hyperparameters as command-line parameters to your model. For example, in *model.py*, we might do:

```
parser.add_argument(
        '--nembeds',
        help='Embedding dimension for categorical variables',
        type=int,
        default=3
    )
```

Note that the initial guess for the variable is the default value. This allows your training script to continue working as it did before. Then, you set the variable from the command-line parameters for use by the training script:

```
args = parser.parse_args()
...
NEMBEDS = args.nembeds
```

It's a good idea to do this for all the hyperparameters we might ever want to tune. A good practice is to never have any hardcoded values in *model.py*—everything there needs to be an input parameter.

## Shorten Training Run

Our training run so far has involved training on the full dataset and then evaluating on the full test dataset. Doing a complete training run like that for hyperparameter tuning is expensive, wasteful, and wrong. Why?

*Expensive*

The point of hyperparameter tuning is to obtain the best set of parameters, not to obtain the best possible model. Once we find the best set of parameters, we can then train a model with those parameters to completion. Therefore, there is no need to carry out a trial to completion. We just need to train it until you know which trial is likely to end up better (see Figure 10-3).

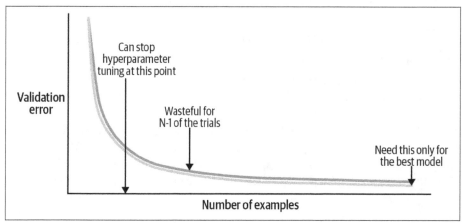

*Figure 10-3. Doing a complete training run for hyperparameter tuning is expensive, wasteful, and wrong.*

*Wasteful*

Under the assumption that your training curves won't cross each other, a better set of parameters will be better throughout the training process, and you can stop the training well before it starts to converge. Use your training budget to do more trials, not to run those trials longer.

*Wrong*

You don't want to evaluate the hyperparameter tuning on the test dataset. You want to compare performance on the validation dataset. Just make sure that the validation dataset is large enough for you to do this comparison between trial models meaningfully.

The way I do these modifications is to add two options to my *model.py*: one to train for a shorter time and another to skip the full evaluation:

```
NUM_EXAMPLES = args['num_examples']
SKIP_FULL_EVAL = args['skip_full_eval']
...
steps_per_epoch = NUM_EXAMPLES // train_batch_size
epochs = NUM_EPOCHS
eval_dataset = read_dataset(eval_data_pattern, eval_batch_size,
                    tf.estimator.ModeKeys.EVAL, num_eval_examples)
model.fit(train_dataset,
                    validation_data=eval_dataset,
                    epochs=NUM_EPOCHS,
                    steps_per_epoch=steps_per_epoch,
                    callbacks=[cp_callback, HpCallback()])
...
if not SKIP_FULL_EVAL:
        test_dataset = read_dataset(test_data_pattern, eval_batch_size,
                                tf.estimator.ModeKeys.TEST, None)
        final_metrics = model.evaluate(test_dataset)
        ...
else:
        logging.info("Skipping evaluation on full test dataset")
```

What's the deal with `steps_per_epoch` and `NUM_EXAMPLES`? Note the x-axis in Figure 10-3. It's not epochs—it's the number of examples. While it's pretty wasteful to train on the full dataset, it can be helpful to get the same number of intermediate metrics that you would get with the full amount of training (I'll explain why in the next step). Because you will also be hyperparameter tuning the batch size, the best way to do this is to use Virtual Epochs (see the Checkpoints pattern in *Machine Learning Design Patterns* by Valliappa Lakshmanan, Sara Robinson, and Michael Munn [O'Reilly] for details). Steps-per-epoch is how we get virtual epochs on large datasets.

## Metrics During Training

The next modification is to write out metrics during the training process. We don't want to just wait until the end before writing out the entire history. If we do this, then Vertex AI will also help us save costs by cutting short unproductive trials.

In Keras, to write out metrics during training we can define and use a callback:

```
METRIC = 'val_rmse'
hpt = hypertune.HyperTune()

class HpCallback(tf.keras.callbacks.Callback):
        def on_epoch_end(self, epoch, logs=None):
                if logs and METRIC in logs:
                        logging.info("Epoch {}: {} = {}".format(
                                        epoch, METRIC, logs[METRIC]))
                        hpt.report_hyperparameter_tuning_metric(
hyperparameter_metric_tag=METRIC, metric_value=logs[METRIC], global_step=epoch)

...
history = model.fit(train_dataset,
                    ...
                    callbacks=[cp_callback, HpCallback()])
```

I'm using the cloudml-hypertune package to simplify the writing of metrics in a form that the TensorFlow ecosystem (TensorBoard, Vizier, etc.) can understand.

## Hyperparameter Tuning Pipeline

Now that we have modified *model.py* to make it easy to do hyperparameter tuning, we could build an MLOps pipeline to tune our model anytime we notice it drifting.

But now, back to the hyperparameter tuning: there are two steps in the orchestration code (in *train_on_vertexai.py*).

First, we create a Vertex AI CustomJob to call the *model.py* with the right parameters:

```
tf_version = '2-' + tf.__version__[2:3]
train_image = (
        "us-docker.pkg.dev/vertex-ai/training/tf-gpu.{}:latest"
        .format(tf_version))
model_display_name = '{}-{}'.format(ENDPOINT_NAME, timestamp)
trial_job = aiplatform.CustomJob.from_local_script(
    display_name='train-{}'.format(model_display_name),
    script_path="model.py",
    container_uri=train_image,
    args=[
        '--bucket', BUCKET,
        '--skip_full_eval', # no need to evaluate on test data
        '--num_epochs', '10',
        '--num_examples', '500000' # 1/10 actual size
    ],
```

```
                requirements=['cloudml-hypertune'],
                replica_count=1,
                machine_type='n1-standard-4',
                accelerator_type=aip.AcceleratorType.NVIDIA_TESLA_T4.name,
                accelerator_count=1,
        )
```

Next, we create and run a hyperparameter tuning job that will use the custom job as an individual trial:

```
hparam_job = aiplatform.HyperparameterTuningJob(
        display_name='hparam-{}'.format(model_display_name),
        custom_job=trial_job,
        metric_spec={'val_rmse': 'minimize'},
        parameter_spec={
            "train_batch_size": hpt.IntegerParameterSpec(
                                    min=16, max=256, scale='log'),
            "nbuckets": hpt.IntegerParameterSpec(
                                    min=5, max=10, scale='linear'),
            "dnn_hidden_units": hpt.CategoricalParameterSpec(
                values=["64,16", "64,16,4", "64,64,64,8", "256,64,16"])
        },
        max_trial_count=4 if develop_mode else 10,
        parallel_trial_count=2,
        search_algorithm=None,   # Bayesian
)
```

Note that I am specifying the metric here to match the METRIC in my *model.py* and that I'm specifying ranges for the parameters.

The parameter train_batch_size is an integer; we ask for it to look for values in the interval [16, 256]—the logarithmic scale instructs the tuner that we would like to try more values at the smaller end of the range rather than the larger end of the range. This is because long-standing experience suggests that smaller batch sizes yield more accurate models.[2] And also because I expect the effect of going from 16 to 32 to be bigger than going from 216 to 232, for example.

The nbuckets parameter is also an integer, but linearly distributed between 5 and 10. The FAA seems to have about 36 grid boxes into which it divides up the airspace (see Figure 9-3). This argues for nbuckets = 6 (since 6 × 6 = 36), but the corridors are significantly narrower in the Northeast part of the United States, and so perhaps we need more fine-grained grid cells. By specifying nbuckets in the range 5 to 10, we are asking the tuner to explore having between 25 and 100 grid cells into which to divide up the United States.

---

2 Geoffrey Hinton, "A Practical Guide to Training Restricted Boltzmann Machines," University of Toronto Department of Computer Science, August 2, 2010. https://oreil.ly/hkiUn.

As for `dnn_hidden_units`, we explicitly specify a few candidates—a two-layer network, a three-layer network, and a four-layer network, and a network with many more nodes. If it turns out that any optimal parameter is near the extrema, we will repeat the hyperparameter tuning with a different range. For example, if it turns out that `nbuckets` = 10 is best, we should repeat the tuning, but trying out `nbuckets` in the range 10 to 15 the next time. Similarly, if a four-layer network turns out to be best, we will need to also try a five-layer and a six-layer network.

By default, the hyperparameter tuning service in Vertex AI (called Vizier) will use Bayesian optimization, but we can change the algorithm to GridSearch if we want.

## Best Trial to Completion

Once we launch the hyperparameter tuning job, we can look at the Vertex AI section of the GCP console to see the parameters come in (see Figure 10-4).

**Hyperparameter tuning trials**

Filter   Enter property name or value

| Trial ID | val_rmse ↑ | Training step | train_batch_size | nbuckets | dnn_hidden_units |
|----------|------------|---------------|------------------|----------|------------------|
| 9        | 0.192      | 9             | 256              | 10       | 64,64,64,8       |
| 10       | 0.192      | 9             | 256              | 7        | 64,64,64,8       |
| 5        | 0.192      | 9             | 256              | 10       | 256,64,16        |
| 1        | 0.194      | 9             | 136              | 8        | 256,64,16        |
| 4        | 0.194      | 9             | 69               | 5        | 256,64,16        |
| 2        | 0.194      | 9             | 74               | 6        | 64,64,64,8       |
| 3        | 0.194      | 9             | 256              | 10       | 64,16,4          |
| 6        | 0.195      | 9             | 33               | 7        | 64,16            |
| 7        | 0.197      | 9             | 16               | 5        | 64,16,4          |
| 8        | 0.199      | 9             | 16               | 5        | 256,64,16        |

*Figure 10-4. Results of hyperparameter tuning in the GCP Vertex AI web console.*

Once we determine the best set of parameters, we can take the best set of parameters and then run the training job to completion. That will give us the model to deploy.

We can automate this as well, of course:

```
best = sorted(hparam_job.trials,
        key=lambda x: x.final_measurement.metrics[0].value)[0]
logging.info('Best trial: {}'.format(best))
best_params = []
for param in best.parameters:
    best_params.append('--{}'.format(param.parameter_id))
    best_params.append(param.value)
# run the best trial to completion
```

```
model = train_custom_model(data_set, timestamp, develop_mode,
                           extra_args=best_params)
```

On doing this, I got a model whose RMSE was 0.195. The improvement (0.196 to 0.195) is relatively minimal. It appears that our initial guesses were not that bad.

# Explaining the Model

Why does the model believe that a certain flight will be late with a probability of 0.83? An active area of research in machine learning is to provide the reasoning that underlies a specific model production in a form that humans can understand.

One of the advantages of deploying a model into Vertex AI is that explainability is easy to add. Several techniques of explainability are supported. The one I like for tabular data is Shapley (*https://oreil.ly/GWzQQ*), which apportions the credit for the prediction among the input features.

To add explainability capabilities, we will have to deploy the model with a configuration file that specifies the input and output tensors. Sending the normal prediction request to the endpoint to which the model is deployed will return a response that contains feature attributions.

## Configuring Explanations Metadata

When we create a model in Vertex AI, we can specify that it should be able to explain its predictions. Broadly speaking, explaining a prediction is more expensive than simply making the prediction because the model has to be invoked with small variants of the original request in order to estimate the affect of different parameters.

Because the model needs to be invoked with variants, we need to configure the model with information from the serving input signature. We can get the serving signature of a TensorFlow/Keras model by using the command-line tool `saved_model_cli`:

```
saved_model_cli show --tag_set serve \
    --signature_def serving_default --dir $model_dir
```

Doing this on our flights model yields the following signature:[3]

```
inputs['arr_airport_lat'] tensor_info:
    dtype: DT_FLOAT
    shape: (-1)
    name: serving_default_arr_airport_lat:0
inputs['arr_airport_lon'] tensor_info:
    dtype: DT_FLOAT
    shape: (-1)
    name: serving_default_arr_airport_lon:0
```

---

3 See the Jupyter Notebook *flights_model_tf2.ipynb*.

```
    ...
The given SavedModel SignatureDef contains the following output(s):
   outputs['pred'] tensor_info:
       dtype: DT_FLOAT
       shape: (-1, 1)
       name: StatefulPartitionedCall_2:0
Method name is: tensorflow/serving/predict
```

Based on the preceding, we can write a file that I'll call *explanations-metadata.json*:

```
{
  "inputs": {
    ...
    "arr_airport_lat": {
      "inputTensorName": "arr_airport_lat"
    },
    "arr_airport_lon": {
      "inputTensorName": "arr_airport_lon"
    },
    ...
  },
  "outputs": {
    "pred": {
      "outputTensorName": "pred"
    }
  }
}
```

Rather than hand-crafting the file, I created it using a short Python program and supplying the names of the columns:

```
cols = ('dep_delay,taxi_out,distance,dep_hour,is_weekday,' +
        'dep_airport_lat,dep_airport_lon,' +
        'arr_airport_lat,arr_airport_lon,' +
        'carrier,origin,dest')
inputs = {x: {"inputTensorName": "{}".format(x)}
          for x in cols.split(',')}
expl = {
    "inputs": inputs,
    "outputs": {
    "pred": {
      "outputTensorName": "pred"
    }
  }
}
print(expl)
with open('explanation-metadata.json', 'w') as ofp:
    json.dump(expl, ofp, indent=2)
```

Now that we have the configuration file that specifies what inputs the model needs when it is invoked on variants of the original query, we can create and deploy the model.

## Creating and Deploying Model

When creating the model, we specify three more options: the explanation method, how many variants of the original query to perform, and the location of the metadata configuration file we created in the previous section:

```
gcloud ai models upload ... \
    --explanation-method=sampled-shapley \
    --explanation-path-count=10 \
    --explanation-metadata-file=explanation-metadata.json
```

Of course, we could do this in Python as well. The Python SDK to create the model supports the first two parameters (*https://oreil.ly/Ki02v*). Instead of passing in a metadata file, we'd pass in the metadata object itself.

Deploying the model is identical to before:

```
gcloud ai endpoints deploy-model $ENDPOINT_ID \
    --region=$REGION \
    --model=$MODEL_ID \
    --display-name=$MODEL_NAME \
    --machine-type=n1-standard-2 \
    --min-replica-count=1 \
    --max-replica-count=1 \
    --traffic-split=0=100
```

Note that we did not have to make any changes to the model code itself in order to add explainability to it.

## Obtaining Explanations

Once the explainability-enhanced model has been deployed, any client can request an explanation. The format of the JSON request doesn't change. Instead of sending the request to the predict method, the request has to be sent to the explain method:

```
PROJECT=$(gcloud config get-value project)
ENDPOINT_NAME=flights_xai
ENDPOINT_ID=$(gcloud ai endpoints list --region=$REGION \
        --format='value(ENDPOINT_ID)' --filter=display_name=${ENDPOINT_NAME})

curl -X POST\
-H "Authorization: Bearer "$(gcloud auth application-default print-access-token)\
-H "Content-Type: application/json; charset=utf-8"\
-d @example_input.json\
"https://...${PROJECT}/locations/${REGION}/endpoints/${ENDPOINT_ID}:explain"
```

When I did it on a flight from GST to JNU, I got the following result:

```
{
  "explanations": [
    {
```

```
      "attributions": [
        {
          "baselineOutputValue": 0.48559775948524475,
          "instanceOutputValue": 0.98635220527648926,
          "featureAttributions": {
            "dep_hour": -0.0019751578569412228,
            "distance": 0.02608233392238617,
            "origin": 0.00673377513885498,
            "arr_airport_lat": 0.065238907933235168,
            "dest": 0.0031582355499267579,
            "taxi_out": 0.017888876795768741,
            "is_weekday": -0.0054439753293991089,
            "dep_airport_lon": 0.15576429069042211,
            "carrier": 0.0063359200954437259,
            "arr_airport_lon": 0.32970959544181822,
            "dep_airport_lat": -0.070850974321365362,
            "dep_delay": -0.03188738226890564
          },
          "outputIndex": [
            0
          ],
          "approximationError": 0.008536300316499771,
          "outputName": "pred"
        }
      ]
    }
  ],
  "deployedModelId": "48598413947699200",
  "predictions": [
    [
      0.986352205
    ]
  ]
}
```

The two most important features are the longitudes of the arrival and departure airport, respectively. This is particularly surprising when we consider (see Figure 10-2) that the AutoML model doesn't consider the airport locations particularly important. This highlights the important difference between global importance (what we saw in Figure 10-2) and local explanation (explaining an individual prediction). There are features that are unimportant in the aggregate but make a lot of difference on specific instances. Because this flight has a departure delay almost identical to the baseline, the model might be making more nuanced predictions based on the remaining features.

What makes the longitude of the airport important for a flight from GST to JNU? Well, GST is Gustavus airport in Alaska and JNU is the airport in Juneau, Alaska. In other words, this is a flight within Alaska. Alaska is a large state, and the distance between the airports (41 miles) is rather unusual. Remember that one of the reasons for gridding the airport locations was to learn nuances like flights within a state. It appears that the model has learned it!

## Summary

In this chapter, we learned how to automate the entire process by creating a Vertex training pipeline. We created a single entry point for the end-to-end training run. At this point, it is easy to make this entry point be the thing that is triggered whenever new code is checked in, when new data is received, or when changes in feature distribution or model evaluation are detected.

After we had a viable machine learning model and features, we carried out hyperparameter tuning to find optimal values of batch size, learning rate, number of buckets, and neural network architecture. We discovered that our initial, default choices were themselves quite good, but that increasing the number of layers provided a minute improvement.

For speed of experimentation, we had trained and hyperparameter-tuned the model on a sample of the full dataset. So, next, we trained the model with the chosen features and hyperparameters on the full dataset.

Finally, we also added explainability to the model and were able to get the contribution of each feature on the predicted outcome.

Remember, however, we briefly explored time-windowed aggregated features (like the average taxi-out time at an airport). However, it was unclear how we could compute it on behalf of online prediction clients. Instead, we used features such as the day of the week and hour of the day extracted from the departure time. In the next chapter, we will look at how to do machine learning, where the input features (like moving averages) have to be computed in real-time.

# Suggested Resources

In this chapter, we discussed how to get ready for MLOps. Implementing MLOps requires knowledge of how to do continuous build and continuous integration with GitHub or GitLab:

- To learn more about continuous build, see this tutorial on GitOps-style continuous delivery with Cloud Build (*https://oreil.ly/ASFrn*).

- To learn more about continuous integration for data processing workflows, see this article on setting up a CI/CD pipeline (*https://oreil.ly/vIEhm*).

- Watch the video "MLOps Best Practices on Google Cloud (Cloud Next '19)" (*https://oreil.ly/cLlbs*) on YouTube.

The Google Cloud whitepaper on MLOps, "Practitioners Guide to MLOps" (*https://oreil.ly/gsjSA*) by Khalid Salama et al., is very comprehensive.

# CHAPTER 11

# Time-Windowed Features for Real-Time Machine Learning

In Chapter 8, we briefly explored incorporating time-windowed features, such as the moving average of taxi-out delay at the originating airport, as an input to the model. We found that the time-windowed features reduced the model error. However, it was unclear how clients (who know only about the flight they are on) would be able to provide the correct value. Because of that, we decided to drop the time-windowed features. In this chapter, we will address that shortcoming by implementing a real-time, streaming machine learning pipeline that uses Cloud Dataflow and Vertex AI.

 All of the code snippets in this chapter are available in the folder *11_realtime* of the GitHub repository (*https://github.com/Google CloudPlatform/data-science-on-gcp*). See the *README.md* file in that directory for instructions on how to do the steps described in this chapter.

## Time Averages

What time-windowed aggregate features did we want to use, but couldn't? Flight arrival times are scheduled based on the average taxi-out time at the departure airport at that specific hour. The machine learning model will learn this average quite easily because we are showing the entire dataset and telling the ML model the name of the origin airport. For example, at peak hours in New York's JFK airport, taxi-out times on the order of an hour are quite common, so airlines take that into account when publishing their flight schedules. It is only when the taxi-out time exceeds the average that we ought to be worried. Such a global average is typically not a feature that we need to incorporate into the model (although it is not harmful if we do).

On the other hand, there are time averages that need to be computed over recent flights. For example, we have an intuition that the average departure and taxi-out delays being experienced at the origin airport will have an impact on whether we are likely to arrive on time. This is even if the flight we are on happens to leave on time. Lots of flights from an airport experiencing delays are typically associated with runway closures due to weather or other reasons. This leads to a congested airspace, and so subsequent flights will also be affected both because the weather delays might persist and because the number of runways might be limited. Unlike the global average taxi-out time, a recent average of departure delay is something that needs to be computed in real time. On historical data, we'd compute it over the hour previous to the departure time of the aircraft. In real time, this computation would be carried out over streaming data.

## Apache Beam and Cloud Dataflow

We will solve the issue of augmenting the dataset with time-windowed aggregate features using Apache Beam.

### Why Apache Beam?

Apache Beam allows us to use the same code for both batch and stream processing—for example, to compute aggregate features on historical data, and then to compute the same aggregate features in real time at prediction time (see Figure 11-1).

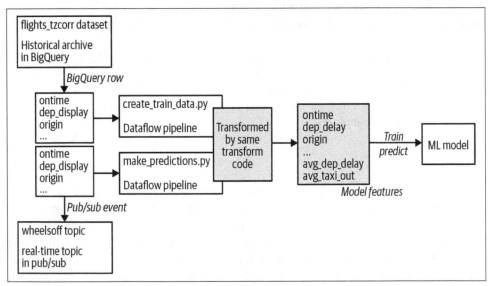

*Figure 11-1. The same transform code is used to transform BigQuery rows in the historical data and Pub/Sub events in real time into the features used by the ML model.*

## Why Dataflow?

Cloud Dataflow is a fully managed service for executing data processing pipelines written using Apache Beam. What does *fully managed* mean? Think BigQuery instead of Cloud SQL. Both allow for SQL queries on the data, but where Cloud SQL was simply a hosted version of MySQL on a cloud virtual machine, BigQuery was totally serverless. This allowed for dramatically larger-scale, instantly available SQL processing with BigQuery.[1] Cloud Dataflow provides a similar, serverless, autoscaling service for programmatic data pipelines.

With Cloud Dataflow, unlike with Cloud Dataproc, we don't need to spin up a cluster in order to carry out data processing. Instead, we simply submit the code and it will get executed and autoscaled to as many machines as needed to accomplish the task effectively. We will get charged for the amount of computational resources that our job involves. Why am I using Cloud Dataflow rather than serverless Spark? Serverless Spark now gives us many of the advantages that only Dataflow used to provide. So, for the majority of use cases, use either serverless Spark or Beam-on-Dataflow depending on which API (Spark or Beam) you are more familiar with. However, in this chapter, we are doing real-time computations and because Apache Beam was designed from the ground up with streaming concepts (Beam stands for *B*atch and St*ream*), Beam is the better choice.

When the model is invoked, the client will know the departure delay of the aircraft that they are on, but how will they know the average departure delay at their airport over the past hour? So, the serving system needs to be routinely computing the average departure and taxi-out delays at all airports. That average needs to be added to the data about the individual flight before the model is asked to make predictions. This is accomplished as shown in Figure 11-1 by invoking the same Apache Beam transform code in both the historical and real-time Dataflow pipelines. The averages can then be used as features in the model.

## Starting points

See Chapter 4 for a gentle introduction to Apache Beam. In Chapter 4, I used Beam Python to move data from Pub/Sub to Cloud Storage (*transform/df07.py*) and compute real-time averages (*realtime/avg03.py*) that were used to drive a dashboard. Those two files are what I'll use as a starting point for developing the Beam pipeline. In that chapter, I skimmed through the streaming code and focused more on visualization concepts. In this chapter, I will remedy that by going through the mechanics of developing a streaming pipeline in more detail.

---

1 Of course, Cloud SQL provides for millisecond-latency transactions while BigQuery is an analytics data warehouse that scales to petabytes. The reasons you'd use the two products are different. I'm just comparing explicit control of the lifecycle of machines in one versus the other.

Similarly, see Chapter 9 for a gentle introduction to TensorFlow and Vertex AI. In Chapter 9, I developed a wide-and-deep model in Vertex AI code in a Workbench notebook and then exported the code into standalone Python files (see *model.py* and *train_on_vertexai.py* in Chapter 9 of the code repository) for operationalization. In this chapter, we'll continue our ML modeling code starting from those two files.

Although I have been recommending that you edit the Python files and do development in Cloud Shell, you might prefer to develop in a Python IDE on your local laptop instead. I use PyCharm on Mac as my Python IDE. To follow along with me:

- Install PyCharm (*https://oreil.ly/4d1VR*) using its installer.
- In PyCharm, create a new virtual environment (*https://oreil.ly/rvCd4*), selecting Python3 as your interpreter.
- In the virtual environment *setup.py*, install the following packages:
  — tensorflow
  — apache-beam[gcp]
  — farmhash
  — google-cloud-aiplatform
  — cloudml-hypertune

Now you will be able to develop and run the Beam and TensorFlow programs from your laptop.

## Reading and Writing

The Beam pipeline code in *transform/df07.py* in Chapter 4 gives us the boilerplate for a Beam pipeline that will run in Dataflow (see *create_traindata.py*):

```
argv = [
    '--project={0}'.format(project),
    '--job_name=ch11traindata',
    '--save_main_session',
    '--staging_location=gs://{0}/flights/staging/'.format(bucket),
    '--temp_location=gs://{0}/flights/temp/'.format(bucket),
    '--setup_file=./setup.py',
    '--autoscaling_algorithm=THROUGHPUT_BASED',
    '--max_num_workers=20',
    '--region={}'.format(region),
    '--runner=DataflowRunner'
]


with beam.Pipeline(argv=argv) as pipeline:
    ...
```

## Reading from BigQuery

This pipeline will need to read events from the BigQuery table `flights_tzcorr` that we wrote out in Chapter 4 and write features to a training CSV file in Cloud Storage:

```
input_table = 'dsongcp.flights_tzcorr'
flights_output = 'gs://{}/ch11/data/'.format(bucket)
events = (
  pipeline
  | 'read_input' >> beam.io.ReadFromBigQuery(table=input_table)
)

(events
  | 'to_string' >> beam.Map(
                  lambda f: ','.join([str(x) for x in f.values()]))
  | 'to_gcs' >> beam.io.textio.WriteToText(
        os.path.join(flights_output, 'all'),
                    file_name_suffix='.csv')
)
```

This is good, but running things on Dataflow and waiting minutes for the workers to spin up and the pipeline to start is no way to develop. I need a smaller local file so that I can develop the transformation code piecemeal. To run locally, I'll need to use `DirectRunner` instead of `DataflowRunner`:

```
if input == 'local':
    argv = [
        '--runner=DirectRunner'
    ]
```

## Local JSON input

In order to have an input file in the right format, let's sample the BigQuery table to a local file:

```
bq query --nouse_legacy_sql --format=json \
    "SELECT * FROM dsongcp.flights_tzcorr WHERE DEP_TIME BETWEEN
    '2015-03-10T10:00:00' AND '2015-03-10T14:00:00' " \
    | sed 's/\[//g' | sed 's/\]//g' | sed s'/\},/\}\n/g' \
    > alldata_sample.json
```

Note that I make sure to extract the data as JSON and remove the extra array brackets because I want a new-line delimited JSON file. This is the file format that we will get from Pub/Sub in the real-time code—we will get back a JSON string corresponding to a single message. Also, rather conveniently, a BigQuery row shows up as a Python dict, which is almost (but not quite) the same format as the JSON string corresponding to what is now in each line of the input file.

Then, we can change the code to read from the sampled file and write to a local file:

```
...
        if input == 'local':
            input_file = './alldata_sample.json'
            flights_output = '/tmp/'
            events = (
                    pipeline
                    | 'read_input' >> beam.io.ReadFromText(input_file)
                    | 'parse_input' >> beam.Map(lambda line:
                                            json.loads(line))
            )
```

At this point, events is a PCollection of dictionaries, the same as we would have gotten if we'd read it from BigQuery.

Run this code to make sure it works and the events in the input file are being written to a CSV file. Now that reading and writing are done, we can turn our attention to the transformations that are needed.

### Filtering

Most data pipelines process a data stream, selecting the data of interest and transforming it in some way. Choosing which data to continue processing is called filtering.

Recall that throughout Chapters 7 to 9, we discarded canceled or diverted flights because they are not associated with an arrival delay. When creating the training dataset in Beam, we have to filter the set of events to contain only those flights that correspond to flights operating normally:

```
def is_normal_operation(event):
    for flag in ['CANCELLED', 'DIVERTED']:
        if flag in event:
            s = str(event[flag]).lower()
            if s == 'true':
                return False;  # cancelled or diverted
    return True  # normal operation


events = (events
    | 'remove_cancelled' >> beam.Filter(is_normal_operation))
```

## Time Windowing

We would like to compute hourly averages every 5 minutes. There are three steps:

- Assign a timestamp to the events.
- Pass sliding windows across the event stream.

- Compute moving averages within each time window.

### Assigning a timestamp

In order to proceed we first have to ensure that all our wheels-off events are time-stamped. This will not be a problem in real time—events get assigned to the time that they are inserted into the Pub/Sub topic. However, this doesn't happen to rows read from BigQuery or lines read from a file.[2] Also, even in real time, the time at which the event gets inserted into Pub/Sub is not the right timestamp. Imagine a message that gets delayed due to network outages or machine failure is re-sent many hours later, and is finally inserted into Pub/Sub. We obviously don't want to include such late-arriving records in our averages, which is what would happen if we use the time of insertion into Pub/Sub.

The way to fix this is to assign the timestamp of the wheels-off event (to be the time at which the aircraft finishes taxiing the runway and its wheels are off the ground):

```
def assign_timestamp(event):
    try:
        event_time = dt.datetime.strptime(event['WHEELS_OFF'],
                                          DATETIME_FORMAT)
        yield beam.window.TimestampedValue(event,
                                           event_time.timestamp())
    except:
        pass


events = events | 'assign_time' >> beam.FlatMap(assign_timestamp)
```

Note that the timestamp that is assigned is the Unix timestamp that we get by parsing the JSON string using `strptime`.

### Sliding windows

We want to compute hourly averages every 5 minutes. To do that, we apply a sliding window onto the event stream:

```
WINDOW_DURATION = 60 * 60
WINDOW_EVERY = 5 * 60

event = (events
   | 'window' >> beam.WindowInto(beam.window.SlidingWindows(
                              WINDOW_DURATION, WINDOW_EVERY))
```

At this point, we have assigned to each event the hourly time window ("between 05:00 and 06:00") within which it lies. But if we run the pipeline at this point, the

---

2 Obviously we don't want to assign all the rows the time at which we read the data!

results will stay the same. It's only when we compute an aggregate value (such as the average) that the windowing starts to show its effect. The average will be computed on each time window separately, and we will end up with a moving average.

## Computing moving average

We don't want a single average departure delay value at 05:00 and another at 05:05. We want the averages to be computed separately for each airport. In order to do that, we need to group by the airport before computing the stats:

```
| 'window' >> beam.WindowInto(beam.window.SlidingWindows(
                        WINDOW_DURATION, WINDOW_EVERY))
| 'by_airport' >> beam.Map(lambda x: (x['ORIGIN'], x))
| 'group_by_airport' >> beam.GroupByKey()
```

This is an idiom you should get familiar with. To group a collection of items, convert them into a couple of tuples where the first element of the tuple is the key to group by (here, we are using ORIGIN), and the second element of the tuple is the item itself:

```
| 'by_airport' >> beam.Map(lambda x: (x['ORIGIN'], x))
```

Then, group by the key. The result will be a collection each item of which is a tuple:

```
DFW, (x1, x2, x3, ...)
DUL, (x1, x2, x3, ...)
```

In this GroupBy tuple, the first element is the key (the origin airport) and the second element is a list of events from that airport in this time window.

We can process the tuple to compute aggregate statistics in a function that I'll call add_stats:

```
def add_stats(element):
    # all averages here are by airport
    airport = element[0]
    events = element[1]

    # how late are flights leaving?
    values = [float(event['DEP_DELAY']) for event in events]
    avg_dep_delay = float(np.mean(values))

    # similar for taxi_out
```

Because the event is just a Python dictionary, we can add the computed statistics to it. However, we have to make sure to add it to a copy of the dictionary because Beam doesn't allow you to modify the input values to a transform function:

```
    for event in events:
        event_plus_stat = event.copy()
        event_plus_stat['AVG_DEP_DELAY'] = avg_dep_delay
        event_plus_stat['AVG_TAXI_OUT'] = avg_taxiout
        yield event_plus_stat
```

The reason we "yield" the event_plus_stat rather than returning it is that there will be multiple events per airport, and so multiple values generated by the add_stats function. Because the input to output mapping is not 1:1, the events_and_stats transform has to be applied with a FlatMap rather than simply a Map:

```
| 'group_by_airport' >> beam.GroupByKey()
| 'events_and_stats' >> beam.FlatMap(add_stats)
```

At this point, we will expect to have exactly as many events as we started with, except that each of the events will have two extra fields—the average departure delay and the average taxi-out time experienced at the airport the flight is departing from over the past hour.

### Removing duplicates

The results on Cloud Storage seem correct, but on closer examination turn out to have repeated flight information:

```
1.0,...,TWF,SLC,...
1.0,...,TWF,SLC,...
1.0,...,TWF,SLC,...
1.0,...,TWF,SLC,...
1.0,...,TWF,SLC,...
```

Why? This has to do with our use of sliding windows. Recall that our sliding window is computed over an hour every 5 minutes. So, every flight is part of several overlapping panes, starting from the second one in Figure 11-2, and therefore, each flight is repeated each time it falls into the pane. We would like the flight to be only part of the second window here.

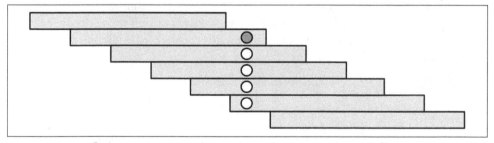

*Figure 11-2. A flight event is part of several hourly time windows. A flight at 12:03 will be part of 11:05 to 12:05, 11:10 to 12:10, 11:15 to 12:15, ..., 12:00 to 1:00.*

This is because the second window is the first window that includes the flight, and we'd like to write the flight event out at the end of that time window. Doing so in subsequent windows will result in duplicate flight objects.

You can clearly see this if you are running it in Dataflow when you look at the size of the input and output of the group-by-airport transform (see Figure 11-3)[3]—but at this point, we are not yet running in Dataflow, so we don't have this information.

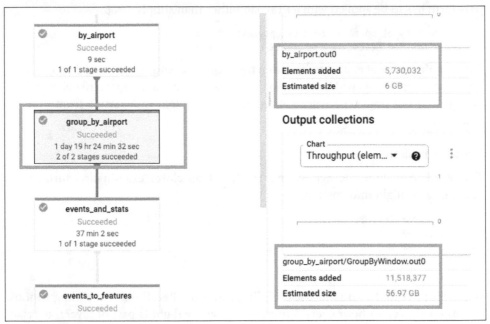

*Figure 11-3. Because a flight event is part of twelve hourly time windows, the size of the collection greatly expands after grouping, from 6 GB to 57 GB.*

The average delay does need to be computed once for every pane (this is why we have a sliding window), but each flight object should be output only once. In order to do that, we should ask Beam to inject the time window being used, and verify that we are in the latest slice:

```
def add_stats(element, window=beam.DoFn.WindowParam):
    ...
    emit_end_time = window.start + WINDOW_EVERY
    for event in events:
        event_time = to_datetime(event['WHEELS_OFF']).timestamp()
        if event_time < emit_end_time:
            event_plus_stat = event.copy()
            event_plus_stat['AVG_DEP_DELAY'] = avg_dep_delay
```

---

3 Look at the size, not the number of elements in the collection—the number of elements is the number of unique airports within each time window. It's hard to compare the number of flights (the input) to the number of airports (the output), but because the data does include (airport, list-of-flights), we can verify that the list of flights is much larger than the flights that we started out with.

```
        event_plus_stat['AVG_TAXI_OUT'] = avg_taxiout
        yield event_plus_stat
```

Once we do this, the duplicates go away, and we get the same number of flights in the output as we had in the input (after removing canceled and diverted flights).

# Machine Learning Training

We don't want to train the ML model with all the raw input values. Instead, we want to use only those features that we used in Chapter 9—those were the features that we determined through experimentation were important. As in earlier chapters, we will also want to add in the data split (train, validate, test) by having different days in different splits.

Once the dataset is created, we can use the code from Chapter 9 (appropriately modified) to train the model and evaluate it.

## Machine Learning Dataset

We start by adding a transform method to convert the raw event data into features:

```
features = (events
    ...
    | 'events_and_stats' >> beam.FlatMap(add_stats)
    | 'events_to_features' >> beam.FlatMap(create_features_and_label)
)
```

### Label

In the transform method, we compute the label, which should be 1.0 if the flight is on-time and zero otherwise:

```
def create_features_and_label(event):
    try:
        model_input = {
            'ontime': 1.0 if float(event['ARR_DELAY']) < 15 else 0,
```

Then, we extract the data that we used in Chapter 9, naming the variables the same as the SQL query did:

```
            # same as in ch9
            'dep_delay': event['DEP_DELAY'],
            'taxi_out': event['TAXI_OUT'],
            'distance': event['DISTANCE'],
            'origin': event['ORIGIN'],
            'dest': event['DEST'],

    ...

            'arr_airport_lat': event['ARR_AIRPORT_LAT'],
            'arr_airport_lon': event['ARR_AIRPORT_LON'],
```

The parts of time we used (the hour of day and day of week) require us to use Python's time library rather than SQL's EXTRACT function, but we do have the equivalent functionality:

```
'dep_hour': to_datetime(event['DEP_TIME']).hour,
'is_weekday': 1.0 if to_datetime(event['DEP_TIME']
                        ).isoweekday() < 6 else 0.0,
'carrier': event['UNIQUE_CARRIER'],
```

Finally, we add in the two time averages we computed in the previous section:

```
'avg_dep_delay': event['AVG_DEP_DELAY'],
'avg_taxi_out': event['AVG_TAXI_OUT'],
}
yield model_input
```

Finally, what do we do if any of the features is not present in the data? A missing key exception is thrown, and we ignore that row:

```
except Exception as e:
    # if any key is not present, don't use for training
    logging.warning('Ignoring {} because: {}'.format(event, e),
                    exc_info=True)
    pass
```

## Data split

Recall that we don't want to use a random split of the rows between training, validation, and test. Instead, we want to use a deterministic method that ensures a date used in training will never be used for testing even in future iterations of the training program. In order to do that in BigQuery SQL, we used the FARM_FINGERPRINT function on the airport code.

Fortunately, this function is available in the Python package farmhash, and we can use it to determine the data split for each row:

```
def get_data_split(date_value):
    # Use farm fingerprint just like in BigQuery
    x = np.abs(np.uint64(farmhash.fingerprint64(str(date_value))
            ).astype('int64') % 100)
    if x < 60:
        data_split = 'TRAIN'
    elif x < 80:
        data_split = 'VALIDATE'
    else:
        data_split = 'TEST'
    return data_split


'data_split': get_data_split(event['FL_DATE'])
```

The managed dataset in Vertex AI will use this column to split the data. However, in case we are training in other frameworks, we want to create separate training, validation, and testing files. We can do this with Beam by filtering the data:

```
for split in ['ALL', 'TRAIN', 'VALIDATE', 'TEST']:
    feats = features
    if split != 'ALL':
        feats = feats | 'only_{}'.format(split) >> beam.Filter(
                                lambda f: f['data_split'] == split)
    (feats
      | '{}_to_string'.format(split) >> beam.Map(
                    lambda f: ','.join([str(x) for x in f.values()]))
      | '{}_to_gcs'.format(split) >> beam.io.textio.WriteToText(
                        os.path.join(flights_output, split.lower()))
    )
```

While we can write only the CSV data, it is probably better if we add a header to the files and name them with a *.csv* suffix. This makes it much easier to use these files for AutoML since we can have AutoML simply parse the file for column names. To do so, we define a CSV header and change the output function:

```
CSV_HEADER = 'ontime,dep_delay,taxi_out,...,avg_taxi_out,data_split'

...

  | '{}_to_gcs'.format(split) >> beam.io.textio.WriteToText(
                        os.path.join(flights_output, split.lower(),
                        file_name_suffix='.csv', header=CSV_HEADER)
```

## Distance bug

On running the pipeline at this point, I encountered a problem—all the files were empty.

The logs indicated an exception about a missing key. The key? DISTANCE.

It turns out that in Chapter 4, I had decided that the wheels-off event would not include the distance on the grounds that at the time the flight is taking off, we don't know whether it is going to get diverted to a different airport:

```
if len(fields["WHEELS_OFF"]) > 0:
    event = dict(fields)  # copy
    event["EVENT_TYPE"] = "wheelsoff"
    event["EVENT_TIME"] = fields["WHEELS_OFF"]
    for f in ["WHEELS_ON", "TAXI_IN",
                "ARR_TIME", "ARR_DELAY", "DISTANCE"]:
        event.pop(f, None)  # not knowable at departure time
```

Unfortunately, I forgot about this, and in subsequent chapters, I did use the nominal distance to the intended destination as an ML feature. We even found that it was a useful feature to use.

There are two ways to address this problem. I can go back and fix the Chapter 4 pipeline that creates the time-corrected data to include the distance field in the wheels-off event. This is the better solution.

Alternatively, I can compute the distance since I know the latitude and longitude of the origin and intended destination. This is simpler, and so, that's what I'm going to do:[4]

```python
def approx_miles_between(lat1, lon1, lat2, lon2):
    # convert to radians
    lat1 = float(lat1) * np.pi / 180.0
    lat2 = float(lat2) * np.pi / 180.0
    lon1 = float(lon1) * np.pi / 180.0
    lon2 = float(lon2) * np.pi / 180.0

    # apply Haversine formula
    d_lat = lat2 - lat1
    d_lon = lon2 - lon1
    a = (pow(np.sin(d_lat / 2), 2) +
         pow(np.sin(d_lon / 2), 2) *
         np.cos(lat1) * np.cos(lat2));
    c = 2 * np.arcsin(np.sqrt(a))
    return 6371 * c * 0.621371  # miles

...

    'distance': approx_miles_between(event['DEP_AIRPORT_LAT'],
                             event['DEP_AIRPORT_LON'],
                             event['ARR_AIRPORT_LAT'],
                             event['ARR_AIRPORT_LON']),
```

### Monitoring and verification

With this done, we can run the Beam pipeline on the full dataset using the Dataflow Runner (see *create_traindata.py* and *flights_transforms.py* in the code repository for full code):

```
python3 create_traindata --input bigquery \
        --project ... --bucket ... --region ...
```

While the pipeline is running, we can use the GCP console, as shown in Figure 11-4, to monitor the progress of the job and examine the logs.

---

4 Besides, it's Chapter 11, and the editor is getting impatient! I'll fix this in the 3rd edition.

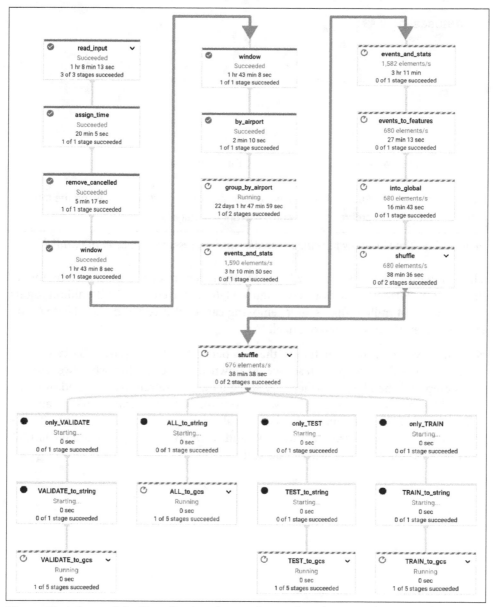

*Figure 11-4. Steps of the Dataflow pipeline to the machine learning dataset with time averages.*

The pipeline took 2 hours and 50 minutes to complete and autoscaled to 20 workers (see Figure 11-5).

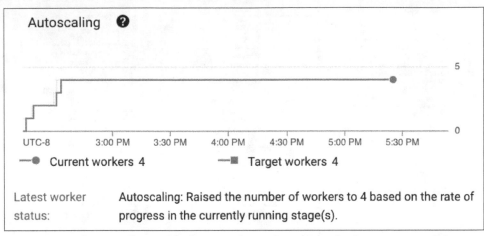

*Figure 11-5. The Dataflow pipeline autoscales and processes the dataset in parallel.*

The number of elements processed at each step is reported, and we can verify that all the data was correctly processed (see Figure 11-6). I started with 5.819 million flights. It became 5.714 million flights after removing canceled/diverted flights. That was the exact number of rows written out in all *.csv*.

Note, however, that the reduction in the number of flights is not from 5.819 to 5.714 million in one fell swoop. Instead, we go down to 5.730 million when we assign a timestamp and then lose a further 15,000 flights when we remove canceled or diverted flights. Why did we lose flights when we assigned a timestamp? It's because we skipped any rows where one of the feature values was missing. Also because it takes an hour to fill up an hourly time window, and so we lost any flights from 00:00 UTC to 01:00 UTC on the first day of our dataset.

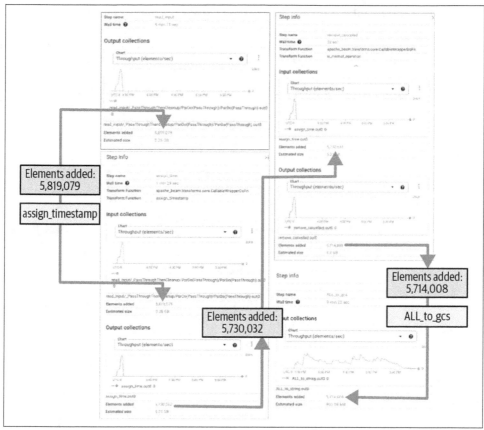

*Figure 11-6. Examine the number of elements in the input and output collections to ensure that no data has been dropped.*

## Training the Model

We can use the same code as we used in Chapter 10. There are just a handful of changes to make.

### Changes from Chapter 10

The code in Chapter 10 reads and writes to paths that contain the string ch9. Here, we'll change it to read and write to paths that contain the string ch11. Instead of deploying to the endpoint flights, let's deploy to a new endpoint named `flights-ch11`. Also, there are now two extra numeric features.

In order to avoid maintaining two similar files, I automated these changes:

```
CHANGES = [
    ("ch10", "ch11"),

    # train_on_vertexai.py
    ("ENDPOINT_NAME = 'flights'", "ENDPOINT_NAME = 'flights-ch11'"),

    # model.py
    ("arr_airport_lat,arr_airport_lon",
     "arr_airport_lat,arr_airport_lon,avg_dep_delay,avg_taxi_out")
]

for filename in ['train_on_vertexai.py', 'model.py']:
    in_filename = os.path.join('../10_vertexai', filename)
    with open(in_filename, "r") as ifp:
        with open(filename, "w") as ofp:
            for line in ifp.readlines():
                for change in CHANGES:
                    line = line.replace(change[0], change[1])
                ofp.write(line)
```

These are the only changes that need to be made to *model.py* and *train_on_vertexai.py*. Apply these changes by running:

```
python3 change_ch10_files.py
```

## AutoML model

Training the AutoML Tables model involves launching the trainer:

```
python3 train_on_vertexai.py --automl \
        --project ... --bucket ... --region ...
```

As in Chapter 9, the trainer writes evaluation data to a table in BigQuery. I can evaluate the resulting model by running the SQL query to compute the RMSE:

```
SELECT
  SQRT(SUM(
      (CAST(ontime AS FLOAT64) - predicted_ontime.scores[OFFSET(0)])*
      (CAST(ontime AS FLOAT64) - predicted_ontime.scores[OFFSET(0)])
      )/COUNT(*))
FROM dsongcp.ch11_automl_evaluated
```

The model took a little over 4 hours to train and resulted in an RMSE of 0.198, whereas the AutoML model in Chapter 9 had an RMSE of 0.199. It appears that the time averages add only a miniscule improvement. Indeed, when we look at the feature importance graph (see longer arrows in Figure 11-7), it appears that the averages do play a role, but not a significant one.

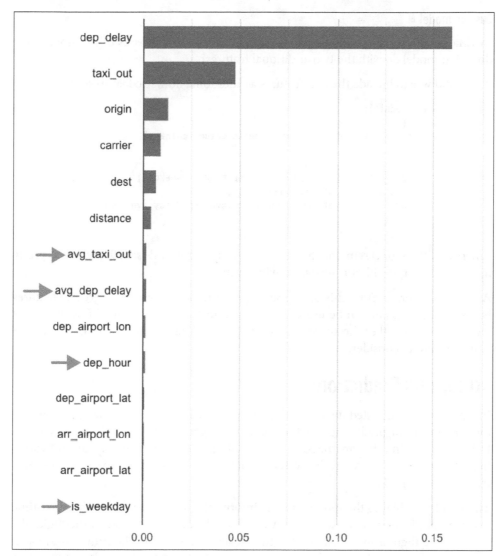

*Figure 11-7. The average delays at the origin airport are not as significant as other features more directly related to the flight itself.*

However, real-time averages may be more useful than the global averages (shown by the shorter arrows in Figure 11-7)—once we have a real-time understanding of what's happening at the airport, the global averages that can be learned from the extracts of time become less important.

### Custom model

In Chapter 10, we also built a custom model using feature crosses of locations. How does that model do with the two additional features?

All we did was to include the two features as additional numeric features:

```
def create_model():
    real = {
        colname: tf.feature_column.numeric_column(colname)
        for colname in
        (
            'dep_delay,taxi_out,distance,dep_hour,is_weekday,' +
            'dep_airport_lat,dep_airport_lon,' +
            'arr_airport_lat,arr_airport_lon,avg_dep_delay,avg_taxi_out'
        ).split(',')
    }
```

The rest of the model remains the same. The resulting RMSE is 0.195, which is pretty much what we got without the two moving averages.

As stated earlier, don't let this discourage you from including time aggregate features in your models. They can be useful in other contexts, and you won't know until you try. However, whether the increased complexity will be worth it is a fair point that you will want to consider.

## Streaming Predictions

In Chapter 9, we ingested historical flight data and used it to train a machine learning model capable of predicting whether or not a flight will be late. We deployed the trained model and demonstrated that we could get the prediction for an individual flight by sending input variables to the model in the form of a representational state transfer (REST) call.

The input variables to the model include information about the flight whose on-time performance is desired. Most of these variables—the departure delay of the flight, the distance the flight is to travel, and the time taken to taxi out to the runway—are specific to the flight itself. However, the inputs to the ML model also included two time aggregates—the average departure delay and taxi-out time at the specific departure airport—that require more effort to compute. In the previous sections of this chapter, we wrote an Apache Beam pipeline to compute these averages on the training dataset so as to be able to train the machine learning model. Then, we trained a TensorFlow model capable of using the input variables to predict whether or not the flight would be late.

The ML pipeline that we wrote deployed this model to a Vertex AI endpoint. Similar to what we did in Chapter 9, we can invoke the service to make predictions. However, the model now expects to see the two time averages in its input. The way we address this is shown in Figure 11-1.

In this section, we will build the real-time Beam pipeline depicted at the bottom of Figure 11-1. The pipeline listens to flight events, computes the time averages, and passes the enriched flight info to the model. It can add the predicted on-time performance of the flight to the flight data and write it out to a database. The resulting table can then be queried by user-facing applications that need to provide information to users of the system interested in their specific flight. Although we could do prediction on behalf of individual users of the service as and when they request the status of their specific flight, this will probably end up being wasteful. It is far more efficient to compute the on-time arrival probability once, at flight takeoff, and then simply look up the flight information as required for specific users.[5] It is worth noting that we are making predictions for a flight only at the time of takeoff (and not updating it as the flight is en route) because we trained our ML model only on flight data at the time of takeoff.

## Reuse Transforms

The advantage of using Apache Beam to compute time averages is that the programming model is the same for both historical data and for real-time data. Therefore, we will be able to reuse most of our training pipeline code in real time.

The pipeline to create the training dataset carries out the following transformations that can be refactored into a method:

```
def transform_events_to_features(events):
    events = events | 'assign_time' >> beam.FlatMap(assign_timestamp)
    events = events | 'remove_cancelled' >> beam.Filter(
                                          is_normal_operation)

    # compute stats by airport, and add to events
    features = (
            events
            | 'window' >> beam.WindowInto(
        beam.window.SlidingWindows(WINDOW_DURATION, WINDOW_EVERY))
            | 'by_airport' >> beam.Map(lambda x: (x['ORIGIN'], x))
            | 'group_by_airport' >> beam.GroupByKey()
            | 'events_and_stats' >> beam.FlatMap(add_stats)
            | 'events_to_features' >> beam.FlatMap(
        lambda x: create_features_and_label(x))
    )
```

---

5 I am assuming that the number of users of our flight delay prediction service will be a factor of magnitude more than the number of flights. This is optimistic, of course, but it is good to design assuming that we will have a successful product.

```
    return features
```

For this method to be callable from both the training and prediction pipelines, we'll put the code in a Python package (look at the file *flights_transforms.py* in the folder *flightstxf* in the code repository) and move all the methods called here—`assign_time stamp`, `is_normal_operation`, and so on—to that file as well.

We can invoke this method from *create_traindata.py* as follows:

```
from flightstxf import flights_transforms as ftxf
...

features = ftxf.transform_events_to_features(events)
```

There is just one small change that we have to make. The training dataset contains the label and the `data_split`, which we won't have during prediction. Let's protect that code with a boolean flag so that those two fields aren't created during prediction:

```
def create_features_and_label(event, for_training):
    model_input = {}

    if for_training:
        model_input.update({
            'ontime': 1.0 if float(event['ARR_DELAY']) < 15 else 0,
        })

    # features for both training and prediction
    model_input.update({
        # same as in ch9
        'dep_delay': event['DEP_DELAY'],
        'taxi_out': event['TAXI_OUT'],
        ...
        # newly computed averages
        'avg_dep_delay': event['AVG_DEP_DELAY'],
        'avg_taxi_out': event['AVG_TAXI_OUT'],

    })

    if for_training:
        model_input.update({
            # training data split
            'data_split': get_data_split(event['FL_DATE'])
        })

    yield model_input
```

## Input and Output

The transform code is the same between training and prediction, so we were able to move it into a common module called from both pipelines. The pipeline input, however, is different. When creating the training dataset, we read the time-corrected Big-Query dataset that contains all the fields.

When doing predictions, though, the streaming pipeline will have to make do with only the data in the `wheelsoff` event. The way that the overall architecture will work is that the streaming pipeline will listen to the `wheelsoff` topic and write predictions for every flight to a database. Client programs (such as the mobile application that a traveler uses) will query the database for the status of the flight that they are on. We have to do it this way because the mobile application will need flight predictions on-demand, whereas the streaming pipeline (and the ML model) cannot operate until the time averages are available. We show the solution architecture in Figure 11-8.

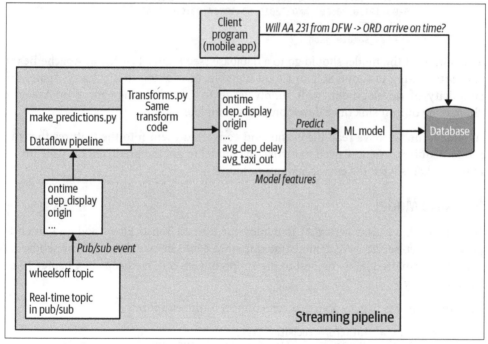

*Figure 11-8. The streaming pipeline writes out predictions for all flights to a database. The mobile application that provides flight information to users queries the database about specific flights.*

Recall from Chapter 4 that the simulator publishes events into a Pub/Sub topic. We can subscribe to this topic and read the events as they stream in using:

```
input_topic = "projects/{}/topics/wheelsoff".format(project)
events = (pipeline
    | 'read_input' >> beam.io.ReadFromPubSub(topic=input_topic,
                            timestamp_attribute='EventTimeStamp')
    | 'parse_input' >> beam.Map(lambda s: json.loads(s))
)
```

As before, however, we want to be able to develop the pipeline locally. An easy way to do this is to remember that we have a historical archive of all the events in `flights_simevents` in BigQuery. We can sample this dataset, create a local file, and use it to develop the pipeline:

```
bq query --nouse_legacy_sql --format=sparse \
    "SELECT EVENT_DATA FROM dsongcp.flights_simevents
    WHERE EVENT_TYPE = 'wheelsoff' AND EVENT_TIME BETWEEN
    '2015-03-10T10:00:00' AND '2015-03-10T14:00:00' " \
    | grep FL_DATE \
    > simevents_sample.json
```

The output of the model should go to a database (see Figure 11-8), and Apache Beam supports writing to Cloud SQL or Cloud Bigtable, in addition to BigQuery. Again, for simplicity of development, we'll simply write to Cloud Storage for now. We can change the output sink once development is complete.

At this point, we have read the events and converted them into the features that the model requires. We now need to invoke the model to get the predicted on-time probability—that is what the end user wants to know!

## Invoking Model

In Chapter 9, we used Vertex AI to deploy the trained TensorFlow model to an endpoint as a web service. We demonstrated that we could invoke the model by sending a correctly formatted JSON request to the endpoint (see *call_predict.py* in Chapter 10 of the repository).

The first step was to get a *stub* that can connect to the endpoint:

```
endpoint = aiplatform.Endpoint.list(
    filter='display_name="{}"'.format(ENDPOINT_NAME),
    order_by='create_time desc'
)[0]
```

In networking parlance, a stub is a local proxy for a remote object. Here, the ML model is deployed and made available as a web application accessible through the endpoint URL. That web application is the remote object. A stub is an object (in Python, Java, JavaScript, etc.) that abstracts away the details of HTTPS invocation—parameter serialization, transport encryption, authentication, and so on—so as to present a simple invocation interface to the client program. The `endpoint` class provided by the Vertex AI client library is the stub.

The next step was to call `predict()` on the endpoint stub (which will take care of the communication details):

```
preds = endpoint.predict(input_data)
probs = [p[0] for p in preds.predictions]
```

In the preceding code snippet, `input_data` is a correctly formatted JSON request:

```
input_data = [
        {"dep_hour": 2, "is_weekday": 1, "dep_delay": 40, "taxi_out": 17,
        "distance": 41, "carrier": "AS",
         "dep_airport_lat": 58.42527778, "dep_airport_lon": -135.7075,
         "arr_airport_lat": 58.35472222,
         "arr_airport_lon": -134.57472222, "origin": "GST", "dest": "JNU"},
        {"dep_hour": 22, "is_weekday": 0, "dep_delay": -7, "taxi_out": 7,
        "distance": 201, "carrier": "HA",
         "dep_airport_lat": 21.97611111, "dep_airport_lon": -159.33888889,
         "arr_airport_lat": 20.89861111,
         "arr_airport_lon": -156.43055556, "origin": "LIH", "dest": "OGG"}
    ]
```

We need to repeat these steps to obtain the probability for every flight. However, we would ideally like to reuse endpoint stubs, instead of looking them up again and again, once for every flight.

Also, as the preceding sample code illustrates, it is possible to send multiple flights to the model endpoint. Sending the flights one-by-one is wasteful. We should batch them up and send in a list of flights.

# Reusing Endpoint

There are two ways that we can reuse the endpoint stub—a shared endpoint stub or a per-worker endpoint stub.

### Shared handle

One way is to create a single endpoint stub and use it from all workers. This is accomplished by using a shared handle that is shared between workers:

```
class FlightsModelInvoker(beam.DoFn):
    def __init__(self, shared_handle):      # ❷
        self._shared_handle = shared_handle  # ❷

    def process(self, input_data):
        def create_endpoint(): # ❹
            from google.cloud import aiplatform
            endpoint_name = 'flights-ch11'
            endpoint = aiplatform.Endpoint.list(
```

```
            filter='display_name="{}"'.format(endpoint_name),
            order_by='create_time desc'
    )[0]

    # call predictions and pull out probability
    endpoint = self._shared_handle.acquire(create_endpoint) # ❸
    predictions = endpoint.predict(input_data).predictions  # ❸
    for idx, input_instance in enumerate(input_data):
        result = input_instance.copy()
        result['prob_ontime'] = predictions[idx][0]
        yield result

...

handle = beam.utils.shared.Shared() # ❶

preds = features | 'pred' >> beam.ParDo(FlightsModelInvoker(handle))
```

❶  In the main pipeline, create a handle of the type beam.utils.shared.Shared and pass that in as a constructor parameter to the DoFn.

❷  In the DoFn, save the handle as an instance variable.

❸  In the process function of the DoFn, acquire the endpoint through the handle every time.

❹  Provide a function that can be called to create the endpoint the first time around.

We would use the shared handle approach if the endpoint stub is very large, very expensive to create, or cannot handle concurrent access from multiple workers. That is not the case here.

 If you are loading an ML model directly from a SavedModel file and calling model.predict() on the in-memory model from within the pipeline, then the considerations flip. Creating the model is very expensive because it involves parsing the model file and creating a set of neural network layers. Models, especially text and image models, can be extremely large. If you are memory limited, you might want to use the same model from multiple workers. Keras model functions are not thread-safe. Given this, you would want to use the shared handle approach, and not the per-worker instance approach that I'm going to use here.

### Per-worker instance

Creating an endpoint stub is just a single network call and is not very expensive. The state of an endpoint stub is essentially just a URL. That is not very large. Moreover, the endpoint stub connects to a web application that runs on Vertex AI, which will autoscale predictions. Therefore, it's better if workers can invoke the endpoint in parallel and not have to wait on each other.

Because we have an inexpensive operation, a small object, and a thread-safe backend, it's better to create an endpoint stub the first time it's needed in a worker thread and then reuse it as long as that worker thread is active.

In order to do so, we should *not* use an instance variable like this because worker state can be passivated and reactivated many hours later on another machine:

```
## THIS IS WRONG. DO NOT DO THIS
class FlightsModelInvoker(beam.DoFn):
    def __init__(self):
        from google.cloud import aiplatform
        endpoint_name = 'flights-ch10'
        self.endpoint = aiplatform.Endpoint.list(
            filter='display_name="{}"'.format(endpoint_name),
            order_by='create_time desc'
        )[0]

    def process(self, input_data):
        predictions = self.endpoint.predict(input_data).predictions
        for idx, input_instance in enumerate(input_data):
            result = input_instance.copy()
            result['prob_ontime'] = predictions[idx][0]
            yield result

...

preds = features | 'pred' >> beam.ParDo(FlightsModelInvoker())
```

In general, instance variables on a Beam function should be set within the __init__ method of a DoFn only for things that can be safely resurrected from a passivated object. The endpoint is not safe to resurrect in this manner because it might contain a number of cached variables.

Instead, we have to hook into the lifecycle of a DoFn. The contract of a DoFn is that the setup method will be called the first time a DoFn is used on a worker. So, we override the setup() method and initialize the endpoint instance variable there:

```
class FlightsModelInvoker(beam.DoFn):
    def __init__(self):
        self.endpoint = None

    def setup(self):
        from google.cloud import aiplatform
        endpoint_name = 'flights-ch10'
        self.endpoint = aiplatform.Endpoint.list(
            filter='display_name="{}"'.format(endpoint_name),
            order_by='create_time desc'
```

```
        )[0]

    def process(self, input_data):
        # call predictions and pull out probability
        predictions = self.endpoint.predict(input_data).predictions
        for idx, input_instance in enumerate(input_data):
            result = input_instance.copy()
            result['prob_ontime'] = predictions[idx][0]
            yield result
```

With this change, we reuse endpoint stubs throughout the lifetime of a worker thread.

## Batching Predictions

While we do need to make predictions for each flight, we do not need to send the flight information to the service one-by-one. Instead of invoking the machine learning service once for each flight, we could batch up requests. If we were to invoke the predictions for 60,000 flights into batches of 60 each, we'd be making only 1,000 requests. Making fewer requests will not only reduce costs, it might also end up increasing the overall performance by having less time spent waiting for a response from the service.

Because it is possible to send multiple flights to the model endpoint, sending the flights one-by-one is wasteful. However, our pipeline uses a ParDo, which will send each element of the features collection one-by-one to the prediction method:

```
preds = (features
    | 'model_predict' >> beam.ParDo(FlightsModelInvoker())
)
```

We can ask Beam to send in a list of elements using the BatchElements method:

```
preds = (features
    | 'batch_instances' >> beam.BatchElements(
                            min_batch_size=1, max_batch_size=64)
    | 'model_predict' >> beam.ParDo(FlightsModelInvoker())
)
```

Recall that all aggregation (sum, mean, max, etc.) happens within a time window—this is why our average departure delay was the average delay over the most recent hour. Unfortunately, batching is also an aggregation. However, we will defeat the purpose if the batches are grouped in any way. So, let's ask Beam to discard the time window information before batching:

```
preds = (features
    | 'into_global' >> beam.WindowInto(beam.window.GlobalWindows())
    | 'batch_instances' >> beam.BatchElements(
                            min_batch_size=1, max_batch_size=64)
    | 'model_predict' >> beam.ParDo(FlightsModelInvoker())
)
```

Note that we have specified a minimum and maximum batch size to the BatchElements method. This allows Dataflow to time how long it takes to invoke the model on different batch sizes and choose an optimal size. When I tried it, Dataflow seemed to settle on sending around 30 flights to the model each time:

```
INFO:root:Invoking ML model on 1 flights
INFO:root:Invoking ML model on 2 flights
INFO:root:Invoking ML model on 4 flights
INFO:root:Invoking ML model on 8 flights
INFO:root:Invoking ML model on 16 flights
INFO:root:Invoking ML model on 32 flights
INFO:root:Invoking ML model on 30 flights
```

For obvious reasons, Dataflow tuning the batch size is better than hard coding the number of elements to batch the features collection into—our model could grow over time, and it might turn out that our hardcoded value is too large at some point.

# Streaming Pipeline

At this point, we have a streaming pipeline that can listen to incoming flight events, compute the likelihood that a flight that's about to take off will arrive on-time, and write the output to Cloud Storage. However, we need to add the arrival probability to a *database*, not just to a file. This is so that the database can be used to serve client applications.

## Writing to BigQuery

Fortunately, it's quite simple to change out the output sink to BigQuery:

```
preds_schema = ','.join([
                'event_time:timestamp',
                'prob_ontime:float',
                'dep_delay:float',
...
                'avg_dep_delay:float',
                'avg_taxi_out:float',
            ])
(preds
            | 'to_bigquery' >> beam.io.WriteToBigQuery(
                    'dsongcp.streaming_preds',
                    schema=preds_schema,
                    # write_disposition=...WRITE_TRUNCATE,
create_disposition=beam.io.BigQueryDisposition.CREATE_IF_NEEDED,
                    method='STREAMING_INSERTS'
                )
)
```

There are two important changes to previous times that we wrote to BigQuery:

- We do not use `WRITE_TRUNCATE`. This is because the streaming pipeline needs to insert new records, not overwrite the table.

- We ask Dataflow to stream the inserts into BigQuery so that information is available in real time. Had we omitted it, Dataflow would have staged the output to Google Cloud Storage and done periodic loads.

Is BigQuery enough for our purpose? Should I not be using Cloud SQL, Cloud Bigtable, or Spanner? I'll answer this question later on in this section. For now, trust me when I say BigQuery is sufficient.

## Executing Streaming Pipeline

Now that the pipeline code has been written, we can start the simulation from Chapter 4 to stream records into Cloud Pub/Sub:

```
cd ../04_streaming/simulate
python3 simulate.py --startTime "2015-02-01 00:00:00 UTC" --endTime \
   "2015-02-03 00:00:00 UTC" --speedFactor 30 --project PROJECT
```

Then, we can start the Cloud Dataflow pipeline that we have just written to consume these records:

```
python3 make_predictions.py --input pubsub \
      --project <PROJECT> --bucket <BUCKET> --region <REGION>
```

With the pipeline running, we can navigate over to the BigQuery console and verify that flight information is indeed getting streamed in:

```
SELECT
   event_time, dest, carrier, prob_ontime
FROM dsongcp.streaming_preds
WHERE origin = 'DFW'
ORDER BY event_time DESC
LIMIT 5
```

The preceding query is looking at flights originating at Dallas/Fort Worth (DFW) and ordering and limiting the result set so that the five latest flights are retained:

| Row | event_time | dest | carrier | prob_ontime |
|-----|-----------|------|---------|-------------|
| 1 | 2015-02-01 04:17:00 UTC | MSY | AA | 0.999135375 |
| 2 | 2015-02-01 04:11:00 UTC | TUL | AA | 0.999612808 |
| 3 | 2015-02-01 04:10:00 UTC | LRD | MQ | 0.229228586 |
| 4 | 2015-02-01 04:07:00 UTC | LAX | AA | 0.809439421 |
| 5 | 2015-02-01 04:02:00 UTC | SEA | AA | 0.994473457 |

The query results change when I execute the query a few minutes later, showing that we are getting new and updated flights (note from the speedFactor that the simulation is run at 30 times the speed of real time):

| Row | event_time | dest | carrier | prob_ontime |
|---|---|---|---|---|
| 1 | 2015-02-01 05:35:00 UTC | PHX | NK | 0.964711547 |
| 2 | 2015-02-01 05:25:00 UTC | LAS | NK | 0.982865453 |
| 3 | 2015-02-01 04:50:00 UTC | ICT | AA | 0.99398911 |
| 4 | 2015-02-01 04:44:00 UTC | LAS | AA | 0.998527884 |
| 5 | 2015-02-01 04:33:00 UTC | LAX | AA | 0.991004586 |

## Late and Out-of-Order Records

Our simulation uses the flight record time to add records into Cloud Pub/Sub in precise order. In real life, though, flight records are unlikely to arrive in order. Instead, network vagaries and latencies will cause late and out-of-order records to happen. In order to simulate these essentially random effects, we should change our simulation to add a random delay to each record.

This can be done in the BigQuery SQL statement that is used by the simulation program to read in the flight records:

```
SELECT
  EVENT_TYPE,
  EVENT_TIME AS ORIGINAL_NOTIFY_TIME,
  TIMESTAMP_ADD(EVENT_TIME,
              INTERVAL CAST (0.5 + RAND()*120 AS INT64) SECOND)
      AS NOTIFY_TIME
FROM
  dsongcp.flights_simevents
WHERE event_type = 'wheelsoff'
ORDER BY original_notify_time ASC LIMIT 5
```

Because RAND() returns a number that is uniformly distributed between 0 and 1, multiplying the result of RAND() by 120 yields a delay between 0 and 2 minutes. Running this query on the BigQuery console, we notice that it works as intended—the records now reflect some jitter:

| Row | EVENT_TYPE | ORIGINAL_NOTIFY_TIME | NOTIFY_TIME |
|---|---|---|---|
| 1 | wheelsoff | 2014-12-31 22:14:00 UTC | 2014-12-31 22:14:42 UTC |
| 2 | wheelsoff | 2015-01-01 04:28:00 UTC | 2015-01-01 04:29:22 UTC |
| 3 | wheelsoff | 2015-01-01 05:21:00 UTC | 2015-01-01 05:21:35 UTC |
| 4 | wheelsoff | 2015-01-01 05:36:00 UTC | 2015-01-01 05:36:28 UTC |
| 5 | wheelsoff | 2015-01-01 05:45:00 UTC | 2015-01-01 05:45:37 UTC |

Note that the first record is delayed by 42 seconds, whereas the second record is delayed by 1 minute and 22 seconds.

## Uniformly distributed delay

A zero delay is highly unrealistic, however. We could change the formula to simulate other scenarios. For example, if we want to have latencies between 90 and 120 seconds, we would change the `jitter` to be `CAST(90.5 + RAND()*30 AS INT64)`. The resulting distribution might look like this:

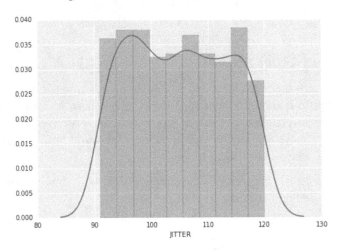

Even this strikes me as being unrealistic. I don't know what the delay involved with the flight messages is,[6] but there seem to be two possibilities: an exponential distribution and a normal distribution.

## Exponential distribution

An exponential distribution is the theoretical distribution associated with the time between events where the events themselves happen at a constant rate. If the network capacity is limited by the number of events, we'd observe that the delay follows an exponential distribution. To simulate this, we can create the `jitter` variable following the formula:

```
CAST(-LN(RAND()*0.99 + 0.01)*30 + 90.5 AS INT64)
```

The resulting distribution would look something like this:

---

6 If we had a real-time feed, we'd of course collect data on delay instead of simply guessing.

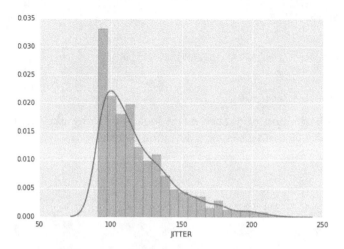

With the exponential distribution, latencies of 90 s are much more common than latencies of 150 s, but a few records will encounter unusually high latencies.

### Normal distribution

A third alternative distribution for the delay is that it follows the law of big numbers, and that if we observe enough flight events, we might observe that the delay is normally distributed around some mean with a certain standard deviation. Of course, the delay has to be positive, so the distribution would be truncated at zero.

Generating a normally distributed random variable is hard to do with just plain SQL. Fortunately, BigQuery allows for user-defined functions (UDFs) in JavaScript. This JavaScript function uses the Marsaglia polar rule to transform a pair of uniformly distributed random variables into one that is normally distributed:

```
js = """
    var u = 1 - Math.random();
    var v = 1 - Math.random();
    var f = Math.sqrt(-2 * Math.log(u)) * Math.cos(2*Math.PI*v);
    f = f * sigma + mu;
    if (f < 0)
        return 0;
    else
        return f;
""".replace('\n', ' ')
```

The preceding JavaScript can be used to create a temporary UDF invokable from SQL:

```
sql = """
CREATE TEMPORARY FUNCTION
trunc_rand_normal(x FLOAT64, mu FLOAT64, sigma FLOAT64)
RETURNS FLOAT64
```

```
LANGUAGE js AS "{}";

SELECT
  trunc_rand_normal(ARR_DELAY, 90, 15) AS JITTER
FROM
  ...
""".format(js).replace('\n', ' ')
```

The resulting distribution of jitter might look something like this (the preceding code used a mean of 90 and a standard deviation of 15):

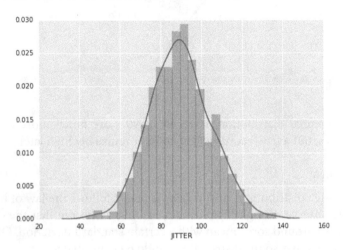

In order to experiment with different types of jitter, let's change our simulation code to add random jitter to the notify_time:[7]

```
jitter = 'CAST (-LN(RAND()*0.99 + 0.01)*30 + 90.5 AS INT64)'

# run the query to pull simulated events
querystr = """\
SELECT
  EVENT_TYPE,
  TIMESTAMP_ADD(EVENT_TIME, INTERVAL @jitter SECOND) AS NOTIFY_TIME,
  EVENT_DATA
FROM
  dsongcp.flights_simevents
WHERE
  EVENT_TIME >= @startTime
  AND EVENT_TIME < @endTime
ORDER BY
  EVENT_TIME ASC
"""
```

---

7 See the jitter variable in *04_streaming/simulate/simulate.py*.

```
job_config = bq.QueryJobConfig(
    query_parameters=[
        bq.ScalarQueryParameter("jitter", "INT64", jitter),
        bq.ScalarQueryParameter("startTime", "TIMESTAMP", args.startTime),
        bq.ScalarQueryParameter("endTime", "TIMESTAMP", args.endTime),
    ]
)
rows = bqclient.query(querystr, job_config=job_config)
```

In the preceding code snippet, I am using parameterized queries in BigQuery by having the query refer to variables as @jitter, @startTime, and so on. These variables are passed in as query parameters by the Python code.

## Watermarks and triggers

The Beam programming model implicitly handles out-of-order records within the sliding window, and by default accounts for late arriving records. Beam has the concept of a *watermark*, which is the oldest unprocessed record left in the pipeline. The watermark is an inherent property of any real-time data processing system and is indicative of the lag in the pipeline. Cloud Dataflow tracks and learns this lag over time.

If we are using the time that a record was inserted into Cloud Pub/Sub as the event time, then the watermark is a strict guarantee that no data with an earlier event time will ever be observed by the pipeline after the watermark. On the other hand, if the event time is user-specified (by specifying a timestampLabel), then there is nothing to prevent the publishing program from inserting a really old record into Cloud Pub/Sub, so the watermark is a learned heuristic based on the observed historical lag. The concept of a watermark is more general than Cloud Pub/Sub, of course—in the case of streaming sources (such as low-power Internet of Things devices) that are intermittent, watermarking helps those delays as well.

Computation of aggregate statistics is driven by a *trigger*. Whenever a trigger fires, the pipeline calculations are carried out. Our pipeline can include multiple triggers, but each of the triggers is usually keyed off the watermark. The default behavior is that the trigger fires when the watermark passes the end of the window and then immediately whenever any late data arrives. In other words, every late-arriving record is processed individually. This prioritizes correctness over performance.

What if we add a uniformly distributed jitter to the simulation? Since our uniform delay is in the range of 90–120 s, the actual difference in delay between the earliest-arriving and latest-arriving records is 30 s. So, Cloud Dataflow has to keep windows open 30 s longer.

The Cloud Dataflow job monitoring web page on the Cloud Platform Console indicates the learned watermark value. We can click on any of the transform steps to view what this value is. And with a uniform delay added to the simulation, the monitoring console shows us that this is what is happening:

| Step summary | | |
|---|---|---|
| Step name | InLatestSlice | |
| System lag | 7 sec | |
| Data watermark | 2015-03-31 (17:11:50) | |
| Wall time | 1 sec | |
| Transform Function | com.google.cloud.traini ng.flights.CreateTraining | |

```
INFO: Sleeping 2.0 seconds
INFO: Publishing 3 wheelsoff till 2015-04-01T00:11:58-00:00
INFO: Publishing 0 arrived till 2015-04-01T00:11:58-00:00
INFO: Publishing 2 departed till 2015-04-01T00:11:58-00:00
INFO: Sleeping 2.0 seconds
INFO: Publishing 2 wheelsoff till 2015-04-01T00:12:00-00:00
INFO: Publishing 1 arrived till 2015-04-01T00:12:00-00:00
INFO: Publishing 1 departed till 2015-04-01T00:12:00-00:00
INFO: Sleeping 2.0 seconds
INFO: Publishing 0 wheelsoff till 2015-04-01T00:12:32-00:00
INFO: Publishing 1 arrived till 2015-04-01T00:12:32-00:00
INFO: Publishing 2 departed till 2015-04-01T00:12:32-00:00
```

We see that the simulation (righthand side of the snapshot) is sending events at 00:12:32 UTC, whereas the watermark shown by the monitoring console is at 17:11:50 Pacific Standard Time. Ignoring the 7 hours due to time zone conversion, Cloud Dataflow is keeping windows open for 42 s longer (this includes the system lag of 7 s, which is the time taken to process the records).

Unlike uniform jitter, small delays are far more likely than larger delays in exponentially distributed jitter. With exponentially distributed `jitter` added to the simulated data in the Cloud Pub/Sub pipeline, the learned watermark value is 22 seconds:

| Step summary | | |
|---|---|---|
| Step name | InLatestSlice | |
| System lag | 5 sec | |
| Data watermark | 2015-03-31 (17:10:37) | |
| Wall time | 0 sec | |
| Transform Function | com.google.cloud.traini ng.flights.CreateTraining | |

```
0: Sleeping 3.0 seconds
0: Publishing 1 wheelsoff till 2015-04-01T00:10:52-00:00
0: Publishing 1 arrived till 2015-04-01T00:10:52-00:00
0: Publishing 1 departed till 2015-04-01T00:10:52-00:00
0: Sleeping 1.0 seconds
0: Publishing 0 wheelsoff till 2015-04-01T00:10:54-00:00
0: Publishing 1 arrived till 2015-04-01T00:10:54-00:00
0: Publishing 1 departed till 2015-04-01T00:10:54-00:00
0: Sleeping 2.0 seconds
0: Publishing 1 wheelsoff till 2015-04-01T00:10:58-00:00
0: Publishing 1 arrived till 2015-04-01T00:10:58-00:00
0: Publishing 3 departed till 2015-04-01T00:10:58-00:00
```

Recall that the default trigger prioritizes correctness over performance, processing each late-arriving record one-by-one and updating the computed aggregates. Fortunately, changing this trade-off is quite easy. Here is a different trade-off:

```
beam.WindowInto(
        beam.window.SlidingWindows(...),
        trigger=AfterWatermark(late=AfterCount(10)),
        allowed_lateness=1800) # 30 minutes
```

Here, the calculations are triggered at the watermark (as before). Late records are processed 10 at a time but only if they arrive within 30 minutes after the start of the plane. Beyond that, late records are thrown away.

## Possible Streaming Sinks

Streaming the output flight records to BigQuery is acceptable for my flight delay scenario, but it may not be the right choice for your data pipeline. You should select the output sink based on four factors—access pattern, transactions, throughput, and latency.

If your primary access pattern is around long-term storage and delayed access to the data, you could simply stream to sharded files on Cloud Storage. Files on Cloud Storage can serve as staging for later import into Cloud SQL or BigQuery for later analysis of the data. In the rest of this section, I will assume that you will need to query the data in near-real time.

Recall that we receive several events for each flight—departed, wheelsoff, etc. Should we have a single row for each flight that reflects the most up-to-date state for that flight? Or can the data be append-only so that we simply keep storing flight events as they come streaming in? Is it acceptable for readers to possibly get slightly out-of-date records, or is it essential for there to be a single source of truth and consistent behavior throughout the system? The answers to these questions determine whether flight updates have to be transactional, or whether flight updates can be done in an environment that provides only eventual consistency guarantees.

How many flight events come in every second? Is this rate constant, or are there periods of peak activity? The answers here determine the throughput that the system needs to handle. If we are providing for eventual consistency, what is the acceptable latency? Once flight data is added to the database, within what time period should all readers see the new data? At the time of writing, streaming into BigQuery supports (*https://oreil.ly/kSryY*) up to 1 GBps with latency on the order of a few seconds. You can achieve a latency on the order of milliseconds by turning on BI Engine in BigQuery. (*https://oreil.ly/GMjhW*) To do so, all we have to do is to go to the BigQuery administration console and purchase a BI Engine capacity reservation (see Figure 11-9).

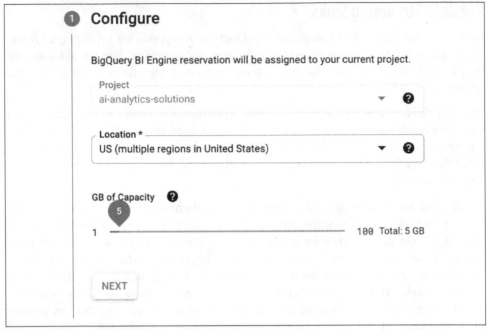

*Figure 11-9. Use BI Engine to provide clients lower latencies when streaming data into BigQuery.*

For throughput needs that are higher than this, or latency requirements that are lower, we need to consider other solutions.

### Choosing a sink

During development, we used Cloud Storage, but as depicted in Figure 11-8, we want the pipeline to write the predictions to a database. What database shall we use?

If transactions are not needed, and we simply need to append flight events as they come in, we can use BigQuery, text files, or Cloud Bigtable:

- As stated in the previous section, streaming flight events directly into BigQuery is a great solution for throughputs of up to 1 GBps and acceptable latencies of a few milliseconds. Many dashboard applications fall into this sweet spot.

- Cloud Dataflow also supports streaming into text files (*https://oreil.ly/DAnpd*) on Cloud Storage. This is obviously useful if the primary use case is to simply save the data, not to analyze it or query it. Recall that we want client programs such as mobile applications to be able to query for a specific flight. So, this won't work for our current use case. However, it is also a solution to consider if periodic batch updates into BigQuery will suffice. For example, we could stream into text files that are sharded by hour, and at the end of the hour, we could do a batch upload of the file into BigQuery. This is less expensive than streaming into BigQuery and can be used if hourly latencies are acceptable.

- Cloud Bigtable is a massively scalable NoSQL database service—it can handle workloads that involve hundreds of petabytes with millions of reads and writes per second at a latency that is on the order of milliseconds. Moreover, the throughput that can be handled by Cloud Bigtable scales linearly with the number of nodes—for example, if a single node supports 10,000 reads or writes in 6 ms, a Cloud Bigtable instance with a hundred nodes will support a million reads or writes in the same 6 ms interval. In addition, Cloud Bigtable automatically rebalances the data to improve query performance and availability.

On the other hand, if transactions are needed and you wish to have a single record that reflects the most current state of a flight, we could use a traditional relational database, a NoSQL transactional database, or Cloud Spanner:

- Cloud SQL, which is backed by MySQL or PostgreSQL, is useful for frequently updated, low-throughput, medium-scale data that you want to access from a variety of tools and programming languages in near-real time. Because relational technologies are ubiquitous, the tools ecosystem tends to be strongest for traditional relational databases. For example, if you have third-party, industry-specific analysis tools, it is possible that relational databases might be the only storage mechanism that they will connect to. Before choosing a traditional relational database solution, though, consider whether the use case is such that you will run into throughput and scaling limitations.

- You can scale to much larger datasets (terabytes of data) and avoid the problem of converting between hierarchical objects and flattened relational tables by using Cloud Firestore, which is a NoSQL object store. Cloud Firestore provides high throughput and scaling by designing for eventual consistency. However, it is possible to get strong (or immediate) consistency on queries that involve lookups by key or "ancestor queries" that involve entity groups. Within an entity group, one gets transactions, strong consistency, and data locality. Thus, it is possible to balance the need for high throughput and many entities while still supporting strong consistency where it matters.

- Cloud Spanner provides a strongly consistent, transactional, SQL-queryable database that is nevertheless globally available and can scale to extremely large amounts of data. Cloud Spanner offers latency on the order of milliseconds, extremely high availability (99.999% availability, which translates to downtimes of around 5 minutes a year), and maintains transactional consistency and global reach. Cloud Spanner is also fully managed, without the need for manual intervention for replication or maintenance.

In our use case, we don't need transactions. Our incoming stream has fewer than a thousand events per second. A few seconds latency between insertion into the database and availability to applications that need the flight delay information is quite tolerable because what we might do is to simply send alerts to our users if their flight is likely to be delayed. BigQuery is fully managed, supported by many data visualization and report-creation products, and is relatively inexpensive compared to the alternative choices. Based on these considerations, streaming into BigQuery is the right choice for our use case.

## Cloud Bigtable

However, just as a hypothetical scenario, what if our stream consisted of gigabytes of flight events per second, and our use case required that the latency be on the order of milliseconds, not seconds? This would be the case if each aircraft were to provide up-to-the-minute coordinate information while it is en route, and if the use case involved traffic control of the air space. In such a case, Cloud Bigtable would be a better choice. Let's look at how we'd build the pipeline to write to Cloud Bigtable if this were the case.

Cloud Bigtable separates compute and storage. Tables in Cloud Bigtable are sharded into blocks of contiguous rows, called tablets. The Cloud Bigtable instance doesn't store these tablets; instead, it stores pointers to a set of tablets. The tablets themselves are durably stored on Cloud Storage. Because of this, a node may go down, but the data remains in Cloud Storage (see Figure 11-10). Work may get rebalanced to a different node, and only metadata needs to be copied.

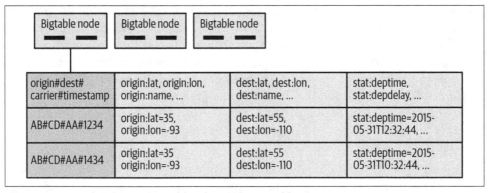

*Figure 11-10. Cloud Bigtable tables sharded into tablets.*

The data itself consists of a sorted key/value map (each row has a single key). Unlike BigQuery, Cloud Bigtable's storage is row-wise, and the rows are stored in sorted order of their key value. Columns that are related are grouped into a *column family*, with different column families typically managed by different applications. Within a column family, columns have unique names. A specific column value at a specific row

---

can contain multiple cells at different timestamps (the table is append-only, so all the values exist in the table). This way, we can maintain a time-series record of the value of that cell over time. For most purposes, Cloud Bigtable doesn't care about the data type—all data is treated as raw byte strings.[8]

The performance of Cloud Bigtable is best understood in terms of the arrangement of rows within a tablet (blocks of contiguous rows into which tables in Cloud Bigtable are sharded). The rows are sorted in order of the keys. To optimize the write performance of Cloud Bigtable, we want to have multiple writes happening in parallel, so that each of the Cloud Bigtable instances is writing to its own set of tablets. This is possible if the row keys do not follow a predictable order. The read performance of Cloud Bigtable is, however, more efficient if multiple rows can be read at the same time. Striking the right balance between the two contradictory goals (of having writes be distributed while making most reads be concentrated) is at the heart of effective Cloud Bigtable schema design.

**Designing tables.**  At the extremes, there are two types of designs of tables in Cloud Bigtable. Short and wide tables take advantage of the sparsity of Cloud Bigtable, while tall and narrow tables take advantage of the ability to search row keys by range.

Short and wide tables use the presence or absence of a column to indicate whether or not there is data for that value. For example, suppose we run an automobile factory and the primary query we wish to support with our dataset is to determine the attributes of the parts (part ID, supplier, manufacture location, etc.) that make up a specific automobile. Imagine that we will have millions of cars, each with hundreds of thousands of parts. We could use the car serial number as the row key, and each unique part (e.g., a spark plug) could have a column associated with it (see Figure 11-11).

| car-serial-no | engine:part1,engine:part2, ... | transmission:part1, transmission:part2, | accessories:part1, accessories:part2... |
|---|---|---|---|
| A134224232 | engine:piston=... | transmission:axle=... | accessories:navigation=... |
| A134323422 | engine:sparkplug=... | transmission:axle=... | accessories:seats=... |

*Figure 11-11. Short and wide table for auto parts.*

Each row then consists of many events and is updated as the automobile is put together on the assembly line. Because cells that have no value take up no space, we

---

8 The exception is for operations like an atomic increment, where Cloud Bigtable expects the data to be an integer.

don't have to worry about the proliferation of columns over time as new car models are introduced. Because we will tend to receive events from automobiles being manufactured at the same time, we should ensure that automobile serial numbers are not consecutive, but instead start with the assembly line number. This way, the writes will happen on different tablets in parallel, and so the writes will be efficient. At the same time, diagnostic applications troubleshooting a quality issue will query for all vehicles made on the same line on a particular day, and will therefore tend to pull consecutive rows. Service centers may be interested in obtaining all the parts associated with a specific vehicle. Because the vehicle ID is the row key, this requires reading just a single row, and so, the read performance of such a query will also be very efficient.

Tall and narrow tables often store just one event per row. Every flight event that comes in could get streamed to a new row in Cloud Bigtable. This way, we can have multiple states associated with each flight (departed, wheels-off, etc.) and the historical record of these. At the same time, for each flight, we have only 20 or so fields, all of which can be part of the same column family. This makes the streaming updates easy and intuitive.

**Designing the row key.** Although the table design of one row per event is very intuitive, we need to design the row key in a way that both writes and reads are efficient. To make the reads efficient, consider that the most common queries will involve recent flights between specific airports on a specific carrier (e.g., the status of today's flight between SEA and SJC on AS). Using multiple rows, with a single version of an event in each row, is the simplest way to represent, understand, and query your data. Tall and narrow tables are most efficient if common queries involve just a scan range of rows. This can be achieved if the origin and destination airports are part of the key, as is the carrier. Thus, our row key can start with:

```
ORIGIN#DEST#CARRIER
```

Having the row key start with these three fields also helps with optimizing write performance. While the tablets associated with busy airports like Atlanta might get some amount of hotspotting, the overload will be counteracted by the many sleepy airports whose names also start with the letter A. An alphabetical list of airports should therefore help distribute the write load. Notice that I have the carrier at the end of the list —putting the carrier at the beginning of the row key will have the effect of overloading the tablets that contain the larger airlines (American and United); because there are only a dozen or so carriers, there is no chance of this load being counteracted by smaller carriers.

Because common queries will involve the latest data, scan performance will be improved if we could store the most current data at the top of the table. Using the timestamp in the most intuitive way: 2017-04-12T13:12:45Z will have the opposite effect. The latest data will be at the bottom of the table. Therefore, we need to store timestamps in reverse order somehow. One way would be to convert timestamps to the number of milliseconds since 1970, and then to compute the difference of that timestamp from the maximum possible long value: (LONG_MAX - milliseconds SinceEpoch).

Where should the timestamp go? Having the timestamp at the beginning of the row key would cause the writing to get focused on just one tablet at a time. So, the time-stamp needs to be at the end of the row key. In summary, then, our row key will be of the form:

```
ORIGIN#DEST#CARRIER#ReverseTimeStamp
```

But which timestamp? We'd like all the events from a particular flight to have the same row key, so we'll use the *scheduled* departure time in the key. This avoids prob-lems associated with the key being different depending on the departure delay.

**Streaming into Cloud Bigtable.**  Creating a Cloud Bigtable instance to stream flight events into can be done using gcloud:

```
gcloud bigtable \
    instances create flights \
    --cluster=datascienceongcp --cluster-zone=us-central1-b \
    --description="Chapter 11" --instance-type=DEVELOPMENT
```

The name of my instance is flights, and the name of the cluster of machines is data scienceongcp. By choosing a development instance type, I get to limit the costs—the cluster itself is not replicated or globally available.

To stream into Cloud Bigtable from Bigtable, we need to create a set of Cloud Big-table *mutations* (each mutation consists of a change to a single cell):

```
class CreateRowFn(beam.DoFn):
    def process(self, event):
        key = "{}#{}#{}#{}".format(event['origin'],
event['dest'],event['carrier'],reverse_ts(event['event_time']))
        result = []
        for name, value in event.items():
            direct_row = row.DirectRow(row_key=key)
            direct_row.set_cell(
                name, value, event['event_time']))
            result.append(direct_row)
        return result

preds | 'to_bigtable' >> beam.io.WriteToBigTable(
            project_id=PROJECT,
            instance_id='flights',
            table_id='predictions'

)
```

With these changes to the pipeline code, flight predictions from our pipeline can get streamed to Cloud Bigtable.

**Querying from Cloud Bigtable.** One of the conveniences of using BigQuery as the sink was the ability to carry out analytics using SQL even while the data was streaming in. Cloud Bigtable also provides streaming analytics, but not in SQL. Because Cloud Bigtable is a NoSQL store, the typical use case involves hand-coded client applications. We can, however, use an HBase shell (*https://oreil.ly/8oyry*) to interrogate the contents of our table.

For example, we can get the latest row in the database by doing a table scan and limiting it to one:

```
scan 'predictions', {'LIMIT' => 1}
hbase(main):006:0> scan 'predictions', {'LIMIT' => 1}
ROW                              COLUMN+CELL
 ABE#ATL#DL#9223370608969975807  column=FL:AIRLINE_ID, timestamp=1427891940,
 ABE#ATL#DL#9223370608969975807  column=FL:ARR_AIRPORT_LAT, timestamp=1427891940
 ABE#ATL#DL#9223370608969975807  column=FL:ARR_AIRPORT_LON, timestamp=1427891940
...
```

Because the rows are sorted in ascending order of the row key, they end up being arranged by origin airport, destination airport, and reverse timestamp. That is why we get the most current flight between two airports that start with the letter A. The command-line shell outputs one line per cell, so we get several lines even though the lines all refer to the same row (note that the row key is the same).

The advantage of the way we designed the row key is to be able to get the last few flights between a pair of airports. For example, here are ontime and EVENT columns of the latest two flights between O'Hare airport in Chicago (ORD) and Los Angeles (LAX) flown by American Airlines (AA):

```
scan 'predictions', {STARTROW => 'ORD#LAX#AA', ENDROW => 'ORD#LAX#AB', COLUMN =>
ROW                                COLUMN+CELL
 ORD#LAX#AA#9223370608929475807    column=FL:EVENT, timestamp=142792
 ORD#LAX#AA#9223370608929475807    column=FL:ontime, timestamp=142792
 ORD#LAX#AA#9223370608939975807    column=FL:EVENT, timestamp=142793
 ORD#LAX#AA#9223370608939975807    column=FL:ontime, timestamp=142793
```

Notice that the `arrived` event has the actual on-time performance (1.00), while the `wheelsoff` event has the predicted on-time arrival probability (0.73). It is possible to write an application that uses a Cloud Bigtable client API to do such queries on the Cloud Bigtable table and surface the results to end users.

# Summary

In this chapter, we augmented the machine learning training dataset with time-windowed aggregate features. We computed the average departure and taxi-out delays at the origin airport over the previous hour. This required us to compute a moving average.

Apache Beam allows us to compute a time-windowed moving average on historical data in the same way as we would on streaming data in real time. Cloud Dataflow allows us to execute data pipelines written using Beam on Google Cloud Platform in a serverless way.

In order to compute the average arrival delay, we need to emit records with a timestamp. We discovered that we had a logical error of repeated lines in our output. This turned out to be because we were computing the arrival delay on sliding windows, and these windows caused each flight object to be present in 12 windows. The solution was to determine the slice of the window that the flight object was in and to emit the flight only if it was the latest slice of the window. With these changes, the pipeline was logically correct and the entire training and evaluation datasets were created.

Invoking a model that requires moving averages requires that the model be invoked from a streaming pipeline that continually computes these moving averages. Sending requests for flights one-at-a-time could prove costly in terms of networking, money, and time. Fortunately, the mechanism that we use to invoke the service batches up the requests to the machine learning service from within our Cloud Dataflow pipeline.

Our pipeline reads data from Cloud Pub/Sub and processes it using code that is identical to that used in training. Using the same code for serving as we used in training helps us mitigate training–serving skew. We also employed watermarks and triggers to get a finer control on how to deal with late-arriving, out-of-order records.

We explored other possible streaming sinks and how to choose between them. As a hypothetical, we considered a Cloud Bigtable sink to work in situations where high throughput and low latency are required. We designed an appropriate row key to parallelize the writes while getting speedy reads.

# Suggested Resources

The Apache Beam documentation includes a section on common pipeline patterns (*https://oreil.ly/miwXT*). These merit careful reading. For example, I learned from the deadletter pattern (*https://oreil.ly/K4eKk*) that the `WriteToBigQuery` transform that I've been using for donkey's years tells you which rows that it failed to write.

Another list worth periodically reviewing is the list of built-in transforms (*https://oreil.ly/iaeqf*) in Apache Beam.

*Streaming Systems* by Tyler Akidau et al. (O'Reilly) is a good way to develop a foundation in streaming systems concepts.

# CHAPTER 12

# The Full Dataset

In Chapters 1–11, we built a system for predicting flight delays so as to provide travelers with guidance on whether they would be likely to make it to their already scheduled meetings. All of the development was carried out on one year of data. In this chapter, I will change the code to process the full dataset.

 All of the code snippets in this chapter are available in the folder *12_fulldataset* of the book's GitHub repository (*https://github.com/ GoogleCloudPlatform/data-science-on-gcp*).

## Four Years of Data

How well the final model performs can be evaluated only on truly independent data. Because we used our "test" data to evaluate different models along the way and do hyperparameter tuning, we cannot use any of the originally ingested data to evaluate the performance of the model.

Fortunately, though, I did *not* actually use all of the available data. In order to keep the datasets small enough that the Dataflow pipelines and ML training jobs would complete in a couple hours, I have limited all my work so far to 2015. I have not used 2016–2021 data in training, model selection, or hyperparameter tuning.

Let's fix this. What I am going to do is to train the ML model on data from 2015–2018 and assume that we put the model into production at the end of 2018. How would that model have fared in 2019? If this works well, it gives us the confidence that we can train the ML model on a few years of data and then apply it in real time. That said, you probably realize why I'm not training the model on 2015–2020 and testing on 2021 data—the world of aviation was turned on its head during 2020–2021 by the

COVID-19 pandemic.[1] We will have to retrain the ML model for a post COVID-19 future.

Even between 2015–2018 and 2019, the environment would have changed; the list of carriers doing business in 2019 is likely to be different from those in 2015. Also, airline schedulers have presumably changed how they schedule flights. The economy would have been different, and this might lead to more full planes (and hence longer boarding times). Still, evaluating on 2019 data is a reasonable thing to do—after all, in the real world, we might have been using our 2015–2018 model and serving it out to our users in 2019. How would our predictions have fared?

In order to evaluate the performance of a model trained on 2015–2018 data in 2019, we need to:

- Create the dataset for training, validation, and testing.
- Train the model on the 2015–2018 dataset.
- Evaluate the model on the 2019 data.

Let's look at each of these steps.

## Creating Dataset

Getting 2015–2019 data ready involves repeating the steps we carried out for our training dataset except doing so on the full dataset (see the *README.md* file in Chapter 12 for details on how to reproduce the steps).

### Dataset split

In order to achieve this desired data split, I changed the splitting code in *flights_transforms.py* to be such that 2019 data is used for test while the rest is split between training (95%) and validation (5%) using `farmhash`:

```
def get_data_split_2019(fl_date):
    fl_date_str = str(fl_date)
    if fl_date_str > '2019':
        data_split = 'TEST'
    else:
        # Use farm fingerprint just like in BigQuery
        x = np.abs(np.uint64(farmhash.fingerprint64(
                            fl_date_str)).astype('int64') % 100)
        if x < 95:
            data_split = 'TRAIN'
        else:
```

---

1 I suppose I could have picked a different dataset for the second edition. But most real-world datasets that are dependent in some way on human behavior exhibit dramatic changes before and after March 2020.

```
            data_split = 'VALIDATE'
        return data_split
```

## Shuffling data

In Chapter 10, when I wrote the TensorFlow code to read in the data, I shuffled the data within an in-memory buffer that is 10 times the batch size:

```
if mode == tf.estimator.ModeKeys.TRAIN:
    dataset = dataset.shuffle(batch_size*10)
    dataset = dataset.repeat()
```

I explained this as being needed for distributed training so that different workers don't always see the same slice of the data. Another reason that we wish to shuffle the data is that it could be clumped based on the way we retrieve and process the records before writing them out. For example, our Beam pipeline processes the data in hourly time windows at each airport. So, successive records are likely to all be from the same airport and the same time. Of course, the file will not be perfectly sorted, just clumped. But such clumping can cause the model to get stuck in a local optimum. So, as our dataset size grows, in-memory shuffling will no longer be sufficient to ensure that a batch remains representative of the overall dataset instead of being from the same time or same airport.

So, let's add a reshuffle operation to *create_traindata.py*:

```
features = (
            features
            | 'into_global' >> beam.WindowInto(
                             beam.window.GlobalWindows())
            | 'shuffle' >> beam.util.Reshuffle()
)
```

Note that I have been careful to remove the time windowing by putting all the elements into the global window. Had I not done that, the reshuffle would have been only within each time window, and the training data would have been clumped by time. With this change, the data will get reshuffled globally before it is written out.

## Need for continuous training

When I ran the pipeline, though, I discovered that the time correction code failed because the *airports.csv* that the script was using was incomplete for the new year. New airports had been built, and some airport locations had changed, so there were several unique airport codes that were not present in the original airports file. We could go out and get the latest *airports.csv*, but this doesn't address a bigger problem. Recall that we used the airport location information in our machine learning model by creating embeddings of origin and destination airports—such features will not work properly for new airports. In the real world, especially when we work with humans and human artifacts (customers, airports, products, etc.), it is unlikely that we will be able to train a model once and keep using it from then on. Instead, models will have to be continually trained with up-to-date data. Continuous training is a necessary ingredient in machine learning. Hence, the emphasis on easy operationalization, versioning, and pipelines in Vertex AI—this is a workflow that you will have to automate.

---

## Continuous Training

What I am doing in this chapter is retraining the model from scratch. I am not using the 2015 model in any way. I am taking the model code and training it on 2015–2018 data.

An alternative approach is called fine-tuning. When we trained our model, we wrote out checkpoints—to train the model with new data, we would start from such a checkpointed model, load it in, and then run a few batches through it, thus adjusting the weights. This allows the model to slowly adapt to new data without losing its accumulated knowledge. It is also possible to replace nodes from a checkpointed graph, or to freeze certain layers and train only others (such as perhaps the embedding layers for the airports). If you've done operations such as learning rate decay, you'd continue training at the lower learning rate and not restart training with the highest learning rate. Vertex AI and TensorFlow are designed to accommodate this.

Fine-tuning is faster than retraining. So, if you are doing continuous training, it is much more common to do fine-tuning than retraining. However, fine-tuning will not provide the same overall benefit as from-scratch retraining. So, the typical approach is to fine-tune the model on a daily or weekly basis with new data, but once the amount of new data has become a significant fraction of the original data (say 5%), go back and train completely from scratch.

---

For now, though, I will simply change the code that looks up airport codes to deal gracefully with the error and impute a reasonable value for the machine learning code:

```
def airport_timezone(airport_id, airport_timezones_dict):
    if airport_id in airport_timezones_dict:
        return airport_timezones_dict[airport_id]
    else:
        return ('37.41', '-92.35', u'America/Chicago')
```

If the airport is not found in the dictionary, the airport location is assumed to be located at (37.41, –92.35), which corresponds to the population center of the United States in central Missouri as estimated by the US Census Bureau (*https://oreil.ly/ShGzD*).

## More powerful machines

Whereas the 2015 data consisted of about 5 million flights, the 2015–2019 dataset consists of 30 million flights. Preparing the data doesn't simply take six times longer on the same set of machines. One of the key steps in the pipeline involves time windowing of grouped elements. Because this is a batched pipeline, Dataflow will need to sort the 30 million flights in order to do time windowing. We can no longer use the default n1-standard-1 machines that we used for the 2015 data. In order for *create_traindata.py* to work, I need more workers each with more memory, more compute, and more storage:

```
--worker_machine_type=m1-ultramem-40 --disk_size_gb=500
```

The M1 class of machines on Google Cloud have higher memory. I'm asking for such a high-memory machine with 40 vCPUs and a persistent disk of 500 GB to store temporary data.

Even with this increased computational power, creating the training dataset seems to take forever—when I ran it, the pipeline got bottlenecked by the ability of the machines to handle the grouped time window (see Figure 12-1). Note that the by_airport transformation that converts the flight events into a tuple (origin, flight) has completed and has output 30 million tuples. On the other hand, the group_by_airport transform is only 79% complete. It is emitting 2,500 elements per second to subsequent stages and has processed 12.5 million airport time-windows so far.

Since the dataset has 30 million records, and we are processing only 2,500 records per second, it will take 12,000 seconds or 3.5 hours to get through this bottleneck. The stage after that computes statistics on each group (time-window at an airport), and that one is processing 800 groups/second. Since there are about 105,000 5-minute intervals in a year and we have 4 years of data and 300 airports, there are 126 million of these groups. At 800 elements/second, it will take 44 hours or around 2 days to finish that step.

In reality, it takes less time because not all airport-hour combinations have flights. For example, many airports do not have flights landing or taking off between midnight and 5:30 a.m. local time. Smaller airports will not have data for many hours. I did run the pipeline to completion, and it took 26 hours, indicating that the true number of groups is about half my estimate.

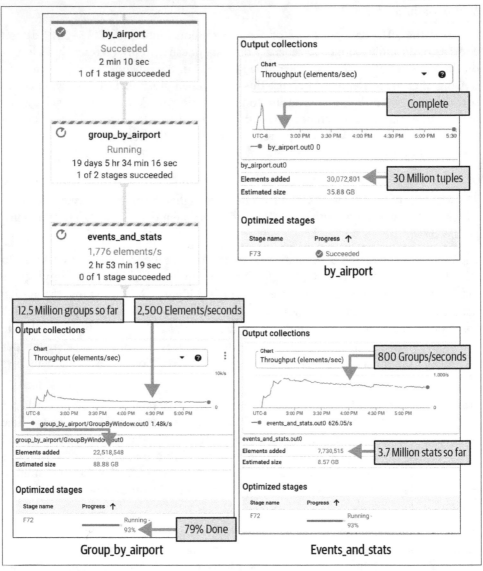

*Figure 12-1. The pipeline to create the full dataset is bottlenecked by the* group_by_air
port *operation, which is able to process only 2,500 elements/second.*

Is there a way to cut down on the time and resources needed? One way would be to compromise on accuracy and process each of the years separately.[2] This would require less powerful machines and allow the pipeline to finish faster.

Since this is so expensive in terms of time and resources, I have placed the full dataset in the data-science-on-gcp bucket. You can copy the data to your bucket instead of running the Dataflow pipeline:

```
gsutil cp \
  gs://data-science-on-gcpedition2/ch12_fulldataset/all-00000-of-00001.csv \
  gs://BUCKET/ch11/data/all-00000-of-00001.csv
```

## Training Model

Once the training dataset is created, we have to choose the model to train. Should we use the AutoML model that got an RMSE of 0.198 or our wide-and-deep model with location-based feature crosses that achieved an RMSE of 0.195? There are good arguments for both.

AutoML uses a number of sophisticated models such as neural architecture search (*https://oreil.ly/eJE7F*), which builds deep learning networks one layer at a time, and TabNet, which is based on a sophisticated approach called sequential attention.[3] These types of models work better the more data you have. Just because we beat AutoML on a dataset of 5 million flights doesn't mean that we will get to beat it using 30 million flights. On the other hand, our location-based feature cross and embeddings will improve in quality if we train them with more data. So, it is conceivable that the custom model will continue to be better than AutoML. There is no way to know. We'd have to try both approaches.

However, there is a key reason I want to use AutoML. Recall that we asked AutoML to write out evaluation data to BigQuery. That capability will come in very handy for *sliced evaluation*—for example, we can easily analyze whether our model performs better on American Airlines flights than on Southwest Airlines. While I could add the necessary code (to write out evaluation data) to our custom model, that's a lot of work.[4] Let's go with AutoML.

---

2 This is a compromise because the time averages at the beginning of the year will be wrong—flights from December 31 will not be available to compute the time average on January 1. Still, this affects only a minuscule number of flights and might be a reasonable compromise to make.

3 Sercan Ö. Arik, Tomas Pfister, "TabNet: Attentive Interpretable Tabular Learning," Proceedings of the AAAI Conference on Artificial Intelligence, 35 no. 8 (May 2021): 6679-6687. https://arxiv.org/pdf/1908.07442.pdf.

4 Can you tell that I'm ready to finish writing the book?

Training took about 5 hours. The feature importance graph on the full dataset was similar to the one obtained from the AutoML model trained on 2015 data (see Figure 12-2). The five most important features in 2015—dep_delay, taxi_out, origin, dest, and carrier—remain the five most important in 2015–2018, although the order of the fourth and fifth features are switched around.

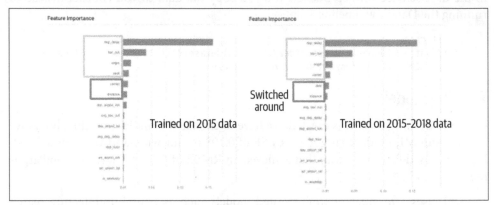

*Figure 12-2. The five most important features in the AutoML model trained on 2015 data are the five most important on 2015–2018 data as well. The first three are identical while features 4 and 5 are switched around.*

The precision and recall curves (see Figure 12-3) seem quite similar.

So far, we have been comparing RMSE (which compares the performance at all thresholds, not just 0.7) and so, we need to evaluate the 2015–2018 model the same way. Let's do that next.

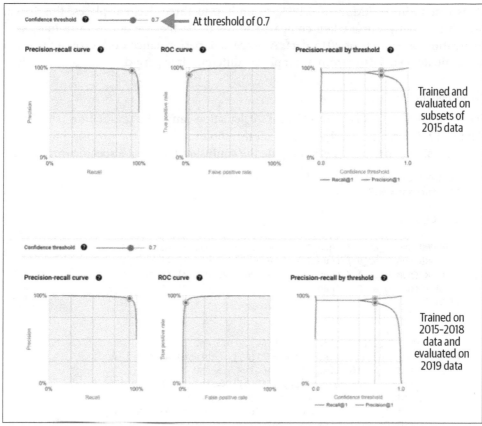

*Figure 12-3. The ML model trained and evaluated on subsets of 2015 data (top) seems to have similar performance to the ML model trained on 2015–2018 data and evaluated on 2019 data.*

## Evaluation

We can dig deeper into the performance characteristics using Vertex Workbench (see *evaluations.ipynb*).

### RMSE

We can start with the query to compute the RMSE:

```
%%bigquery
SELECT
  SQRT(SUM(
      (CAST(ontime AS FLOAT64) - predicted_ontime.scores[OFFSET(0)])*
      (CAST(ontime AS FLOAT64) - predicted_ontime.scores[OFFSET(0)])
      )/COUNT(*)) AS rmse
FROM dsongcp.ch10_automl_evaluated
```

This results in an RMSE of 0.1998. Rounding to three decimal places, this is 0.2, which is slightly worse when compared to the 0.198 that we got from training and evaluating on subsets of 2015 data. As expected, performance does drop a bit when we evaluate on a dataset from a completely different time period.

### Confusion matrix

The difference between this RMSE calculation and the evaluation shown in Figure 12-3 is that the RMSE is over all thresholds, whereas the precision and recall are for a single threshold. Let's compute the confusion matrix at a specific threshold:

```
DECLARE thresh FLOAT64;
SET thresh = 0.7;

SELECT
  *,
  ROUND(num_1_as_1 / (num_1_as_1 + num_1_as_0), 2) AS frac_1_as_1,
  ROUND(num_1_as_0 / (num_1_as_1 + num_1_as_0), 2) AS frac_1_as_0,
  ROUND(num_0_as_1 / (num_0_as_1 + num_0_as_0), 2) AS frac_0_as_1,
  ROUND(num_0_as_0 / (num_0_as_1 + num_0_as_0), 2) AS frac_0_as_0
FROM (
    SELECT
      thresh,
      COUNTIF(CAST(ontime AS FLOAT64) > 0.5 AND
      predicted_ontime.scores[OFFSET(0)] > thresh) AS num_1_as_1,
      COUNTIF(CAST(ontime AS FLOAT64) > 0.5 AND
      predicted_ontime.scores[OFFSET(0)] <= thresh) AS num_1_as_0,
      COUNTIF(CAST(ontime AS FLOAT64) <= 0.5 AND
      predicted_ontime.scores[OFFSET(0)] > thresh) AS num_0_as_1,
      COUNTIF(CAST(ontime AS FLOAT64) <= 0.5 AND
      predicted_ontime.scores[OFFSET(0)] <= thresh) AS num_0_as_0
    FROM dsongcp.ch10_automl_evaluated
)
```

The result shows that 4% of on-time flights are misclassified as being late, and 13% of late flights are misclassified as being on time:

| Row | thresh | num_1_ as_1 | num_1_ as_0 | num_0_ as_1 | num_0_ as_0 | frac_1_ as_1 | frac_1_ as_0 | frac_0_ as_1 | frac_0_ as_0 |
|-----|--------|-------------|-------------|-------------|-------------|--------------|--------------|--------------|--------------|
| 1 | 0.7 | 5633570 | 245409 | 184545 | 1204708 | 0.96 | 0.04 | 0.13 | 0.87 |

### Impact of threshold

We can expand this to multiple thresholds using an array in SQL:

```
WITH counts AS (
    SELECT
      thresh,
      COUNTIF(CAST(ontime AS FLOAT64) > 0.5 AND
      predicted_ontime.scores[OFFSET(0)] > thresh) AS num_1_as_1,
```

```
        COUNTIF(CAST(ontime AS FLOAT64) > 0.5 AND
        predicted_ontime.scores[OFFSET(0)] <= thresh) AS num_1_as_0,
        COUNTIF(CAST(ontime AS FLOAT64) <= 0.5 AND
        predicted_ontime.scores[OFFSET(0)] > thresh) AS num_0_as_1,
        COUNTIF(CAST(ontime AS FLOAT64) <= 0.5 AND
        predicted_ontime.scores[OFFSET(0)] <= thresh) AS num_0_as_0
    FROM UNNEST([0.5, 0.7, 0.8]) AS thresh, dsongcp.ch10_automl_evaluated
    GROUP BY thresh
)

SELECT
    *,
    ROUND(num_1_as_1 / (num_1_as_1 + num_1_as_0), 2) AS frac_1_as_1,
    ROUND(num_1_as_0 / (num_1_as_1 + num_1_as_0), 2) AS frac_1_as_0,
    ROUND(num_0_as_1 / (num_0_as_1 + num_0_as_0), 2) AS frac_0_as_1,
    ROUND(num_0_as_0 / (num_0_as_1 + num_0_as_0), 2) AS frac_0_as_0
FROM counts
ORDER BY thresh ASC
```

which returns:

| Row | thresh | num_1_ as_1 | num_1_ as_0 | num_0_ as_1 | num_0_ as_0 | frac_1_ as_1 | frac_1_ as_0 | frac_0_ as_1 | frac_0_ as_0 |
|-----|--------|-------------|-------------|-------------|-------------|--------------|--------------|--------------|--------------|
| 1 | 0.5 | 5763136 | 115843 | 258138 | 1131115 | 0.98 | 0.02 | 0.19 | 0.81 |
| 2 | 0.7 | 5633570 | 245409 | 184545 | 1204708 | 0.96 | 0.04 | 0.13 | 0.87 |
| 3 | 0.8 | 5498807 | 380172 | 146200 | 1243053 | 0.94 | 0.06 | 0.11 | 0.89 |

As we'd expect, the fraction of on-time flights that we get correct decreases the higher we make our threshold. Conversely, the fraction of late flights that we get correct increases.

## Impact of a feature

We can also check whether what the model understood about the data is reasonable. For example, the relation between model prediction and departure delay can be obtained using:

```
SELECT
    ROUND(predicted_ontime.scores[OFFSET(0)], 2) AS prob_ontime,
    AVG(CAST(dep_delay AS FLOAT64)) AS dep_delay,
FROM dsongcp.ch10_automl_evaluated
GROUP BY prob_ontime
ORDER BY prob_ontime ASC
```

The query pulls out the average departure delay associated with each predicted probability. For example, what is the average departure delay associated with model predictions of 0.8? We can plot the converse graph as well:

```
SELECT
    ROUND(predicted_ontime.scores[OFFSET(0)], 2) AS prob_ontime,
```

```
    AVG(CAST(dep_delay AS FLOAT64)) AS dep_delay,
  FROM dsongcp.ch10_automl_evaluated
  GROUP BY prob_ontime
  ORDER BY prob_ontime ASC
```

Both graphs, when plotted, are eminently smooth and reasonable (see Figure 12-4). At higher on-time probabilities, we see lower departure delays. And at lower departure delays, we see higher probabilities. This is what we would expect.

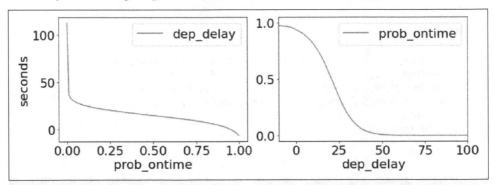

*Figure 12-4. The average departure delay associated with probabilities predicted by the model (left) and the average prediction for specific departure delays (right).*

### Analyzing errors

We can also analyze the difference in the relationship of departure delay to errors in the model:

```
WITH preds AS (
  SELECT
    CAST(ontime AS FLOAT64) AS ontime,
    ROUND(predicted_ontime.scores[OFFSET(0)], 2) AS prob_ontime,
    CAST(dep_delay AS FLOAT64) AS var,
  FROM dsongcp.ch10_automl_evaluated
)

SELECT
  prob_ontime,
  AVG(IF((ontime > 0.5 and prob_ontime <= 0.5) or
              (ontime <= 0.5 and prob_ontime > 0.5), var, NULL)) AS wrong,
  AVG(IF((ontime > 0.5 and prob_ontime > 0.5) or
              (ontime <= 0.5 and prob_ontime <= 0.5), var, NULL)) AS correct
FROM preds
GROUP BY prob_ontime
ORDER BY prob_ontime
```

Plotting this shows that our model has a very similar dependency on departure delay (see Figure 12-5). This makes sense because departure delay is the most important feature. When we look at the next best feature (taxi-out time), differences start to show up. It's clear that the model makes more errors when the taxi-out time is small but the flight nevertheless arrives late.

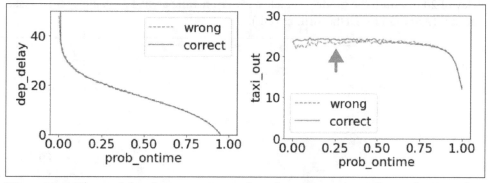

*Figure 12-5. The model makes more errors when the taxi-out time is lower than usual but the flight nevertheless arrives late.*

### Categorical features

Analyzing the impact of categorical features is more difficult—there are more than 300 airports, and it's difficult to make sense of so many different values.

To understand whether the model learned the difference between airports, we can examine the model behavior in terms of the probability that it predicts for a given departure delay at two different airports: New York's JFK airport and Seattle's SEA airport (see Figure 12-6). A 25-minute delay at Seattle is associated with a lower on-time arrival probability than the same delay at JFK. The model discounts long departure delays at New York—these are common enough that airline schedulers take them into account when publishing scheduled arrival times.

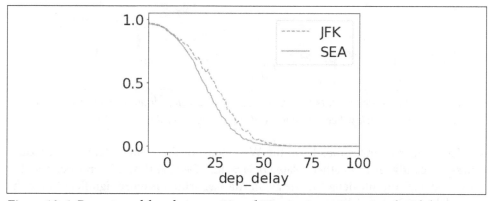

*Figure 12-6. Departure delays between 10 and 50 minutes are associated with lower probabilities predicted by the model in Seattle versus New York's John F. Kennedy airport.*

Because there are only a handful of carriers, we can plot the probability versus departure delay relationship of all the carriers. As you can see in Figure 12-7, at a departure delay of 20 minutes, the model predicts a lower on-time arrival probability for Alaska Airlines (AS) than for Delta Airlines (DL).

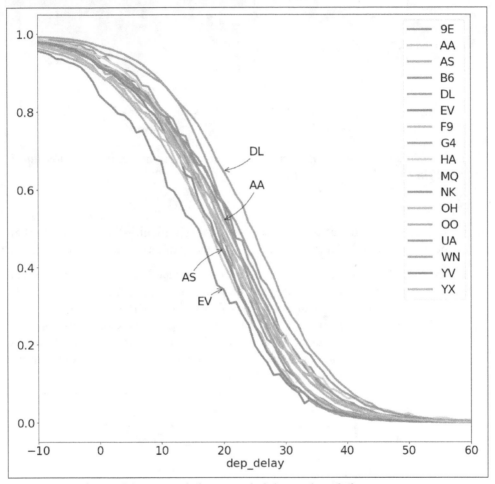

*Figure 12-7. The model outputs different probabilities when different carriers encounter the same departure delay. See it in color online (https://oreil.ly/dsgcp_12-7).*

Alaska Airlines operates mostly on the West Coast of the United States and encounters significantly fewer weather-related delays than Delta Airlines. Therefore, it makes sense that a 20-minute departure delay on Alaska Airlines is more significant than the same delay on Delta Airlines.

It appears that our 2015–2018 model would have performed quite well in 2019. 2020, with its COVID-19 pandemic, is of course a completely separate story. Hopefully, we would have been continuously evaluating the predictions, caught the deterioration of the model once many flights started to get canceled, and taken our model out of production.

## Summary

In this chapter, we looked at how to train the model on the full dataset and how to evaluate model performance. Having now built an end-to-end system, work moves on to continually improving it and constantly refreshing it with data.

## Suggested Resources

When developing and evaluating ML models, keep responsible AI principles and practices (*https://oreil.ly/0JN81*) in mind.

# Conclusion

In Chapter 1, we discussed the goals of data analysis, how to provide data-driven guidance using statistical and machine learning models, and the roles that will be involved with such work in the future. We also formulated our case study problem—of recommending whether a traveler should cancel a scheduled meeting based on the likelihood of the flight that they are on being delayed.

In Chapter 2, we automated the ingest of flight data from the Bureau of Transportation Statistics website. We started out by reverse engineering a web form, writing Python scripts to download the necessary data, and storing the data on Google Cloud Storage. Finally, we made the ingest process serverless by creating a Cloud Run application to carry out the ingest and made it invokable from Cloud Scheduler.

In Chapter 3, we discussed why it was important to bring end users' insights into our data modeling efforts as early as possible. We achieved this by building a dashboard in Data Studio and populated this dashboard from Cloud SQL. The dashboard was used to explain a simple contingency table model that predicted on-time arrival likelihood by thresholding the departure delay of the flight.

In Chapter 4, we simulated the flight data as if it were arriving in real time, used the simulation to populate messages into Cloud Pub/Sub, and then processed the streaming messages in Cloud Dataflow. In Cloud Dataflow, we computed aggregations and streamed the results into BigQuery. Because Cloud Dataflow follows the Beam programming model, the code for streaming and batch is the same, and this greatly simplifies the training and operationalization of machine learning models in the rest of the book.

In Chapter 5, we carried out interactive data exploration by loading our dataset into Google BigQuery and plotting charts using Vertex Workbench. The model we used in this chapter was a non-parametric estimation of the 30th percentile of arrival delays. It was in this chapter that we also divided up our dataset into two parts—one part for training and the other for evaluation. We discussed why partitioning the dataset based on date was the right approach for this problem.

In Chapter 6, we created a Bayes model on a Cloud Dataproc cluster. The Bayes model itself involved quantization in Spark and on-time arrival percentage computation using Apache Pig. Cloud Dataproc allowed us to integrate BigQuery, Spark SQL, and Apache Pig into a Hadoop workflow. Because we stored our data on Google Cloud Storage (and not HDFS), our Cloud Dataproc cluster was job-specific and could be job-scoped, thus limiting our costs. At the end of the chapter, we briefly looked at serverless Spark, which promises to allow us to forget about cluster management completely.

In Chapter 7, we built a logistic regression machine learning model using Apache Spark. The model had three input variables, all of which were continuous features. On adding categorical features, we found that the resulting explosion in the size of the dataset caused scalability issues. There were also significant hurdles to taking the logistic regression model and making it operational in terms of achieving low-latency predictions.

In Chapter 8, we built machine learning models in SQL using BigQuery ML. We found that the scalability of BigQuery made it possible to use sparse categorical features and sophisticated models such as gradient boosted trees quite easily. BigQuery ML also allowed us to separate out the transformations needed, so that we could ensure that those transformations were carried out during inference as well.

In Chapter 9, we used TensorFlow to create a wide-and-deep model with hand-crafted features. This resulted in a high-performing model for predicting the on-time arrival probability.

In Chapter 10, we scaled out the training of the TensorFlow model using Vertex AI, carried out hyperparameter tuning, and deployed the model so as to be able to carry out online predictions and get explainability. We also automated the entire process by creating a Vertex AI training pipeline.

In Chapter 11, we built a Cloud Dataflow pipeline to compute time-aggregate features to use as inputs to the machine learning model. This involved the use of time windows. We also created a streaming pipeline to invoke the deployed model as a microservice, batching up calls to it and adding flight predictions as we receive and process flight data in real time.

In Chapter 12, we evaluated the model on completely independent data, learning that continuous training of our ML model is a necessity.

Throughout this book, as we worked our way through a data science problem end-to-end, from ingest to machine learning, the realization struck me that this is now a lot easier than it ever has been. I was able to do everything from simple thresholds, to Bayesian techniques, to deep neural networks, with surprisingly little effort. At the same time, I was able to ingest data, refresh it, build dashboards, do stream processing, and operationalize the ML model with very little code. At the start of my career,

80% of the time to answer a data science question would be spent building the plumbing to get at the data. Operationalizing a machine learning model was something on the same scale as developing it in the first place. Google Cloud Platform, though, is designed to allow you to forget about infrastructure, and operationalizing a machine learning model is something you can fold into the model development phase itself. The practice of data science has become easier thanks to the advent of serverless data processing and machine learning systems that are integrated into powerful statistical and visualization software tools.

I can't wait to see what you build next.

# Considerations for Sensitive Data Within Machine Learning Datasets

The content of this appendix, written by the author and Brad Svee, was published as a solution paper on the Google Cloud Platform documentation website (*https://oreil.ly/qvXek*).

When you are developing an ML program, it's important to balance data access within your company against the security implications of that access. You want insights contained in the raw dataset to guide ML training even as access to sensitive data is limited. To achieve both goals, it's useful to train ML systems on a subset of the raw data, or on the entire dataset after partial application of any number of aggregation or obfuscation techniques.

For example, you might want your data engineers to train an ML model to weigh customer feedback on a product, but you don't want them to know who submitted the feedback. However, information such as delivery address and purchase history is critically important for training the ML model. After the data is provided to the data engineers, they will need to query it for data exploration purposes, so it is important to protect your sensitive data fields before making it available. This type of dilemma is also common in ML models that involve recommendation engines. To create a model that returns user-specific results, you typically need access to user-specific data.

Fortunately, there are techniques you can use to remove some sensitive data from your datasets while still training effective ML models. This article aims to highlight some strategies for identifying and protecting sensitive information, and processes to help address security concerns you might have with your ML data.

# Handling Sensitive Information

Sensitive information is any data that you and your legal counsel want to protect with additional security measures such as restricted access or encryption. For example, fields such as name, email address, billing information, or information that could allow a data engineer or malicious actor to indirectly deduce the sensitive information are often considered sensitive.

Standards such as HIPAA and PCI-DSS specify a set of best practices for protecting sensitive data, while also informing customers about the way their sensitive data is supposed to be handled. These certifications allow customers to make informed decisions about the security of their information.

Handling sensitive data in ML datasets can be difficult for the following reasons:

- Most role-based security is targeted toward the concept of ownership, which means a user can view and/or edit their own data but can't access data that doesn't belong to them. The concept of ownership breaks down with ML datasets that are an aggregate of data from many users. Essentially, data engineers need to be granted view access to an entire set of data in order to effectively use the dataset.

- Encrypting or reducing the resolution of sensitive fields is often used as a preventive measure, but isn't always sufficient for an ML dataset. The aggregate dataset itself often provides the means of breaking the encryption through frequency analysis attacks (*https://oreil.ly/BjnMY*).

- Random tokenization, suppression, or removal of the sensitive fields from the dataset can degrade effective ML model training by obscuring necessary data, resulting in poor performance of your predictions.

Organizations often develop tools and a set of best practices in order to strike an appropriate balance between security and utility. To help protect sensitive data in ML datasets, keep in mind the following three goals, which are discussed in the rest of this document:

- Identify sensitive data in the dataset with a high level of confidence.

- Protect sensitive data without adversely impacting the project. This can be accomplished by removing, masking, or coarsening the data you have determined to be sensitive.

- Create a governance plan and best practices documentation. This allows your data engineers as well as customers to make appropriate decisions about your sensitive data, particularly those scenarios where the sensitive data cannot be identified reliably, masked, or removed.

These three goals are discussed in detail in the following sections, which focus on scenarios where your datasets remain private within your company. This article does not cover scenarios where the datasets are meant to be shared publicly.

Sensitive data might exist in your environment in several scenarios. The following sections cover five of the most common scenarios and present methods you can use to identify sensitive data in each.

## Sensitive Data in Columns

Sensitive data can be restricted to specific columns in structured datasets. For example, you might have a set of columns containing a user's first name, last name, and mailing address. In this case, you identify which columns have sensitive data, decide how to secure them, and document these decisions.

## Sensitive Data in Natural Language Datasets

Sensitive data can be part of an natural language dataset, and it can often be detected using known patterns. For example, credit card numbers in chat transcripts can be reliably detected using a common regular expression pattern for credit card numbers. Regular expression detection errors, leading to misclassification, can be minimized using more complex tools like the Google Data Loss Prevention API (DLP API) (*https://oreil.ly/GAG14*).

## Sensitive Data in Free-Form Unstructured Data

Sensitive data can exist in free-form unstructured data such as text reports, audio recordings, photographs, or scanned receipts. These datasets make it considerably more difficult to identify your sensitive data, but there are many tools available to help you:

- For free-text documents, you might use a natural language processing system such as the Cloud Natural Language API (*https://oreil.ly/8GIeF*) to identify entities, email addresses, and other sensitive data.

- For audio recordings, you can use a speech-to-text service such as the Cloud Speech API (*https://oreil.ly/V2jDD*), and subsequently apply the natural language processor.

- For images, you can use a text-detection service such as the Cloud Vision API (*https://oreil.ly/4ar4W*) to yield raw text from the image and isolate the location of that text within the image. The Vision API can provide the coordinates for locations of some targeted items within images, and you might use this information, for example, to mask all faces from images of a cash register line before training a machine learning model to estimate average customer wait times.

- For videos, you can parse each video into individual picture frames and treat them as image files, or you can use a video processing tool such as the Cloud Video Intelligence API (*https://oreil.ly/024qh*) along with the Cloud Speech API to process the audio.

These techniques are still subject to the review and approval of your own legal counsel and depend on how well your systems are able to process free text, transcribe audio, understand images, and segment video in order to identify potential sensitive data. The Google APIs listed previously, as well as the DLP API, are powerful tools you can incorporate into your preprocessing pipeline. However, these automated methods are imperfect, and you will want to consider maintaining a governance policy to deal with any sensitive information that remains after scrubbing.

## Sensitive Data in a Combination of Fields

Sensitive data can exist as a combination of fields, or manifest from a trend in a protected field over time. For example, a standard practice to reduce the likelihood of identifying a user is to blur the last two zip-code digits, reducing the zip code from five to three ("zip3"). However, a combination of zip3 associated with work and a zip3 associated with a home address might be enough to identify users with unusual home-work combinations. Similarly, a zip3 home address trend over time might be enough to identify an individual who has moved several times.

Identifying whether a dataset is truly protected in the face of a frequency analysis attack requires statistical expertise. Any scenario dependent upon human experts presents scalability challenges and can paradoxically require the same data engineer scrubbing the data to inspect the raw data for potential problems. Ideally, you would create automated ways to identify and quantify this risk, a task beyond the scope of this article.

Regardless, you should work with your legal counsel and data engineers to assess your exposure to risk in these scenarios.

## Sensitive Data in Unstructured Content

Sensitive data sometimes exists in unstructured content because of embedded contextual information. For example, a chat transcript might include the phrase "I called yesterday from my office. I had to go to the eighteenth floor lobby by the Cafe Deluxe Espresso, because the fourth floor has poor mobile reception."

Based on the context and scope of your training data and advice of your legal counsel, you might want to filter aspects of this content. Due to the unstructured nature and large set of complex combinations of phrases that could enable similar inferences, this is a difficult scenario to address with programmatic tools, but it is worth considering tighter governance around access to the entire unstructured dataset.

For model development it is often effective to take a subsample of this data that has been scrubbed and reviewed by a trusted person and make it available for model development. You would then be able to use security restrictions and software automation to process the full dataset through the production model training process.

# Protecting Sensitive Data

After you have identified your sensitive data, you must determine how to protect it.

## Removing Sensitive Data

If user-specific information is not necessary for your project, consider deleting all that information from the dataset before it is provided to the data engineers building your ML model. However, as discussed earlier, there are cases where removing the sensitive data dramatically reduces the value of the dataset and in these cases, sensitive data should be masked using one or more of the techniques discussed in the following section.

Depending on the structure of the dataset, removing sensitive data requires different approaches:

- When data is restricted to specific columns in structured datasets, you can create a view that doesn't provide access to the columns in question. The data engineers cannot view the data, but at the same time the data is "live" and doesn't require human intervention to de-id it for continuous training.

- When sensitive data is part of unstructured content, but it's identifiable using known patterns, it can be automatically removed and replaced by a generic string. This is how the DLP API addresses this challenge.

- When sensitive data exists within images, videos, audio, or unstructured free-form data, you can extend the tools you've deployed to identify the sensitive data to mask or remove it.

- When sensitive data exists because of a combination of fields, and you have incorporated automated tools or manual data analysis steps to quantify the risk posed by each column, your data engineers can make informed decisions about retaining or removing any relevant column.

## Masking Sensitive Data

When you can't remove sensitive data fields, it might still be possible for your data engineers to train effective models with the data in a masked format. If your data engineers determine that some or all of the sensitive data fields can be masked without impacting the ML training, you can use several techniques to mask the data:

- The most common approach is to use a substitution cipher, which involves replacing all occurrences of a plain-text identifier by its hashed and/or encrypted value. It is generally accepted as a best practice to use a strong cryptographic hash such as SHA-256 (*https://oreil.ly/RKGjO*), or a strong encryption algorithm such as AES-256 (*https://oreil.ly/OzrII*) to store all sensitive fields. It is important to remember that using a salt with your encryption will not create repeatable values and is detrimental to ML training.

- Tokenization is a masking technique that substitutes an unrelated placeholder value for the real value stored in each sensitive field. The mapping of the placeholder value to the real value is encrypted/hashed in a completely different and presumably more secure database. It is worth noting that this method works for ML datasets only if the same token value is reused for identical values. In this case, it is akin to a substitution cipher and is vulnerable to frequency analysis attacks. The primary difference is that tokenization adds an additional layer of protection by pushing the encrypted values into a separate database.

- Another method of protecting data with multiple columns uses Principal Components Analysis (*https://oreil.ly/HvmbK*) (PCA) or other dimension-reducing techniques to combine several features and then carry out ML training on only the resulting PCA vectors. For example, given three different fields (age, smoker —represented as 1 or 0—and body-weight), the data might get condensed into a single PCA column that uses the following equation:

  *1.5 age + 30 smoker + 0.2 × body-weight*

  Somebody who is 20 years old, smokes, and weighs 140 pounds generates a value of 88. This is the same value generated by someone who is 30 years old, doesn't smoke, and weighs 215 pounds.

  This method can be quite robust because even if one identifies individuals who are unique in some way, it is hard to determine what makes them unique without an explanation of the PCA vector formula. However, all PCA processing reduces the data distribution and trades accuracy for security.

As previously noted, it is sometimes possible to break a substitution cipher using *a priori* knowledge of the frequency with which different identifiers occur "in the wild," and deriving inferences from the actual occurrence of the various encrypted identifiers. For example, the distribution of first names in a public dataset of baby names (*https://oreil.ly/2blCy*) can be used to infer the likely set of names for a particular encrypted identifier. Given that bad actors might have access to the complete dataset, encryption, hashing, and tokenization are vulnerable to frequency analysis attacks. Generalization and quantization (*https://oreil.ly/uJ1bc*) use a many-to-one mapping in their substitution, and the corresponding inference is slightly weaker but still vulnerable to a frequency analysis attack. Because ML datasets have a number of corresponding variables, the frequency analysis attack can use joint-probabilities of occurrence (*https://oreil.ly/6b4tr*), potentially making the cipher much easier to crack.

Therefore, all masking methods have to be combined with an effective auditing and governance mechanism to restrict access to all ML datasets that could potentially contain sensitive data. This includes datasets where all the sensitive fields have been suppressed, encrypted, quantized, or generalized.

## Coarsening Sensitive Data

Coarsening is another technique used to decrease the precision or granularity of data in order to obscure sensitive data within the dataset, while maintaining comparable benefits versus training your model with the pre-coarsened data. The following fields are particularly well-suited to this approach:

*Locations*
Population density varies across the globe, and there is no easy answer to how much you should round off location coordinates. For example, decimal-based latitudes and longitudes, rounded off to single-digit precision (e.g., –90.3, approximately within 10 km), might be sufficient to pinpoint residents of rural areas with large farms. When rounding is insufficient for coordinates, you can use location identifiers such as city, state, or zip code. These cover much larger areas, making it harder to distinguish one single individual. Choose a large enough bucket size to adequately obfuscate the unique characteristics of any one row.

*Zip codes*
US zip codes in a 5 + 4 form can identify a household, but can be coarsened to include just the first three digits ("zip3"). This limits the ability to identify a specific user by putting many users into the same bucket. Again, you might want to quantify this risk since extremely large datasets enable increasingly sophisticated attacks.

*Numeric quantities*
Numbers can be binned to make them less likely to identify an individual. For example, an exact birthday is often not required, just the decade or month a user was born. Therefore, ages, birthdays, and similar numeric fields can be coarsened by substituting ranges.

*IP addresses*
IP addresses are often part of any machine learning workflow that involves application logs, and they are often treated like physical addresses in terms of sensitivity. A good coarsening technique is to zero out the last octet of IPv4 addresses (the last 80 bits if using IPv6). This has the same function as rounding off the

latitude/longitude or reducing a street address to a zip code, trading geographic accuracy for more protection. Engage in IP address coarsening as early in the pipeline as possible: you might even be able to modify your logging software to mask or suppress IP addresses before writing them to disk.

# Establishing a Governance Policy

If your datasets have any amount of sensitive data, I recommend that you consult legal counsel to establish some sort of governance policy and best practices documentation. The details of your policy are left to you, and there are many resources available, such as the PCI Security Standards Council's Best Practices for Maintaining PCI DSS Compliance (*https://oreil.ly/M2Uja*), and the ISO/IEC 27001:2013 security technique requirements (*https://oreil.ly/J7l6k*). The following list also contains a number of common concepts you can consider when establishing your policy framework:

- Establish a secure location for governance documentation.
- Exclude encryption keys, hash functions, and other tools from your documentation.
- Document all known sources of incoming sensitive data.
- Document all known locations of stored sensitive data along with what type of data is present. Include all remediation steps that have been taken to protect it.
- Document known sensitive data locations where remediation steps are difficult, inconsistent, or impossible. This covers situations where it is suspected that frequency analysis attacks could be used.
- Establish a process to continually scan for and identify new sources of sensitive data.
- Document the roles and (possibly) individual employee names who have been granted temporary or permanent access to sensitive data. Include information as to why they required the access.
- Document the processes by which employees request access to sensitive data. Specify where they can access sensitive data; if, how, and where they can copy it; and any other restrictions associated with access.
- Establish a process to regularly review who has access to what sensitive data and determine whether access is still required. Outline what to do when employees leave or change roles as part of an off-boarding process.
- Establish a process to communicate, enforce, and regularly review the policies.

# Index

## A

## B

## About the Author

**Valliappa (Lak) Lakshmanan** is the director of analytics and AI solutions at Google Cloud, where he leads a team building cross-industry solutions to business problems. His mission is to democratize machine learning so that it can be done by anyone anywhere. Lak is also the author or coauthor of *Practical Machine Learning for Computer Vision*, *Machine Learning Design Patterns*, *Data Governance: The Definitive Guide*, and *Google BigQuery: The Definitive Guide* (all O'Reilly).

## Colophon

The animal on the cover of *Data Science on the Google Cloud Platform* is a buff-breasted sandpiper (*Calidris subruficollis*). While most sandpipers are considered shorebirds, this species is uncommon near the coast. It breeds in tundra habitat in Canada and Alaska, and migrates thousands of miles to South America during winter, flying over the Midwest region of the United States. Some small flocks can be found in Great Britain and Ireland.

Buff-breasted sandpipers are small birds, about 7–9 inches in length and with an average wingspan of 18 inches. They have brown plumage on their backs, as well as light tan chests that give them their common name. During mating season, the birds gather on display grounds (called "leks") where the males point their bills upward, raise their wings to show the white undersides, and shake their body. They may mate with multiple females if successful. Female sandpipers have separate nesting grounds, where they lay eggs on the ground in a shallow hole lined with moss, leaves, and other plant matter. Insects are the primary food source of the sandpiper; it hunts by sight by standing still and making a short run forward to catch the prey in its short thin bill.

Outside of breeding season, buff-breasted sandpipers prefer habitat with short grass: plowed fields and golf courses are common resting places for the birds as they pass through or winter in developed areas. They are currently classified as Near Threatened due to pesticide use, as well as habitat loss in their Arctic breeding grounds. Many of the animals on O'Reilly covers are endangered; all of them are important to the world.

The cover illustration is by Karen Montgomery, based on a black and white engraving from *British Birds III*. The cover fonts are Gilroy Semibold and Guardian Sans. The text font is Adobe Minion Pro; the heading font is Adobe Myriad Condensed; and the code font is Dalton Maag's Ubuntu Mono.

CPSIA information can be obtained
at www.ICGtesting.com
Printed in the USA
JSHW020810120422
24813JS00004B/12